M000305462

THE METAMORPHOSIS OF AJAX

A NEVV DIS-
COVRSE OF A STALE
SVBIECT, CALLED THE
Metamorphosis of AIAX:

VVritten by MISACMOS, *to his friend
and cosin* PHILOSTILPNOS,

Sur John Harmgton writ this of Sumersetshere

AN CHO RA SPEI.

AT LONDON,
Printed by Richard Field, dwelling
in the Black-friers.
1 5 9 6.

Lumley

SIR JOHN HARINGTON'S
A NEW DISCOURSE
OF A STALE SUBJECT,
CALLED THE
METAMORPHOSIS OF AJAX

A Critical

Annotated Edition

by

ELIZABETH STORY DONNO

New York: Columbia University Press
London: Routledge & Kegan Paul
1962

Library of Congress
Catalog Card Number: 61-16779

Printed in Great Britain

To Dan

CONTENTS

ABBREVIATIONS

APC	*Acts of the Privy Council*
Carew MSS	*Calendar of Carew MSS*
Cal. Pat. Rolls	*Calendar of the Patent Rolls*
CSP	*Calendar of State Papers: Domestic, Ireland, Venetian*
HMC	*Historical Manuscripts Commission* *Rutland MSS* *Salisbury MSS*
L&E	*Letters and Epigrams of Sir John Harington*, ed. N. E. McClure, Philadelphia, 1930
L&P, Henry VIII	*Letters and Papers, Henry VIII*
NA	*Nugae Antiquae*, ed. Thomas Park, London, 1804
OF	*Orlando Furioso*, tr. Sir John Harington
Tilley	M. P. Tilley, *A Dictionary of the Proverbs in England in the Sixteenth and Seventeenth Centuries*, Ann Arbor, 1950

In addition, I have made use of standard abbreviations for dictionaries and periodicals.

PREFACE

PROMPTED TO BE 'one of the first English . . . to make the title of his worke the worst part of it,' Sir John Harington blazoned his second published work with indecorous Elizabethan puns, giving it the title *A New Discourse of a Stale Subject, Called the Metamorphosis of Ajax*.[1] The result in 1596 was a quick rush of interest. Today, however, it is a work more talked about than read. Unlike readers of his own robust age, those of succeeding ages seem to have been deterred by its purported subject matter, while the historians of literature, missing its more serious appeal as well as much of the humour, have too readily dismissed it as a Rabelaisian trifle.

Part of the neglect has doubtless stemmed from its inaccessibility, since there has been no adequate modern edition. But a greater part has stemmed from the nature of the work itself, for the text is a tissue of learned and topical references. Courtly scandals, literary extravagances, current social ills, religious intolerance and controversies are glanced at, often covertly, in merry or mocking fashion. A modern reader, wishing to recapture the lively topicality of the work, needs to have many of these allusions explained. For when allusions lose currency, they also lose point, and to grasp Harington's play of wit, his easy erudition, and his satirical thrusts, a modern reader must be brought back to the immediate Elizabethan context.

Seen not only as a diverting frolic but also as a vivid social document, the *Metamorphosis of Ajax* merits re-establishment in the scheme of Elizabethan literature. It places its author among those writers who, taunting foibles and eccentricities, sharply delineated the manners and sensibilities of the age. Yet Harington was no black-browed satirist but a cultivated young courtier whose fresh bright turns of phrase are everywhere

---

[1] Stale: cf. *MWW*, II.iii.31 and Ajax: a jakes. Cf. *LLL*, v.ii.580–1.

ix

stamped with his own winning personality and incorrigible gaiety.

In endeavouring to make the work accessible, I have aimed at producing a reader's edition. Although provided with an *apparatus criticus* that I hope will be both interesting and useful, this edition is not intended to supplant the sixteenth-century editions as bibliographical source material (something I believe no modern edition can do). Luckily, part of Harington's manuscript which furnished the copy for the printer has survived, and its variants from the copy-text, duly recorded in the notes, afford information of a kind to appeal to anyone interested in the connection between a writer and his printing house.

In the explanatory notes I have endeavoured to provide material useful for understanding the Elizabethan complex of the work. I have tried not only to identify topical allusions but also to recreate their context; this has resulted in elaborate notes, particularly in the *Apologie* where Harington furnishes an abundance of personal comment about his contemporaries. The numerous literary references cited in the notes give ample evidence of his breadth of reading. At first glance, a reader may wonder at their extent and diversity, but at second glance, it seems to me, he will marvel at the ease with which Harington incorporated such varied source material into his text.

The Introduction includes a biographical account which is intended simply to place Harington in his social milieu. It provides no new material; for that we must await the full-length biography on which M. H. M. MacKinnon is currently at work. But the vexing problems of the authorship of the three parts and of the anonymous sequel, *The Ulysses upon Ajax*, of the priority of editions, of licensing and possible piracy are discussed at some length and, I hope, with resulting clarification.

I should like to express my gratitude to those who gave me assistance in the preparation of this edition. To trace copies of a work, the parts of which have frequently been bound separately or bound without regard for the edition of which they were intended to be a unit is a troublesome task, and I am grateful to many librarians who arranged to send me photostats or microfilm or who checked points for me. My specific obligations are recorded in the notes, but I should also like to thank

Professors Ruth Hughey, William A. Jackson, and M. H. M.
MacKinnon, who sent me useful information; I am indebted
in many ways to members of the Folger staff but to none more
than to Dr. James G. McManaway for his unfailing help. I
should also like to extend my thanks to the Trustees of the
British Museum for their kind permission to include readings
from Harington's manuscript; to the Trustees of the Shakespeare Folger Library for permission to reprint the title page
and illustrations from the Lumley copy as well as a selection
of Harington's annotations in both the Lumley and the Nares
copies; I am also grateful to Sheffield University and the
University of Texas for kind permission to include a selection
of Harington's annotations from their copies. Lastly, to Peter
Allen, Procope S. Costas, Allen T. Hazen, S. F. Johnson,
William Nelson, and Maurice J. Valency for help in a host of
ways, I can no other answer make but thanks, and thanks and
ever thanks.

ELIZABETH STORY DONNO

New York, N. Y.
June, 1960

N.B. The year of Harington's birth has been established as
1560 by Ruth Hughey, *The Arundel Harington Manuscript of
Tudor Poetry* (Columbus, Ohio: The Ohio State University
Press, 1960), 1, 26n. W. T. MacCaffrey's 'Talbot and Stanhope: an Episode in Elizabethan Politics' (*Bulletin of the
Institute of Historical Research*, May, 1960, 73–85), which
appeared too late for me to consult, should be used to supplement my note on the Stanhope-Shrewsbury quarrel, pp. 230–
31.

INTRODUCTION

HARINGTON'S LIFE

BIRTH AND BREEDING decreed that John Harington (1560–1612) should be intimately connected with the brilliant world of the Elizabethan court and the equally brilliant world of Elizabethan letters. His mother, Isabella, the daughter of Sir John Markham, Lieutenant of the Tower, had been one of the six maids of honour to the Princess Elizabeth at Hatfield, and she remained a member of the Queen's Privy Chamber until her death in 1579.[1] His father, also John Harington, was a cultivated gentleman, a poet, a translator, and in the words of his son 'much skilled in musicke,' which 'he learnt in the fellowship of good Maister Tallis.'[2] He had served in the household of Henry VIII, married the King's illegitimate daughter[3] Ethelreda Malte (upon whose death he acquired extensive holdings in Somerset and Berkshire),[4] and then entered the service of the dashing and unscrupulous Thomas Seymour, Lord High Admiral. Upon Seymour's arrest in 1549, Harington too was sent to the Tower where, questioned about the matrimonial intrigues of Seymour, he denied that he ever knew of any conference of love or marriage between the Lady Elizabeth and the

---

[1] Harington, *A Tract on the Succession to the Crown*, ed. C. R. Markham (London, 1880), pp. 40–1.

[2] *L&E*, p. 64.

[3] The evidence for this derives primarily from family tradition (*Miscellanea Genealogica et Heraldica*, n. s., IV, 191; III, 18; *L&E*, p. 64). The daughter of Joan Dyngley (who subsequently married one Dobson), Ethelreda or Audrey Malte is referred to by John Malte (tailor to Henry VIII) as his bastard daughter. In support of tradition is the unquestionable fact that the King made extensive grants of land to Malte and Ethelreda and the heirs of her body (*L&P, Henry VIII*, XIX, Pt. 1, 630; XXI, Pt. 2, 96). The date of the marriage is uncertain, but from a licence recorded for 11 Nov. 1547 granting Harington the advowson of the rectory of Kelston which was part of Ethelreda Malte's holdings, it would seem that 1547 is correct (*Cal. Pat. Rolls, Edward VI*, I, 1547–8, 53).

[4] *L&P, Henry VIII*, XVI, 423; XIX, Pt. 1, 630; XXI, Pt. 2, 96; *Cal. Pat. Rolls, Philip and Mary*, III, 1555–7, 93, 95–6.

Lord Admiral.[5] In 1554 he was again sent to the Tower, this time by Bishop Gardiner, 'for only carrying a letter to the Princess Elizabeth,' even as Isabella Markham was taken from her service by the same prelate and detained as a heretic.[6] Elizabeth consequently looked with favour upon the marriage of her two faithful servitors[7] and later stood godmother to their eldest son.

'Boye Jacke,' as Queen Elizabeth affectionately called him, began his education at Eton under two future bishops, the Provost William Day and his assistant William Wickham who showed the young scholar 'as fatherly a care, as if he had bene a second tutor' to him.[8] Here, with his schoolfellows Thomas Arundell and Edward Hoby, Harington practised Latin by translating the account of Elizabeth's sufferings from the *Book of Martyrs*, a work which was then presented to the Queen.[9] Here too he began to court 'his sweet wanton Muse.'[10]

Upon leaving Eton, Harington proceeded to King's College, Cambridge, where he received his B.A. in 1577/8 first in *ordo senioritatis*.[11] In 1578 Burghley wrote exhorting him to become proficient in 'all tonges and sciences' and to follow in the steps of Sir John Cheke, 'one of the sweetest flowers that hath coomen in my tyme' out of Cambridge.[12] He remained in residence until 1581, in turn, a truant scholar, an eager

---

[5] *HMC, Salisbury MSS*, XIII, 26.

[6] *L&E*, p. 127; *NA*, II, 67-8.

[7] The date of Harington's marriage to Isabella Markham is also uncertain. In a letter he wrote in 1554 to Bishop Gardiner from the Tower, Harington states that his wife is the Lady Elizabeth's servant (*NA*, I, 64). Since Isabella Markham was a maid of honour, this remark has frequently been understood to refer to her. However, Ethelreda was still alive in 1555 (*Cal. Pat. Rolls, Philip and Mary*, III, 1555-7, 95-6). Therefore, we must assume that Ethelreda also served Elizabeth in some capacity and that Harington's marriage to Isabella Markham occurred after 1555.

[8] Both Harington's schoolmasters were to become Bishops of Winchester and figure in his lively account of contemporary bishops entitled *A Supplie or Addicion to the Catalogue of Bishops to the year 1608;* this was first printed in 1653 as *A Briefe View of the State of the Church of England*. It is reprinted in *NA*, II, 1-318.

[9] Notes to Bk. XLV of the *OF*. [10] Epigram 427, *L&E*, pp. 321-2.

[11] J. and J. A. Venn, *Alumni Cantabrigienses* (Cambridge, 1922), Pt. I, II, 310.

[12] *NA*, I, 131-5.

spectator at the college plays, a meritorious student of Greek and Latin, and in his last year a reader of Justinian under Thomas Bynge, Regius Professor of Civil Law.

During these sportive and academic years he became acquainted not only with future courtiers like Sir Ralph Horsey and the Earl of Essex, but also with a number of men who were to become dignitaries in the church. His tutor was a 'grave and learned man,' Dr. Samuel Fleming, whose defence of humane letters against the more precise divines who 'would have the word and church and all goe naked (saving for some aporne, perhaps of fig-leaves)' Harington recalled twenty-five years later.[13] The influence of Dr. Fleming perhaps, as well as his own inclination, coloured his later judgment of Dr. John Still, Bishop of Bath and Wells, who examined him for his baccalaureate: 'I hold him a rare man for preaching, for arguing, for learning, for lyving,' he wrote Prince Henry; 'I could only wish, that in all theise he would make lesse use of logique, and more of rhetoricke.'[14] He remembered how Dr. William Chaderton, later Bishop of Lincoln, had been beloved among the students 'the rather, for he did not affect any sowre and austere fashion, either in teaching or government, as some use to do; but well tempered both with courage and curtesie.'[15] And he recalled the skill at tennis of the young Robert Bennet, later Bishop of Hereford, who when he came to be a Bachelor of Divinity 'would tosse an argument in the schooles better than a ball in the tennis-court.'[16]

Leaving Cambridge, Harington proceeded like other fashionable young men to London, there to become a 'punie' at Lincoln's Inn. His father's death in 1582 curtailed his legal studies, and he returned to the family estate at Kelston where a fine manor house had been begun, the gardens graced with a fountain like that described in Ariosto.[17] In September 1583[18] he married Mary, daughter of Sir George Rogers from nearby Cannington (who had died the same year as the elder Harington) and the redoubtable Lady Jane. He now established the pattern

---

[13] *NA*, II, 207.

[14] *Ibid.*, p. 165.

[15] *Ibid.*, p. 114.

[16] *Ibid.*, p. 186.

[17] See *A New Discourse*, p. 56.

[18] *Somerset Parish Records*, ed. W. P. W. Phillimore (London, 1905), VI, 94.

he was to follow for the rest of his life—periods of residence at court pursuing 'ambition's puff ball' followed by a return to his obligations at Kelston as a member of the landed gentry, devoted to county duties, to his books, to his 'Sweet Mall,' and in due time to his 'boys and maids.'

In 1586, Harington left Kelston, together with his personal servant Thomas Combe and his brother-in-law Edward Rogers, to make his first trip to Ireland as one of the 'undertakers' for repeopling the province of Munster; they returned, according to Thomas Combe, 'overtaken.' But his interest had been stirred by the superstitions and habits of the people, and he was later to affirm that it seemed as if his very *genius* led him to that country.[19] The sympathetic attitude Harington maintained toward the Irish, while in accord with his characteristically tolerant outlook, was in strong contrast to that of many of his contemporaries.

In 1591, his spirited translation of the *Orlando Furioso* appeared in a fine folio printed by Richard Field, handsomely illustrated. Fittingly, he dedicated it to the Queen since he had undertaken the task of translating the work as a 'penance' imposed 'by that saint, nay rather goddesse, whose service I am only devoted unto.'[20] This clearly substantiates the tradition that, having translated the ribald twenty-eighth canto for the delectation of her maids of honour, he had been enjoined by the Queen to translate the whole. Yet it seems clear that the initial impetus for the work on which he had spent 'some yeeres & months, & weeks, and dayes' stemmed from his father's warm interest in poetry. This explains Harington's inclusion of his father's translation of the first stanza of Book XIX and the fifty stanzas translated by his brother Francis for a 'proofe of his veine in this kind.'[21] Even as the elder Harington, from his practice of collecting in manuscript the poetry and prose of his contemporaries, had established a family pattern,[22] so had he instilled in his two sons the habit of writing and translating verse.

---

[19] *A Short View of the State of Ireland*, ed. W. D. Macray in *Anecdota Bodleiana* (Oxford, 1879), p. 9.

[20] *An Apologie*, p. 256.   [21] Notes to Bks. XIX and XXXII.

[22] For an account of the various manuscript collections of the Harington family, see Ruth Hughey, 'The Harington Manuscript at Arundel Castle and Related Documents,' *Library*, XV (1934–5), 388–444.

In 1593/4, in a fashion typical of that quarrelsome, litigious age, the volatile temper of the young courtier exploded in angry charges against his brother-in-law Edward Rogers. Among the ten articles Harington preferred against him were that he had boasted 'that he pulled out a handful of hair from the said John Harington's beard,' that on meeting Francis Harington he had 'jostled him for the wall,' and that on Twelfth Eve he had told the said John Harington that he would have certain trees he had taken out of his ground 'out of his throat,' to which Harington characteristically responded 'there grew none there.'[23] Harington then concluded his charges with a dire allusion to the bloodshed that had ensued in Somerset a few years earlier at the murder of Nicholas Turbervile by one John Morgan.[24] The ill feeling continued to mount after the death of Lady Rogers (1602), and Harington remained at odds with his wife's 'naturall (yet to unnaturall)' brother until 1604, when the Star Chamber suit brought by Rogers was at the King's will submitted to speedy arbitration.[25]

Throughout this period, whether at Kelston or at court, Harington was busy commenting on the events of his immediate world in epigrams which were, by turns, witty, incisive, or satiric, and in 1596 his second published work, *The Metamorphosis of Ajax*, appeared.

Given scant time to put on his boots, he was summoned by Essex in 1599 to be a captain of horse in the ill-fated expedition to Ireland. His cousin Robert Markham wrote from court, directing him to keep a journal 'unknown to any in the company' and urging discretion: 'mind your bookes, and make your jestes, but take heed who they light on.'[26] Harington responded zestfully to his Irish experience. He presented a copy of his Ariosto to the two sons of Tyrone and disputed a point of theology with 'Teroans preests' in the presence of the Earl himself.[27] He wrote to Thomas Combe of his lucky escape from bodily hurt and of the knowledge he had acquired:

In the camp, where drinking water, and milk, and vinegar, and aqua vitae, and eating raw beef at midnight, and lying upon wet green

[23] *Salisbury MSS*, Pt. IV, 472–3.   [24] In 1579/80; see *APC*, XI, 391.

[25] *L&E*, pp. 112–14; 115–17; *Salisbury MSS*, Pt. XVI, 437–8.

[26] *NA*, I, 241–3.   [27] *A Short View of the State of Ireland*, pp. 17–18.

corn oftimes, and lying in boots, with heats and colds, made many sick; yet myself (in a good hour be it spoken and a better heard) was never sick; neither in the camp nor the castle, at sea or on land. Besides all this, to vaunt myself at large, to you; I have informed myself reasonably well of the whole state of the country, by observation and conference; so that I count the knowledge I have gotten here worth more than half the three hundred pounds this jorney hath cost me: and as to warr, joyning the practise to the theory, and reading the book you so prays'd, and other books of Sir Griffin Markham's,[28] with his conference and instructions, I hope at my coming home to talk of counterscarpes, and cazamats, with any of our captains.[29]

On 30 July he was knighted by the Earl of Essex.[30]

Following Essex's unscheduled return in September, Harington arrived at court 'in the very heat and height of all displeasures.' Threatened with the Fleet, he answered 'that coming so late from the land-service, I hoped that I should not be prest to serve in her Majesty's fleet in Fleet-street.'[31] The journal he had been advised to keep helped to clear him in the eyes of the Queen, but when she bade him go home, as he later wrote, 'I did not stay to be bidden twise; if all the Iryshe rebels had been at my heels, I shoude not have had better speede, for I did now flee from one whom I both lovede and fearede too.'[32]

Despite her alternate smiles and frowns, Harington's allegiance to the Queen never wavered, but he had long favoured King James's claim to the succession. In 1584 he had refused to sign the Bond of Association, although such a refusal was 'ill taken' by the Earl of Leicester and gave rise to the suspicion of being 'Scottishe.'[33] At Christmas, 1602, he sent the King a gift—Latin and English verses designed to please that pedant's heart and a curious perfumed lantern decorated with symbolic figures and bearing the legend of the thief on the

---

[28] There are no listings in the STC for Sir Griffin Markham, although several books on military subjects are credited to his second cousin, the indefatigable Gervase Markham. Since all of these are dated 1616 and later, long after Sir Griffin's exile (see below), they perhaps represent a refurbishing of Sir Griffin's earlier efforts.

[29] L&E, pp. 73–4.   [30] CSP, Ireland, IX (1600), 234.

[31] L&E, p. 79.   [32] Ibid., p. 123.

[33] Tract on the Succession, p. 37.

cross, 'Lord, remember me when thou comest into thy kingdom.'[34] At this time also he wrote a prose tract defending
James's right to the throne. Taking up the views of representa-
tives of the Protestant, Puritan, and Catholic factions, he
showed how their arguments led logically to support of the
Scottish king. Filled with personal recollections and anecdotes,
the work was very likely never intended for publication. Harington remarks in it that he is writing to his dearest friend, and the
manuscript, annotated by Tobie Matthew, Archbishop of York,
remained in the chapter library until it was edited in 1880 by Sir
Clements Markham under the title *Tract on the Succession to
the Crown*. However, Sir Robert Cecil, a secret supporter of
James, read the work and filled three large pages in a minute
handwriting entitled 'Some notes for remembrance out of his
Sir Jo. Harrington's book on the behalf of the K. of Sc.
succession.'[35]

Up to this point Harington's wit, irrepressible spirits, and
disarming candour had determined his outlook and action.
Despite periodic disillusionment, he had been irresistibly
attracted to the glitter of the Elizabethan court. Despite the
fact that he had not received any position at court, he had
adhered to the Renaissance view that devotion to letters was a
sure means of advancement, and he had remained tolerably
content with the Queen's 'approbation, esteeme, and rewarde.'[36]

After James's accession his views darkened. He wrote to Lord
Thomas Howard before setting out in April, 1603, for Kelston:

Thus muche I have livede to see, and (in good soothe) feel too, that
honeste prose will never better a mans purse at cowrte; and, had
not my fortune been in *terra firma*, I might, even for my verses, have
daunced bare foot with Clio and her school-fellowes untill I did
sweat, and then have gotten nothinge to slake my thirste, but a
pitcher of Helicons well. E'en let the beardless god Apollo dip his
own chin in such drinke; a haire of my face shall have better
entertainmente.[37]

Arrived there, he noted in his journal:

Here now wyll I reste my troublede mynde, and tende my sheepe
like an Arcadian swayne, that hathe loste his faire mistresse; for in

---

[34] Folger MS, V.a. 249 (formerly 4455), pp. 257–63.
[35] *Salisbury MSS*, Pt. XIV, 245.   [36] *L&E*, p. 100.   [37] *Ibid.*

soothe, I have loste the beste and faireste love that ever shepherde knew, even my gracious Queene; and sith my goode mistresse is gone, I shall not hastily put forthe for a new master. I heare oure new Kynge hathe hangede one man before he was tryede; 'tis strangely done: now if the wynde blowethe thus, why may not a man be tryed before he hathe offended.—I wyll keepe companie with none but my *oves* and *boves*, and go to Bathe and drinke sacke, and wash awaie remembraunces of paste times in the streams of Lethe.[38]

A series of personal difficulties ensued. His old uncle Thomas Markham had been forced into debt by the extravagances of his son-in-law Sir John Skinner, and Harington had bound himself security for £4,000. Unable to raise the required sum, he was imprisoned in 1603 for several months until, fearful of the plague, he contrived to escape from the Gatehouse and arranged to settle with his creditors. The Star Chamber suit with his brother-in-law followed. Meanwhile, his cousin, Sir Griffin Markham, who had been apprehended for his share in the 'Bye' plot, designed to gain greater tolerance for Catholics, was convicted of treason and exiled. His confiscated property was then made over to Harington by the King for settlement of the Markhams' debts.[39]

Having solved his financial and family difficulties, Harington looked about for an occupation. In the autumn of 1601 he had sought unsuccessfully to be made Colonel of the County of Somerset and at the time had requested Cecil's aid to counteract the wish of the Council for a younger man and the charges of some 'pure speryted fellows' that he was backward in religion.[40] In 1605 he again addressed Cecil, now Viscount Cranbourne, and Charles Blount, now Earl of Devonshire, with the proposal that he be made Chancellor of Ireland and Archbishop of Dublin. He accompanied his letter with a brief-discourse[41] written in his characteristic vein and designed to explain his offer and project his views about Ireland. Remembering the case of Sir Christopher Hatton, he was aware that his study of Civil Law at Cambridge and his brief tenure at Lincoln's Inn (albeit he had studied Littleton 'but to the title of discontinuance') might suffice for the position of Chancellor,

---

[38] *NA*, I, 180.

[39] *CSP, Dom.*, VIII (1603–10), 125.

[40] *L&E*, pp. 88–90.

[41] *A Short View of the State of Ireland.*

yet he faced the question of his qualifications for spiritual office: 'yt may bee objected that the example ys strawnge for a Knight, a layman, and one moche conversant in lyght studyes and poetry, to bee made a Byshop and a Preest; but that ys not new or strawnge'; and he cites examples, including that of his own ancestor, Sir James Harington, who had been a knight first and a priest afterwards.[42] It remained his lot, however, 'to lyve a pryvat man' and 'to rejoyse,' as he modestly observed, 'that Brytany hath so many hunderds more worthy then myselfe.'[43]

By this date he had already expended some efforts in behalf of Prince Henry, having written a commentary for him on the sixth book of Virgil.[44] In June 1605 he presented him with a fine autograph copy of his *Epigrams*, accompanied by a youthful picture of himself wearing a 'Pecque Devaunt' beard.[45] His popular verse translation of the *Regimen Sanitatis Salernitanum*, published anonymously in 1607 under the title *The Englishmans Doctor*,[46] was perhaps undertaken for the entertainment of the Prince[47]; he speaks of it later as if it were familiar when, apologizing to the Prince for his extensive use of 'physick metaphors,' he explains that he has lately been looking over his *Schola Salerni*.[48] This apology occurs in his interesting *Supplie or Addicion to the Catalogue of Bishops*, written for Prince Henry in 1607–8. Purportedly a history of Elizabethan and Jacobean bishops, it is enlivened throughout by warm personal recollections and colourful comments gathered both from his reading and from his experiences at court. Among the letters he wrote to the Prince during this period is the engaging account of his dog Bungey[49]; and in 1609 he sent him a copy of the *Orlando Furioso*, which Field had reprinted two years before.

---

[42] *Ibid.*, pp. 19-20.   [43] *Ibid.*, p. 2.

[44] Mentioned in *A Short View of the State of Ireland*, p. 20, which he sent to Viscount Cranbourne on 20 April 1605; it has been reputed lost, but see 'Research in Progress,' *PMLA*, LXXI, No. 2 (April 1956), 284.

[45] Folger MS V.a. 249. He is wearing a single drooping earring and a 'Pecque Devaunt' in the delightful miniature by Hoskins.

[46] Reprinted by F. R. Packard and F. H. Garrison as *The School of Salernum*, (N.Y., 1920).

[47] *L&E*, p. 38. However, he had been interested in the work as early as 1595-6. See *A New Discourse*, p. 156 ff.

[48] *NA*, II, 124.

[49] *L&E*, pp. 132-4.

The polishing of his translation of the Psalms occupied his last years. Whether at Kelston with his family or meeting his old friends in nearby Bath, Harington no doubt became, as he had prophesied, *laudator temporis acti*. He died in November 1612, 'sicke of a dead palsy,' at the age of fifty-two. Lady Mary and seven of his eleven children survived him.

Such are the biographical facts of the Queen's witty godson. His *Orlando Furioso* was the first notable translation of a Renaissance heroic poem. Following closely upon the publication of Books I–III of the *Faerie Queene*, it contributed to the vogue for Italian heroic romances. His 'Briefe Apologie of Poetrie' prefacing that work is a witty example of Renaissance criticism, and his fluent use of the *ottava* established its popularity as a verse form for poets like Daniel and Drayton. His teeming supply of epigrams circulating in the court also set the fashion for that genre, and Harington together with Ben Jonson must be ranked as the most skilful of the epigrammatists. His miscellaneous writings,[50] including his informative and diverting letters, provide a vivid index to the Elizabethan world, since he was a man more than ordinarily acquainted with the great men of the court, with the landed gentry, with ecclesiastical dignitaries, and with men of letters. Moreover, since so many of his writings were essentially private, directed either to individuals or to a select group of readers, they reveal intimate aspects of personality which are hidden from us in the case of many of his contemporaries. As a courtier he recorded the pulse of the Elizabethan and Jacobean world both in the court and in the country with keen observation and inimitable style. As translator, scholar, and epigrammatist, he was esteemed by his contemporaries for his wit and erudition, proving himself to be, as Thomas Fuller later observed, 'a poet in all things save in his wealth.'

---

[50] Some of these appear in the collection entitled *Nugae Antiquae*, first edited by Henry Harington (Vol. I, 1769; Vol. II, 1775; Vol. I–III, 1779 and again in 1792) and again by Thomas Park in two volumes in 1804.

The Metamorphosis of Ajax

The complex literary and bibliographical problems of *The Metamorphosis of Ajax* stem from several factors relating to the manner of its publication in 1596. First of all, the work consists of three parts:

> *A New Discourse of a Stale Subject, Called the Metamorphosis of Ajax*
> *An Anatomie of the Metamorpho-sed Ajax*
> *An Apologie*

These were published as a unit in the first edition, but the first two parts (with the *Apologie* probably appended to the *Anatomie*) were also issued separately as trade publications with a separate title page for the *Anatomie*. The second edition of the three parts can also be shown to have been intended as a unit, but these apparently were the only two editions to include all three parts. There were subsequent editions of both *A New Discourse* and *An Apologie*. The problem of these various editions is discussed in the bibliographical section below.

Secondly, there is the question of authorship. As Harington mentioned in a letter to Lady Russell dated 14 August 1596,[1] he had put forth his 'fantasticall treatise' under a covert name, that is, Misacmos, the name which appears on the title page of the *New Discourse*. There is no difficulty in establishing the identity of Misacmos and Harington: numerous biographical and personal allusions in the work and the rebus on his name at the end of the *Anatomie* proclaim his authorship. Moreover, the manuscript which was used by the printer has been preserved among the Harington Papers now in the British Museum[2]; from this we see that the prefatory letter written by Philostilpnos was originally addressed to 'Cosen Harington' (later changed to 'Sir') and that Harington's signature appeared at the end of his answer to the letter. In addition, he wrote a

---

[1] *L&E*, pp. 65–6.
[2] BM Add. MS 46368. For a description, see below.

number of epigrams which either refer to the *Metamorphosis* or again make use of the pen name Misacmos.[3] Finally, the allusions of his contemporaries, testifying directly or indirectly to his authorship, show that the designations Misacmos and Ajax clung to him pertinaciously.[4]

The author of the *Anatomie* is indicated on the title page by the initials *T.C.*, *i.e.*, Thomas Combe, Harington's personal servant whose name appears in full in the MS and whose contribution had been anticipated by two references in the *New Discourse* to the drawings which he was to supply (pp. 57; 172).

Commentators have recognized the purported authorship of Thomas Combe[5] but have assumed that this was merely a further disguise on the part of Harington. However, the likelihood of Combe's actual authorship is indicated by the fact that, besides being in the service of Harington, he also appears to have been a fellow translator.

The *Anatomie*, which occupies only one sheet in each edition, consists of a prefatory address to 'M.E.S.,' two pages of illustrations (the Anatomie proper), and a short apology. In the address and the apology Thomas Combe sets forth some personal information: he describes himself as serving two 'prentiships,' one in poetry and one in painting (p. 190), as having been not only 'Poeticall,' like his master, but also 'Pictoricall' (p. 203), and, most significantly, as having been 'a dealer in Emblemes' (p. 204). He points up this latter assertion by concluding his text with an emblem or rebus on Harington's name.

---

[3] *L&E*, pp. 164–6; 167; 177–8; 190; 192; 198; 241–2; 299–300; 305; 309.

[4] *E.g.*, Nashe, Marston, Jonson, John Davies of Hereford, and John Chamberlain. For Harington's sharp response to a lengthy attack by the poetaster Robert Joyner published in *Itis* in 1598, see his epigrams on pp. 185, 201–2 in *L&E*.

[5] A. E. M. Kirwood in ' "The Metamorphosis of Aiax" and its Sequels (*Library*, XII, 1931–2) says that although Combe 'may be given the credit of the drawings, it is unlikely that he had any further part in the work; Harington's authorship is everywhere apparent' (p. 222). He also describes the prefatory letter in the *New Discourse* which is signed *Philostilpnos* as Harington's letter to himself (p. 214). Philostilpnos is the 'M.E.S.' to whom the *Anatomie* is addressed: solely on the basis of internal evidence, he can be identified as Harington's cousin, Master Edward Sheldon. This is substantiated by Harington's annotation in the Nares-Folger copy. Since there is no evidence, internal or external, to preclude the collaboration of either Sheldon or Combe, we should, it seems, accept the text itself as a *datum*.

Is there any evidence to substantiate his claims? The Stationers' Register for 9 May 1593 records an entry to Richard Field of 'a booke intituled *The Theater of fyne Devises conteyninge an hundred morrall Emblemes* translated out of French by THOMAS COMBE.'[6] This record is supported by Francis Meres's statement in *Palladis Tamia*, where he names Thomas Combe among the three English emblematists he cites.[7] Although no copy of the original edition of *The Theater of fyne Devises* seems to have survived, it must have appeared around the date of Field's entry, certainly before the appearance of the *Anatomie* in 1596 and Meres's *Palladis Tamia* in 1598. However, a copy of the 1614 edition (STC 15230), which was also printed by Field and ascribed to Combe, has survived.[8]

If then the identification of Thomas Combe of the *Anatomie* with the translator is conclusive, there is no reason to question his authorship as set forth on the title page of the *Anatomie*. He too was a poet-translator.[9]

Harington's authorship of the third part, the *Apologie*, which does not have a separate title page, is clearly revealed by its contents. In it Misacmos elucidates and emphasizes the points made in the *New Discourse* under the pretence of answering charges brought against that work by certain detractors.

Thus the authorship and basic unity of the three parts are clear: the *New Discourse* written by Misacmos (*i.e.*, Harington)

---

[6] Ed. Arber, II, 631. Guillaume de La Perrière's *Le Théâtre des Bons Engins*, published in Paris in 1539.

[7] Ed. D. C. Allen (Scholars' Facsimiles & Reprints, N.Y., 1938), fol. 285ᵛ.

[8] In the Henry Huntington Library. Combe's translation includes La Perrière's original dedication, an address to the reader, and the emblems, each with a two-line poesy and a woodcut enclosed in a decorative border, followed by a stanza in ottava rima. Emblem 32 illustrates the proverb that eagles 'disdaine to litigate with flies'; this may be compared with Combe's application of it in the *Anatomie*: 'Well, yet I trust how ever my master speeds, I shall do wel inough. *Aquila non capit muscas*' (p. 201 and note).

[9] Apart from the few facts in the *Anatomie* and some remarks in Harington's letters, I have been unable to trace any definite information about Combe. It should be observed that Harington's third son, George, married Mary Combe, daughter of a Thomas Combe, Gentleman, of Lincombe near Bath. In his will (dated 9 March 1655) Thomas Combe left to his grandson Charles Harington 'my bedstead, cupboard, books, &c., and my gold signet ring, &c., charging him to live in unity with his brother Edward' (*Misc. Gen. et Her.*, n. s. 3, IV, 192; F. Brown, *Abstracts of Somersetshire Wills*, s. IV, 1889, 13).

sets forth his invention; T. C. (*i.e.*, Thomas Combe) provides the drawings or *Anatomie* of that invention; and Misacmos then offers a defence—the *Apologie*—to counter (in anticipation) accusations regarding his intent in writing the *New Discourse*.

It is also necessary to distinguish Harington-Misacmos from the author of a subsequent pamphlet entitled *Ulysses upon Ajax, Written by Misodiaboles to his friend Philaretes*. Two editions of this work, both printed for Thomas Gubbins, were published in 1596 (STC 12782 and 12783). For some reason this pamphlet has been repeatedly assigned to Harington (see STC), though there is not a shred of evidence to connect him with the work and much to argue against the attribution.

To begin with external evidence, Harington's contemporary, John Davies of Hereford, wrote an epigram which clearly indicates that the *Ulysses* was by another hand.[10] Although this epigram was not published until 1617, it seems very likely to have been written c. 1596 when the publication of the two works would have occasioned Davies's interest.

Although, as stated above, Harington's MS of the *New Discourse* (with some lacunae), the *Anatomie* (complete), and the *Apologie* (in part) has been preserved, there is nothing in the MS papers relating to the *Ulysses*. As we have seen, Harington wrote epigrams referring to the *Metamorphosis* and to himself as Misacmos, yet there are no references to the *Ulysses* in his *Epigrams*, and, finally, the *Ulysses* was not included in the large-paper presentation copies Harington annotated and presented to his friends.[11]

---

[10] I Dare not say your Wit was wisdom pointed,
When you in *Aiax* had your Wit annoynted:
Sith by no small Fooles, yet accompted wise,
Such straines of Wit are held but Fooleries:
But, this I say, and say what well I wot,
Ulisses upon *Aiax* plaid the Sot:
For, what you put in *Aiax* was more woorth,
By odds, than what *Ulisses* then put forth.
Epigram 233, *Wits Bedlem*

[11] Isaac Reed, who at one time owned the copy Harington had presented to his uncle Thomas Markham, appended to it an uncut copy of the *Ulysses* and bound the collection in russia (*Proceedings and Papers of the Oxford Bibliographical Society*, II, 1927–30, 212). The presentation copy which Robert Nares once owned has been bound with a copy of Singer's 1814 reprint of the *Ulysses*. The Lumley and Sheffield copies include only the three parts of the *Metamorphosis*.

As for internal evidence, the argument from style has resulted in directly opposed viewpoints. S. W. Singer, for example, who edited a modernized text in 1814, even though he knew and cited Davies's epigram, insisted on the 'similarity of style' of the *Metamorphosis* and the *Ulysses*. Harold V. Routh in the *CHEL* also claimed that the similarity of style was unmistakable.[12] On the other hand, Douce commented on the *Ulysses* on the flyleaf of his copy, 'seems to have been undertaken by a different and very inferior writer,'[13] and McClure in his edition of the *Letters and Epigrams* more recently observed that 'a consideration of the style shows this ascription [to Harington] to be incorrect.'[14] Arguments of style, unsupported by evidence from the text, have clearly been of little value in determining the identity of its author.

An examination of the contents of the *Ulysses* does provide some useful evidence. First, the *Ulysses* is an attack, albeit good-humoured, upon the *Metamorphosis*, wherein the author in a direct address to Misacmos challenges him to a combat of wits (A2–A4). Addressing himself then to Philaretes, Misodiaboles proceeds systematically to criticize Harington's methods and remarks, defending in the process individuals whom Harington had mocked, for example, 'a father so reverend,' *i.e.*, Dr. Laurence Humphrey, on C7^v–C8; Master Dalton on E4^v–E5; and 'mayster *Plat* mine old and honest friende' on E5 (whereas Harington had directly affirmed that he and Plat were of no great acquaintance, p. 165).

Secondly, there is the question of scurrility. Harington maintains a certain reticence in his treatment. This can definitely be ascertained by checking his sources with the modifications he introduced when citing them. For example, he is careful to translate the epigrams of Sir Thomas More by decorous paraphrase (pp. 99, 100); his memory of Heywood's epigrams on two occasions is 'no better' than he 'would have it' (p. 104); he forbears to quote a ribald epigram of Sir John Davies since 'without his consent it is no good manners to publish it' (p. 103); he leaves questionable passages, whether

---

[12] Cambridge, 1919, IV, 533.
[13] Microfilm of Douce H91.
[14] P. 16, n. 4.

they derive from merry Martial or learned divines like Dr. Humphrey or Dr. Rainolds (p. 104), in their original Latin; in recounting an amusing if impolite anecdote about an Italian lady and her physician, he likewise leaves the key line in Italian. Thus Harington's method is to work by suggestion, equivocation, puns, and witty allusions. The reason is manifest: he is writing for a courtly circle of readers. As he had admitted in his letter to Lady Russell, the first two leaves (*i.e.*, sheets) contained almost nothing but 'skurrill and toying matter,' but the rest he considered 'pleasaunt and harmeles,' and he had taken occasion earlier to read 'the moste part of it' aloud to her.[15] Thus by means of circumlocution and indirection Harington intended to keep his work within the bounds of propriety, fit not only for courtiers of either sex but also for 'the magnificent majestie of a Mayden Monark.'

The *Ulysses upon Ajax* affords a direct contrast: here there is no reliance on circumlocution or indirection; the vocabulary is earthy and explicit. As its author himself pointed out, Harington was 'a courtier in regard, I a courtier in hope.'

Who then was Misodiaboles, and who was Philaretes to whom the pamphlet was addressed?[16] I can offer no definite answer, but it is possible to glean some indications from the personal allusions recorded in the *Ulysses*. In distinguishing himself from Harington, Misodiaboles says:

Would *Misacmos* be famous? why I yeeld him the meanes: he is a courtier in regard, I a courtier in hope: he riche in ancient demeasne, I in good demesne: he sprightly and wittie; I diligent & pleasant: a ladie blest his children, and God and our Lady my Lady mothers sonnes: he a *Lincolnes Inne* man, I belonging to *Lincolne*. If any oddes be, he hath the interest of mony, I of Reading. (A2ᵛ-A3)

---

[15] *L&E*, p. 65.

[16] I have not come across the use of *Misodiaboles* in any other work of the period; *Philaretes*, however, was not an uncommon pen name. It was used, for example, by the author of the prefatory letter to J. C.'s *Alcilia: Philoparthen's Loving Folly* which appeared in 1595 (reprinted in A. H. Bullen, *Some Longer Elizabethan Poems*, pp. 319–62). In 1602 it was adopted by the author (a doctor) of a pamphlet entitled *Work for Chimny-sweepers: or A Warning for Tabacconists*, printed by T. Este for Thomas Bushell; this pamphlet, in turn, was answered in the same year by another doctor (?Roger Marbecke) who declared he did not know the identity of Philaretes: *A Defence of Tabacco: with a friendly answer to the late printed Booke called Worke for Chimny-Sweepers*, etc., printed by Richard Field for Thomas Man.

From this we can conclude that the author has no children and that he is in some way connected with Lincoln—city? county? Oxford college? He further shows a familiarity with Brasenose College (C1^v), especially in 'Doctour *Colmers*' time (D3), *i.e.*, Dr. Clement Colmer, fellow of Brasenose 1568-9; Bursar 1575-9. In 1579 Colmer was incorporated at Cambridge.[17]

However, the most telling indication of his identity comes in his reference to Harington's attack (*Apologie*, O6–O6^v, pp. 243-4) on Richard Young, the hated justice of peace for Middlesex, whose energies had been directed to ferreting out religious suspects. On O6^v (p. 244) Harington had prudently refrained from printing Young's name, leaving a lacuna in the text which, for a modern reader at least, robs the passage of meaning.[18] Having detected these allusions, the author of the *Ulysses* in a statement that suggests his name may also have been *Young* warns Harington of his need for greater religious conformity:

And (by the way for your selfe) a *Yoong* that will be olde, (saith thus) in behalfe of olde *Yoong* that except you presentlie put one a habit of more conformity, if some his enimies maie promote you, you shall bee the next dog shall be sacrifisd in the *Lupercalia*, and therfore provide your selfe for it; (except you get a better tong into you[r] heade; or a modester pen in your hande.) (C7^v)

Whoever Misodiaboles was, it seems quite clear that he was not Harington.

One unfortunate result stemming from the failure to distinguish Harington's work from the *Ulysses upon Ajax* is that its general indecency has been allowed to colour the evaluation of the *Metamorphosis*.

What was Harington's intent in writing the *Metamorphosis*? His motives, as we shall see, were varied, as varied as the several literary strands he wove together to fashion a work carrying the dominant impress of his humanistic training.

By means of his annotations in the presentation copies, we

---

[17] *Brasenose College Register* (Oxford, 1909), I. 39. In this connection it may be noted that Harington has some twenty epigrams directed against one Lynus; in Epigram 13, Bk. III, he associates him with 'Brazen-nose.' As to the identity of Lynus, see G. C. Moore Smith's speculations in *TLS*, 19 March 1927, p. 160.

[18] He has supplied this lacuna by hand in all presentation copies.

17

can reconstruct the genesis of the *Metamorphosis*. The setting was the splendid residence in Wiltshire belonging to Sir Matthew Arundell which Harington termed the 'wonder of the West,' Wardour Castle. Here on one occasion had gathered six persons, of whom 'five, for beuty, for birth, for vallew, for witt, and for wealth' were not to be matched in many places of the realm. Here the device was 'first both thought of and discoursed of, with as brode termes as any belongs to it' with 'all save one' being 'enterlocutors in the dialogue.' In addition to Harington, these included the host, Sir Matthew; his son Thomas, Harington's old schoolfellow at Eton, now elevated to the rank of Count of the Holy Roman Empire; Sir Henry Danvers; the Earl of Southampton; and Lady Mary Arundell, wife of Thomas and sister of Southampton, the doubtless silent member of the group. We can date this jocular conversation some time before October 1594 when one of the interlocutors, Sir Henry Danvers, having climaxed a family feud with murder, escaped to France through the help of Thomas Arundell and the Earl of Southampton.[19]

Having thus conceived his unworthy 'conceyt' in worthy surroundings, Harington next proceeded to have the device constructed and installed in his fine manor house at Kelston. Then, at the entreaty of his cousin Philostilpnos, he was persuaded to expel all 'private bashfulnesse' and record his invention for a 'publicke benefite.' Emphasis on the utility of his invention remains a persistent, and more than mock-serious, element in the work; and the need to justify a literary treatment of so base a topic afforded him a traditional framework within which he could also incorporate his other motives in writing.

As he makes clear in his prefatory letter, Harington keys his treatise to the kind of ingenious display piece popular in the Renaissance, the encomium on a trivial or unworthy subject. Aptly described as a kind of intellectual gymnastics, this form of writing had had a long vogue, dating back to the Greek rhetoricians, and it received a new infusion of vitality during the Renaissance through the efforts of the humanists. To preface such a work with a listing of other examples in the genre became standard, and Harington duly notes seven

---

[19] See notes to p. 59.

examples, thereby gaining an opportunity to highlight the particular merits of his own feat: it will not be so wise as the first example he has noted—Erasmus's *Praise of Folly*—but it will be 'civiller,' 'truer,' 'honester,' 'chaster,' 'modester,' and 'clenlyer' than the others; and thus he may be reckoned (in Horace's ironic phrase) *sapientum octavus*.

Harington's inclusion of Rabelais among the seven and his suggestion that, in terms of the priority of subject matter at least, he should precede the Frenchman in his catalogue suggests that he was to some degree consciously imitating the Rabelaisian mode. In his study, *Rabelais in English Literature*, Huntington Brown asserts that the first two Englishmen who knew how to value and imitate Rabelais were John Eliot and Harington; he feels, furthermore, that the particular qualities of Rabelais that Harington captured were the 'charm of his miscellaneous learning, his mock-gravity, and his healthy coarseness.'[20]

In accordance with a humanistic technique, the structure of the *New Discourse* is ordered: first, he defends the use of homely terms by 'most autenticall authorities and examples'; second, he shows that 'the matter itself has been an object of concern in all ages'; and, finally, he shows the 'forme, and how it may be reformed.' Since the times are captious and there is a need to stop carping mouths, Harington adopts the art of *copia*, marshalling an array of 'Emperours, Kings, Magistrats, Prophets, Poets All-hallowes, and all prophanes, even from the Bible to the bable' to ennoble his argument. But if he relies on the skill of art to make his treatise mannerly (clothing it 'like an ape in purple'), he also provides an escape clause by reliance on the humanistic principle of *decorum* that dictates slovenly eloquence for a slovenly matter.

However, Harington never loses sight of the basic utility of his invention. This justifies the appending of the *Anatomie* with its diagrams instructing a workman how to assemble the device. This accounts for his repeated insistence on its usefulness in poor cottages, stately houses, or the goodliest palaces of the realm.[21] In the *Apologie*, when he discusses the type of person

---

[20] Cambridge, Mass., 1933, p. 65.
[21] That his efforts brought results in the palace at Richmond is indicated by Epigram 44, Bk. I, *L&E*, p. 165.

to whom he would be content that both the discourse and the device be shown, he stresses his interest in the individual who is not only a builder but also a housekeeper:

Then I will come home to his house to him, I will reade him a lecture of it, I will instruct his workeman, I will give him plots and models, and do him all the service I can: for that is a man of my own humor, & a good common wealthsman. . . .

Accordingly, when he selects the jurors who are to pass judgment on the *New Discourse*, he selects those who, in addition to being his friends and relatives, are all conspicuous examples of that particularly Elizabethan species, great builders and house-keepers. Thus, in emphasizing the true merits of his invention, Harington somewhat alters the cast of essential triviality characteristic of the mock encomium while still retaining its method and technique.

Although he clearly preserves the formal outlines of the treatise, he makes use of the digressive technique characteristic of popular writers like Stubbes and Nashe and Lodge. Nashe, most particularly, had the habit of seizing on a topic as a loose device on which to hang diverting matter, lively anecdotes, and wayward comments, in the course of which, his tide of digressive eloquence having ebbed, he made a conspicuous point of returning to his original topic. This practice Harington imitates.

Harington further exploits the discursive method in order to present the 'true intent' of the book, which, in sum, is a satire of contemporary persons and practices. That his readers should not miss this intent, he states it in direct terms at the end of the *New Discourse*. The prologue and the first part are directed chiefly 'against malcontents, Epicures, Atheists, heretickes, & carelesse & dissolute Christians, and especially against pride and sensualitie'; the second part, largely an account of Roman rulers who had exhibited concern for the problem of sanitation, 'gives a due praise without flatterie, to one that is worthie of it, and a just checke without gall to some that deserve it'; the third part 'as it teacheth indeed a reformation of the matter in question, so it toucheth in sport, a reprehension of some practises too much in custome,' namely, monopolies.

Again, in order to make quite certain his objectives have not been passed over by his readers, Harington adds the *Apologie* where he answers eleven specific charges directed against him for writing the *New Discourse*; of these several are intended to emphasize the personal satire. He pleads guilty to the accusation that he has taken this 'laughing libertie' to grace some that had favoured him and to grate against some that had galled him. Three other accusations he denies but with equivocal statements intended to reinforce their point. The accusations are that he has thought 'to scoffe at some Gentlemen that have served in some honorable services, though with no great good successe'; that he has sought 'to discredit the honest meaning & laudable endevours of some zealous & honest men, that seeke for reformation, & labour faithfully & fruitfully in the word'; and that he has intended 'some scorne to great Magistrats & men in authority, either alive or deceassed, under covert names to cover som knavery.'

Furthermore, in the comments about his prospective jurors, he offers brief personal sketches of his friends; these are mainly complimentary, but he also offers a vindication of two who had incurred suspicion because of their Catholic sympathies. Indeed, he goes to considerable pains to defend his uncle Thomas Markham and, more briefly, Hatton, Bancroft, and others who had been victims of a libel.

If then he made his satiric intent explicit, were the objects of his satire equally clear to his readers? We know, for example, that the Queen had conceived 'much disquiet' on being told he 'had aimed a shafte at Leicester.'[22] Yet this particular shaft has never been detected. The reason is perhaps to be found in the obliqueness of his method.

The handling of the section on the various Roman rulers (which is, I think, a mine of undetected allusions) suggests Harington's technique, *i.e.*, to marshal pertinent facts and anecdotes from the historians which would have, at the same time, suggestive overtones for his contemporaries. Thus, in accordance with his sources, he contrasts Lucius Brutus with Marcus Brutus whom he seems to refer to by the phrase *ultimus Romanorum*, an epithet usually applied to Cassius. Yet this contrast of historical figures clearly includes a topical

---

[22] *NA*, I, 240.

overtone. For in the *Apologie* among his various detractors are two who were particularly touched in honor because they had been 'likened to Brutus and Cassius, and called *ultimi Ruffian-orum.*' Again, it is quite clear that the 'due praise' extended to the sixteenth-century English parallel of Trajan is intended for the Earl of Essex who 'perhaps at this houre is not farre from Trajans countrey,' a reference to the expedition to Cadiz.

Since Harington does adhere to historical sources, apparently relying on a cluster of skilfully selected details to reveal his topical reference, it is impossible in most cases for us to detect the allusion with any certainty; in many instances it must have been equally difficult for his readers, even for those most caught up in the social and political intrigues of the courtly world. And therein lay his real protection from the charges of 'scandaling.'

Thus we can summarize his methods and motives: taking the mock encomium as his form, Harington develops it according to a humanistic technique, tinged, however, with a Rabelaisian strain. But ingenuity and erudite display in the cause of an unworthy subject are counter-balanced to some degree by repeated emphasis on the utility of his invention. He also employs the discursive, anecdotal technique characteristic of popular writing both in order to enliven his treatise and to include an abundance of topical satire. Yet, unlike Nashe, he never allows these digressions to overshadow his essential concept of form and unity.

His style consequently is an amalgam of the popular and the learned. The tone is sprightly and direct with the easy and, frequently, loose syntax characteristic of informal conversation. References to Livy or Suetonius, Horace or Ovid blend with recollections out of Heywood or one of the old jest books, and the spice of contemporary allusion is scattered throughout.

Harington delights in word play, in the exploitation of sounds, in witty equivocations; his range of vocabulary, especially in terms of the novel and unexpected, is notable. As George Peele had observed in 1593, 'Harrington well letter'd and discreet . . . naturalized / Strange words, and made them all free-denyzons.'[23] Offsetting this flair for the unexpected is

---

[23] 'The Honour of the Garter,' Prologue, ll. 41-2, *Life and Works*, ed. D. H. Horner (New Haven, 1952).

an equally marked reliance on the proverbial and the familiar.[24]

Wit and scholarship, as Nashe had noted, are to be found in the *Metamorphosis of Ajax*, and these two elements, together with a gay impudence, characterize the whole: *ridentem dicere verum quis vetat?*

EDITIONS

The First Edition of the Three Parts

The first edition, carrying the imprint of Richard Field, is the only complete edition published with continuous signatures. It is a small octavo consisting of the three parts: *A New Discourse of a Stale Subject, Called the Metamorphosis of Ajax* (A–K⁸); *An Anatomie of the Metamorpho-sed Ajax* with a separate title page (L⁸); and *An Apologie* (M–P⁸ Q², last leaf blank).

Large-paper copies

Of the large-paper copies printed on thick ruled paper, two are complete, the Markham-Wrenn and Lumley-Folger copies. In addition, there is a mutilated copy at Sheffield University (lacking text for P1–2, P7–8, Q1) and an incomplete copy including only the *Anatomie* and *Apologie* (lacking the last leaf of text), the Nares-Folger copy.[1] Each of these includes

---

[24] There are some seventy-odd examples of proverbs in his text.

[1] By using a copy of the third edition of *A New Discourse*, Nares created a complete text; the three parts were then slightly trimmed, the pages inlaid, and bound into a single volume. Nares has written on the flyleaf: 'The few marginal Notes inserted in the beginning [of the copy of the third edition of the *New Discourse*], were cut from an old, large-paper, ruled copy, too much mutilated & dirtied to be preserved; & have much [the] appearance of having been written by the author himself, or by his order. It had evidently been a presentation Copy. The *Anatomie* & *Apologie* are part of the same copy, and have also a few MS. notes.' This is dated 1813. The last leaf of the text of the *Apologie* which is missing has been supplied by hand.

S. W. Singer had apparently seen the Nares-Folger or Sheffield copies (or one with a comparable annotation), since he includes a MS annotation on p. 21 of his edition which appears in these copies but not in the Lumley or Markham copies. Yet the only source he mentions for the MS notes he included is the Markham copy; these, he says, were printed 'from an accurate transcript furnished by a friend' (p. ix).

annotations written in Harington's Italian hand.

There is convincing evidence to show that the edition represented by these copies is the first and that it included all three parts.

1. Successive editions of *A New Discourse* and *An Apologie* are progressively made more compact.

2. In the dedication of the copy presented to his uncle Thomas Markham,[2] which is dated 3 August 1596, Harington refers to the remarks he has made about Markham which occur in the *Apologie* (P1–P3); this shows that all three parts were in print prior to the date of the dedication and that they constituted a unit.

3. The use of continuous signatures for the complete work is clear evidence that the three parts were intended to form a unit.

4. The watermark is the same in all sheets of the Lumley-Folger, Markham-Wrenn, and Sheffield copies;[3] although the Nares-Folger copy has been trimmed for inset, the same watermark as in the other copies appears on sheets M and N of the *Apologie*.

5. Certain characteristic Latin spellings follow Harington's MS (*e.g.*, *indolencia* for *indolentia*); many of these were normalized for the second edition.

6. The text of *A New Discourse* begins on a new sheet, characteristic of a first edition.

7. Further support for the identification of the A–K[8]

Since he failed to examine the Markham copy personally, Singer was unaware of the differences between the first edition of *A New Discourse* and the subsequent derived editions. Consequently, he used for a copy-text the non-imprinted fourth edition collated with a copy of the non-imprinted third edition, even though he knew Richard Field had been the publisher of the first (pp. vii, viii). An even more startling consequence of his having failed to examine the Markham copy was that he was totally unaware that it contained the first edition of the *Apologie*. Therefore, he again used one of the derived editions for his copy-text, apparently having assumed it to be the earliest (p. viii).

[2] 'To the Right worshipfull / Thomas Markham. / Esquyre this / bee dd. / I wil not say moche to you in the / beginning of my booke becaus I / have sayd perhaps more then en- / ough of yow in the end. / I pray yow take yt wel for I doubt / not but some wil take it ill, but yf / they doe yt wil be becaus they doe / ill understand yt; yor interest is / moch in the work becaus yt is moste / in the wryter. so I end the iij^d of / August. 1596. / By the Autor.'

[3] Miss Jean Cassel and Dr. W. B. Todd kindly checked the Markham-Wrenn copy for me, Miss Sigrid Mandahl and Mr. J. E. Tolson the Sheffield copy.

edition of *A New Discourse* as the first is to be found in the letter written by Harington to Lady Russell dated 14 August 1596. Remarking that the work had been written 'not long since,' he asks Lady Russell to send a copy to Burghley and refers to his mention of 'Tiballs' on page 118. To judge from the date of the Markham dedication, the work had probably been off the press only some ten to twelve days at the time of Harington's letter, which accords well enough with his statement that it had been written 'not long since.' Since the A–K[8] edition is the only one where the reference to 'Tiballs' falls on page 118, Harington's letter provides collateral evidence for identifying it as the first.

Trade copies

In addition to the large-paper copies, there is still extant a complete edition of the three parts printed on ordinary paper at Lambeth Palace,[4] as well as individual copies of *A New Discourse* (Chapin; BM C.21.a.2) and the *Anatomie* (Bodley, Douce H91[5]). As stated above, the *Anatomie* has its own title page, indicating its author by the initials T.C., *i.e.*, Thomas Combe, Harington's personal servant, but the third part of the work has only the caption-title *An Apologie*, followed by a series of twelve subtitles.[6]

It is clear, furthermore, that the trade copies of *A New Discourse* were issued prior to the *Anatomie*. This is shown by the fact that the gibes Harington directed at the resourceful Hugh Plat (I3 ff. of *A New Discourse*) caused him to answer in a brief publication entitled *Sundrie new and Artificiall remedies against Famine*,[7] which, in turn, was noticed by T.C. in the *Anatomie*.

Stung by Harington's remarks, Plat apparently determined to retaliate at once; consequently, he sprinkled references to

---

[4] Professor James L. Clifford kindly checked this copy for me, and Mr. E. G. W. Bill, the Librarian, states that the volume, still in its original binding, belonged to Archbishop Bancroft.

[5] Professor Herbert Davis kindly checked this copy for me.

[6] Even when the four subsequent editions of the *Apologie* were published, no title page was added.

[7] Entered to Peter Shorte 23 August 1596 (*S.R.*, III, 69). The entry clearly must have been made some weeks *after* publication.

'M. Ajax,' the sobriquet which was to remain Harington's ever after, in the last few pages of this brief pamphlet, a work which he doubtless had ready at hand. Nor was Plat answering a manuscript that had been circulated, for from his remarks we can conclude that *A New Discourse*, which consisted of ten sheets, was in print and being sold—at a cost of 1*s*. 8*d*. Speaking of his own literary efforts, Plat says,

[If] I could fal into *M. Ajax* veine, and had some of his glib paper, & gliding pens, I might soon scribble ten sheets, and sell everie sheet for two pence, towarde necessarie charges.[8] (E1)

Sometime then after the publication of *Sundrie remedies against Famine*, the *Anatomie*, which was in print prior to 3 August, appeared. In it, T.C. takes occasion to refer to Plat's reaction in his 'booke against famine' (L3, following MS).

Thus, we may conclude that Field, in line with normal printing-house practice, ran off his trade copies of *A New Discourse* before printing the large-paper copies.[9] After a brief interval, sufficient for Plat's pamphlet to have appeared in print, Field printed the *Anatomie* and the *Apologie*.

The Second Edition of *A New Discourse*

Edition II (not listed in STC) [12779.1]

The second edition was also printed by Richard Field with an almost identical title page (some variation in spacing; some wrong-font letters) but in a more compact form (A–I[8] K[2]).[10]

---

[8] In the *Apologie* Harington terms the *New Discourse* 'a booke that was not to be sold in Paules churchyard, but onely that he [one of his detractors] had borowed it of his friend' (M2 and verso).

[9] This is substantiated by the fact that a marginal reference Harington added to G7 is not in the Chapin copy of the trade issue, but it is in the BM trade copy (C.21.a.2) and in the copies on large paper.

Apparently the large-paper copies were all intended as presentation copies; though the four mentioned above are the only ones traced, it seems not unlikely that Harington presented copies to a number of the friends he mentions in the course of the work. One would assume, for example, that he had sent a copy to be presented to Burghley along with the letter that he wrote Lady Russell requesting her to do so.

[10] In addition to Field's printer's device (McKerrow 192), Edition II uses the same distinctive floral initials, ornaments, and tail piece (McKerrow 179) which had appeared in Edition I.

Copies: Hitch-Folger; Huntington 59769; White-Harvard; Farmer-Bindley-Wrenn; Bodley, Malone 509.

Although a careful reprint which corrects some errors, this second edition, in turn, introduces a few new ones, omits the marginalia appearing on H1ᵛ of Edition I, and introduces a number of changes in paragraphing and typographical arrangement. Furthermore, the woodcuts on C7 and G7, although close copies of the originals (D1ᵛ and H4), show certain differences which indicate that they were not printed from the blocks which had been used in the original edition.

Subsequent Editions of *A New Discourse*

Edition III (STC 12780), with no imprint

Although the STC distinguishes 12780 and 12781 on the basis of the spelling of *priuie* vs *priuy* in the last line of the text (I2ᵛ), this means of distinguishing the two has caused much confusion and resultant errors of listing. The confusion arises from the fact that there are two states of the final quarter sheet of 12780 and each setting of I2ᵛ illustrates the two spellings.[11]

Apparently either because of an accident at press or the need to run off more copies, the settings of I1 and I2 were reimposed. This necessitated the resetting of the marginal notes on I1 recto and verso and I2 recto and a complete resetting of the text of I2ᵛ. As a result, I2ᵛ shows the variant spellings in the last line:

		Copies
a	*priuy faults,*	Nares-Folger [listed as 12781]
		Douce H91
		Lincoln Cathedral
b	*priuie faults.*	Huntington 20122

---

[11] A. E. M. Kirwood examining only the copies in the British Museum was led to assert that C.21.a.5 and G10364 representing 12780 and 12781 were really the same edition, differing only in the settings of I1 and I2 (p. 222, n. 1, and p. 232). This is (partially) true for these two BM copies, but the STC is correct in recognizing two distinct, non-imprinted editions—STC 12780 and 12781. BM C.21.a.5 is a copy of Edition IV (12781), while BM G10364 should properly be classified as a composite issue since it consists of Edition IV (12781) up through H8, but I1 and I2 have been supplied from the *b* state of Edition III (12780).

The priority of *a* seems to be established by the fact that the marginal settings of *a* conform in their arrangement to those in Edition I from which the text was set while *b* does not. Furthermore, the arrangement of the marginal notes in the *b* setting of Edition III is followed by the compositor of Edition IV who set his text page-for-page from a copy of Edition III.[12]

Edition III which lacks an imprint is signed A–H⁸ I². That this edition was printed after II is indicated by its more compact arrangement and by the fact that the woodcuts on C6 and G1ᵛ were printed from the same blocks as those in Edition II.[13]

However, III derives directly from Edition I:

1. It includes the marginalia on F7ᵛ which was omitted in Edition II. It follows the readings of Edition I even in its errors, as *indolencia* (B8) for the *indolentia* of II. (Nares-Folger copy corrected by hand), and its attempt at such an ill-conceived

---

[12] Cf. the arrangement of marginal notes in Edition I and Edition III:

Edition I	Edition III (12780)	
	a setting	*b* setting
K7	I1	I1
Allusion to the former words.	Allusion to the former wordes.	Allusiō to the former words
K7ᵛ	I1ᵛ	I1ᵛ
A fit rule to be kept, and breedes all misrule when it is broken, specially by honorable persons.	A fit rule to be kept, and breeds all misrule, when it is broken especially by honorable person.	A fit rule to be kept, and breeds al misrule when it is broken specially by honorable persons.
K8	I2	I2
That is to say, What a foole was S. Peter?	That is to say, What a foole was S. Peter?	That is to say what a soole [long *s*] was S. Peter

[13] Kirwood further concluded from the fact that the woodcuts in his 12780–1 edition differ from those in the first (12799) that the later edition was pirated (p. 221). His assertion, however, that the different woodcuts constitute the 'strongest evidence of piracy' must be discounted, since woodcuts from the same blocks had appeared in Field's reprint. See below.

correction as the following shows that III could only have derived from I:

> I side note I6 'flatteree' (corrected by hand, Lumley-Folger and Sheffield copies)
> II side note H8 'flattered' (the correct reading)
> III side note H2 'flatterie'

2. Further, III follows Edition I in typographical arrangement, whereas II introduces a number of variations, chiefly in paragraphing. These are shown in the following table (P stands for paragraph):

I			III			II		
	line			line			line	
A3ᵛ	19	no P	A3ᵛ	19	no P	A3	17	P
A6	4	no P	A5ᵛ	13	no P	A5	23	P
D4	4	no P	C8	8	no P	D1	20	P
D4	17	no P	C8	20	no P	D1ᵛ	4	P
D4ᵛ	20	no P	C8ᵛ	17	no P	D2	5	P
D5	3	no P	C8ᵛ	26	no P	D2	14	P
D5ᵛ	Epigram 4 ll.		D1	Epigram 4 ll.		D2ᵛ	Epigram 8 ll.	
D6ᵛ	14	no P	D2	18	no P	D3ᵛ	16	P
D7	16	no P	D2ᵛ	14	no P	D4	15	P
G8ᵛ	Quote italics		F6ᵛ	Quote italics		G3ᵛ	Quote roman	
K4	8	no P	H6ᵛ	20	no P	I5ᵛ	18	P
K7ᵛ	7	no P	I1ᵛ	10	no P	K1	16	P

Thus Edition III with its two settings of I1 and I2 derives directly from the first edition but utilizes the woodcuts which had appeared in Edition II.

Composite Editions III and IV

There are two composite editions: (1) consists of Edition III (12780) up through sheet H; the edition is then completed by Edition IV (12781) for leaves I1 and I2. Copies: Wrenn (Wh/H244/596nc)[14] and Bodley, Malone 510. (2) consists of Edition IV (12781) up through sheet H; the edition is then

---

[14] Cited hereafter simply as Wrenn.

completed by the *b* state of Edition III (12780) for leaves I1 and
I2. Copies: BM G10364 and Bodley L79 Art (11).

Thus, we may conclude that the same printer was responsible
for 12780 and 12781, since at some stage in assembling these
editions the *b* setting of I1 and I2 of 12780 and the I1 and I2
setting of 12781 were indiscriminately used.

Edition IV (STC 12781) with no imprint

Edition IV also lacks an imprint and is also signed A–H⁸ I²,
but it may be distinguished from III as the 'omicron' edition.
Copies: Folger [called 12781a]; Yale Medical Library; BM
C.21.a.5; Bodley E 106 Linc. (5).

1. The heading of the Prologue in Editions I, II, and III
reads: 'The Prologve / To the Reader of / the [*the* omitted in
III, followed by IV] Metamorphώ sis of A IAX' whereas IV
reads 'Metamorph*o*sis' (my italics).

2. This inordinately careless page-for-page reprint of
Edition III blindly follows the errors in III while effecting
further degeneration of the text in terms of both literals and
substantives. A few examples suffice to make this clear.

    a. A8ᵛ, ll. 3–4 read: 'hee massacred a whole / flocke of sheepe
       not Ewes,' whereas II and III correctly follow I (which,
       in turn, follows the MS) in reading: 'he massacred a
       whole flock of good nott Ews.'

    b. D4, l. 23 reads 'of mewing a woodcock,' whereas the
       other editions read 'inewing': a substitution of one
       hawking term, here inapplicable, for another.[15]

    c. E1ᵛ, l. 14 follows III in repeating the error '*purgarie &*
       reficere cloacam.'

    d. F3ᵛ (missigned F4 in all copies traced), ll. 18–19 repeat
       III's error 'that though now to the cleane of al thinges /
       are cleane,' whereas I and II read 'that though now to the
       cleane all things are cleane.'

---

[15] To *inew* (or enew) is to drive a fowl into the water; to *mew* is to inclose a
hawk in a cage during moulting time, here, inaptly, applied to the object of
the hunt, the woodcock.

e. H2, margin, follows III in reading 'flatterie' in place of the 'flatteree' of I or the correct 'flattered' of II.

Edition IV, furthermore, offers a perplexing situation in terms of the variants for sheet I. I1ʳ exists in two states, each of which shows a correction and each of which introduces a new error.[16] Yet no copy I have seen corrects ll. 12–13 which read '*Of faults, priuies, and sinks and draughts to | write*' where *faults* should be *vaults*. I2ᵛ has the same setting in all copies.

I1ᵛ exists in two states, the corrected state being represented by Folger [12781a] plus copies of Composite III (Bodley, Mal. 510 and the Wrenn copy).[17] I2ʳ exists in three states,[18] suggesting that two represent corrections, a situation which, although not unusual, does seem a trifle odd in an edition which is rife with errors.

Thus Edition IV is a careless reprint of Edition III, but it too uses the woodcuts that had appeared in Edition II.

---

[16]

	Folger [12781a] plus Bodley, Mal. 510, and Wrenn	Yale Medical L. BM C.21.a.5 Bodley E 106 Linc. (5)
I1ʳ		
l.16	piruie	priuie
l.21	noted do	note do

[17]

I1ᵛ		
l.4	swarue	swaure
margin	whenit	when it
l.22	of his person	nif his person
l.23	if the same	of the same

[18]

	Folger [12781a] Bod., Mal. 510	Yale Med. L. BM C.21.a.5 Bod. E 106 Linc. (5)	Wrenn
I2ʳ			
margin	Miscacmos	Misacmos	Misacmos (positioned like Yale, etc.)
l.5	exhortation	exhortation	exhortation
margin	to say	ro say	to say

The priority of editions of *A New Discourse* may be summarized as follows:

I

STC 12779. A–K^8, with imprint of Richard Field.
Trade copies: Lambeth
Chapin
BM C.21.a.2
Large-paper State
Copies: Markham-Wrenn
Lumley-Folger
Sheffield

II

Not in STC [12779.1]
A–I^8 K^2, with imprint of Richard Field.
Copies: Hitch-Folger
Huntington 59769
White-Harvard
Farmer-Bindley-
Wrenn
Bodley, Malone 509

III

STC 12780. A–H^8 I^2, no imprint. Two settings of I1 and I2.
Copies: Nares-Folger
Bodley, Douce H91
Lincoln Cathedral
Huntington 21022

IV

STC 12781. A–H^8 I^2, no imprint. 'Omicron' edition.
Copies: Folger [12781a]
Yale Medical Lib.
BM C.21.a.5
Bodley, E 106 Linc. (5)

N.B. As recorded on pp. 29–30, four other copies are composite, partly Edition III and partly Edition IV.

An Anatomie

There are two editions of the *Anatomie*. Both consist of one sheet in octavo signed L⁸, and both were published by Richard Field and carry his imprint on the title pages. The priority of Edition I, not listed in STC [A12772], is established by its appearance in the complete text published with continuous signatures and is easily distinguished from Edition II (STC 12772). The text of the second edition is a page-for-page reprint and in its correction of misprints is superior to Edition I.

[A12772] I	12772 II
Trade copies: Lambeth	BM G10364 (3)
Bod., Douce H91	Hitch-Folger
Large-paper State	Huntington 59766
Copies: Markham-Wrenn	Chapin
Lumley-Folger	Farmer-Bindley-
Sheffield	Wrenn
Nares-Folger	Bristol Pub. L.
	White-Harvard (with corrected title page)[19]

Title page *not* dated	dated 1596
Title page, l.16 *atq*;	*atque*
L2 ornamental initial inverted	ornamental initial correct

The emblems on L8 differ; in [A12772] the I of DEI alone comes under the fastening of the emblem, whereas in 12772 both the E and I are directly under it.

---

[19] The corrected title page of the second edition illustrates the care which Field's proofreader took: he corrected misspellings (*Poetre* for *Poetrie*, l. 12; *Pria-/ctiser* for *Prac-/tiser*, ll. 12–13) and he altered the spelling of *tripartite* (l. 4) to *tripertite*, the spelling found in I.

An Apologie

As indicated above, the *Apologie* has only a caption-title followed by a series of twelve subtitles placed above the beginning of the text. In order to classify the subsequent editions, I have used the readings of subtitles 1 and 10 which vary between *retractation-retraction* and *confirmation-confirmatiō*.

Edition I 'retractation . . . confirmation,' signed M–P⁸ Q² (last leaf blank). Not in STC [A12774]. Copies: Markham-Wrenn; Lumley-Folger; Sheffield; Nares-Folger; Lambeth (trade copy).

That this is the first edition is attested by its appearance with the first editions of *A New Discourse* and *An Anatomie*, the three parts being published with continuous signatures.

Edition II 'retractation . . . confirmation,' signed 2A–2C⁸ 2D³ (2D⁴ probably blank). STC 12774. Copies: Huntington 59767; Chapin; White-Harvard; Farmer-Bindley-Wrenn.

Although lacking a separate title page, this may safely be assigned to Richard Field as the third part of his reprint.

1. On M3ᵛ of the original edition, there is a marginal reference to page '44' of *A New Discourse*. The Farmer-Bindley-Wrenn copy of Edition II of the *Apologie* also reads '44', but other copies (Huntington 59767; Chapin; and White-Harvard) were corrected to '41,' thus bringing the marginal note into conformity with the proper passage in the more compact arrangement of the second edition of *A New Discourse* printed by Field. Furthermore, only Editions I and II, carrying Field's imprint, have pagination. (Since Editions III and IV of *A New Discourse* are more compact than II, the only edition to which the corrected paginal reference '41' could apply in any case is to Edition II printed by Field.)

2. The head ornament on 2A1 was frequently used by Field (see Kirwood, 'Richard Field, Printer, 1589–1624,' where the ornament is listed as number six in the order of frequency[20])

---

[20] *Library*, XII (1931–2), 28. Consisting of an arabesque with hearts at the centre, this is to be distinguished, as Kirwood points out, from a similar head ornament used by other printers which consists of an arabesque strip with hearts at the end. The latter ornament appears in the third and fourth editions of the *Apologie*.

and appears in the first edition of the three parts on signatures C1, E3, H7^v, and M1 and in the second edition of *A New Discourse* on B7 and D7^v.[21]

On the basis then of these indications that Field was the printer of this edition, the use of the doubled signatures becomes clear: the reprint of the *Apologie* is signed to indicate its continuation of the other two reprinted parts carrying Field's imprint.

Subsequent Editions of *An Apologie*

Edition III 'retractation . . . confirmatiō,' signed 2A–2C^8 2D^3 (2D^4 probably blank). Not listed in STC [12774.1]. Copies: Folger copy bound with [12781a]; Huntington 61279; Yale Medical Library; BM G10364 (2); Bodley Douce H91; Bodley L79 Art (12).

Edition IV 'retraction . . . confirmation,' signed 2A–2C^8 2D^3 (2D^4 probably blank). STC 12773. Copies: BM C.21.a.5; BM C.37.b.8; Huntington 61363.

Edition V 'retraction . . . confirmation + floral spray initial,'[22] signed 2A–2C^8 2D^3 (2D^4 probably blank). Not in STC [12773.1]. Copy: Hitch-Folger.

These three editions, all of which are signed 2A–2C^8 2D^3, derive directly or indirectly from the second edition. Although closely following II, they are not exact page-for-page reprints; Edition V, furthermore, differs from II, III, and IV in a host of minor readings, proving conclusively that V could not have

---

[21] The watermarks of the three parts of the second edition, unfortunately, offer no help since they have been lost in the spine because of the octavo format; furthermore, the copies I have examined have also been trimmed. This is true of the Huntington copies of the three parts, which Dr. French Fogle, formerly of the Huntington, was kind enough to check for me.

[22] In contrast with the floral spray initial of V, Editions II, III, and IV all have the same factotum on 2A1. This factotum is not uncommon; it appears, for example, in the *Ulysses upon Ajax* (STC 12783) carrying Thomas Gubbins's imprint. The head ornament of Edition V also appears in various arrangements in the first edition of the *Ulysses* (STC 12782).

been the source for any other edition.[23] The evidence tends to support the view that III and IV derive independently from II, so that, although they are here called III and IV, their *actual* priority cannot be determined. Edition III, moreover, is characterized by the conscientious, if inept, efforts of its compositor to rectify various incorrect readings.

That all editions subsequent to II derive directly or indirectly from II seems sufficiently attested by the following examples:

1. Like II, Editions III, IV, and V omit various marginal references on 2B4 and verso, 2C3^v, 2C4, 2C7, and 2C8^v [N7, O8, O8^v, P4, and P6 of the original edition].

2. On 2B3, l. 1 of Editions II, III, IV, and V reads 'if the graund Iurie were *prickt* by a bad Sheriffe,' whereas the original edition reads *packt* [my italics].

3. On 2B5^v, ll. 13–14; 17–18 of II, III, IV, and V inadvertently repeat the subject 'you / you had a brother of Lincolnes Inn' and 'you / you haue a learned writer of your name,' whereas the original edition in each case reads simply 'you.' (Edition V in each case adds a comma.)

4. Edition I (N7, ll. 5–7) reads:

> Here is one *Misacmos*, that is accu- / sed by some diligent officers and good / seruants of the state. . . .

Edition II (2B4, last line) reads:

> Here is one *Misacmos*, that is accused /
>   [catchword] ser-

---

[23] Cf. the following random examples where Editions II, III, and IV have identical readings (although varying in orthography), but where V shows modifications resulting from a careless compositor:

		II, (III, IV)	V
2A5	2	'this that he hath'	'this hee hath'
	11	'You did thinke'	'You thought'
	14–15	'neither do / I meane'	'neither mean I'
2B1^v	15–16	'the town / is drawne by this reuell'	'the / towne is drawn by this leuel'
2C6	24–25	'did / not I tel you again, that I would laugh too'	'did / not I tel you againe, I would laugh too'
	29–30	' if you do not / say well of it'	' if you say / not wel of it'
2D3	2	'the two last verses'	'the last two verses'
	6–7	'that looked like *Ia- / nus* picture'	'looking like / *Ianus* picture'

($2B4^v$) seruants of the state. . . .

    Editions IV and V follow II.

    Edition III ($2B4$, last line) reads:

        Here is one *Misacmos*, that is an accused /

                [catchword] seruant

($2B4^v$) seruants of the state. . . .

This not only illustrates the ultimate derivation of Editions III, IV, and V from II, but also the haphazard effort of the compositor of III to make a correction for $2B4$ while simply reverting to following the text for $2B4^v$; it also shows that Editions IV and V could not have been printed from III.

Thus it seems clear that Edition II was the source for all subsequent editions and that Edition IV was printed from II rather than from III.

That Edition V ('retraction . . . confirmation + floral spray initial') derives from IV ('retraction . . . confirmation') is supported by the following points:

    1. The reading 'retraction' in subtitle 1.

    2. Edition II ($2A2$, last line) reads:

                they perused the

                [no catchword]

($2A2^v$) pictures. . . .

Edition III follows II but with the addition of the catchword 'pictures.'

Edition IV ($2A2$, last line) reads:

                they perused the

                [catchword] pictures

($2A2^v$) tures. . . .

Edition V is the same as IV.

    3. Finally, the running head on $2A8$ of Edition V has been set from an uncorrected forme of Edition IV (*e.g.*, BM C.21.a.5) and reads 'The Prologie' (both swash capitals), whereas the corrected forme of IV (*e.g.*, Huntington 61363) reads 'An Apologie' (swash A in An). Thus it seems clear that Edition V derives from IV.

What then is the evidence to support the view that III derives directly from II rather than from IV? No one point, it should be recognized, is incontrovertible, but the cumulative evidence seems convincing.

1. The reading 'retractation' in the first subtitle is more simply explained by its following of II, also 'retractation,' than by its departure from IV's 'retraction' and, as a result, restoring the original reading.

2. The correct reading on 2A2 and 2A2^v involved with the catchword and turn of the page (see above) is also more simply explained by III's following of the correct reading in II than by assuming it results from a correction of the reading in IV.

3. Of fourteen changes in paragraphing introduced by Edition II, III follows II in every case, whereas IV in two cases does not. Again, the simpler explanation is that III derives directly from II.

4. The text of the *Apologie* ends with a quotation from Aesop which has the correct reading *gallinaceous* in Edition I. Edition II prints *gallinatius*.
Edition III follows II in the arrangement of the lines but compounds the error to *gallinatious*.
Editions IV and V, which vary the line arrangement found in II and III, print *galinatius*. Again, the simpler explanation is that III derives directly from II.

5. Finally, the signatures of Edition II have arabic numbers except for sheet 2A which has small roman.
Editions IV and V use arabic throughout, as does Edition III except for one signature on sheet 2A which follows II in the use of small roman (Aa iii).

Thus, the bits and pieces of evidence seem to support the view that Edition III derives directly from II, not from IV.

The priority of editions of *An Apologie* may be summarized as indicated on p. 39.

LICENSING AND PRINTING

In the Stationers' Register for 30 October 1596 there is an entry to Richard Field

for his copie intituled *a newe discourse of a stale subiect called 'the Metamorphosis of AIAX'* with the *'Anatomy and Apologie of the*

I

Not in STC [A12774]
'retractation . . . confirma-
tion,' signed M–P^8 Q^2 (last
leaf blank), printed by
Richard Field.
Trade Copy: Lambeth
Large-paper State
Copies: Markham-Wrenn
   Lumley-Folger
   Sheffield
   Nares-Folger

II

STC 12774.
'retractation . . . confirma-
tion,' signed 2A–2C^8 2D^3,
printed by Richard Field.
Copies: Huntington 59767
   Chapin
   White-Harvard
   Farmer-Bindley-
    Wrenn

III IV

Not in STC [12774.1] STC 12773.
'retractation . . . confirma- 'retraction . . . confirma-
tiõ,' signed 2A–2C^8 2D^3. tion,' signed 2A–2C^8 2D^3.
Copies: Folger Copies: BM C.21.a.5
  Huntington 61279   BM C.37.b.8
  Yale Medical Lib.   Huntington 61363
  BM G10364 (2)
  Bodley, Douce H91
  Bodley, L79 Art
   (12)

V

Not in STC [12773.1]
'retraction . . . confirmation
+ floral spray initial,' signed
2A–2C^8 2D^3.
Copy: Hitch-Folger

39

same' wrytten by MYSACMOS to his frend and Cozen PHILO-STILPNOS.[1] [no sum stated]

The entry brings up the vexed question of licensing. Since the end of the eighteenth century, it has been asserted from time to time that a licence for *A New Discourse* had been refused. In every case the basis for the statement is the same: that Harington had written the words 'Seen and disallowed' on the copy he dedicated to Thomas Markham which was dated 3 August.[2]

How seriously should Harington's assertion be taken?[3] Was it perhaps merely a playful vaunt? In the light of the 'purported' and the 'true intent' of the *New Discourse*, this seems to me a possibility, *i.e.*, having played with scandalous matter, he now presented the complete work to his uncle with a notation designed to stress how scandalous he had been. It should be remembered that Harington constantly emphasized rather than minimized the questionable aspects of his treatise and that he had devoted eight pages at the end of *A New Discourse* and the entire *Apologie* precisely to making this emphasis. His method was that of an author markedly taking pains to anticipate, and therefore to direct, his readers' reactions: they will find it, he affirms, fantastical, scurrilous, and satiric (*A New Discourse*, K4ᵛ–K8). Since he had lain 'allmost buryed in the Contry these three or fowre yeere,' he hoped, as he said, by means of his

---

[1] III, 73. It should be noted that the entry, apart from the inserted '*with the "Anatomy and Apologie of the same"* ' gives the title of the printed book. More than thirty years ago W. W. Greg observed in 'Some Notes on the Stationers' Registers' that there were instances of books being entered in the Register after publication (*Library*, VII, 1926–7, 378–80); the same point was made by G. B. Harrison ('Books and Readers, 1591–4,' *Library*, VIII, 1927–28, 273) and, more recently, by Leo Kirschbaum (*Shakespeare and the Stationers*, Columbus, 1955, pp. 22, 328, n. 45), although he felt the practice must have been rare.
The identity of wording of an entry with the title page is taken as a clear indication that the printed book rather than the manuscript had been submitted. Thus, the entry of Hugh Plat's pamphlet which, as we have seen, must have been made *after* publication is also the same as the title: '*Sundrye newe and artificiall Remedies against famyne wrytten* by H. P. Esquier *vppon th*[e] *occasion of this present Dearthe*' (III, 69).

[2] Steevens, Herbert, Reed, Beloe, Heber, Hazlitt, and Lowndes all refer to the Markham copy.

[3] Kirwood, while doubting that the book could have been officially approved, nevertheless points out that Harington's notation is the sole evidence that a licence had been refused ('The "Metamorphosis of Aiax",' *Library*, XII, 215–16).

writing to give some occasion to make himself both 'thought of and talked of.'[4]

Furthermore, there is some evidence to show how those at court had thought of and talked of the work and its author. In a letter written after September 1598 and before the end of March 1599 when Harington, 'speciallie commended' to Essex' notice by the Queen,[5] accompanied the expedition to Ireland, Robert Markham set down an account of the current reaction:

Since your departure from hence, you have been spoke of, and with no ill will, both by the nobles and the Queene herself. Your book is almoste forgiven, and I may say forgotten; but not for its lacke of wit or satyr. Those whome you feared moste are now bosoming themselves in the Queene's grace; and tho' her Highnesse signified displeasure in outwarde sorte, yet did she like the marrowe of your booke. Your great enemye, Sir James, did once mention the Star-Chamber, but your good esteeme in better mindes outdid his endeavors, and all is silente again. The Queen is minded to take you to her favour, but she sweareth that she believes you will make epigrams and write *misacmos* again on her and all the courte; she hath been heard to say, 'that merry poet, her godson, must not come to Greenwich, till he hath grown sober, and leaveth the ladies sportes and frolicks.' She did conceive much disquiet on being tolde you had aimed a shafte at Leicester: I wishe you knew the author of that ill deed; I would not be in his beste jerkin for a thousand markes. You yet stande well in her Highnesse love, and I hear you are to go to Ireland with the Lieutenant, Essex. . . .[6]

There are among Harington's epigrams dealing with the subject one addressed: '*To the Queenes Majestie, when shee found fault with some particular matters in* Misacmos *Metamorphosis,*' one addressed '*To Master* Cooke, *the Queenes Atturney, that was incited to call* Misacmos *into the Starre-chamber, but refused it; saying, he that could give another a Venue, had a sure ward for himselfe*' and a second one '*To the Queene when she was pacified, and had sent* Misacmos *thankes for the invention,*'[7] where he jauntily intimates that he might be

---

[4] *L&E*, p. 66.

[5] Essex to Harington, *NA*, I, 245.

[6] *Ibid.*, 239–40.

[7] *L&E*, pp. 164–5; 165; 167.

given a 'small sute' as a reward for his 'enditings.' Does this evidence indicate more than that the Queen, prompted by a hostile courtier, evinced some displeasure at the antics of her merry godson?

There is also the unquestioned fact that Field published two editions of the *New Discourse*, both of which carried his imprint; that Dr. Bancroft licensed the *Apologie*, mentioning Field by name, on 29 August,[8] some twenty-five days after all three parts had first appeared in print; and that two months later Field entered the three parts in the Stationers' Register. If a licence had been refused at the time of the dedication copy, it would seem that Field's subsequent actions would have constituted a flagrant defiance of authority.[9] They suggest, on the contrary, that he had not encountered any serious difficulty with the authorities.

There is the additional fact to be reckoned with that two editions of *A New Discourse* were also published without imprint. Who was their printer[10] and why did they lack imprint? Kirwood has suggested that these editions (conflated in his account into one) were pirated,[11] the work of an unscrupulous printer who wished to profit from the popularity of the work. The strongest evidence of piracy, he felt, was the difference between the woodcuts in the first edition printed by Field and those in the non-imprinted edition[s]. However, Field's second edition, which Kirwood had not seen, had used these same woodcuts. Consequently, it would seem that the printer of the later editions must have issued his work with the

---

[8] The imprimatur appears at the end of the MS of the *Apologie* and reads: 'This Apologye I have p[er]used and doe think it may well be printed by M[r] Richard ffeild or any other printer. At Lambeth this xxix[th] of August 1596 Ric: Bancrofte.' It may be noted that the words 'think it may well' have been written above two scored words which appear to be 'allow to' (BM Add. MS. 46368).

[9] In 1589, the first year in which he issued books under his own imprint, Field was fined twice for actions contrary to the Stationers' regulations; one of these violations was printing a book contrary to order (Arber, II, 860), for which he was fined 10s. Cited in Kirwood, 'Richard Field, Printer, 1589–1624,' *Library*, XII, 8.

[10] As I have indicated in the earlier discussion, the third and fourth editions must have been the work of the same printer since, in the process of assembling, sheets of one edition were interchanged with those of the other.

[11] See p. 27, n. 11, and p. 28, n. 13.

consent of Field. Perhaps, having published two editions, Field felt amenable to farming out his rights to the book.[12]

The following postulated sequence of the publishing of the *Metamorphosis of Ajax* seems reasonable and accords with the known facts. In July 1596 Field undertook to publish Edition I, perhaps largely intended for Harington's personal use. Trade copies of *A New Discourse* were offered for sale before the *Anatomie*, but the complete edition, including all three parts, was in print by 3 August. A flurry of interest in the work then prompted Field to publish a second edition, probably around 29 August when Bancroft's imprimatur was obtained. At the end of October, as indicated by the record in the Stationers' Register, Field considered publishing a third edition but instead of doing so he may have farmed out his rights to the work. This would account for his failure to complete the entry in the Stationers' Register by the payment of the fee of 6d. The second printer-publisher, utilizing the blocks for the woodcuts belonging to Field, then printed two editions of the *New Discourse* and, we may assume, the three editions of the *Apologie*.

Who he was can only be conjectured. Possibly it was Thomas Gubbins, the publisher of the two editions of the *Ulysses upon Ajax*. Since the *Ulysses* assumes a knowledge of the *New Discourse*, its publisher might reasonably be interested in seeing that a stock of the latter was currently available. But this is only a guess.

Why these editions appeared without imprint I cannot explain. Indeed, it seems that there can be no final but only reasonably informed answers to the questions of both licensing and printing of all the editions subsequent to the first two. However, since the woodcuts in Edition II of *A New Discourse* printed by Field appear in Editions III and IV, I suggest that the accusation of 'piracy' must be ruled out. I also suggest that, since Field printed two editions of the complete work and since Bancroft's imprimatur on the *Apologie* dated 29 August indicates that Field was in no difficulty over having published the first edition, the assertion that a licence had been refused must also be rejected.

---

[12] Kirwood has pointed out that 1596 was Field's busiest year, in which he reached the highest output of his entire career both as publisher and as printer ('Richard Field, Printer, 1589–1624,' *Library*, XII, 24).

THE MANUSCRIPT

Included among the nineteen volumes of Harington Papers purchased by the British Museum in 1947 is the MS of the *Metamorphosis of Ajax*. As I have indicated above, it is not complete: the *New Discourse* lacks a number of pages and only the last part of the *Apologie*, amounting to some eighteen pages of the original edition, remains; the *Anatomie*, however, is complete.

Despite its abbreviated state, the MS is of interest on several counts. Including as it does notes to the printer, it indicates to what degree Harington, who in McKerrow's phrase was 'more likely than many authors to know what he wanted and to see that he got it,' made concessions to the exigencies of the press; it tells much about the state of copy the printer had to work with; it indicates Harington's second thoughts not only as shown in the changes in the MS but also the changes he made in reading proof; and, finally, it reveals the practice of a reputable printing house in handling the problem of spelling, punctuation, etc.

The MS[1] is written throughout in Harington's secretary hand with passages to be set in italic indicated in his very clear Italian hand; the writing is on the whole careful, but some insertions and additions were apparently hurriedly written, and the *Apologie* in general shows an unstructured loose script characteristic of some parts of the MS of the *Orlando Furioso*.[2] Many of the additions were written on odd sheets, and Harington has inserted a variety of symbols and notes calling attention to the fact: 'this that follows muste come in at this marke'; 'heer comes in the letter'; 'here comes in the picture of the chimny'; or 'looke at this marke.' There are many interlineations as well as additions in the side margins. On two occasions Harington went so far as to turn the page end for end to squeeze in additional lines, much no doubt to the irritation of the compositor. One instance, indicative of his method of composition, shows a space in the MS for the number

---

[1] First described in print by Ruth Hughey, 'The Harington Manuscript at Arundel Castle,' *Library*, xv, 403-4.

[2] Facsimile of BM Add. MS 18920 in two vol., published by MLA, 1930.

of a Psalm he had forgotten, together with a blank portion of a line apparently to be filled in with the Latin to precede the English; the text, which reads perfectly well, was printed as if there had been no lacunae. Sometimes he crossed out passages and later, deciding to include them, wrote *Stet* alongside; once or twice, the compositor ignored the deletion and set the original word or phrase, a fact not particularly serious in most cases. However, this confusion of deleted and non-deleted matter led to a curious error in the *Apologie* which is discussed below.

Harington's spelling tends to be both old-fashioned and phonetic: he very frequently uses *y* for *i* and, almost invariably, *w* for *u* as *yow, yowr, howse, grownd, fowntayn.* Indicative of his pronunciation are spellings like *awngell, dawnger, grawnt, parson* (for *person*), and *sarvyce.* Although he varies his practice in respect to final *e*, his prevailing tendency is to use it in common words like *mee, bee, hee*; on the other hand, he most frequently adopts the short forms, *wold* and *shold.*

He is markedly casual about capitalization, particularly after a full stop which is often indicated by both a point and a virgule. This casualness extends at times to proper names, and he writes *bath Bridge* and *greenwitche*; at other times he capitalizes words like *Gentlemen, Coach, Pallace, Pagans,* and *lady of Ladyes.*

His punctuation is generally rhetorical, and when recognized as such it does not offer much difficulty; but sometimes, caught up in the immediacy of communication, he does not indicate a stop until he has completed his entire thought. This habit leads, in turn, to sporadic paragraphing with passages running on for pages without a break.

As a result, despite certain recognizable tendencies, Harington's spelling, capitalization, punctuation, and paragraphing tend to be both haphazard and inconsistent.

An interesting aspect of the MS is the clear indication that with revision came discretion: often a specific name has been scored and a general or veiled reference substituted. This is revealed not only in the changes made in the MS but also in changes he introduced into the proof.

That he read proof for the *New Discourse* is shown by the addition of a marginal allusion to Lady Russell on G7; this reference is not in the MS or in the Chapin copy, but it is in

45

the BM (C.21.a.2) and Lambeth copies on ordinary paper and
in the copies on large paper. Other stylistic changes made in
proof are recorded in the textual notes. The addition of
marginalia not in the MS indicates that he also read proof for
the *Anatomie,* but there is no such definite evidence for the
Apologie and some indication that he did not read proof for
this section of the work. Since a large portion of the MS of the
Apologie is lacking, its evidence cannot be conclusive; the slight
differences between the existing MS and the printed text may
have been the result of authorial changes, but they could,
conceivably, have derived from the compositor. Furthermore,
on P3ᵛ and P4 the error mentioned above occurs: here two lines
from stanza 98, Canto XXVII, of the *Orlando Furioso* have
been introduced into the middle of an ottava from Canto
XXVIII, causing an obvious jumbling of sense. The error
came about because, having deleted the entire stanza from
Canto XXVIII, four lines of which appeared at the bottom of
fol. 56ᵛ and four lines at the top of 57, Harington then wrote
his substitute passage of two lines at the bottom of fol. 56ᵛ,
and the printer simply set all ten lines. It seems unlikely that as
translator of the quoted passages Harington would have missed
such a striking error if he had read proof, especially since he
later scored the passages in all presentation copies of the
Apologie. On the other hand, this error was not corrected in
the second edition in which there is an example of a very
minor change that must have come from Harington.

If the compositor (whether one or more) was severely taxed
by Harington's copy, did he, none the less, endeavour to follow
directions noted in the MS? An interesting case in point occurs
in the passage where Harington details fifteen homely functions,
each of which was presided over by a classical deity (p. 89
below). The functions are listed in order, followed by a sentence
declaring that the names of the deities are set down by themselves to satisfy the curious, and the list of deities is recorded.
The printed text follows the MS scrupulously, but the compositor ignored the marginal instruction: 'print the latten and
englyshe thus. Lacturtia / for sucking /.' Why? It would seem
that not having noticed the marginal note (or uncertain how to
handle it since it would involve omitting a sentence), the
compositor set his type according to the MS, and when

Harington came to read proof he either failed to note that the change had not been made or, more probably, he considered it not sufficiently worth the necessary resetting of type.

A note to the printer in the *Anatomie* indicates Harington's awareness of the economy of space: designed to occupy only one sheet, including the title page, the *Anatomie* concludes with the emblem on Harington's name, and Harington has directed Field to omit a passage of nine MS lines 'rather then roome shall want for the lytle picture in the end.' Four earlier lines had been omitted, perhaps for the same reason.

The printer's handling of the MS is shown in the marks dividing the text according to signatures and in many cases noting the turn of the page. The signatures are indicated by *prima* for the first page of a signature, thereafter by the correct letter and number up to sixteen. The turn of the page is marked by a large bracket enclosing the word or—in the case of word division—the part of the word beginning the next page. This suggests that the text must have been set *seriatim*. Furthermore, since the MS includes many interlineations, corrections, and insertions, it would have been difficult for the printer to cast off his copy accurately.

That the Prologue which occupies sheet B was originally intended to precede the two prefatory letters which, with the title page, occupy sheet A is shown by the changes in the printer's marks and also by Harington's change in the MS where a passage in the Prologue refers to the letter 'followinge.' This has been scored and 'precedent' substituted.

Not all of the signatures have been indicated in the MS, and there are two or three cases where the turn of the page does not conform exactly, perhaps because of adjustment in proof. There are no printer's marks in the *Anatomie*, although, as we have seen, it includes Harington's note to the printer; the *Apologie* has all the signatures for the extant sheets and the turn of the page in every case conforms to that of the first edition.

Clearly, it was the practice of Field's house to normalize spelling, and the compositor obviously tried to normalize capitalization and the use of italics. On the other hand, he tended to follow Harington's punctuation, although freely adding whenever he thought the sense required it, and he generally followed the paragraphing of the MS in the first edition. When it came to the second edition, as I have indicated above, Field's compositors introduced many variations in paragraphing which, according to modern standards, constitute an improvement.

MODERN EDITIONS

S. W. Singer edited a modernized version of the *New Discourse*, the *Anatomie*, the *Apologie* and the *Ulysses upon Ajax* which was published in 1814 by the Whittingham Press in a limited edition of one hundred copies. Since Singer did not examine the first edition of *A New Discourse* or the *Apologie*, his text includes a great many errors, and there are no textual or explanatory notes.

Peter Warlock [Philip Heseltine] and Jack Lindsay edited an old-spelling text including only the *New Discourse* and *Anatomie* which was published in an edition of 450 copies by the Fanfrolico Press in 1927. This curtailed edition again is not reliable. Although it contains no textual notes, it does include some explanatory notes which are to be commented on only for the extent and variety of their errors.

THIS EDITION

The copy-text used is that of the first edition, printed by Richard Field, for which Harington read proof, at least for two parts, *A New Discourse* and *An Anatomie*. This has been collated with a microfilm copy of the MS used by the printer (BM Add. MS 46368) and with the second edition, also printed by Richard Field. Although it introduces new errors, the second edition makes some corrections and gives some slight evidence of minor authorial revision. The other editions of *A New Discourse* and *An Apologie*, all of which lack an imprint, derive from either the first or second editions. They contain no authorial revision and have no independent authority; consequently, they have not been included in the collations.

A study of the changes from MS to the first edition of *The Metamorphosis*, as shown in the textual notes, indicates that Harington like other authors relied on printing house normalization (*e.g.*, italicizing of foreign words and phrases,

48

capitalization after terminal punctuation, etc.), and, more importantly, that he made corrections of the text, additions, and deletions at press. To this extent the printed text, representing Harington's considered judgment, must be recognized as having a stronger authority than the MS. On the other hand, despite the fact that Field's was a reputable and careful printing house, there are instances of compositors' inadvertencies (omissions, eye transpositions, misreadings) as well as omissions dictated by considerations of space, the latter most notably in the *Anatomie*. These omissions have been restored in this edition. Other changes between the MS and the printed text may fairly readily be accounted for and offer no great difficulty to an editor, but in some cases the reading selected must remain a matter of editorial judgment.

There are in addition Harington's annotations to the four presentation copies. Where these represent textual emendations, I have generally incorporated them in my text; where, in the majority of cases, they are elucidations intended for Harington's personal circle of friends, they have been reserved for the explanatory notes.[1] The aim of this edition is to present a complete and correct old-spelling text, which does not merely reprint Harington's eccentricities of spelling as found in the MS nor, it is to be hoped, submit to what has been called the tyranny of the copy-text. It is intended to be both eclectic and critical.

Punctuation, paragraphing, and capitalization. Harington's punctuation in the earlier MS of the *Orlando Furioso* has been described by one scholar as merely decorative and by another as beneath contempt, and it is to be admitted that the punctuation of *The Metamorphosis*, whether of the MS or the text, may perhaps offer some difficulty to a modern reader. However, since there seems no sound reason for modernizing punctuation in an old-spelling edition, I have followed the copy-text, correcting only manifest errors, and in such few cases I have noted the fact in the collations. The paragraphing is that of the copy-text, as is the capitalization, but errors in quotations with proper names have been corrected and noted. Since the changes

---

[1] One exception is the completing of a marginal note in the *Apologie* (O6ᵛ) where the (discreet) omission of a topical reference results in an unintelligible reading.

in punctuation, paragraphing, and capitalization from MS to first edition and from first edition to second edition are of the same order as the changes in orthography, they have not, apart from errors noted in the copy-text, been included in the collations.

Typographical conventions. S is used for long *s*, *w* for *vv*, and the modern usage of u/v and j/i has been followed. Ligatures have been ignored. The variation in size and kind of type in the different sections has also been ignored; the use of wrong font type has been silently corrected as well as errors in the use of italics for titles and foreign words and phrases since these were clearly a matter of the printer's inadvertence.

Standard Elizabethan abbreviations have been retained, as M. for Master, but contractions like y^r, y^e, and words using the tilde have been silently expanded, as have abbreviations of Latin words involving the use of symbols.

Corrections. Latin and Greek words and phrases have been corrected and noted. For example, Harington characteristically uses *c* for *t* medially in Latin words (*Tacius, indolencia, gracia,* although both *Marcial* and *Martial*). Since many of these were normalized in the first edition and others in the second, I have consistently normalized and indicated the fact in the collation. On the other hand, I have followed the orthography of the copy-text in quotations from the modern vernaculars.

Misprints have been corrected and recorded when they occur in the copy-text, but the Elizabethan practice of the 'misplaced' apostrophe is retained.

Finally, there are several instances of changes in the use of contracted forms (tis/it is, tother/the other, he/a) which are perhaps properly spelling variants but which create a distinct stylistic effect. These changes *may* have been the result of printing house normalization *or* of Harington's changes in proof (there are examples of such stylistic modifications in the MS); as a result, although I have followed the copy-text, I have included these variants in the collation. Conversely, the variation in the spacing of the pun on AJAX/A JAX found in the second edition has not been recorded.

Form of the collation. When I have departed from a reading in the copy-text, I have given the source of that reading by the use of the appropriate siglum immediately following the lemma.

Where no siglum appears immediately following the lemma, it is to be understood that the reading of the nonspecified text agrees with that of the copy-text. Thus

his] this *B*

means that *his* appears in the MS as well as in the copy-text. The orthography is that of the copy-text or, if I have departed from it, that of the first text cited. I have substituted the phrase *not in* for *omitted* in pointing out minor omissions in the MS. This is perhaps a more precise indication of the facts, since Harington made additions at press and since certain omissions in the MS may have been the result of historical accident (some of the MS was written on odd sheets of paper, and some of the margins have been cropped). When a portion of the MS is lacking, the extent of the omission is indicated in the textual notes.

Where there is no doubt as to the textual reading referred to, as in the case of a misprint, I have omitted the lemma.

Explanatory Notes. I have endeavoured to identify Harington's sources and allusions, and I have used Elizabethan translations whenever it seemed useful to quote his classical or foreign sources. Where scored passages in the MS offer a key to an allusion, I have quoted these as well as Harington's annotations in the presentation copies. His annotations overlap in a few instances, and where this is so I cite from only one copy. I have glossed difficult Elizabethan words, particularly where Harington's is the first or antedates the first example cited in the *OED* which is the source for all definitions unless otherwise indicated. All modern references to classical works, unless otherwise noted, are to editions in the Loeb Classical Library series.

The marginal notes of the copy-text are in this edition placed immediately below the text-page and are indicated by raised letters.

Sigla

A   First edition, printed by Richard Field

B   Second edition, printed by Richard Field. This includes some authorial corrections

MS   BM Add. MS 46368

Markham-Wrenn ⎫
Lumley-Folger ⎬ Presentation copies with Harington's
Nares-Folger   ⎬   annotations
Sheffield   ⎭

A NEW DISCOURSE OF A STALE SUBJECT, CALLED THE METAMORPHOSIS OF AJAX:

Written by *Misacmos*, to his friend and cosin *Philostilpnos*.

A LETTER WRITTEN
BY A GENTLEMAN
OF GOOD WORTH,

to the Author of this booke.

SIR[1] I HAVE HEARD speech[2] of your house,[3] of your pictures, of
your walks, of your ponds, and of your two boats, that came one
by land, and the other[4] by sea, from London bridge, and met
both at Bath bridge: all which God willing (if I live another
sommer) I wil come of purpose to see; as also a swimming
place,[5] where if one may beleeve your brother Fraunces,[6]

---

[1] *Sir*] The MS originally read 'Cosen Harington' which was then scored and
'S^r' written above the line.

[2] speech] *MS*; much *A, B*

[3] *of your house*] This was located in the small parish of Kelston, situated on
the Avon three and a half miles north-west of Bath. The property had come into
the possession of the Haringtons as a result of the marriage of Harington's
father to Ethelreda Malte alias Dyngley, the illegitimate daughter of Henry VIII.
Here Harington's father had begun a fine manor house, reportedly according to
a design of the Italian architect Giacomo Barozzi of Vignola. which Harington
completed at considerable expense (John Collinson, *The History and Antiquities
of the County of Somerset*, Bath, 1791, I, 127–8).

[4] thother] *MS*

[5] *swimming place*] Also called a fountain by the Elizabethans. Bacon points out
the distinction between a fountain which 'sprinkleth or spouteth water' and the
kind called a 'bathing pool' consisting of 'a fair receipt of water, of some thirty
or forty foot square, but without fish, or slime, or mud' (*Works*, ed. Spedding,
Ellis, and Heath, N.Y., 1872, XII, 241–2).

[6] *Fraunces*] Harington's younger brother received his B.A. from Corpus
Christi College, Oxford, in 1581 and probably studied also at the Middle Temple
(Joseph Foster, *Alumni Oxoniensis, 1500–1714*, Oxford, 1891, II. 653). He too
shared the poetical inclinations characteristic of the family, indicated by his
translation of the first fifty stanzas of Bk. XXXII of the *OF* (Notes to Bk. XXXII).

Diana[7] did bath her, & Acteon, see her without hornes. But to deale plainly with you, there be three speciall things that I have heard much boasted of, and therefore would willinglyest see. The one a fountaine standing on pillers, like that in Ariosto,[a] under which you may dyne & suppe; the second a shooting close with a xii. score marke to every point of the card,[9] in which I heare you have hit a marke that many shoot at, viz: to make a barren stony land fruitfull with a little cost; the third is a thing that I cannot name well without save-reverence,[10] & yet it sounds not unlike the shooting place, but it is in plaine English a shyting place.[11] Though, if it be so sweet and so cleanely as I heare, it is a wrong to it to use save reverence, for one told me, it is as sweet as my parlor, and I would thinke discortesie, one should say, save-reverence my parlor. But if I might entreat you (as you partly promist me at your last being here) to set down the maner of it in writing, so plaine as our grosse witts here may understand it, or to cause your man

---

[a] 43. Can.[8]

---

[7] *Diana . . .*] Perhaps a reference to Harington's entertainment of the Queen at Kelston in 1592 (John Nichols, *Progresses and Public Processions of Queen Elizabeth*, London, 1823, III, 250–1).

[8] See *OF* XLII, 72–75 (not XLIII). An engraving of the fountain at Kelston is included in Collinson, I, facing 41 (pointed out by M. Trotter, 'Harington's Fountain,' *MLN*, LVIII, Dec., 1943, 614–6).
The engraving shows the base of the fountain supported on four columns to form a kind of pavilion which would provide a sheltered area for dining. On a central shaft rising from the base there is an elaborately ornamented basin spilling forth the water supplied from a tun mounted at the top of the shaft. A hare holding a ring in its outstretched paw is perched on the tun which has the date 1567 inscribed upon it. Thus it is evident that the hare, the ring, and the tun which Thomas Combe depicts in the emblem at the end of the *Anatomie* (p. 204) had long been used as a family device.

[9] *a shooting . . . card*] A distance of 'xii score' yards was standard for shooting at prick. Harington's archery range was apparently circular in shape and of sufficient size to afford the standard range at every point of the compass.

[10] *save-reverence*] An apologetic term used to introduce any unpleasant or indecorous remark. Cf. 'Of a Precise Lawyer' (*L&E*, pp. 179–80).

[11] *it is . . . place*] Harington has written in the margin of the Markham-Wrenn copy: 'a shooting / place written / with Pitha- / goras letter,' *i.e.*, the Greek upsilon, transliterated as the Greek *y*. It was used by Pythagoras as a symbol of the two divergent paths of virtue and vice.

56

M. Combe[12] (who I understand can paint pretily) to make[13] a draught, or plot thereof to be well conceaved, you should make many of your friends much beholding to you, & perhaps you might cause reformation in many houses that you wish wel unto, that will thinke no scorne to follow your good example. Nay to tell you my opinion seriously, if you have so easie, so cheap, & so infallible a way for avoyding such annoyances in great houses; you may not only pleasure many great persons, but do her Majestie good service in her pallace of Greenwitch & other stately houses, that are oft annoyed with such savours, as where many mouthes be fed can hardly be avoided. Also you might be a great benefactor to the Citie of London, and all other populous townes, who stand in great neede of such convayances. But all my feare is that your pen having bene inured to so high[14] discourse,

Of Dames, of Knights, of armes, of loves delight.[15]

will now disdaine to take so base a subject,

Of vaults, of sinkes, privies & draughts to write.

But herein let a publik benefit expell a private bashfulnes, & if you must now and then breake the rules *de slovilitate morum,*[16] with some of these homely words, you see I have broken the ise[17] to you, and you know the old saying, pens may blot, but they cannot blush.[18] And as olde Tarlton[19] was wont to saie, this same excellent word save-reverence, makes it all manerlie. Once this I dare assure you, if you can but tell a homelie tale of this in prose as cleanlie, as you have told in verse a baudie tale

---

[12] *M. Combe*] Harington's personal servant whose 'pictoricall' talents were utilized in the *Anatomie.* Harington's close, friendly relationship with Combe is revealed in the long letter which he wrote to him from Ireland in 1599 (*L&E,* pp. 71–6).

[13] to make] *MS*; make *A, B*   [14] high] high a *B*

[15] *Of Dames . . .*] *OF* I.i which appeared with a dedication to the Queen in 1591.

[16] *de . . . morum*] I am unable to explain *slovilitate*; the intended meaning, however, is clear.

[17] *broken the ise*] Tilley I3.   [18] *pens . . . blush*] Tilley P183.

[19] *Tarlton*] Richard Tarlton, the popular improvisator who endeared himself not only to the Queen and court but to all London. He died in poverty in 1588, leaving one son named Philip, the 'godson of Sir Philip Sydney' (Tarlton's letter to Walsingham, *CSP, Dom.,* II, 1581–90, 541).

or two in Orlando mannerlie, it maie passe among the sowrest censurers verie currantlie.[20] And thus expecting your answer hereto, at your convenient leysure, I commit you to God this of 1596.[21]

Your loving cosin.[22]
Φιλοστιλπνος.[23]

THE ANSWER TO THE LETTER.

My good Cosin, if you have heard so well of my poore house with the appurtenaunces, it were to be wished for preservation of your better conceit thereof; that you would not see them at all, they will seeme to you so far short of the report: for I do compare my buildings and my writings together, in which though the common sort thinke there is some worth and wit, yet the graver Censurers[24] do finde many faults and follies.[25] And no marvell, for he that builds and hath gathered litle, and writes and hath read little, must needes be a bad builder, and a worse writer. But whereas you are disposed either in the way of prayse, or of play, to extoll so much the basest roome of my house, as though you preferred it afore the best; your commendation is not much unlike his curtesie that being invited by a crabbed-favord host to a neat house, did spit in his hostes face

---

[20] *passe . . . currantlie*] *i.e.*, be accepted; see p. 78, n. 51.

[21] 1596] 1595 *MS*

[22] *Your . . . cosin*] The identification of Harington's 'loving cosin' as Master Edward Sheldon is clearly established not only by personal references in the text (*e.g.*, Thomas Combe's addressing of the *Anatomie* to 'M. E. S. Esquier' and the reference to his son 'prety Wil,' p. 179), but also by Harington's own annotation in the Nares-Folger copy.

Edward Sheldon, son and heir of the wealthy recusant Ralph Sheldon of Boeley, Worc. (who is directly referred to in the *Apologie*, pp. 238–240), was Harington's close contemporary, 'aet⁵. 8 in 1569.' He married Harington's cousin Elizabeth Markham, daughter of Thomas Markham of Ollerton, Notts., sometime before 1588/9 when their son William was born (*Visitation of the County of Worcester*, ed. W. P. W. Phillimore, Publications of the Harleian Society, XXVII, London, 1888, 127–9, and *Familiae Minorum Gentium*, III, Publications of the Harleian Society, XXXIX, London, 1895, 965–7). There is also a letter of Harington's addressed to 'Cosen Sheldon,' unidentified in McClure (*L&E*, pp. 142; 410).

[23] Φιλοστιλπνος] Φιλοστιλπνοτης *MS*; *i.e.*, 'lover of cleanliness,' see p. 79.

[24] Censurers] *MS, B*; Censures *A*   [25] follies; *A*

because it was the fowlest part of the house.[26] But such as I have you shall be welcome to, and if I may know when you will begin your progresse, I will pray my brother to be your guide, who will direct your jestes[27] in such sort, as first you shall come by a fine house that lackes a mistresse,[28] then to a fayre house that mournes for a master,[29] from whence, by a straight way called

---

[26] *his curtesie . . . house*] The source for this popular story is Diogenes Laertius who records it both of Diogenes the Cynic (vi.32) and of Aristippus (ii.75). Erasmus recounts it of Aristippus (*Apophthegmes*, tr. N. Udall, 1564, E8ᵛ–F1); in his *Anatomie of Abuses*, 1583, Stubbes tells it simply of a 'certen . . . Philosopher' (ed. F. J. Furnivall, London, 1879, Pt. I, 47); while Nashe in *Pierce Penilesse* credits it to Diogenes (*Works*, ed. R. B. McKerrow, Oxford, 1958, I, 182).

[27] *jestes*] Variant of gests, the various stages of a journey, especially of a royal progress.

[28] *as first . . . mistresse*] Harington's annotation in the Nares-Folger copy reads: 'Sʳ H. Lea at / Ditchly.' Champion of the Tilt established in honour of Queen Elizabeth's accession and a long-time courtier, Sir Henry Lee (1533–1611) possessed large holdings in Oxfordshire and Bucks., where he was recognized as a grazier of considerable importance. Ditchley, the centre of his Oxfordshire estate, was located only four miles from the royal manor of Woodstock to which he had been appointed lieutenant in 1571; here, having built a fine house, he entertained the Queen in 1592. The death of his wife Anne, daughter of William Lord Paget, in 1590, no doubt accounted for his fanciful depiction of himself in 1592 as a 'newe religious Hermite,' but Sir Henry early consoled himself with Mistress Anne Vavasour, a former Gentlewoman of the Bedchamber whose reputation had already been tarnished by a scandalous liaison with the Earl of Oxford (E. K. Chambers, *Sir Henry Lee*, London, 1936, *passim*). The following epigram by Harington seems to refer to this; since 'Laelius,' representing a Latinization of Lee, was applied to Sir Henry by his contemporaries (see n. 18, p. 69), 'Lelia' would thus refer to Anne Vavasour:

Of Lelia

When lovely *Lelia* was a tender girle,
She hapt to be deflowred by an Earle;
Alas, poore wench, she was to be excused,
Such kindnesse oft is offered, seld refused.
But be not proud; for she that is no Countesse,
And yet lies with a Count, must make account this,
   All Countesses in honour her surmount,
   They have, she had, an honourable Count.

(*L&E*, p. 269)

[29] *then . . . master*] 'Davers': Harington annotation in the Nares-Folger copy. This refers to the banishment of Sir Charles Danvers (or Davers, as it was frequently spelled in the sixteenth century) and his younger brother Sir Henry of Dauntsey, Wilts., for the murder of Henry Longe. Climaxing a bitter feud between the two families, the slaying of Henry Longe in Oct. 1594 occurred, according to an account in the State Papers, at the hands of Sir Henry while 'defending his brother, Sir Charles, against Long and his company' (*CSP, Dom.*, IV, 1595–7, 34, but see DNB for reference to another account). Following the

the *force way*,[30] you shall come to a towne that is more then a towne,[31] where be the waters that be more then waters.[32] But from thence, you shall passe downe a streame that seemes to be no streame,[33] by corne fields that seeme no fields,[34] downe a street no street,[35] in at a gate[36] no gate, over a bridge no bridge, into a court no court, where if I be not at home, you shall finde perhaps a foole no foole.[37]

But whereas you prayse my husbandry, you make me remember an old schoolefellow of mine in Cambridge, that having lost five shillings abroad at Cardes, would boast he had

fray, the two brothers fled to the Earl of Southampton at Tichfield where they took refuge in a nearby lodge; as news of the murder circulated, with the aid of Southampton and his brother-in-law Thomas Arundell plus the connivance of minor officials, the Danverses escaped into France shortly before they were to be apprehended. (See the record of witnesses in *Salisbury MSS*, V, 84–90, and for Harington's relationship with Southampton and Arundell, see note 68, p. 174.)

Both brothers received the sentence of banishment and Sir Henry 'was duly attainted by outlawry of murder' (*Salisbury MSS*, VI, 69), but by June 1598 the bells in various parishes were ringing 'in triumph' for their pardon (*ibid.*, VIII, 244).

They returned to England where Sir Charles was to lose his life in the Essex rebellion and Sir Henry to attain honour and dignity under James and Charles as Baron Danvers and Earl of Danby.

[30] *force way*] Or fosse way, one of the great Roman highways so called from the fosse or ditch on either side of it. Harrison describes its slopewise course 'over the greatest part of this Iland' (Holinshed, *Chronicles*, 1587, I, L1ᵛ–L2).

[31] *you . . . towne*] 'Bathe,' Harington annotation: Nares-Folger copy.

[32] *where . . . waters*] 'the / hot bathes,' Harington annotation: Nares-Folger copy. Camden says, 'Within the Citie it selfe there buble and boile up three springs of hote water, of a blewish or sea colour, sending up from them thin vapours and a kind of a strong sent withall, by reason that the water is drilled and strained through veines of Brimstone and a clamy kind of earth called *Bitumen*. Which springs are very medicinable and of great vertue to cure bodies over-charged and benummed (as it were) with corrupt humors' (*Britain*, tr. Philemon Holland, 1610, V2).

[33] *But . . streame*] 'becaus yt is / so stil,' Harington annotation: Nares-Folger copy.

[34] *by corne . . . fields*] 'becaus they / be so stony,' Harington annotation: Nares-Folger copy.

[35] *downe . . . street*] 'becaus they / bee all so / fantasticall,' Harington annotation: Nares-Folger copy.

[36] at a gate] at gate *MS*

[37] *where . . . foole*] 'becaus she / ys so shrowd,' Harington annotation: Nares-Folger copy; this is of course Harington's wife, Mary. Cf. the epigrams, '*To my wife, from Chester*' and '*To his wife, in excuse he had call'd her foole in his writing*' (*L&E*, pp. 221–2; 226).

saved two candels at home, by being out of his chamber; for such be most of my savings. But[38] this one point of husbandry, though it may well be called beggerly: yet it is[39] not for all that contemptible and thus it was. Finding a faire and flat field, though verie stonie, as all this country is; I made some vagrant beggers[40] (of which by neighbourhood of the Bathes here comes great store) to gather all the stones that might breake our arrowes, and finding an easie meane to water the ground with a fat water[41]; I have betterd my ground (as you say) and quite rid me of my wandring guests, who will rather walke seven myle about, then come where they shall be forst to worke one halfe houre.

Now Syr, to come to the chiefe point of your desire, which requires a more ample answer, but for a preamble you must be content with this. You tell me, belike to encourage me, that my invention may be beneficiall, not only to my private friends, but to townes and Cities, yea even to her Majesties service for some of her houses: trust me I do beleeve you write seriously as you terme it herein, and for my part I am so wholly addicted, to her highnesse service, as I would be glad, yea even proud; if the highest straine of my witte, could but reach, to any note of true harmony in the full consort of her Majesties service, though it were in the basest key that it could be tuned to. And if I should fortune to effect so good a reformation, in the pallace of Richmond, or Greenwich (to which Pallace, many of us owe service for the tenure of our land) I doubt not but some pleasant witted Courtier of either sex, would grace me so much at least; as to say, that I were worthy for my rare invention, to be made one of the Privie (and after a good long parenthesis come out with)[42] chamber, or if they be learned and have read *Castalios Courtier*[43] they will say, I am a proper scholer, and

---

[38] But] *MS*; Yet *A, B*   [39] yet it is] yet is *MS*

[40] *vagrant beggers*] The 'beggars of Bath' became proverbial. Cf. Tilley B250.

[41] *a fat water*] Turbid.

[42] parenthesis . . . with)] *MS*; parenthesis) *A, B*

[43] *Castalios Courtier*] A not uncommon sixteenth-century spelling of Castiglione whose *Il Cortegiano* was first published in 1528; the noteworthy translation by Sir Thomas Hoby, father of Harington's 'old schoolfellow' of Eton (Notes to Bk. XLV of *OF*) appeared in 1561.

well seene in *latrina lingua*.[44] But let them mocke that list, *qui moccat moccabitur*.[45]

> *Who strike with sword, the scabbard them may strike:*
> *And sure love craveth love, like asketh like*.[46]

If men of judgement thinke it may breed a publike benefite, the conceit thereof shall expell all private bashfulnesse; and I will herein follow the example of that noble Lady, that to save the liberties of Coventry,[b] rode naked at noone through the streets thereof, and is now thought to be greatly honored, and nothing shamed thereby.

Further whereas you embolden my pen, not to be abasht at the basenesse of the subject, and as it were leading me on the way, you tell me you have broken the yce[48] for me, to enter me into such broad phrases, as you thinke must be frequent herein: I will follow your steppes and your counsell, neither will I disdaine to use the poore helpe of save reverence if neede be, much like as a good friend of yours and mine, that beginning to dispraise as honest a man as him selfe, to a great Noble man,

---

[b] Camden in his *Britannia*.[47]

[44] *well seene . . . lingua*] Harington is referring to the section dealing with the courtier's use of *facetiae* or witty pleasantries of language: 'Un' altra sorte è ancor, che chiamiamo *bischizzi*, e questa consiste nel mutare ovvero accrescere o minuire una lettera o sillaba; come colui che disse: Tu dei esser piú dotto nella lingua *latrina* che nella greca' (ed. V. Cian, Florence, 1947, II, lxi, 1–4). Some sixteenth-century translations (including Hoby's) miss the point by reading 'latina' for 'latrina' (*e.g.*, the multilingual edition published by John Wolfe in 1588 where not only the French and English but the Italian has the incorrect reading, R2ᵛ).

[45] *moccat moccabitur*] Harington apparently derives this word from the Italian *moccare*—'to mocke, flout, or skoffe' (John Florio, *A Worlde of Wordes*, 1598, T6ᵛ).

[46] *Who strike . . .*] Cf. OF XXVIII.80.7–8. Both expressions were proverbial, Tilley S1047 and L286.

[47] 'The first Lord of this Citie [Coventry], so farre as I can learne, was this *Leofricke*, who being very much offended and angrie with the Citizens, oppressed them with most heavy tributes, which he would remit upon no other condition, at the earnest suite of his wife *Godiva*, unlesse she would her selfe ride on horse-backe naked through the greatest and most inhabited street of the Citie: which she did in deed, and was so covered with her faire long haire, that (if we may beleeve the common sort) she was seene of no bodie, and thus she did set free her Citizens of *Coventry* from many payments for ever' (tr, Holland, 3A6ᵛ).

[48] *you . . . yce*] See p. 57, n. 17.

said, he is the veryest knave, saving your Lordship: But the noble man (ere the wordes were fully out of his mouth,) said, save thy self knave or be hangd, save not me. Even so I must write in this discourse, sometime indeede as homly (saving your worship) as you shall lightly see, and yet I will endevour to keepe me within the boundes of modestie, and use no wordes, but such as grave presidents in Divinitie, Law, Phisicke, or good Civilitie, will sufficiently warrant me.

Sure I am that many other country men, both Dutch, French, & Italians, with great prayse of wit, though small of modestie, have written of worse matters.[49] One writes in prais of follie.[50] 2. an other in honour of the Pox.[51] 3. a third defendes usurie.[52] 4. a fourth commends Nero.[53] 5. a fift extolls and instructs bawderie.[54] 6. the sixt displayes and describes *Puttana*

---

[49] *Sure I am . . . matters*] The exercise of wit and ingenuity through display pieces such as the encomia dealing with trifling or unworthy subjects was a common literary practice during the Renaissance. In 1619, for example, Caspar Dornavius [Dornau] gathered together a collection which included over six hundred titles, some by classical authors but the majority of them dating from the Renaissance and varying in form and scope from what we should properly call epigrams to works of the extent of More's *Utopia: Amphitheatrum Sapientiae Socraticae Joco-Seriae hoc est* etc., Hanover.

In addition to those written in Latin, there were of course examples in the various vernaculars. Furthermore, as McKerrow has pointed out in his notes to Nashe's *Lenten Stuffe* which includes such a list, it became almost traditional for the author of a work on a light subject to include a listing of other such works. (Cf. Nashe III, 176 ff. and McKerrow's notes in IV, 389–94 and 438–9; Harvey's list in *Pierce's Supererogation*, ed. Grosart, II, 244; and for a general discussion H. K. Miller, 'The Paradoxical Encomium with Special Reference to Its Vogue in England, 1600–1800,' *MP*, LIII, Feb. 1956, 145–78.)

[50] *in prais of follie*] The *Moriae Encomium* of Erasmus, included in Dornavius.

[51] *in honour of the Pox*] E.g., the 'Capitolo del Mal Francese' by Francesco Bino [Bini] (*Opere Burlesche*, Rome, 1771, I, 304–11); the *Blason de la Vérolle*, now lost (cited by R. E. Pike, 'The "Blasons" in French Literature of the Sixteenth Century,' *The Romanic Review*, XXVII, 1936, 240); and Francesco Beccuti's *Cicalamenti del Grappa . . . delle lodi delle donne et del mal Francioso*, Mantua, 1545 (cited in Nashe, Supplement, V, 55).

[52] *defendes usurie*] The *Dialogo della Usura* of Sperone Speroni which caused its author some difficulty with the ecclesiastical authorities (*Dialoghi*, Venice, 1552, H3ᵛ-I3).

[53] *commends Nero*] The *Neronis Encomium* of Girolamo Cardano, included in Dornavius.

[54] *extolls . . . bawderie*] Since Aretino's name is so frequently associated in the period with works of bawdry, this may refer to his *Raggionamenti*, although it is not properly an encomium. *A New Booke Intituled The blasing of Bawdrie* by R. C. Citizen was published in London in 1574, but this too is not an encomium.

Errante,[55] which I here will come forth shortly in English.
7. A seventh (whom I would guesse by his writing, to be
groome of the stoole to some Prince of the bloud in Fraunce)
writes a beastly treatise onely to examine what is the fittest
thing to wype withall,[c] alledging that white paper is too smooth,
brown paper too rough, wollen cloth too stiffe, linnen cloth
too hollow, satten too slipperie, taffeta too thin, velvet too
thick, or perhaps too costly: but he concludes, that a goose
necke to be drawne betweene the legs against the fethers, is the
most delicate and cleanly thing that may be.[d] Now it is possible
that I may be reckned after these seven, as *sapientum octavus*,[58]
because I will write of A Jakes, yet I will challenge of right (if
the Heralds should appoint us our places) to go before this
filthy fellow, for as according to Aristotle, a ryder is an *Architectonicall* science to a sadler, & a sadler to a stirop maker &c.[59]
so my discourse must needes be Architectonicall to his, sith I
treat of the house it self, & he but of part of that is to be done in
the house, & that no essential part of the businesse:[e] for they say
"there be three things that if one neglect to do them, they will
"do themselves; one is for a man to make even his recknings,
"for who so neglects it will be left even just nothing; an other
"is to mary his daughters for if the parents bestow them not,

---

[c] This matter is discoursed by Rables, in his 13. chap. of his first[56] booke.[57]

[d] *Un moyen de me torcher le cul le plus Seigneurial, le plus excellent, le plus
expedient que jamais fut veu.*

[e] This may be omitted in reading.

---

[55] *Puttana Errante*] There are two works with this name: *La Puttana Errante*,
a poem of 185 stanzas by Lorenzo Veniero and *La Puttana Errante ovvero
dialogo tra Maddalena e Giulia*, which was formerly ascribed to Aretino
(Domenico Fusco, *L'Aretino Sconosciuto ed Apocrifo*, Turin, 1953, pp. 45–9).

[56] first] *MS*; fift *A, B*

[57] Allusions to Rabelais appear from the 1570's on, but, as Huntington Brown
has pointed out in his study of *Rabelais in English Literature* (Cambridge, Mass.,
1933), there is not always sufficient evidence to indicate how familiar the
writers actually were with the difficult French text. And there is no clear
evidence of an English translation before that of Urquhart. He credits John
Eliot, author of *Ortho-Epia Gallica* (1593), and Harington as being the 'first
two Englishmen who knew how to value and imitate' the French writer (see
Introd. p. 19). He also observes that Harington has 'proportionately *more*
learned references than Rabelais' (pp. 55–70).

[58] *sapientum octavus*] Horace's ironic epithet, *Sat.*ii.3.296.

[59] *Aristotle . . . maker &c*] Elaboration of *Nichomachean Ethics* i.1.

"they will bestow them selves;[60] the third is that, which the
"foresaid French man writes of: which they that omit, their
"lawndresses shall finde it done in their linnen. Which mishap
"a faire Lady once having, a serving man of the disposition of
"Mydas Barber,[61] that could not keepe counsell had spyed it,
"& wrate in the grossest termes it could be exprest, upon a wall,
"what he had seene; but a certaine pleasant conceited Gentle-
"man,[62] corrected the barbarisme, adding ryme to the reason in
"this sort.

> *"My Lady hath polluted her linneall vesture:*
> *"With the superfluitie, of her corporall disgesture.*

But soft, I feare I give you to great a tast of my slovenly
eloquence, in this sluttish argument. Wherfore to conclude, I
dare undertake, that though my discourse will not be so wise as
the first of those seven I spake of, that prayses folly: yet it shall
be civiller then the second, truer then the third, honester then
the fourth: chaster then the fift, modester then the sixt, and
clenlyer then the seventh. And that you & other my[63] good
friends may take the lesse offence at it, I will cloth it (like an
ape in purple,)[64] that it may be admitted into the better company; & if all the art I have cannot make it mannerly enough,
the worst punishment it can have, is but to employ it in the
house it shall treat off, onely craving but that favour, that
a noble man was wont to request of your good father in law,[65]
to teare out my name before it be so employed; and to him that
would deny me that kindnesse, I would the paper were nettles,
and the letters needles for his better ease: or that it were like
to the Friers booke dedicated as I take it to *Pius quintus*; of

---

[60] *an other . . . selves*] Burghley repeats this advice to his son Robert: 'Marry
thy daughters in time, lest they marry themselves' (*Certaine Precepts*, 1616/17;
reprinted in John Strype, *Annals of the Reformation*, Oxford, 1824, IV, 477).
The earliest example cited in Tilley is from Robert Burton, D47.

[61] *Mydas Barber*] Ovid *Metam.* xi.182 ff.

[62] *a certaine . . . Gentleman*] Harington had originally included a parenthesis
reading 'sometyme my chamberfellow, and now a doctor of Phisyck' but
later scored it.

[63] other my] other of my *B*

[64] *like . . . purple*] Tilley A266 where Harington's example is the earliest
cited, but cf. A262 and A263.

[65] *father in law*] Thomas Markham. See note 22, p. 58.

which one writes merily, that his holinesse finding it was good for nothing else, imployed it (in steed of the goose necke) to a homely occupation, and forsooth the phrase was so rude, the style so rugged, and the Latin so barbarous, that therewith as he writes, *scortigavit sedem Apostolicam.* He galled the seat Apostolicke: and so I commend me to you, till I send you the whole discourse.[66]

Your loving cosin and true friend.

μισακμος.[67]

---

[66] discourse.] discourse; from my howse at *the rest scored MS*

[67] μισακμος] Misachnos *MS. Ff. by signature* John Haryngton; μισακμος, *i.e.,* 'hater of filth,' see n. 62, p. 80.

THE PROLOGUE
TO THE READER OF
the Metamorph*ŵ*sis of AJAX.[1]

GREAT CAPTAINE AJAX, as is wel knowen to the learned, and shall here be published for the unlearned, was a warrier of Graecia; strong, heddy, rash, boysterous, and a terrible fighting fellow, but neither wise, learned, stayd, nor Politicke. Wherefore falling to bate with Ulisses, & receiving so foule a disgrace of him, to be called foole afore company,[a] & being bound to the peace,[3] that he might not fight with so great a Counseller; he could indure it no longer, but became a perfit mal-content,[4] viz. his hat without a band, his hose without garters, his wast without a girdle, his boots without spurres, his purse without coyne, his head without wit, and thus swearing he would kill and slay[5]; first he kild all the horned beasts he met, which made Agamemnon and Menelaus now, more affrayed then Ulisses, whereupon he was banished the townes presently, and then he went to the woods and pastures, and imagining all the fat

[a] Ovid *Meta.* Lib. 12.[2]

[1] of the . . . Ajax] not in *MS*   [2] This should read *Lib.* 13.

[3] *bound to the peace*] Harington's usage here is earlier than the instance cited in the *OED*.

[4] *mal-content*] One who manifests his disaffection—be it political, social, or personal—by a singularity of deportment.

[5] *his hat . . . slay*] Several of these elements become standard in delineations of the malcontent. Lodge, for example, echoes Harington's description in *Wits Miserie*, a work which followed *The Metamorphosis*, appearing some time after 5 Nov. 1596, the date of the dedicatory epistle: 'This is a right malecontent Devill, You shall alwaies find him his hat without a band, his hose ungartered, his Rapier *punto r'enverso*, his lookes suspitious and heavie, his left hand continually on his dagger' (*Works*, ed. Sir E. Gosse, Hunterian Club, 1883, IV, 23). There are many such descriptions in the seventeenth century.

sheep he met, to be of kin to the coward Ulisses, because they
ran away from him, he massacred a whole flock of good nott
Ews.[6] Last of all having no body else to kill, poore man killed
him selfe; what became of his bodie is unknowen, some say
that wolves and beares did eate it, & that makes them yet such
enemies to sheepe and[7] cattell. But his bloud as testifieth
Povidius[b] the excellent Historiographer was turnd into a
Hiacint, which is a very notable kind of grasse or flower as
many of owr great grasyers with the well lyned powches know
very well.[9]

Now there are many miracles to be marked in this Metamorphosis, to confirme the credit of the same: for in the grasse
it selfe remaines such pride of this noble bloud, that as the
grasyers have assured me of their credites (and some of them
may be trusted for 100000 pounds) the ruther beastes[10] that
eate to greedily hereof will swel till they burst, the poore sheepe
stil for an old grudge, would eate him without salt[c] (as they
say)[12] but if they do, they will soone after rot with it.

Further I read that now of late yeares, a French Gentleman
son to one *Monsieur Gargasier*,[d] & a yong Gentleman of an
excellent spirit & towardnesse, as the reverent Rabbles (*quem
honoris causa nomino*, that is, whom I should not name without

---

[b] Lib. supra dicto.[8]

[c] Salt recovers baned sheepe.[11]

[d] Rabbles lib. I. cap. 13. *Come Gargasier cognoit l'esprit excellent de Gargantua
a l'invention d'un torche cul.*[13]

---

[6] *and imagining . . . Ews*] Cf. Horace *Sat.* ii.3.197–8; *nott Ews* are a variety
of hornless sheep.

[7] annd *A*

[8] *Metam.* xiii.394–8.

[9] flower . . . well.] *MS*; flower. *The rest om. A, B*

[10] *ruther beastes*] Variant of 'rother beasts,' *i.e.*, oxen or cattle.

[11] Sheep diseased with 'rot,' a disease affecting the liver of sheep fed on
moist pasture-lands.

[12] *would eate . . . say*] In his *Alvearie or Quadruple Dictionarie*, 1580, John
Baret describing that which is odious or hateful says: 'A Proverbe used, when a
man hateth one even with a deadlie hate, and as our phrase of speach is, He
could willingly eate his heart with salt' (2T2). Harington's usage apparently
suggests an even more fierce hatred. Cf. also Tilley S78.

[13] *Come* follows the MS, Harington perhaps unconsciously substituting the
Italian form for *comment. Gargasier* is his version of Grandgousier.

save-reverence) writeth in his first booke 13. Chap. but the
storie you shall find more at large in the xiiii. book of his tenth
Decad.[e] This young Gentleman having taken some three or
a foure[14] score pills to purge melancholy,[15] every one as big as a
Pome Cyttern,[16] commanded his man to mowe an halfe acre
of grasse, to use at the privy, and notwithstanding that the
owners (to save their hay perhaps) sware to him it was of that
ancient house of A JAX, & therefore reserved of purpose onely
for horses of the race of Bucephalus,[17] or Rabycano,[18] yet he
would not be perswaded: but in further contempt of his name,
used a phrase that he had learned at his being in the low
Countreys, and bad *Skite upon AJAX*. But suddenly (whether
it were the curse of the people, or the nature of the grasse I
know not) he was stricken in his Posteriorums[19] with S.

---

[e] Lib. Fictitius.

---

[14] or a foure] or foure *B*

[15] *pills to purge melancholy*] This is adopted as the title of a curious
pamphlet published in ?1599: *A Pil To purge Melancholie: or, A Prep[a]rative
to a Purgation: or, Topping, Copping, and Capping: take either or whether: or,
Mash them, and squash them, and dash them, and diddle come derrie come daw
them, all together* (unique copy in the Pforzheimer Library). See Cyrus L. Day's
'Pills to Purge Melancholy' (*RES*, VIII, 1932, 177–84) where the recurrent use
of this phrase in titles of the seventeenth and eighteenth centuries is traced back
to this Elizabethan pamphlet and ultimately to Harington's earlier usage.

[16] *Pome Cyttern*] A variety of citrus fruit: 'yf they [citrons] be very great
and round lyke Pompeons [melons], they call them Pomecydrons' (Heresbach's
Foure Bookes of Husbandry, tr. Barnaby Googe, 1577, M4).

[17] *Bucephalus*] The horse of Alexander the Great (Plutarch 'Alexander' 6).

[18] *Rabycano*] Astolfo's horse in the *OF* XXII.5. It was also the name given to
Sir Henry Lee's horse:

> Hardy *Laelius*, that Great *Garter-Knight*,
> Tiltting in Triumph of *Elizas* Right.
> (Yeerely the Day that her deere Raigne began)
> Most bravely mounted on proud *Rabican*,
> All in guilt armour, on his glistening Mazor
> A stately Plume, of Orange mixt with Azure,
> In gallant Course, before ten thousand eyes,
> From all Defendants bore the Princely Prize.

(Joshua Sylvester, *Devine Weekes and Workes*, 1605, quoted in Chambers,
Sir Henry Lee, p. 141.)

[19] *Posteriorums*] Cf. *priorums* below. Aristotle's two works, the *Analyticorum
posteriorum* and the *Analyticorum priorum*, were popularly referred to as the
'posteriorums' and the 'priorums.' Harington's punning use of these terms is
in the one case the first and in the other earlier than the first example cited in
the *OED*.

69

Anthonies fier[20]; and dispairing of other helpe, he went on Pilgrimage in hope of remedy hereof to Japana, neare Chyna: where he met a French Surgeon, in the Universitie of Miaco[21] that cured him both of that & the Verol,[22] that he had before in his priorums; with the Momio,[23] of a Grecian wench, that Ulysses buried in his travell, upon the cost of the further Aethiopia: and so he came back againe by *Restinga des ladrones*,[24] thorough *S. Lazaro*,[25] and crossing both the Tropickes, *Cancer*, & *Capricorne*, he came by *Magellanes*, swearing he founde no straightes there; but came from thence straight home. And so in 24. houres saile, and two or three od yeares beside, he accomplished his voyage, not forgetting to take fresh wine and water at *Capon de bona speranza*. Yet ere he could recover his health fully, he was fayne to make divers vowes (for now he was growen verie[26] religious with his long travell.) Among which one was, that in remembrance of China, of all meates, he would honour the Chine a beef most; an other was, that of all offices of the house, he should do honour to that house of office, where he had committed that scorne to AJAX: and that there, he should never use any more such fine grasse, but rather, teare a leafe out of Holinsheds *Chronicles*,[27] or some of the bookes that lye in the hall; then to commit such a sinne against AJAX. Wherefore immediatly on his comming

---

[20] *S. Anthonies fier*] Erysipelas.

[21] *Miaco*] *i.e.*, Kyoto, ancient capital of Japan.

[22] *Verol*] Syphilis.

[23] *Momio*] *i.e.*, momia, a medicinal substance derived from mummified bodies. John Sanderson who visited Egypt in 1586 described the momia: 'They gave no noysome smell at all, but ar like pitch, beinge broken; for I broke of[f] all parts of the bodies to see howe the flesh was turned to drugge, and brought home divers heads, hands, arms, and feete for a shewe. . . . One little hand I brought into Ingland to shewe, and presented it my brother, who gave the same to a doctor in Oxford' (*Travels*, Hakluyt Society, 2nd s., LXVII, London, 1931, 44–5).

[24] *Restinga des ladrones*] *i.e.*, the Mariannas, discovered by Magellan in 1521 and by his crew called *Islas de los Ladrones* because of the thieving propensity of the natives. An Ortelius map of 1587 gives *Restinga di ladrones* (*Theatrum Orbis Terrarum*, Antwerp, 1595, fol. 1).

[25] *S. Lazaro*] *i.e.*, the Philippines, also discovered by Magellan in 1521 and named by him the Archipelago of San Lazarus.

[26] veri *A*

[27] *Chronicles*] The first edition appeared in 1577, an enlarged edition under the supervision of John Hooker alias Vowell in 1587.

home, he built a sumptuous privie, and in the most conspicuous place thereof, namely just over the doore; he erected a statue of AJAX, with so grim a countenance, that the aspect of it being full of terrour, was halfe as good as a suppositor: and further, to honour him he chaunged the name of the house, and called it after the name of this noble Captaine of the greasie[28] ones (the Grecians I should say) AJAX: though since, by ill pronunciation, and by a figure called *Cacophonia,*[f] the accent is changed and it is called a Jakes.

Further when the funerall oration was ended, to do him all other complements, that appertained to his honour; they searcht for his petygrew,[30] and an excellent Antiquarie, and a Harold, by great fortune, found it out in an old Church booke in the Austen Friers at Genova: and it was proclaimed on this fashion.

> AJAX sonne of Telamon.
> sonne of Aeacus.
> sonne of Juppiter.[g]
> Juppiter,[32] *aliâs dictus* Picus.
> sonne of olde[33] Saturne.
> *Aliâs dictus* Stercutius.[h]

---

[f] *Hic desunt non pauca de sermone ath clerum.*[29]

[g] Thus farre Ovid.[31]

[h] Thus much lib. 6.[34] S. Aug. *de Civitate Dei.* Stercutius the god of doung.

---

[28] *greasie*] Obscene.

[29] ?*ath[eorum] cler[icor]um.* Cacophonia—Latinized form of κακοφωνία, a rhetorical term used to describe the disagreeable sound formed from the conjunction of certain syllables.

[30] *petygrew*] Archaic form of pedigree.   [31] *Metam.* xiii.21–8.

[32] Juppiter] *scored MS*   [33] olde] *not in MS*

[34] This should read *lib.* 18. In constructing his fanciful genealogy, Harington has perhaps understandably forgotten his correct reference: Augustine while scoffing at the supererogatory functions of the pagan gods in Bk. vi mentions Pilumnus; Vives in his commentary adds that the brother god of Pilumnus was Picumnus who 'found out the mannuring of grounds, and therefore was called *Sterquidinus,*' a fact that no doubt stuck in Harington's memory (*Of the Citie of God: with the Learned Comments of Jo. Lod. Vives,* tr. John Healey, 1610, Y6-Y6ᵛ; that Harington was using an edition of St. Augustine with Vives's commentary, first published in Basel in 1522 and dedicated to Henry VIII, is indicated by his later references on pp. 90 and 113).

In Bk. xviii, Ch. 15, Augustine describing the succession of '*Picus Saturnes* sonne' to the rule of Laurentum says: '*Sterces* was *Saturnes* father, hee that

Which when it was made knowen unto the whole fraternitie of the brethren, there was nothing but rejoycing and singing,[35] unto their god *Sarcotheos*[36] a devout *Shaame*[37] in honour of this *Stercutius* the great great grand-father of A JAX. Which Sonet hath a marvellous grace in their countrey, by meanes they do greatly affect these same *similiter desinentia*,[38] every Frier singing a verse and a brother aunswering him in the tune following amounting just to foure and twentie, which is the misticall number of their order.

But by the way, if any seveare *Catoes* take exceptions, and any chast *Lucretias*[39] take offence at the matter or musick here following, let them pardon me, that sought but to keepe *decorum*, in speaking of a slovenly matter, and of slovenly men somewhat slovenly.

Vos verò viri eruditi si quae hic scurriliter nimis dicta videbuntur, ignoscite: aequissimum enim est, ut quam voluptatem scelerati male faciendo capiant, eandem (quoad fieri potest) male audiendo amittant. Videtis autem cuiusmodi farinae homines taxare instituimus: non pios, doctos, sanctos, continentes, sed luxuriosos, hereticos, barbaros, impios. Quibus ego me per omnem vitam acerrimum hostem, ut & verum μισακμον[40] semper profitebor. Nostis proverbium, Cretisandum cum Cretensibus,[41] &

---

invented manuring of the ground with dung, which of him was called *Stercus*: Some say they called him *Stercutius*. Well howsoever hee gotte the name of *Saturne*, hee was the same *Sterces* or *Stercutius* whome they deified for his husbandry' (3N3ᵛ). Cf. Harington's epigram, '*Of* Cloacina *and* Sterquitius' (*L&E*, p. 167).

[35] *MS lacking from* unto *to p. 76, with* A.

[36] *Sarcotheos*] Bodygod, apparently Harington's coinage.

[37] *Shaame*] Not in the *OED*. Is it intended as a humorous conflation of *psalm* and *sham*? Lodge uses the verb *shawme* (illustrated in the *OED* only as the name of a medieval instrument) to describe an Englishman devoted to 'belly-cheere': 'he shawmes like a cow had broke her forelegs' (*Works*, IV, 85).

[38] *similiter desinentia*] A rhetorical trick of using words with similar or like endings.

[39] Lucrecias *A*   [40] μισακμον] See note 62, p. 80.

[41] *Cretisandum . . . Cretensibus*] Cf. 'Cretensis Cretensem. One false merchaunte deceyveth an other. The men of Crete were in olde tyme moche reproved for theyre falshode and deceite' (Richard Taverner, *Proverbes* or *adagies with newe addicions gathered out of the Chiliades of Erasmus*, 1539, Bl). Cf. Tilley C822.

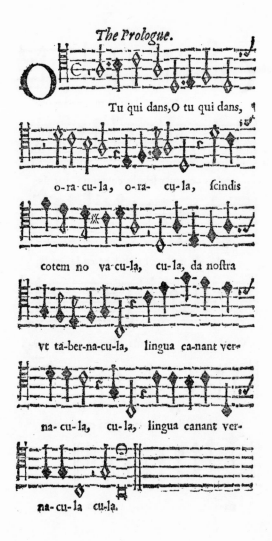

The Prologue.

Tu qui dans, O tu qui dans,

o-ra-cu-la, o-ra- cu-la, ſcindis

cotem no va-cu-la, cu-la, da noſtra

vt ta-ber-na-cu-la, lingua ca-nant ver-

na-cu-la, cu-la, lingua canant ver-

na-cu-la cu-la.

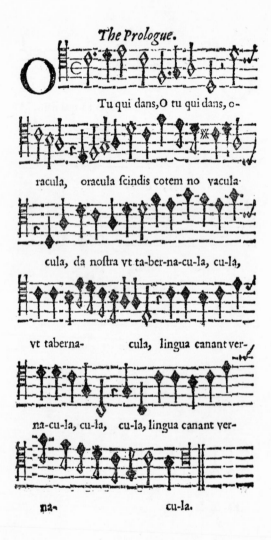

The Prologue.

Tu qui dans, O tu qui dans, o-

racula,   oracula ſcindis cotem no vacula-

cula, da noſtra vt ta-ber-na-cu-la, cu-la,

vt taberna-   cula, lingua canant ver-

na-cu-la, cu-la,   cu-la, lingua canant ver-

na-   cu-la.

74

certè hoc dignum est patella operculum.[42] *Nam similes habere debent labra lactucas.*[i]

1. *O tu qui dans oracula*
2. *Scindis cotem novacula*
3. *Da nostra ut tabernacula*
4. *Lingua canant vernacula*
5. *Opima post gentacula*
6. *Huiusmodi miracula*
7. *Sit semper plaenum poculum.*
8. *Habentes plaenum loculum*
9. *Tu serva nos ut specula*
10. *Per longa & laeta saecula*
11. *Ut clerus & plebecula*
12. *Nec nocte nec diecula*
13. *Curent de ulla recula,*
14. *Sed intuentes specula*
15. *Dura vitemus spicula*
16. *Jacentes cum amicula*
17. *Quae garrit ut cornicula*
18. *Seu tristis ceu ridicula*
19. *Tum porrigamus oscula*
20. *Tum colligamus floscula*
21. *Ornemus ut caenaculum*
22. *Et totum habitaculum*
23. *Tum culi post spiraculum.*
24. *Spectemus hoc spectaculum.*[44]

---

[i] Such lippes, such lettuce.[43]

---

[42] *hoc dignum . . . operculum*] Cf. *OF* XVI.6, side note and Tilley C742.

[43] Proverbial for 'like has met like,' derived from an alleged saying of Marcus Crassus when he saw an ass eating thistles. Cf. Tilley L326.

[44] *O tu . . . spectaculum*] The twenty-four verses of this 'Blacke Sauntus' or 'monkes hymne to *Saunte Satane*,' Harington asserted in a letter to Burghley in 1595, he had found in an old book of his father's: 'My father was wont to say, that Kynge Henry was used, in pleasante mood, to sing this verse; and my father (who had his good countenance, and a goodlie office in his courte, and also his goodlie Esther to wife) did sometyme receive the honour of hearing his own songe: for he made the tune which my man Combe hath sent herewith; having been much skilled in musicke, which was pleasing to the King, and which he learnt in the fellowship of good Maister Tallis, when a young man' (*L&E*, p. 64).

The hymn was translated by Sir John Hawkins (disregarding the play on *cula-culum*) and included in his five-volume history of music.

> O thou who utt'ring mystic notes,
>   The whetstone cut'st with razor,
> In mother-tongue permit our throats,
>   Henceforth to sing and say, Sir!
>
> To rich, material breakfasts join
>   These miracles more funny—
> Fill all our cups with lasting wine,
>   Our bags with lasting money!
>
> To us a guardian tow'r remain,
>   Through ages long and jolly;
> Nor give our house a moment's pain
>   From thought's intrusive folly!
>
> Ne'er let our eyes for losses mourn,
>   Nor pore on aught but glasses;
> And sooth the cares that still return,
>   By couching with our lasses;

Then sutable to this hymne, they had a dirge for A JAX, with a prayer to all their chief Saints whose names begin with A.

Sauntus Ablabius
Sauntus Acachius
Sauntus Arrius
Sauntus Aerius
Sauntus Aetius

} Some of these denyed the godhead of Christ with Arrius, some the authoritie of Bishops as Aerius: which you may see in Prateolo *de vita haereticorum*.[45]

Who loud as tatling magpies prate,
Alternate laugh and lour,
Then kiss we round each wanton mate,
And crop each vernal flow'r,

To deck our rooms, and chiefly that
Where supper's charms invite;
Then close in chimney-corner squat,
To see so blest a sight!

(*A General History of the Science and Practice of Music*, London, 1776, v, 437–8.)

[45] *Prateolo . . . haereticorum*] Gabriel Prateolus [Dupréau] (1511–88) was a French ecclesiastic and humanist who expressed a vigorous reaction to the Reformation; although he published works on grammar and philology, his most important undertaking was a lengthy survey of heresy (*Dictionnaire de théologie catholique*, Paris, 1935, XII[2]).

De Vitis, Sectis, et Dogmatibus Omnium Haereticorum (Cologne, 1569) treats over five hundred heresies, including all those in Harington's list: *Ablabius* or *Ablavius*, a bishop of Nicaea (c. A.D. 430), taught that remission of sins could only be obtained by baptism; hence penitence and self-mortification were useless.

Acachius or Acacius, a bishop of Caesarea in Palestine (c. A.D. 338), established a branch of Arianism which refused to accept either the orthodox doctrine of 'homoousion' or the view that the 'filius Dei' was of the same nature as other created beings.

Arrius or Arius, a priest of Alexandria, the most notable heretic of all, impugned the divinity of Christ by denying that he was co-substantial and co-eternal with God. Excommunicated as the result of the Council of Nicaea in 325, Arius was ordered to be reinstated in 336. For an account of his sudden death on the evening before his reinstatement, see p. 92, n. 54.

Aerius—founder of a fourth-century presbyterian sect which maintained there was no difference between a priest and a bishop, thus denying episcopal rank.

Aetius—friend of the apostate Julian and a bishop (c. 363), upheld the extreme Arian view that the Second and Third Persons of the Trinity differed in substance and will from the First Person.

Ora pro *A JAX*

Sauntus Almaricus	Almaricus denied the resur-
Saunti Adiaphoristae[46]	rection of the body, which
Saunti[47] 11000 *Anabaptistae*	is an heresie that marres
Et tu Sauntiss. Atheos	all, as S. Paule saith I. Cor.
	15. 14. That then our faith
	were vaine.

And so ended the blacke *Sauntus*.

By all which you may see, that it is but lacke of lurning, that makes some fellowes seeke out stale English Etymologies of this renowmed name of A Jax. One imagined, it was called so of blacke jackes; because they looke so slovenly, that a mad French man wrote, we did carrie our drinke in our bootes: but that is but a bald Etymologie, and I will never agree, that Jacke, though he were never so blacke, should be thus slaundered. But if you stand so much upon your English, and will not admit our Greeke, and our Romane tongue, you shall see I will cast about, to have one in English for you. First then, you have heard the olde proverbe (age breedes aches): now[48] you must imagine, that an old man, almost fouresquare yeare old, and come to the Psalme of *David, Labor & dolor*,[49] being

---

Almaricus or Amalricus, a late twelfth-century theologian and dialectician of Paris, taught a doctrine of pantheism, affirming that 'Deum sic locutum fuisse in Ovidio, sicut in Augustino.'

Adiaphoristae—followers of Melanchthon who held that certain Lutheran tenets were of an 'indifferent' nature—*adiaphora*—and therefore should not become the subject of controversy.

Anabaptistae—constituted an extreme antisacerdotal sect which appeared in Germany, Holland, and Switzerland at the beginning of the Reformation. Advocating communism and the right to rebel, they followed the 'heretic' Luther in rejecting infant baptism.

Atheos—'Athei sunt, qui nullum esse Deum credunt, caeci & excordes, quíque Dei providentiam è rebus humanis tollunt, omnia utique agi fato, animasque unà cum corporibus interire arbitrantes' (See Prateolus, A2–I3ᵛ and J. H. Blunt, *Dictionary of Sects, Heresies, Ecclesiastical Parties, and Schools of Religious Thought*, Philadelphia, 1847).

[46] Adiaphoristae] Albigenses *MS*

[47] Saunti] *not in MS*

[48] aches) now *A; age breedes aches*] Tilley A66, where Harington's example is the earliest cited.

[49] *Labor & dolor*] Psalm 89:10 (Sixtine-Clementine Bible, 1592, which became the authorized vulgate).

somewhat costive, at the house groned so pitifully, that
they thought hee had bene sicke: whereupon one ran to him
to hold his head, and asked him what he ayled. He told them,
he ayled nothing, but onely according to the proverbe, he
complained, that age breeds aches, and minding to speake it
shorter, by the figure of abbreviation, or perhaps by the rule,
Quod potest fieri per pauciora, non debet fieri per plura.[50] (I pray
you pardon me for being againe in my Latin) oh saith he,
maisters make much of youth, for I tell you age akes, age akes.
I feele it, age akes. Upon which patheticall speech of his,
delivered in that place, the younger men that bare him speciall
reverence, termed the place age akes: which agrees fully in pronunciation, though it may be since, some ill orthographers
have mis-written it, and so now it passeth currant[51] to be
spoken and written A Jax. And because as the saying is,
loquendum cum vulgo, we must now take him as we finde him,[52]
with all his faults.

But yet for reformation of as many as we can; and specially
of one fault he is much subject unto, you must remember that
this Ajax was always so strong a man, that this[53] strength
being an inseparable accident to him, doth now onely remain
in his breath, and that in diverse extremities, & contrarie
fashions.[54] Sometime with the heate of his breath he will be
readie to overcome a strong man; another time he will take a
weake man at the vauntage, and strike him behind with such a
cold, that he shalbe the worse for it a moneth after. Now many
have wrastled with him, to seeke to stop his breath and never
maime him; but he makes them glad to stop their noses, and
that indeed is some remedie, for such whose throats have a
better swallow, then their heads have capacitie. As some men
that are forced at sea to drinke stinking puddle water, do winke
and close their nosthrils, that they may not offend three sences
at once.

---

[50] *Quod . . . plura*] Nashe uses a variant of this in *Strange Newes,* I, 288;
McKerrow has identified it as a legal maxim (IV, 174).

[51] *passeth currant*] *i.e.,* accepted as genuine. This is the earliest example
cited in the *OED.*

[52] *we must . . . him*] Tilley T29

[53] this] *MS;* his *A, B*

[54] fashions] fashion *MS*

Now againe, some arme them selves against A JAX with perfumes, but that me thinke doubles the griefe, to imagine[55] what a good smell this were, if the other were away: as he that should have had 10000 pound with an ugly Mopsa,[56] sayd, not without a great sigh; Oh, what a match were this, were the woman away?[57] But the devise that shalbe hereafter discovered, will so confound this gentleman with the strong breath, that save we carrie about us some traitors, that are ready to take his part, he should never be able so much as to blow upon you. Yet I wold have the favourable readers (of what sort soever) thus farre satisfied, that I tooke not this quarrell upon me voluntarily, but rather in mine owne defence; & standing upon the *puntilio* of honour, having bene chalenged, as you may partly see in the letter precedent, by one, as it seemes, of the Captaines owne countryman: for his name is *Philostilpnos*, which I thought at first, was a word to conjure a spirit, till at last, a fellow of mine of Cambridge, told me the *Philo* was Greeke, and that he[58] would say in English, that he loveth cleanlinesse.[59] Now I being bound by the Duello, having accepted the challenge, to seeke no advantage, but even to deale with him at his owne weapon, entred the lists with him, and fighting after the olde English maner without the stockados,[60] (for to voyne[61] or strike below the girdle, we counted it base and too cowardly) after halfe a score downright blowes, we grew to be friends, and I was content to subscribe, Yours &c. And to the ende I may answer him in the same

---

[55] imagine] thinke *MS*

[56] *Mopsa*] Familiar to readers of the *Arcadia* as the daughter of the 'arrant doltish clowne' Dametas and his wife Miso; here used generically.

[57] *Oh, what . . . away*] Heywood, *A dialogue conteyning . . . proverbes*, Pt. II, Ch. I, 51–2 (*Works*, ed. B. A. Milligan, Illinois Studies in Language and Literature: XLI, Urbana, 1956).

[58] he] a *MS*   [59] loveth cleanlinesse] loves cleannes *MS*

[60] *stockados*] From Italian *stoccata*: a thrust in fencing.

[61] *voyne*] variant of *foin*: to thrust. Camden credits one Rowland York, involved in the betrayal of Deventer, with being 'the first that with high admiration for his boldnesse brought into *England* that deadly manner of foyning with the rapier in single fight; whereas the *English* till this time fought with long swords and bucklers, striking with the edge, and thought it no manly part either to foyne, or strike beneath the girdle' (*Elizabeth*, tr. R. Norton, 1635, 2G2; the original edition in Latin appeared in 1615). Cf. Harington in the *OF*, 1634, XL.78.1–2: '*Rogero* never foyned, and seldome strake, / But flatling.'

language, I am called *Misacmos*,[62] which is cosin and allie to his name; and it signifies a hater of filthinesse, and to all such as are of kin to either of our names or condicions, we commend this Discourse ensuing.

Ad Zoilum & Momum.

Cease maisters anie more,
    To grudge, chafe, pine & freat,
Lo stuffe for you good store
    To gnaw, chew, bite, and eate.[63]

---

[62] *Misacmos*] As Allan Gilbert has pointed out, there is no precise equivalent in Greek for the pen name Harington adopted. He apparently derived it from μισ and αὐχμός, meaning filth or squalor; transliterated, this would result in 'Misauchmos.' Like Spenser, Harington did not feel the 'pedant's compulsion to exactness' and simplified the form ('Sir John Harington's Pen Name,' *MLN*, LVIII, Dec. 1943, 616–17).

[63] bite and, eate *A*

A SHORT ADVERTISMENT OF THE AUTOR
TO THE READER.

The discourse ensewing is devided into three parts or sections
(as it were breathing places) least it may seeme confused,
or to tedious too be read all at once.

1   The first justifies the use of the homelyest wordes.
2   The second prooves the matter not to be contemptible.
3   The third shews the forme, and how it may be reformed.

1   The first begins gravely, and ends lightly.
2   The second begins pleasantly, and ends soberly.
3   The third is mixt both seriously and merily.

1   I would pray you to weigh the grave autorities reverently,
for they are true and autenticall.
2   I would wish you to regard the pleasaunt histories respectively, for they be honest and commendable.
3   I would advise you to use the mery matters modestly, for
so they may be faultlesse and harmlesse.

1   If you meane not to read it, then disp13rayse it not, for that
would be counted folly.
2   Till you have fully read it, censure it not, for that may be
deemed rashnesse.
3   When you have read it, say both of us have lost more time
then this in our dayes, and that perhappes would be
judged the right.[1]

---

[1] *MS lacking for p. 81.*

THE METAMORPHOSIS
OF A JAX.

THERE WAS a very tall & serviceable gentleman, somtime Lieutenant of the ordinance, called *M. Jaques Wingfield*[2]; who coming one day, either of businesse, or of kindnesse, to visit a great Ladie in the Court; the Ladie bad her Gentlewoman aske, which of the *Wingfields* it was; he told her *Jaques Wingfield*: the modest gentlewoman, that was not so well seene in the French, to know that *Jaques*, was but *James* in English, was so bashfoole, that to mend the matter (as she thought) she brought her Ladie word, not without blushing, that it was *M. Privie Wingfield*; at which, I suppose the Lady then, I am sure the Gentleman after, as long as he lived, was wont to make great sport.

I feare the homely title prefixed to this treatise (how warlicke a sound so ever it hath) may breed a worse offence, in some of the finer sort of readers; who may upon much more just occasion condemne it, as a noysome and unsavory discourse: because, without any error of equivocation, I meane indeed, to write of the same that the word signifies. But if it might please them a litle better to consider, how the place we treate of (how homely soever) is visited by them selves, once at least in foure and twentie houres, if their digestion bee good, and their constitution sound; then I hope they will do me that favour, and them selves that right, not to reject a matter teaching their owne ease and cleanlinesse, for the homelinesse of the name;

---

[2] *M. Jaques Wingfield*] The third son of Sir Richard Wingfield of Kimbolton, James Wingfield had been Master (not Lieutenant) of the Ordinance in Ireland with 'longe and good service' as well as Constable of Dublin Castle for thirty years; he died in 1587. In the official documents of the period, he is commonly referred to as Jaques, Jakes, or James (*APC*, xv, 33–5; *HMC, Carew MSS* i, *passim;* and Thomas Wright, *Queen Elizabeth and Her Times*, London, 1838, i, 86).

and consequently, they will excuse all broade phrases of speech, incident to such a matter, with the old English proverbe that ends thus; *For Lords and Ladies do the same.*[3] I know that the wiser sort of men wil consider, and I wish that the ignorant sort would learne; how it is not the basenesse, or homelinesse, either of words, or matters, that make them foule & obscenous,[4] but their base minds, filthy conceits, or lewd intents that handle them. He that would scorne a Physition, because for our infirmities sake, he refuseth not sometime the noisome view of our lothsomest excrements, were worthy to have no helpe by Physicke, and should breake his devine precept, that saith; Honour the Physition, for necessities sake God hath ordained him.[5] And he that would honour the makers of[6] *Aposticchios,*[7] or rebatoes,[8] because creatures much honored use to weare them, might be thought, perhaps full of curtesie, but voyd of wit.

Surely, if we would enter into a sober, and sad consideration of our estates,[9] even of the happiest sort of us, as men of the world esteeme us; whether we be noble, or rich, or learned, or beautifull, or healthy, or all these (which seldome happeneth) joyned together: we shall observe, that the joyes we enjoy in this world, consist rather *in indolentia*[10] (as they call it) which is an avoyding of grievances and inconveniences, then in possessing any passing great pleasures; so durable are the harmes, that our first parents fal hath layd on us, and so poore the helpes that we have in our selves: finally so short, & momentanie the contentments that we fish for, in this Ocean of miseries, which either we misse, (fishing before the net, as the proverbe is)[11] or if we catch them, they prove but like Eeles,

---

[3] *For Lords . . . same*] I have not traced this.

[4] *obscenous*] Harington's usage in his 'Briefe Apologie' (*OF*, 1591, $ 7) is the earliest instance cited in the *OED*.

[5] *Honour . . . him*] Ecclus. 38:1.   [6] *of of A*

[7] *Aposticchios*] Florio defines aposticcio as '*made by art or wrought by the hand, counterfait*' (*A Worlde of Wordes*, B5ᵛ).

[8] *rebatoes*] A kind of stiff collar worn by both sexes from 1590 to 1630.

[9] *of our estates*] 'A sober / considera / cion': Harington annotation in the Sheffield copy.

[10] indolentia] *B;* indolencia *MS, A.* Cf. Cicero de Finibus ii.4.11 and ii.6.

[11] *fishing . . . is*] Tilley F335.

sleight & slipperie. The chiefest of all our sensual pleasures, I meane that which some call the sweet sinne of letcherie,[12] though God knowes, it hath much sowre sawce to it; for which notwithstanding, many hazard both their fame, their fortune, their friends, yea their soules; which makes them so oft breake the sixt commaundement,[13] that when they heare it read at Church, they leave the words of the Communion booke, and say, *Lord have mercie upon us, it grieves our hearts to keepe this Law.* And when the Commination is read on Ashwednesday, wherein is read, *Cursed be he that lyeth*[14] *with his neighbours wife,* and let all the people say, *Amen*; all[15] these people either say nothing, or as a neighbour of mine said, *he hem*[a]; I say this surpassing pleasure, that is so much in request, and counted such a principall solace, I have heard confessed before a most honourable person, by a man of middle age, strong constitution, and well practised in this occupation, to have bred no more delectation to him (after the first heate of his youth was past) then to go to a good easie close stoole, when he hath had a lust thereto (for that was his verie phrase.) Which being confessed by him, and confirmed by many; makes me take this advantage thereof in the beginning of this discourse, to preferre this house I mind to speake of,[b] before those which they so much frequent; neither let any disdaine the comparison. For I remember, how not long since, a grave & godly Ladie, and grand-mother to all my wives children,[17] did in their hearings, and for their better instruction,

---

[a] Some say amend, and so done, were very wel said.[16]

[b] A jak's house preferred before a bawdie house.

---

[12] *sweet . . . letcherie*] Cf. 'That same sweet sinne, that some but deeme a Jest' in the epigram, '*Sir* John Raynsfords *confession*' (*L&E*, p. 202); Notes to Bk. IV, *OF*; and below, p. 136.

[13] *sixt commaundement*] According to the Latin division followed by the Lutherans and the Roman Catholics.

[14] lyeth] lyes *MS*   [15] all] *MS*; *om. A, B*   [16] said *A*

[17] *a grave . . . children*] 'the Lady / Rogers som- / tyme caled / the fayre / Nonne of / Cannington,' Harington annotation: Nares-Folger copy. After the suppression of the monasteries, the manor and rectory of Cannington in Somersetshire with the advowson of the vicarage and many other lands and tenements were given by Henry VIII to Edward Rogers; the property continued in the family until c. 1670 (Collinson, I, 233). Cf. the epigram '*A Tale of a Bayliffe distraining for rent. To my Ladie* Rogers' where Harington also calls her 'The faire Nun' (*L&E*, pp. 183–5).

tell them a story; which though I will not sweare it was true,
yet I did wish the auditorie would beleeve it; namely, how an
Hermit being caried in an evening, by the conduct of an Angell,
through a great citie, to contemplate the great wickednesse daily
and hourely wrought therein; met in the street a gongfarmer[18]
with his cart full laden, no man envying his full measure. The
poore Hermit, as other men did, stopt his nosthrils, & betooke
him to the other side of the street, hastening from the sower
cariage all he could; but the Angell kept on his way, seeming
no whit offended with the savour. At which while the Hermit
marvelled, there came not long after by them, a woman gor-
geously attyred, well perfumed, well attended with coaches,
and torches, to convey her perhaps to some noble mans
chamber. The good Hermit somewhat revived with the faire
sight, and sweet savour, began to stand at the gaze. On the
other side, the good Angell now stopped his nose, and both
hastened him selfe away, and beckened his companion from
the place. At which the Hermit more marvelling then before,
he was told by the Angell, that this fine courtesan laden with
sinne, was a more stinking savour afore God & his holy Angels,
then that beastly cart, laden with excrements. I will not spend
time to allegorize this storie, onely I will wish all the readers
may find as sure a way to cleanse, and keepe sweete the noblest
part of them selves, that is, their soules; as I shall shew them a
plaine and easie way, to keepe sweet the basest part of their
houses, that is, their sinkes.[19] But to the intent I may binde my
selfe to some certaine method, I will first awhile continue as I   1
have partly begun, to defend by most autenticall authorities
and examples, the use of these homely words in so necessary
matters. Secondly, concerning the matter it selfe, I wil shew   2
how great, and extraordinarie care hath bene had in all ages, for
the good ordering of the same. Lastly, for the forme, I will set
downe the cheapest, perfectest, & most infallible, for avoyding   3
all the inconveniences the matter is subject to; that hitherto (if
I and many more be not much deceived) was ever found
out.

When I was a truantly scholer in the noble University of

---

[18] *gongfarmer*] A dung carter.
[19] *sinkes*] Receptacles for filth or ordure; cf. p. 88, n. 32. *Marginal numbers om. B*

Cambridge[20] (though I hope I had as good a conscience as other of my pew-fellowes, to take but a litle learning for my money) yet I can remember, how a very learned and reverent Devine held this question in the schooles. *Scripturae stylus non est barbarus.* The style, or phrase of the Scripture is not barbarous. Against whom one replyed with this argument.

> *That which is obscenous, may be called barbarous:*
> *But the Scripture is in many places obscenous:*
> *Therefore the Scripture may be called barbarous.*

To which syllogisme was truly answered (as I now remember, denying the *minor*) that though such phrases to us seeme obscenous, and are so when they are used to ribauldrie, or lasciviousnesse, yet in the Scripture they are not only voyd of incivilitie, but full of sanctitie; that the Prophets do in no place more effectually, more earnestly, nor more properly beate downe our pride and vanitie, and open to our eyes the filthinesse, and horror of our sinnes, then by such kind of phrases, of which they recited that, where it is sayd, that the sinnes of the people were, *quasi pannus menstruatae universae justitiae nostrae,*[c] that a common or strange woman (for so the Scripture covertly termeth a harlot)[22] hath her quiver open for everie arrow[23]; that an old lecherous man, is like a horse that neigheth after every mare,[24] &c. To which I could adde many more, if I affected copiousnesse in this kind; some in broad speeches, some in covert termes, expressing mens shame, mens sinnes, mens necessities. *Quinque aureos anos facietis pro quinque*

---

[c] Esa. 64[21]

---

[20] *When I . . . Cambridge*] Harington was matriculated as a fellow commoner from King's College in 1576 and received his B.A. 1577/78, first in the *ordo senioritatis*; this was a kind of honours list, apparently granted on the basis either of social position or intellectual pre-eminence. He received his M.A. in 1581 (J. and J. A. Venn, *Alumni Cantabrigienses* Pt. I, Cambridge, 1922, II, 310; I, vii).

[21] Isa. 64:6.

[22] *that a . . . harlot*] Ecclus. 9:10; Prov. 5:20; 23:27.

[23] *hath . . . arrow*] Ecclus. 26:15. Cf. Harington's epigram utilizing this metaphor, '*Of an Heroicall awnswer of a great Roman Lady to her husband*' (*L&E*, p. 298).

[24] *that an . . . mare*] Jer. 5:8.

satrapis, which our English of Geneva translates very modestly Ye shall make five golden Emeralds[25] for five Noblemen or Princes. Which word I am sure, many of the simple hearers, & readers, take for a precious stone of the Indians, set in gold; and so they shal still take it for me, for that ignorance, may perhaps do them lesse hurt in this matter, then further knowledge; but yet what a special Scripture that is to Gods glory and their shame, appeares by Davids prophecie in the 77.[26] Psalme, where he saith; *Percussit inimicos suos in posteriora, opprobrium sempiternum dedit illis.*[27] Hee smote his enemies in the hinder parts, & put them to a perpetuall shame; in remembrance whereof, in some solemne lyturgies, untill this day the same Chapter of *Aureos anos* is read.

What should I speake of the great league betweene God and man, made in Circumcision? impressing a painful *stigma*, or caracter in Gods peculiar people,[28] though now, most happily taken away in the holy Sacrament of Baptisme. What the word signified, I have knowne reverent and learned men have bene ignorant; and we call it very well Circumcision, and uncircumcision, though the Remists (of purpose belike to varie from

---

[25] *Quinque . . . Emeralds*] I Sam. 6:4. Harington's pun on the use of 'emerods' for αἱμορροΐδες in the Genevan version (found also in the Bishops' Bible (I Kings 6:4) and later in the King James's version) would be clearer to a modern reader with one of the older spellings for the 'precious stone of the Indians,' *e.g.*, emerode, emorade, emeraud.

However, it should be pointed out that on p. 159 where he is speaking of various physical maladies, including haemorrhoids, the MS reading is also *emralds*; here, however, the printer correctly substituted 'hemeroids.' Thus *emerald* was either homophonic with *emerod*, a view supported by seventeenth-century lists of homophones (*emeralds*, ME *emrauds* paired with *emrods*, 'haemorrhoids'; E. J. Dobson, *English Pronunciation 1500–1700*, Oxford, 1957, II, 923), or the term was popularly used for the disease. Cf. the use of *pearl* for a kind of cataract:

Had every verse a pearl in the eye, it should be thine.

(Middleton, *The Spanish Gypsy*, II.i.164, ed. A. H. Bullen, London, 1885) and the still current use of *carbuncle*:

Thou art a boil,
A plague sore, or embossed carbuncle
In my corrupted blood.

(*Lear* II.iv.226–8.)

[26] 77.] three score & xvij[th] *MS*   [27] 77. . . . *illis*] 77:66

[28] *impressing . . . people*] Gen. 17:7–14.

Geneva) will needes bring in Prepuse[29]; which word was
after admitted into the Theater with great applause, by the
mouth of Maister Tarlton the excellent Comedian; when many
of the beholders that were never circumcised, had as great cause
as Tarlton, to complaine of their Prepuse. But to come soberly,
and more nearely to our present purpose; In the old Testament,
the phrase is much used of covering the feete,[30] and in the
newe Testament, he that healeth & helpeth all our infirmities,
useth[31] the word *draught*[32]; that that goeth into the man, is
digested in the stomacke, and cast out into the draught.[d]
Lastly, the blessed Apostle S. Paule,[34] being rapt in contempla-
tion of divine blisfulnes, compares all the chief felicities
of the earth, esteeming them (to use his owne word) as *stercora*,
most filthy doung, in regard of the joyes he hoped for. In
imitation of which zealous vehemency, some other writers have
affected to use such phrase of speech, but with as il successe,
as the asse[35] that leapt on his maister at his coming home,
because he saw a litle spaniell, that had so done, very[36] much
made on[37]: for indeed, these be counted but foule mouthd
beasts for their labors.

---

[d] εἰς ἀφεδρῶνα[33]

---

[29] *and we . . . Prepuse*] The Rhemists so-called because the seminary established at Douay for the purpose of educating young English Roman Catholics
as missionary priests was temporarily removed to Rheims (1578 to 1593); there
the Catholic translation of the New Testament was published in 1582. Harington's gibe here is directed at the translation of Rom. 2:25 where the Rhemist
version renders the ἀκροβυστία or 'uncircumcision' of the original as 'prepuce'
(*The English Hexapla*, London, 1872).

[30] *of covering the feete*] A periphrasis for *purgare ventrem*. Cf. I Sam. 24:3
(cited by Harington, p. 107) and Judges 3:24. Harington has annotated the
Sheffield copy:' because / the Jews / ware short / garments / that cove- / red
not yᵉ / feet but / when they stooped. / and Horac / sayth / Curtis Ju / deis
oppe- / dere': *Sat.* i.9.69.

[31] useth] used *B*

[32] *the word draught . . .*] Matt. 15:17; Mark 7:19. Cf. *T&C* V.i.82:
    Sweet draught! 'Sweet,' quoth 'a? sweet sink, sweet sewer!

[33] *om. A, B*   [34] *S. Paule . . .*] Phil. 3:8.

[35] *as the asse . . .*] This story appears in Adriano Banchieri's *La Nobilità
dell' Asino*, Englished 1595, to illustrate the proverb, 'He plaies the Asses
pastime with me' (G2ᵛ, from a photostat of the Huntington copy at the Folger
Shakespeare Library), where, following Banchieri, it is incorrectly attributed to
Apuleius. The source is the Aesopian fable of the ass and the little dog.

[36] very] *MS*; *om. A, B*   [37] on] of *B*

But to conclude these holy autorities, worthy to be alledged in most reverent and serious manner; and yet here also I hope without offence; let us come now to the ridiculous, rather then religious customes of the Pagans, and see, if this contemptible matter I treat of, were despised among them; nay rather observe, if it were not respected with a reverence, with an honour, with a religion, with a dutie, yea with a deitie, & no marvel. For they that had Gods and Goddesses, for all the necessaries of our life, from our cradles to our graves, viz. 1. for sucking, 2. for swathing, 3. for eating, 4. for drinking, 5. for sleeping, 6. for husbandrie, 7. for venerie, 8. for fighting, 9. for physicke, 10. for mariage, 11. for child-bed, 12. for fire, 13. for water, 14. for the thresholds, 15. for the chimneys; the names of which I do set downe by them selves, to satisfie those that are curious. 1. *Lacturtia*, 2. *Cunina*, 3. *Edulica*, 4. *Potina*, 5. *Morpheus*, 6. *Pan*, 7. *Priapus*, 8. *Bellona*, 9. *Aesculapius*, 10. *Hymen*, 11. *Lucina*, and *Vagitanus*, 12. *Aether*, 13. *Salacia*, 14. *Lares*, 15. *Penates*. I say, you must not thinke, they would commit such an oversight, to omit such a necessary, as almost in all languages, hath the name of necessitie, or ease: wherefore they had both a God and a Goddesse, that had the charge of the whole businesse; the God was called *Stercutius*,[38] as they write, because he found so good an employment for all maner of doung,[39] as to lay it upon the land: or perhaps it was he, that first found the excellent mysterie of the kinde setting of a Parsnip[40] (which I wil not here discover, because I heard of

---

[38] *the God . . . Stercutius*] Cf. Tommaso Garzoni's *The Hospitall of Incurable Fooles*: 'And the Romanes might well bee numbred amongst those three elbowed Fooles, in offering divine sacrifice to such an harlot, as was *Flora*, and adoring *Stercutio* for a god, no lesse unwoorthily, then shamfully constituting him a patron, and Protector of *Ajax*, and his commodities' (B3-B3ᵛ). The translation which appeared in 1600 has been assigned to Edward Blount and also to Nashe; the dedication of the original is dated 1586.

[39] maner of doung] manner downge *MS*

[40] *that first . . . Parsnip*] Although one might expect to find some such bizarre notion as Nashe sets forth about the growing of asparagus (I, 174), the only information I have been able to find about the 'excellent mysterie' of the parsnip is of the very practical kind set forth by Dydymus Mountaine [Thomas Hill] that 'the seedes of the Parsnep and Carote, require one manner of diligence in the sowing, and to bee bestowed in a ground painefully digged, well turned in with dung, and workemanly dressed before' (*The Gardeners Labyrinth*, 1586, 2C3ᵛ).

a truth, that a great Ladie that loved Parsnips verie well, after she had heard how they grew, could never abide them, and I would be loth, to cause any to fall out of love with so good a dish.)[41] Neverthelesse (except they will have better bread then is made of wheate[42]) they must (how fine so ever they be) give *M. Stercutius* leave, to make the land able to beare wheate. But the Goddesse was much more especially, and properly assigned for this busines, whose name was *Dea Cloacina*, her statue was erected by *Titus Tatius*,[43] he that raigned with *Romulus*, in a goodly large house of office (a fit shrine for such a Saint) which *Lodovicus Vives* cites out of *Lactantius*.[44] But he that wil more particularly enform him selfe of the originall of all these pettie Gods and Goddesses; as also of the greater, which they distinguisht by the name of *Dii consentes*, which are according to old *Ennius* verse, devided into two rankes of Lords and Ladies.

> *Juno, Vesta, Minerva, Cerésque Diana, Venus, Mars,*
> *Mercurius, Neptunus, Jovis, Vulcanus, Apollo.*[e]

Of all which S. Augustin writes most divinely, to overthrow their divinitie; and therefore I referre the learned and studious reader, to his fourth and sixt bookes *de Civitate Dei*, where the originall, and vanitie of all these Gods and Goddesses is more largely discoursed: with a pretie quippe to *Seneca* the great Philosopher, who being in heart halfe a Christian, as was thought; yet because he was a Senator of Rome, was faine (as S. Augustine[f] saith) to follow that he found fault with, to do

---

[e] These Gods were of the privy counsell[45] to Juppiter, 23. Chap. 4. booke.
[f] S. Augustine 6. booke 10. chap.[46]

---

[41] them) . . . dish. *MS, A, B*   [42] *except they . . . wheate*] Tilley B622.
[43] Tacius *MS, A, B*

[44] *Lodovicus Vives . . . Lactantius*] In his annotations to Bk. IV, Ch. 8, *The Citie of God*, Vives says of Cloacina, 'her statue was found by *Tatius* (who raigned with *Romulus*,) in a great Privy or Jakes of Rome and knowing not whose it was, [he] named it after the place, *Cloacina*, of *Cloaca. Lactant[ius]*' (P4).

[45] *These . . . counsell*] Vives in his note on the 'dei consentes' in Bk. IV, Ch. 23, cites Ennius's listing of the twelve gods and goddesses and adds: '*Jupiter* using them as counsellours in his greatest affaires as *Augustine* saith heere' (R3).

[46] 10. chap. L. *A, B* ?*from misreading symbol for insert in MS*

that he disliked, to adore that he detested. But come we to my stately Dame *Cloacina*, and her Lord *Stercutius*, though these were not of the higher house, called *Consentes*; yet I hope for their antiquity, they may make great comparison: for he is sayd to have bene old *Saturne*, father to *Pycus* that was called *Juppiter*; and *Cloacina* was long before *Priapus*, and so long before *Felicitie*, that S. Augustine writes merily, that he thinkes verily, *Felicitie* forsooke the Romanes, for disdaine that *Cloacina* and *Priapus* were deified so long before her; adding *Imperium Romanorum propterea grandius, quam felicius fuit.*[47] The Romane Empire therefore was rather great, then happy. But howsoever Lady *Felicitie* disdaines her, no question but Madame *Cloacina* was alwayes a verie good fellow: for it is a token of speciall kindnes, to this day among the best men in France, to reduce a Syllogisme *in Bocardo*[48] together. Insomuch as I have heard it seriously told, that a great Magnifico of Venice being Ambassador in France, and hearing a Noble person was come to speake with him, made him stay til he had untyed his points; and when he was new set on[49] his stoole, sent for the Noble man to come to him at that time; as a verie speciall favour.[50] And for other good fellowships I doubt not, but from the beginning it hath often happened, that some of the Nymphes of this gentle goddesse, have met so luckily with some of her devout chaplens, in her chappels of ease, and payd their

---

[47] *Imperium . . . fuit*] Harington's quotation varies slightly from the original where it is given in the form of a question, Bk. IV, Ch. 23 (*Corpus Christianorum Series Latina* XLVII, Turnholt, 1955, 14, Pt. I, 117).

[48] *to reduce . . . Bocardo*] The process used in logic to bring a syllogism into a different but equivalent form, specifically into one of the moods of the first figure (see pp. 200–201 where Combe plays with the various moods and figures of logic). *Bocardo* is a mnemonic word representing by the arrangement of its vowels the fifth mood of the third figure of syllogisms; it also gave its name to a prison in Oxford.

In Bocardo, however, here clearly seems to signify 'privy,' a meaning not included in the *OED*. Cf. the same usage in the *Ulysses* (STC 12782), D7, and the following example from Middleton's *The Family of Love* 1.3.5–9: 'she that paints a day-times, and looks fair and fresh on the outside, but in the night-time is filthier than the inside of Bocardo, and is indeed far more unsavory [to those] that know her, forsooth' (ed. A. W. Bullen, London, 1885).

[49] on] of *MS*

[50] *and when . . . favour*] This 'French courtesy' is frequently alluded to. Cf. Montaigne, *Essays*, tr. Florio (London, Everyman's Library, 1946), I, 29, and Nashe, I, 177.

privie tithes so duly, and done their service together with such devotion; that for reward, she hath preferred them within fortie weeks after to *Juno Lucina*, and so to *Vagitana*, *Lacturtia*, and *Cunina*, for even to this day, such places continue verie fortunate.[51] And whereas I named devotion, I would not have you thinke, how homely soever the place is, that all devotion is excluded from it. For I happening to demand of a deare friend of mine, concerning a great companion of his, whether he were religious or no, and namely if he used to pray; he told me, that to his remembrance he never heard him ask any thing of God, nor thanke God for any thing; except it were once[52] at a Jakes, he heard him say, he thanked God, he had had a good stoole.[53] Thus you see, a good stoole might move as great devotion in some man, as a bad sermon; & sure it sutes very well, that *Quorum Deus est venter, eorum templum sit cloaca.* He that makes his belly his God, I wold have him make a Jakes his chappell. But he that would indeed call to mind, how Arrius, that notable and famous, or rather infamous hereticke, came to his miserable end upon a Jakes;[54] might take just

---

[51] *for even . . . fortunate*] Apparently a current scandalous allusion. Cf. Harington's epigram '*Against* Cayus *that scorn'd his Metamorphosis*':

> Last day thy Mistris, *Cayus*, being present,
> One hapt to name, to purpose not unpleasant,
> The Title of my mis-conceived Booke:
> At which you spit, as though you could not brooke
> So grosse a Word: but shall I tell the matter
> Why? If one names a Jax, your lips doe water.
> There was the place of your first love and meeting,
> There first you gave your Mistris such a greeting,
> As bred her scorne, your shame, and others lafter,
> And made her feele it twenty fortnights after:
> Then thanke their wit, that makes the place so sweet,
> That for your *Hymen* you thought place so meet.
> But meet not Maids at Madam *Cloacina*,
> Lest they cry nine moneths after, Helpe *Lucina*.

> (*L&E*, pp. 190–1.)

[52] once] *MS; om. A, B*

[53] *For I . . . stoole*] On p. 253 of the *Apologie*, Harington tells this story of his uncle Thomas Markham.

[54] *how Arrius . . . Jakes*] 'he died / on a draught': Harington annotation in the Sheffield copy. Everard Digby, a Cambridge divine whose views in respect to the despoiling of church properties were obviously compatible with those of

occasion even at that homely businesse, to have godly thoughts; rather then as some have, wanton, or most have, idle. To which purpose I remember in my riming dayes, I wrote a short Elegie upon a homly Embleme;[55] which both verse and Embleme, they have set up in *Cloacinas* chappell, at my house verie solemnely.[56] And I am the willinger to impart it to my frends because I protest to you truely, a sober Gentleman protested to me seriously; that the conceit of the picture & the verse, was an occasion to put honest and good thoughts into his mind. And Plutark defends with many reasons, in his booke called *Symposeons*,[g] that where the matters them selves often are unpleasant to behold, their counterfeits are seene not without delectation.[57]

Wherefore, though I graunt manie places and times are much fitter for true devotion, yet I dare take it upon me; that if we would give the Devil no kinder entertainment in his other suggestions, then this father gave him in his causlesse reproofe

---

[g] *Lib. 5. quaest. I.*

Harington (see p. 151), in *his Dissuasive From Taking away the lyvings and goods of the Church*, 1590, uses the same epithet in referring to the demise of Arius 'that notable heretike ... as he went in the streete with great pride, and countenance of many friends: of a sodaine he went aside to the privie, where his belly violently burst in sunder, his guts came out, and he fell downe dead most miserably, as it was presently seene of all the people' (Y1-Y1ᵛ).

[55] *a short Elegie ... Embleme*] Included in the collection of epigrams published after his death as well as in the manuscript copy presented to Prince Henry.
The emblem (see Illus.) includes two proverbs. In his *Worlde of Wordes*, Florio defines *sprinto* as '*kickt, winsed, or spurned*' and *spinto* as '*thrust, pusht, shouldred, prickt, provoked, urged, prest, or driven out*' (2K4ᵛ and 2K3ᵛ). The first proverb, accordingly, might literally be rendered: 'Kickt but not prickt.' For the second, see Tilley A55.

[56] *MS lacking* And *through* delectation.

[57] *And Plutark ... delectation*] 'In pastimes and sports, presented to the eie and the eare, the pleasure consisteth not in seeing or hearing, but in the understanding: for an odious and unpleasant thing it is, to heare a henne keepe a creaking or cackling, and a crow untowardly and untunably crying; and yet hee that can well and naturally counterfet either the cackling of an henne, or the crying of the crow, pleaseth and contenteth us woonderfull well: semblably, to looke upon those who are in ptisicke or consumption, is but a lovelesse sight; and yet we joy and take delight to see the pictures or images of such persons; for that our understanding is pleased and contented with the imitation & resemblance of them, as a thing proper and peculiar unto it' (*The Philosophie, commonlie called The Morals*, tr. Philemon Holland, 1603, 304).

A godly father sitting on a draught,
To do as neede, and nature hath us taught;
Mumbled (as was his maner) certen prayr's,
And unto him the Devil straight repayr's:
And boldly to revile him he begins,
Alledging that such prayr's are deadly sins;
And that it shewd, he was devoyd of grace,
To speake to God, from so unmeete a place.
The reverent man, though at the first dismaid;
Yet strong in faith, to Satan thus he said.
Thou damned spirit, wicked, false & lying,
Dispairing thine own good, & ours envying:
Ech take his due, and me thou canst not hurt,
To God my pray'r I meant, to thee the durt.
Pure prayr ascends to him that high doth sit,
Down fals the filth,[58] for fiends of hel more fit.

(for he gave it him in his teeth, take it how he would.) I say we should not so easily be overthrowne with his assaults, as dayly we are, for lacke of due resistance.[h] But come we now to more particular & not so serious matter; have not many men of right good conceit, served them selves with diverse pretie emblemes, of this excrementall matter, as[59] that in Alciat,[60] to shew that base fellowes oft-times swimme in the streame of good fortune, as well as the worthiest:[61]

Nos quoque poma[i] natamus.[62]

---

[h] For want of the good take heed.
[i] *Poma*, signifies horsdong aswell as apples.[63]

---

[58] filth] durte *MS*
[59] matter. As] *A*

[60] *emblemes . . . Alciat*] The reference is clearly to the emblem entitled 'Adversus naturam peccantes' which first appeared in a collection published in Venice in 1546; considered offensive, it was thereafter frequently omitted or relegated to appendices or printed without the device. A 1621 edition published by Peter Paul Tozzius in Padua restored it to the text proper (LXXX) with an even more explicit device (Mario Praz, *Studies in Seventeenth-Century Imagery*, London, 1947, II, 7); the same cut was used in a Latin-Italian edition also published in Padua in 1626.

The sixteenth-century commentators observed that Alciati's emblem derived from Martial's Epigram i.37 (quoted by Harington on p. 98), and the Italian and French translations make this clear by translating the 'choenice' of the original as 'la coppa d'oro' and 'un vaisseau de prix' (*Emblemati*, Padua, 1626, H1[v] and *Les Emblemes*, Cologne, 1615, N8[v]).

> Turpe quidam factu, sed & est res improbu dictu,
>   Excipiat si quis choenice ventris onus.
> Mensuram legisque modum hoc excedere sanctae est,
>   Quale sit incesto pollui adulterio.

(*Emblematum Libellus*, Venice, 1546, D2[v]).

[61] worthiest. *A*

[62] *Nos . . . natamus*] Cf. Tilley A302. This is apparently an example of an elliptical proverb. The English translation of the Latin given in Withals's schoolboy dictionary is, 'Wee apples swimme quoth the horseturds' (John Withals, *A Dictionary in English and Latine*, 1634, 2O5[v]; first published in 1553, it was augmented in 1586 and again in 1602: see STC listings). Cf. '*Nos poma natamus*, dissero gli sterchi cavallini, galleggiando insieme ai pomi' (Gustavo Strafforello, *La Sapienza del Mondo*, Turin, 1883, III, 284). Both Strafforello and Wilhelm Binder in his *Novus Thesaurus Adagiorum Latinorum* (Stuttgart, 1866), 2257, give its origin as German.

[63] Poma . . . apples] *poma* bee horsdung. *MS*

Or as the old proverb, as wel as emblem, that doth admonish men not to contend with base and ignominious persons.

> *Hoc scio pro certo, quod si cum stercore certo*
> *Vinco ceu vincor, semper ego maculor.*

> *I know if I contend with dirtie foes,*
> *I must be soild,*[64] *whether I win or lose.*[65]

Which Emblem had almost hindered me the writing of this present discourse, save that a good friend of mine told me, that this is a fansie and not a fight, and that if it should grow to a fight; he assured me I had found so excellent a ward against his chiefe dart, which is his strong breath, that I were like to quit my hands in the fray, as well as any man. But to proceede in these rare Emblemes; who hath not read or heard, of the Picture made in Germanie, at the first rising of Luther? where to shew as it were by an Emblem, with what drosse, and draffe, the Pope & his partners fed the people; they caused him to be purtraied in his Pontificalibus riding on[66] a great sow, and holding before her taster, a dirty pudding: which dirtie devise, Sleidan the historian verie justly and gravely, both reports and reproves;[67] yet it served a turne for the time, and made great

---

[64] soild] foild *MS, A, B*

[65] *I know . . . lose*] Harington utilized this proverb in an epigram addressed 'To Doctor Harvey of Cambridge' (*L&E*, p. 199).

[66] no] of *MS*

[67] *Emblem . . . reproves*] The emblem 'very fonde in dede, but yet as it were a prophesye of the thyng to come' is described as follows: 'The Bisshop in hys prelates apparell sitteth upon a greate sowe with manye dugges, whyche he diggeth in with his spurres: havyng two fyngers of hys right hand nexte hys thume stretched ryghte up as the maner is, he blesseth suche he chaunceth to mete with: In hys lefte hande he holdeth a new smokinge tourde, at the smell wherof the sowe lyfteth up her snowte, and with her wyde mouthe and nose thirlles catcheth after her praye: but he in derysion, blamyng the beast full bytterly, I shall ryde thee, saieth he, with my spurres, whether thou wylt or noe. Thou haste troubled me longe aboute a counsell, that thowe myghtest rayle on me at thy pleasure, and accuse me franckelye. Beholde nowe, thys same is that counsell, that thou so greatlye desyrest: by the sowe he sygnifyeth Germany. These tryfles of hys, many men taunted, as unsemely for hym, and not verey modest: But he had hys reasons whye he did so, & was thought to have had a greater foresyghte in thynges' (tr. John Daus, *A Famouse Cronicle of oure time, called Sleidanes Commentaries*, 1560, 2Q6ᵛ).

sport to the people. But when this May-game[68] was done, an hundred thousand of them came home by weeping crosse;[69] so as the poore sow was not only sold by the eares, but sould by a drumme,[70] or slaine by the sword. Yet the Flanders cow, had more wit then the Germane sow: for she was made after an other sort, viz. the Mirrour of Princes feeding her, the Terror of Princes spurring her, the Prince of Orange milking her,[71] or after some such fashion, for I may faile in the particulars; but the conclusion was, that Monsieur d'Allanson (who indeed with most noble endevour, thogh not with so happie successe, attempted them) would have pulled her backe by the taile, and she filed his fingers.[72] And thus much for Emblemes. Now for poesie (though Emblemes also are a kind of poesie) I rather doubt, that the often usage of such words, will make the Poets be condemned; then that the Poets authorities, will make the wordes be allowed: but if their example can give anie countenance to them, they shall want none. It is certaine, that of all poems, the Epigram is the plesawntest,[73] & of all that writes Epigrams, Martiall is counted the wittyest.[74] He in his

---

[68] *May-game*] Merrymaking or foolery.

[69] *came . . . crosse*] Proverbial for repenting of an undertaking. See Tilley W248 and L460. Nares notes that there were at least three crosses of this name, located near Oxford, Stafford, and Shrewsbury.

[70] *sould . . . drumme*] Betrayed publicly.

[71] *the Mirrour . . . her*] Harington originally had written: 'her sacred Majesty of England feeding her, the kynge of Spayn spurring her, the Prince of Orenges milking her'; as a result of the Pacification of Ghent in 1576, the Low Countries united in opposition to Spain under William of Orange; from 1577 the Queen had given aid to the Dutch rebels.

[72] *Monsieur . . . fingers*] In August of 1578 Francis of Valois, Duke of Alençon, had signed a treaty with the Estates General whereby he was proclaimed *Défenseur de la Liberté Belgique contre la tyrannie Espagnole* in return for military assistance; in Sept. 1580 he was made sovereign of the Low Countries; in 1583 the 'folly of Antwerp' occurred. Reacting to his endeavour to gain control of important cities, the burghers not only slew half the French forces but forced Alençon to flee across the French frontier; there he spent the rest of his life attempting to recover his position.

Although it was recognized that Alençon had been at fault, Elizabeth took the position that the Dutch had wronged him and continued to champion him (Conyers Read, *Mr. Secretary Walsingham*, N.Y., 1925, I, 403; II, 40–1; 107; 108; cf. Stow, *Annales*, 1615, 3M2ᵛ-3M3).

[73] plesawntest] *MS*; wittiest *A, B*   [74] wittyest] *MS*; pleasantest *A, B*

38. ep.[75] of his first book, hath a distichon, that is very plyable to my purpose; of one that was so stately, that her close stoole was of gold, but her drinking cup of glasse.

> *Ventris onus puro, nec te pudet excipis auro:*
> *Sed bibis in vitro, carius[76] ergo cacas.[j]*

And in the same book, to a[77] gentlewoman that had a pleasure, to have her dogge licke her lips, as many do now a dayes.

> *Os, & labra, tibi lingit Maneia catellus:[78]*
> *Non miror merdas, si libet esse cani.[k]*

> *Thy dog still licks thy lips, but tis no hurt:*
> *I marvell not, to see a dog eate durt.*

Further in his third booke, he mocks one of his fellow Poets, that drave away all good companie with his verses, everie man thought it such a penance to heare them.

> *Nam tantos rogo quis ferat labores,*
> *Et stanti legis, & legis sedenti,*
> *Currenti legis, & legis cacanti,*
> *In Thermas fugio sonas ad aurem &c.[l]*

> *Alas my head with thy long readings akes,*
> *Standing or sitting, thou readst every wheare,*
> *If I would walke, if I wold go t' A JAX,*
> *If to the Bath, thou still art in mine eare.*

Where by the way, you may note that the French courtesie I spake of before, came fyrst[81] from the Romanes; sith in Martials time, they shunned not one the others companie, at Monsieur A JAX. But now it may be some man will say, that these wanton and ribald phrases, were pleasing to those times of licentiousnes,

---

[j] I. 38.   [k] I.74.[79]   [l] 3.44.[80]

---

[75] *38. ep.*] In modern editions this is i.37 and varies slightly from Harington's text.

[76] charius *MS, A, B*   [77] to a] to the *B*

[78] Catellus *A, B*, Catellis *MS*   [79] i.83.

[80] iii.44.9–12.   [81] fyrst] *MS; om. A, B*

and paganisme that knew not Christ; but now they are abhorred
and detested, and quite out of request. I would to God with
all my heart, he lyed not that so said; and that indeed religion
could roote out as it should do, all such wanton and vaine
toyes (if they be all wanton and vaine) yet I am sure, that even
in this age, and in this realme, men of worth and wit, have used
the wordes and phrases, in as homely sort as Martial, some in
light, some in serious matter. Among Sir Thomas Mores
Epigrams, that flie over all Europe for their wit and conceit,[82]
the very last[83] (to make a sweet conclusion) is this.

> Sectile ne tetros porrum tibi spiret odores;
>   Protinus à porro fac mihi cepe vores;
> Denuo foetorem si vis depellere cepe:
>   Hoc facile efficient allia mansa tibi;
> Spiritus at si post etiam gravis, allia restat;
>   Aut nihil, aut tantum, tollere merda potest.

Which for their sakes that love garlicke, I have taken some
paines with, though it went against my stomacke once or twise.

> If leeks you leeke, but do their smell disleeke,
> Eat onions, and you shall not smell the leeke:
> If you of onions would the sent expell,
> Eat garlick, that shal drown the onions smell;
> But against garlikes savour, at one word,
> I know but one receipt. whats that? go looke.

Nay[84] fie, will you name it, and reade it to Ladies, thus you
make them blame me that meant no lesse. But to come againe to
pleasant Sir Thomas, he hath another Epigram, that though

---

[82] *Among . . . conceit*] The *Epigrammata* were printed twice by Froben in
1518 and again in 1520. After More's death, they appeared in the collected
Latin works, *Thomae Mori lucubrationes*, Basel, 1563 and in the *Opera*, Louvain,
1565–6, with some omissions (*The Latin Epigrams of Thomas More*, ed. L.
Bradner and C. A. Lynch, Chicago, 1953, xiii–xix).

[83] *the very last*] This is 238 of the Bradner-Lynch text. Harington is citing
either the 1520 or 1563 edition, indicated by his reading in l.3.
When Harington included this epigram in the presentation copy for Prince
Henry in 1605, he took cognizance of the royal point of view by changing the
last line to read:
'I know but one receipt, what's that? Tobacco.' Folger MS V.a. 249, p. 50.

[84] Nay] Now *B*

this was but a sowre one, I durst as live be his halfe at this as at that, and it is about a medicine for the collicke.

> *Te Crepitus perdit nimium si ventre retentes,*[85]
> *Te propere emissus servat item crepitus:*
> *Si crepitus servare potest, et perdere numquid,*
> *Terrificis crepitus, regibus aequa potest.*[86]

Thus il-favoredly in English, for I will tell you true, my Muse was afraid to translate this Epigram: and she brought me out three or foure sayings against it, both in Latine and English[m]: and two or three shrewd examples, both of this last poet,[n] who died not of the collicke, and of one Collingbourne, that was hanged for a distichon of a Cat, a rat, and a dogge.[89] Yet I opposed *Murus aheneus esto nil conscire sibi,*[90] and so with much a do, she came out with it.

> *To breake a litle wind, sometime ones life doth save,*
> *For want of vent behind, some folke their ruine have:*
> *A powre it hath therefore, of life, and death expresse:*
> *A king can cause no more, a cracke*[91] *doth do no lesse.*

And when she had made it in this sorie fashion, she bad me wish my friends, that no man should follow Sir Th. Mores

---

[m] *Non est bonum ludere cum sanctis.* It is good to play with your fellows. *An nescis longas regibus esse manus.*[87]

[n] He was beheaded.[88]

---

[85] retentes] *MS*; retentus *A, B*

[86] *Te ... potest*] This is 21 in the Bradner-Lynch text, identified as a translation from the *Anthologia Palatina* xi.395.

[87] A common variation of the proverbial *Non est bonum ludere cum diis* and Ovid *Heroides* xvii.166. *English note not in MS.*

[88] *English note not in MS.* More was executed in 1535.

[89] *Collingbourne ... dogge*]
> I am that Colingbourne
> Whych rymed that whych made full many mourne:
> The Cat, the Rat, and Lovel our Dog,
> Do rule al England, under a Hog.

('The Poet Collingbourne,' *The Mirror for Magistrates*, ed. L. B. Campbell, Cambridge, 1938, ll. 67–70.)

[90] *Murus ... sibi*] Horace *Epistle* i.1.60–1.

[91] *cracke*] 1) *ventris crepitus* and 2) a lad

humour, to write such Epigrams as he wrate, except he had the spirit, to speake two such apothegmes[o] as he spake, of which the last seemes to fal fit into our text. The first[94] was, when the King sent to him to know if he had chaunged his mind; he answered, yea: the King sent straight a counseller to him, to take his subscription to the sixe Articles.[95] Oh sayd he, I have not changed my mind in that matter, but onely in this; I thought to have sent for a Barber, to have bene shaven ere I had died, but now if it please the King, he shal cut off head, and beard, and all together. But the other[96] was milder, and pretier; for after this, one coming to him as of good will, to tell him he must prepare him to die, for he could not live: he called for his urinall, and having made water in it, he cast it, & viewed it (as Physicians do) a pretie while; at last he sware soberly, that he saw nothing in that mans water, but that he might live, if it pleased the King; a pretie saying, both to note his owne innocencie, and move the Prince to mercie: and it is like, if this tale had bin as frendly told the King, as the other[97] perhaps was unfrendly enforced against him, sure the King had pardoned him. But alas what cared he, or[98] (to say truth) what neede hee care, that cared not for death? But to step backe to my teshe[99] (though every place I step to, yeelds me sweeter

---

[o] Two[92] Apothegmes of[93] Sir Thomas More.

---

[92] Two] *not in MS* [93] of] *not in MS*

[94] *The first . . .*] Cf. Camden, *Remaines*, 1629, Q7.

[95] *to take . . . Articles*] Since the Act of the Six Articles was not enacted until 1539, this is a *lapsus memoriae* or perhaps a confusion on the part of Harington between the Six Articles and the oath of supremacy. See p. 102, n. 102.

[96] *But the other . . .*] Cf. Camden, *Remaines*, Q7^{v}.

[97] the other] tother *MS* [98] or] *om. B*

[99] *teshe*] *i.e.*, text. The *OED* states it is a word of uncertain origin and conjectures that, if it means 'task,' it may derive from OF *tasche*. Quite clearly 'teshe' is intended as a humorous approximation of 'text,' representing a substandard pronunciation which was perhaps an identifying characteristic of a certain contemporary preacher. Cf. the following epigram where Harington juxtaposes the two words:

Of a certayn man

There was not certaine when, a certaine Preacher,
that never learn't, and yet became a teacher
And having thus in latten read a text,
of *Erat quidam homo*, much perplext.

discourse) what thinke you by Haywood,[100] that scaped hanging with his mirth, the King[101] being graciously and (as I thinke) truely perswaded, that a man that wrate so pleasant and harmlesse verses, could not have any harmfull conceit against his procedings, & so by the honest motion of a Gentleman of his chamber, saved him from the jerke of the six stringd whip.[102] This Haywood for his Proverbs & Epigrams, is not

> Hee seemd the words with dilligence to skan,
> In english thus. There was a certaine man.
> But now (quoth he) good people note you this,
> He saith there was, he doth not say there is,
> For in this age of ours it is most certayn,
> Of promise, oath, worde deed no man is certayn
> Yet by my teshe (quoth he) this comes to pass,
> That surely once a certaine man there was,
> But yet I thinke in all the Byble no man
> Can find this text. *There was a certaine woman.*

(Folger MS V.a. 249, pp. 252–3; printed as *text* throughout in the published editions, including *L&E*, p. 262.)

Conclusive evidence is to be found in the MS, fol. 22, l. 6, where Harington originally wrote 'text,' scored it, and substituted 'tesh.' Other instances of its use in the *Metamorphosis* are to be found on pp. 111, 118, 131, 172, and 235.

The author of the *Ulysses*, in accordance with his habit of citing Harington's humorous spellings (*e.g.*, 'bashfoole,' 'monapole'), also writes: 'But returne we to *Misacmos* teshe' (D5ᵛ); the only other example recorded in the *OED*, that found in the second edition of Richard Braithwait's *Essayes upon The Five Senses*, 1635, seems to be a misprint for 'test': 'the more the age wherein they liv'd, dispenc'd with their crimes, the more numerous and odious they were; when they came to the Tesh' (O11).

[100] *Haywood . . .*] John Heywood was indicted for treason 15 Feb. 1544 for attempting to deprive the king of 'his dignity, title and name of "Supreme Head of the English and Irish Church",' for attempting to depose and deprive the king of 'his Majesty, state, power and royal dignity,' and for attempting 'to subvert, frustrate, and annihilate the good and praiseworthy statutes and ordinances of our aforesaid lord the King' (James Gairdner, *Lollardy and the Reformation in England*, London, 1908, II, 411–2). Heywood was granted a general pardon on June 26 and July 6 made a public recantation at Paul's Cross (*L&P, Henry VIII*, XIX, Pt. 1, 504; 531–2).

[101] *the King*] Puttenham remarks somewhat churlishly on the favour shown by Henry VIII to Heywood, 'who for the myrth and quicknesse of his conceits more then for any good learning was in him came to be well benefited by the king' (*The Arte of English Poesie*, ed. G. D. Willcock and A. Walker, Cambridge, 1936, p. 60).

[102] *six stringd whip*] This was the Act of the Six Articles (originally enacted in 1539; modified in 1544), '*for abholyshyinge of diversitie of opinions, in certayne artycles concernynge Christen religion*' whereof 'it was named the whyp wyth syxe strynges, and of some other and that of the moste part, it was named the bloudy statute, for of truthe it so in shorte tyme after skourged a great nomber in the citie of London' (Edward Hall, *Henry VIII*, ed. C. Whibley, London,

yet put downe by any of our countrey, though one doth in
deede come neare him, that graces him the more in saying he
puts him downe.[103] But both of them have made sport with as
homely words as ours be; one of a Gentlewomans[104] glove,[*p*] save
that without his consent it is no good manners to publish it:
but old Haywoods sayth:

> Except wind stand, as never wind stood,
> It is an ill wind blowes no man good.[106]

And another not unpleasant, one that I cannot omit.

> By word without writing one let out a farm,
> The lessee most leudly the rent did retaine,
> Whereby the lessor wanting writing had harme:
> Wherfore he vowd, while life did remaine,
> Without writing never to let thing againe.
> Husband quoth the wife, that oath againe revart,
> Else without writing you cannot let a crack.
> God thanke thee sweet wife,[107] quoth he, from my hart:
> And so on the lips did her lovingly smacke.[108]

[*p*] M. Davies.[105]

1904, II, 285, and *Tract on the Succession*, p. 98). Cf. Robert B. Bolwell, *The Life
and Works of John Heywood* (N.Y., 1921), p. 40, followed by R. de la Bère,
John Heywood Entertainer (London, 1937), p. 33, where it is pointed out that
Harington has apparently confused the Act of the Six Articles with the Act of
Supremacy.

[103] *This Haywood . . . downe*] John Davies's Epigram 29, '*In Haywodum*':
> Haywood that did in Epigrams excell,
> Is now put downe since my light Muse arose:
> As Buckets are put downe into a Well,
> Or as a schoole boy putteth downe his hose.

(Reprinted in *The Works of Christopher Marlowe*, ed. T. Brooke, Oxford, 1946,
p. 635. Cf. Harington's epigram '*To Mr: John Davys*' (*L&E*, p. 306). See also
Milligan, pp. 6–7 for Thomas Bastard's epigrams on Davies's 'putting down' of
Heywood.)

[104] *a Gentlewomans*] his mistres *MS*

[105] John Davies's Epigram 14, '*In Leucam*' (*The Works of Christopher
Marlowe*, p. 631). This clearly establishes 1596 as a date anterior to the publication of Davies's epigrams, contrary to the theory set forth by J. M. Nosworthy
('The Publication of Marlowe's *Elegies* and Davies' *Epigrams*,' *RES*, n.s. IV,
1953, p. 261).

[106] *Except . . . good*] Harington's more decorous rendition of Epigram 72 of
The firste hundred of Epigrammes.

[107] *wife*] malkin *MS*

[108] *By word . . . smacke*] Epigram 32 of *The firste hundred of Epigrammes*.
Harington, whose memory is no better than he would have it, has expanded the
original seven lines to nine in order to temper Heywood's more forthright language.

Such a thing it was, but not having the booke here, and my memory being no better then I would have it, I have stumbled on it as well as I can. But now to strike this matter dead with a sound authoritie indeed, and in so serious a matter as under heaven is no weightier,[109] to such a person, as in the world is no worthier,[110] from such a scholer, as in Oxford was no learneder,[111] marke what a verse here is, an[112] Eucharisticall and Pareneticall verse.[113] He saith:

> *Italici Augiae*[114] *stabulum foedamque cloacam,*
> *A te purgari Romanaque* σκύβαλα[115] *tolli.*[116]

If he had said[117] *stercora,*[118] I could have guessed[119] wel enough what it had meant,[a] but that the Greeke hath in some

---

[a] M. Raynolds much more seemly useth the metaphor, li. 1. c. 8. p. 290. *Iesuitae fimum in ipsius caput retorquere.*[120]

---

[109] *and in . . . weightier]* i.e., religion.

[110] *to such . . . worthier]* i.e., the Queen.

[111] *from such . . . learneder]* Dr. Laurence Humphrey (c. 1527–1589/90), a vigorous Protestant, became President of Magdalen College, Oxford, Dean of Gloucester, Vice-Chancellor of the University, and ultimately Dean of Winchester; he was unable, says Camden, to attain any higher preferment 'haply for that he did not consent with the Church of *England* concerning things indifferent' (*Elizabeth*, 2K2).

[112] is, an] *B*; ?is in a. an *MS*; is in an *A*

[113] verse] *om. with lacuna MS. Pareneticall*—hortatory. This is earlier than the example cited in the *OED*. Harington derives it from the title of Latin verses Humphrey presented to the Queen at Woodstock on 11 Sept. 1575: 'Carmen eiusdem Laur. Humfredi eucharisticum & paraeneticum de initio regni R. Elisabethae, et de auspicatiss. anno decimo octavo Novemb. die 17, &c.'

[114] Augaei *A*   [115] σκυβαλα *A*

[116] *Italici . . . tolli]* ll. 31–2 of *Carmen eiusdem . . . (Oratio ad Sereniss. Angliae, Franciae, & Hyberniae Reginam ELIZABETHAM . . . .* It is reprinted in Nichols, *Progresses*, 1, 583–99). 'Doctor / Humfry / to her / Matie': Harington annotation in the Sheffield copy.

[117] had said] said *MS*   [118] stercora] *lacuna in MS*

[119] have guessed] *MS*; guess *A, B*

[120] *Note not in MS.* John Rainolds (1549–1607), a fellow of Corpus Christi, Oxford, had been appointed in 1586 to a temporary lectureship established by Walsingham to confute Roman tenets, particularly those of Father Robert Bellarmine. 'No sooner,' says his biographer, were the dictates of Bellarmine 'taken in writing by his auditors, but, by some of Secretary Walsingham's intelligencers residing at Rome, they were sent by post in packets to the court, and from thence speeded to Dr. Reinolds, who, acquainting his auditory with

eares a better emphasis. Thus writes their great Campiano
μάστιξ that confounds all the *Puritano Papistas*.[121] And[122] yet
to say truly, I make no great boast of his authoritie to my text.
If I had alledged him in Divinitie, I wold have stood lustily to
it, and sayd αὐτὸς ἔφα[123] but for verses in praise of his Mistresse,
there be twentie of us may set him to schoole: for be it spoken
without disgrace[124] or dispraise to his poetrie, such a metaphor
had bene fitter for a plaine Dame, abhorring all princely pompe,
and not refusing to weare russet coates, then for the magnificent majestie of a Mayden Monark. Beleeve me, I would faine
have made him speake good rime in English, but (as I am a
true μισακμος) I beate my braines about it, the space that one
may go with the tyde from London bridge, downe where the
Priest fell in upon the mayd, and from thence almost to
Wapping, and yet I could not couch it into a cleanly distichon.
But yet because I know Mistresse *Philostilpnos* will have a great
mind to know what it meanes, I will tell her by some handsome
circumlocution. His meaning is, that a Ladie of Ladies, did for
zele to the Lord of Lords, take the like pains to purge some
Popish abuses, as the great giantly Hercules did for Augeus.
Now what maner of worke that was, in the processe of this

---

the very days in every month and week, in which Father Robert handled such
a point, addressed himself immediately to make a punctual answer thereunto;
insomuch that . . . [it] may be truly affirmed of Cardinal Bellarmine's books of
controversies, that they were *prius damnati quàm nati*' (Thomas Fuller, *Abel
Redevivus*, London, 1867, II, 225 ff.). Cf. the *Apologie*, p. 207.

In 1593 Rainolds became Dean of Lincoln, and in 1598 he was elected
President of Corpus Christi. Harington's brother Francis had been tutored by
Rainolds at Oxford ('A Supplie or Addicion,' *NA*, II, 208, and *Tract on the
Succession*, p. 113).

The Latin is telescoped from Bk. I, Ch. 8 (T1ᵛ), of *De Romanae Ecclesiae
Idololatria* which was published in 1596 with a dedication to Essex.

[121] *their great . . . Papistas*] In 1582 and again in 1584 Humphrey published
attacks on Catholic practice and doctrine, directed mainly against Edmund
Campian who, said Humphrey, although dead still bites (*Jesuitismi Pars Prima:
sive de Praxi Romanae Curiae*, 1582, A4ᵛ). In 1584 his *Jesuitismi Pars Secunda:
Puritanopapismi* . . . appeared. *Puritanopapismi* was apparently Humphrey's
coinage (*Tract on the Succession*, p. 4).

[122] Aud *A*

[123] αυτος εφα; 'The master said,' used by the disciples of Pythagoras
(Diogenes Laertius, 'Pythagoras' viii.46).

[124] disgrace] disparage *MS*

discourse one way or other, you shall see me bring it in,[125] though yet I know not where wil be the fittest place for it: here yet you see by the way I have told the mans meaning reasonable mannerly, yet still me thinke I can say of his metaphor,

> *That still (me thinke) he usde a phrase as plyant,*
> *That said, his Mistres was for wit a giant.*[126]

But I pray you let me go backe againe to merie Martiall: for I should have one more of his, if I have not lost it. *Ad Phoebum.* Oh here I have it.

> *Utere lactucis & mollibus utere malvis,*
> *Nam faciem durum, Phoebe, cacantis, habes.*[r]

He advises him to take somwhat to make him soluble, for his face looked as if he were asking, who should be M. Mayor next[128] yeare. But I thinke this jest was borrowed of

---

[r] 3. 68.[127]

---

[125] *you shall . . . in*] Harington has annotated the Lumley-Folger copy 'pag: 45/linea.9' in reference to his comments on the cleaning of the stables of Augeus (p. 119 of this edition).

[126] *That . . . giant*] Although I have been unable to identify this allusion, it would seem from other contemporary references that the metaphor was a recognized source of literary ridicule. Cf. the following couplet to Sir John Davies's Epigram 25, the first four lines of which deride a sonnet by Drayton (*Ideas Mirror*, 1594, No. 8):

> Me thinks that gull did use his tearmes as fit
> Which tearm'd his love a giant for her wit.

(ed. Brooke, p. 634.)

In his conversations with Jonson, Drummond records: 'That S. J. Davies played in ane Epigrame on Drayton, who in a Sonnet concluded his Mistriss might been the ninth [tenth] worthy & said he used a phrase like Dametas in Arcadia, who said for wit his mistresse might be a Gyant' (*Ben Jonson*, ed. Herford and Simpson, Oxford, 1925, I, 137). The editors state that the reference is 'untraced, and probably an error,' adding that Drummond perhaps confused Dametas with the gull mentioned in Davies's epigram (p. 162). However, it seems likely that Harington, Davies, and Jonson were alluding to a common source.

[127] iii.89.

[128] next] *MS*; the next *A, B*

Vespasyans[129] foole,[130] or else the foole borrowed it of him:
but the jest is worthy to be received into this discourse. This
foole had jested somewhat at all the boord, save Vespasian
him selfe; and belike he thought, it was ill playing with
edge tooles,[131] and Emperours; but Vespasian commaunded
him, & promised him franke pardon, to breake a good jest
upon him. Well Sir (then said the foole) I will but tarie till
you have done your busines; whereby he quipped the
Emperours ill feature of face, that even when he was meriest,
looked as if he had bin wringing hard on a close stoole. But
let us seeke some better authorities then Epigrams and Jesters:
sure I am I shall find in historie, which is called *nuncia vetustatis*,
vita memoriae,[132] the reporter of antiquities, the life of memory,
many phrases, expressing the same action, and not thinking
their style any whit abased thereby. He that writes the first
booke of Samuel[s] tels, that David did cut off the lap of Saules
coate, and leaves not to tell, what Saule was then doing. The
writer of Bassianus life telles, how he was not onely privily
murdred, but murdred at the privie.[134] Heliogabulus body was
throwne into a Jakes,[135] as writeth Suetonius.[t] Lastly the best,

---

[s] I. Sam. 24. *Spelunca quam ingressus est Saul, ut purgaret ventrem.*[133]

[t] Suetonius.[136]

---

[129] Vespasyans] *MS*; Vespasianus *A, B*

[130] *But I . . . foole*] Suetonius 'Vespasian' 20. Cf. 'Mery Tales, Wittie
Questions and Quicke Answeres,' No. 111, *Shakespeare Jest-Books*, ed. W. C.
Hazlitt, London, 1864, I, 126, which begins 'SUETONIUS sheweth that
Titus the father,' obviously an error for 'Titus his father.' The jest is followed
by Martial's epigram.

[131] *ill . . . tooles*] Tilley J45.

[132] *nuncia . . . memoriae*] Cicero *de Orat.* ii.9.36.   [133] I Sam. 24:3.

[134] *The writer . . . privie*] Traditionally, the writer of the 'Vita' of Antoninus
Caracallus (or Bassianus, the elder son of Septimius Severus) was Aelius
Spartianus, one of the six reputed authors of the *Scriptores Historiae Augustae*,
first published by Phillipus de Lavagna in 1475 (Sir John Sandys, *A Short
History of Classical Scholarship*, Cambridge, 1915, p. 198, and Introduction
to the Loeb edition).
The passage to which Harington refers appears twice: 6.7 and 7.1–2.

[135] *Heliogabulus . . . Jakes*] The 'Vita' of Antoninus Elagabalus, 17.1–9 in
the *Scriptores Historiae Augustae*.

[136] *Note not in MS*; *as writeth Suetonius*] According to tradition, the author
was Aelius Lampridius writing at the request of the Emperor Constantine (Intro.
Scriptores Historiae Augustae, pp. xii–xv). During the sixteenth century,
however, this late collection of imperial biographies was frequently appended

and best written part of all our Chronicles, in all mens opinions; is that of Richard the third, written as I have heard by Moorton, but as most suppose by that worthy, and uncorrupt Magistrate, Sir Thomas More,[137] sometime Lord Chancelor of England, where it is written; how the King was devising with Terill, how to have his nephewes privily murdred, & it is added, he was then sitting on a draught[138] (a fit carpet for such a counsel.)[139] But to leave these tragicall matters, and come to comicall; looke into your sports of hauking & hunting, of which noble recreations, the noble Sir Philip Sidney was wont to say; that next hunting, he liked hauking worst[140]; but the faulconers and hunters would be even with him, and say, that these bookish fellowes, such as he, could judge of no sports, but within the verge,[141] of the faire fields of *Helicon*, *Pindus*, and *Pernasus*. Now I would aske you Sir, lest you should thinke

---

to those of Suetonius, and the whole given some such title as *Historiae Vitae Caesarum*. (For editions, see J. G. T. Graesse, *Trésor de livres rares et précieux*, Dresden, 1862, III, 302-3.) The title *Historia Augusta* was first applied by Casaubon in 1603.

[137] *written . . . More*] R. W. Chambers says of this passage: 'John Harrington [*sic*] had heard many things. It is curious that his "I have heard," written nearly a century after the death of Morton, should be taken as outweighing the evidence of Rastell, one of More's closest intimates, to say nothing of Grafton and Ascham and Bale and Harpsfield. Yet even if we were to dismiss all these, and judge the matter on Harrington's evidence only, there could be no doubt. For Harrington admits [states] that "most" suppose More to be the author, and we have only to turn to the internal evidence to find the attribution to Morton quite impossible and that to More confirmed' (*The English Works of Sir Thomas More*, ed. W. E. Campbell, London, 1931, I, 34).

[138] *he . . . draught*] 'The History of King Richard the Third' (*ibid.*, I, 450).

[139] counsel. *A*; *MS lacking from* But *to p. 110* Thus you

[140] *the noble . . . worst*] Cf. Spenser on Sidney's apparently well-known distaste for the sport:

> Besides, in hunting such felicitie,
> Or rather infelicitie he found:
> That every field and forest far away,
> He sought, where salvage beasts do most abound.
> (*Astrophel*, ll. 79–82.)

(Cited in D. H. Madden, *The Diary of Master William Silence*, N.Y., 1907, p. 211, n. 2.)

[141] *verge*] An area extending to a distance of twelve miles round the king's court, subject to the jurisdiction of the Lord High Steward.

I never read Sir Tristram.[142] Do you not sometime (beside the fine phrase, or rather Metaphor, of inewing a woodcocke)[143] talke, both of putting a heron to the mount,[144] and then of his slicing?[145] tell of springing a pheasant and a partridge, & find them out by their dropping? Do you not further, to judge of your haulks health, looke on her casting?[146] if it be black at one end, and the rest yellow, you feare she hath the phillanders[147]; if it be all blacke, you shall see and smell, she is not sound. Lastly, you have a speciall regard to observe, if she make a cleane mute.[148] Moreover for hunting, when you have harbourd a stagge, or lodged a bucke, doth not the keeper, before he comes to rouse him from his lodging, (not without some ceremonie) shew you his femishing,[149] that thereby you

---

[142] *Sir Tristram*] The terms of venery are frequently spoken of as derived from Sir Tristram's precepts: 'It hath bin long received for a truth, that Sir *Tristram*, one of King Arthures Knights, was the first writer and (as it were) the founder of the exact knowledge of the honorable and delightfull sport of hunting; whose tearmes in Hunting, Hawking, and measures of blowing, I hold to be the best and fittest to be used. And these first principles of Sir *Tristram* yet extant, joyned with my owne long experience in Hunting for these fiftie two yeares now last past, have mooved me to write more at large, of hunting the Bucke and other Chases, than Sir *Tristram* did' (Sir Thomas Cockaine, *A Short Treatise of Hunting*, 1591, London, Shakespeare Association Facsimiles, No. 5, 1932, A3; cf. George Turbervile, *The Noble Arte of Venerie or Hunting*, 1576, reprinted as *Turbervile's Booke of Hunting*, London, Tudor & Stuart Library, 1908, p. 153).
'The first principles' appear to be 'extant' only in terms of having passed into the common vocabulary of hunting and hawking.

[143] *inewing a woodcocke*] Or enewing, driving a fowl into water.

[144] *putting . . . mount*] To cause it to rise from the ground.

[145] *slicing*] 'Muting' or dung.

[146] *Do you . . . casting*] 'For by the casting [vomit] is founde, whither the hawke do neede eyther upwarde, or downward scowrings, or stones, or any suche like remedie' (Turberville, *The Booke of Faulconrie or Hauking*, 1575, E6ᵛ).

[147] *phillanders*] Intestinal worms (*ibid.*, Q6ᵛ).

[148] *Lastly . . . mute*] 'The mischiefes and diseases that grow within the bodies of Hawkes, may best be discerned & knowen by their excrement' (*ibid.*, O3ᵛ; cf. H2ᵛ).

[149] *femishing*] 'Of an Harte therefore, and of all Deare the ordure is called *Fewmets* or *Fewmishing*' (Turbervile, *Booke of Hunting*, p. 239). Turbervile devotes a chapter to the 'judgement and knowledge' that may be derived from examining the fewmishing of a deer (ch. 23), and describes how huntsmen should present their fewmishings unto the Prince or master of the game in the field: 'And when the Prince or other chiefe hath hard them and seene their fewmishings, he or she may then chose which of the Hartes he will hunt, and which he or she thinkes most likely to make him or hir best sport' (p. 94).

may judge, if he be a seasonable[150] deare? And soone after, followes the melodious crie of the houndes,[151] which the good Ladie could not heare, because the dogs kept such a barking. And when al this is done, and you are rehearsing at dinner what great sport you have had: in the middest of your sweet meates, in comes Melampus,[152] or Ringwood,[153] that sang the base that morning, and in the returne home, lighted upon some powderd[154] vermin,[155] and layes a chase under the table, that makes all as sweet as any suger-carrion; and all this you willingly beare with, because it is your pastime. Thus you must needes confesse, it is more then manifest, that without reproofe of ribaldrie, or scurrilitie, writings both holy, and prophane, Emblemes, Epigrams, Histories, and ordinarie and familiar communication; admits the use of the words, with all their apurtenances; in citing examples whereof, I have bene the more copious, because of this captious time, so readie to back-bite every mans worke, and I would forewarne men not to bite here, lest they bite an unsavorie morsell. But here me think

---

[150] *seasonable*] Proper to be hunted and killed. Cf.

> He is no woodman that doth bend his bow
> To strike a poor unseasonable doe.
>
> (*Rape of Lucrece*, 580-1.)

[151] *And soone . . . houndes*] Harington's kinsman Gervase Markham was among those Elizabethans who responded to the music of the hounds: 'If you would have your Kennell for sweetnesse of cry, then you must compound it of some large dogges, that have deepe solemne mouthes, and are swift in spending, which must as it were beare the base in the consort, then a double number of roaring, and loud ringing mouthes, which must beare the counter tenor, then some hollow plaine sweete mouthes, which must beare the meane or middle part: and soe with these three parts of musicke you shall make your cry perfect . . . amongst these you cast in a couple or two of small singing Beagles, which as small trebles may warble amongst them: the cry will be a great deale the more sweeter' (*Country Contentments*, 1631, B4ᵛ; cited in Cockaine's *Short Treatise*, p. xvii).

[152] *Melampus*] A common name for a dog, meaning 'Blackefoote' (Abraham Fraunce, *The Third part of the Countesse of Pembrokes Yvychurch;* cited in T. W. Baldwin, *William Shakspere's Small Latine & Lesse Greeke*, Urbana, 1944, II, 431). It was also the name of a celebrated Greek seer who understood the language of birds.

[153] *Ringwood*] Also a common name for a dog. Cf. *MWW* II.i.122: 'Like Sir Actaeon he, with Ringwood at thy heels.' (Also discussed in Baldwin, II, 431-2).

[154] *powderd*] i.e., seasoned.

[155] *vermin*] In addition to 'Hares and Coneys,' according to Turbervile, other vermin or 'stinking chases' included 'Foxes, Badgers and such like' (*Booke of Hunting*, pp. 97-8).

it were good to make a pause, & (as it were at a long diner)
to take away the first course; which commonly is of the coursest
meate, as powdred biefe and mustard, or rather (tó compare it
fitter) fresh biefe and garlicke; for that hath three properties,
more suting to this discourse: viz. to make a man winke, drinke,
and stinke.[156] Now for your second course, I could wish I had
some larks, & quailes, but you must have such as the market I
come from will affoord, alwayes remembred, that our retiring
place, or place of *rende vous* (as is expedient when men have
filled their bellies) must be Monsieur A Jax, for I must still
keepe me to my tesh: wherfore as I say, here I will make the
first stop, and if you mislike not the fare thus far, I will make
the second course, make you some amends.

THE SECOND SECTION,

proving the matter not to be *contemptible*.[1]

It hath bene in the former part hereof sufficiently proved,
that there is no obscenitie, or barbarisme in words concerning
our necessaries: but now for the place, where these necessaries are to be done, perhaps some will object, that it was never
of that importaunce, but that it was left to each mans owne care
to provide, for that which concerned his owne peculiar necessitie. It is not so, for I can bring very autenticall proofes out of
auncient recordes, and histories; that the greatest magistrates
that ever were, have employed their wits, their care, and their
cost, about these places; as also have made diverse good lawes,
proclamations, and decrees about the same: & all thereto
belonging; as by this that ensues shall more plainely appeare.
In the handling wherof, I will use a contrary method to the
former: for I wil begin now with prophane stories, and end
with divine. First therefore most certaine it is, that mischiefes

---

[156] *fresh biefe . . . stinke*] 'A homly / Proverb of / garlike. / horace saith
O Dura messo- / rum ilia' [*Epodes* 3.4]: Harington annotation in the Sheffield
copy. Cf. his directive in *The School of Salernum*:

> And scorne not *Garlicke*, like to some that thinke
> It onely makes men winke, and drinke, and stinke.
> (P. 86.)

and Tilley G40.

[1] *Heading not in MS*

make us seeke remedies, diseases make us find medicines, and evil maners make good lawes. And as in all other things, so by all likelihood in this we now treate of, when companies of men began first to increase, and make of families townes, and of townes cities; they quickly found not onely offence, but infection, to grow out of great concourse of people, if speciall care were not had to avoyd it. And because they could not remove houses, as they do tents, from place to place, they were driven to find the best meanes that their wits did then serve them, to cover, rather then to avoyd these annoyances: either by digging pits in the earth, or placing the common houses over rivers; but as Tully[2] saith of Metaphors, that they were like our apparell[a]; first devised to hide nakednesse, then applied for comelinesse, and lastly abused for pride: so I may say of these homely places, that first they were provided for bare necessitie, for indeed till Romulus time I find little mention of them; then they came to be matters of some more cost, as shall appeare in examples following; & I thinke I might also lay pride to their charge: for I have seene them in cases of fugerd sattin,[4] and velvet[5] (which is flat against the statute of apparell[b]) but for

---

[a] Simile.[3]

[b] *33. Henry 8.*[6] For it is no reason M. AJAX[7] should have a better gowne then his Mistresse.

---

[2] *as Tully . . .] de Orat.* iii.38.155

[3] *om. A, B*

[4] *fugerd sattin*] From AF 'satayn fugaree.' Halliwell defines it as 'figured or branched satin' (*Dictionary of Archaic and Provincial Words*, London, 1881). Harington uses it again in an epigram to his wife:

'a fugerd Sattin petticote Carnation'
Folger MS V.a. 249, p. 165.

This spelling was modernized in the 1615 edition of the *Epigrams* (E2ᵛ) and in *L&E* (p. 279).

[5] *for I . . . velvet*] Cf.

ffyve close stooles of black velvet quilted, with panns.
ffower of Flaunders worke, two of blacke velvet plaine.
A close stoole of black velvet, laced and fringed with black silck.
A low stoole of blacke vellet, quilted with black silck, with a panne.
ffyve close stooles of black velvet.
Eight close stooles with locks to them.
A close stoole of black velvet, garnished with lace and fringe of silver, gould, and black silck.
ffower close stooles, in fashion of chaiers of green clothe.
A close stoole of black vellet, garnished with black silck and silver.
Six other close stooles, two dozen of pewter chamber potts.

sweetnesse or cleanlinesse, I never knew yet any of them guiltie of it; but that if they had but wayted on[8] a Ladie in her chamber a day, or a night, they wold have made a man (at his next entrance into the chamber) have sayd, so, good speed ye. Now, as scholers do daily seeke out new phrases, and metaphors; & Tailors do oft invent new vardingales, and breeches: so I see no reason, but Magistrates may as well now as heretofore, devise new orders for cleanlinesse, & wholesomnesse. But now to the stories, I alledged before, as it were at the second hand, out of Lactantius;[9] how *Titus Tatius*[10] that was king with *Romulus*, erected the Statue of the Goddesse *Cloacina*, in a great Privie, made for that purpose. I find after this in the storie of Livy, how Tarquinius Pryscus, a man of excellent good spirit, but husband to a wife of a more excellent spirit[11]; a man that wan a kingdom with making a learned oration,[12]

(From the inventory of household stuff at Kenilworth, prepared after the death of Leicester, printed in George Adlard, *Amye Robsart and the Earl of Leycester*, London, 1870, p. 243.)

[6] Contrary to the usual sixteenth-century method of reference to the enacting of a statute, Harington here identifies it by reference to the calendar year [15]33 rather than to the regnal year: 24 Henry 8, c. 13. This act for the 'Reformacyon of Excesse in Apparayle,' for example, forbade anyone but the king and the royal family to wear purple silk or cloth of gold tissue (with certain exceptions), for anyone below the degree of Baron to wear 'any Velvett of the Colours of Crymesyn Scarlet or Blewe,' and for anyone unless he could expend 100 pounds a year to wear 'any satene damaske silke chamlett or taffata in his gowne cote' (*Statutes of the Realm*, ed. Alexander Luders *et al.*, London, 1810, III, 430–2).

[7] M AJAX *A*   [8] on] of *MS*

[9] *But . . . Lactantius*] See p. 90 and n. 44.   [10] Tacius *A*

[11] *how Tarquinius . . . spirit*] Livy i.34.1–5. 'So hee grew much more prowd for his matching in marriage with *Tanaquil*, a dame of a right noble house descended, and who could hardly beare a lower estate and degree than that wherein she was borne. When shee was once married, and saw the Tuscanes to disdain *Lucumo* [Tarquinius], for that his father was a stranger and banished person, she could not indure that indignitie. But forgetting all kind affection to her native countrey, so shee might see her husband raised to high promotion, shee resolved and plotted to leave Tarquinii and depart. To which purpose and dessignement, Rome seemed a place most fit and convenient of all others' (tr. Philemon Holland, 1600, D1).

[12] *a man . . . oration*] Livy i.35.2–6. 'Hee himselfe (as men say) was the first, that both ambitiously sought for the crowne, and also to win the hearts of the commons, divised and framed an eloquent Oration.' As a result, 'the people of Rome with exceeding great consent elected him their king' (Holland, D1ᵛ).

and lost it with hearing a rude one[13]; a king, that was first crowned by an Eagle,[14] counselled by an Augure,[15] and killed by a traitor; whose raigne and his ruine, were both most strangely foretold. This worthie Prince is reported by that excellent historian, to have made two provisions for his citie, one for warre, the other for peace, both verie commendable: for warre a stone wall about the towne, to defend them from outward invasions; and for peace, a goodly Jakes within the towne, with a vault to convey all the filth into Tyber, to preserve them from inward infection.[16]

Not long after him raigned Tarquinius, surnamed the Proud,[17] a tyrant I confesse, and an usurper,[18] and husband

---

[13] *and lost it . . . one*] Livy i.40.5–7. The murder of Tarquinius was plotted by the two sons of Ancus, Tarquinius's predecessor: 'There were for the purpose to do this feat, two passing stout and sturdie heardmen chosen, who having such rusticall yron tooles about them, as they were woont both of them to occupie, and made a great shew of a most tumultuous brawle and fray in the very porch of the court gate; by which means, they drew all the kings officers, sergeants, & guard about them: then as they called with a lowd voice, both the one and the other upon the king, in such wise, as the noise was heard within the pallace, they were convented before his highnes. . . . Then one of them for the nones, as it was before agreed, began his tale: and while the king, as wholly bent to give eare turned aside towards him, the other lift his axe aloft, and strooke the king on the head, and leaving it sticking there still in the wound, they whipt out both of them together, and ran their waies' (Holland, D3).

[14] *a king . . . Eagle*] Livy i.34.8. 'As *Tarquinius* sat with his wife in the chariot [at the outskirts of Rome], behold an Eagle came gently flying downe from aloft, & tooke up his bonnet from his head, and soaring over the chariot with a great noise, and clapping of her wings, as if shee had been sent from heaven to doe this feat, set it gainely and handsomely on his head againe: which done, shee mounted on high, and flew away' (Holland, D1).

[15] *counselled by an Augure*] Livy i.36.3–6.

[16] *One . . . infection*] Livy. i.36.1 and 38.5–6.

[17] *Tarquinius . . . Proud*] Livy i.49.1. Servius, the son-in-law of Tarquinius Priscus, succeeded him as king, thus dispossessing Lucius Tarquinius (later called Superbus), the son or grandson of Tarquinius Priscus.

[18] *a tyrant . . . usurper*] Livy i.47.7–8 and 48.1–4. Endeavouring to gain the kingdom, Tarquinius with a strong guard forcibly entered the Forum and sitting in Servius's chair delivered a bitter invective against him. Servius, entering in the midst of it, challenged Tarquin's right: 'Then *Tarquinius* being put to his shifts, and forced to trie the utmost, seeing no other remedie, tooke *Servius* by the middle, as being himselfe much younger and stronger farre, carried him out of the counsell house, and threw him downe from the staires head to the foot, and so returned again into the Senate house, to get the Senators together' (Holland, D5ᵛ).

to a dragon rather then a woman[19]: but himself surely, a man
valiant in warre, provident in peace,[20] and in that young
world, a notable politician: of whom Livy takes this speciall
note, that coming to the crowne without law, and fearing
others might follow his example, to do that to him, he had done
to another: he was the first, that appointed a guard for his
person, the first that drew publike matters to private hearings,
the first that made private warres, private peace, private con-
federacies; the first that lessened the number of the Senators;
the first, that when any of them dyed, kept their roomes voyd,
with manie excellent Machiavillen lessons[21]; which, who so
would be better instructed of, let him read but his accusing of
Turnus,[22] his stratageme against the Gabians,[23] &c. But the
matter I would praise him for, is none of all these, but only,
because he built a stately temple, and a costly Jakes; the words
be, *Cloacámque maximam receptaculum omnium purgamentorum
urbis*, a mightie great vault to receive all the filth of the citie.[24]
Of which two works, joyning them both together, Livy saith
thus, *Quibus duobus operibus, vix nova haec magnificentia
quicquam adequavit*. Which two great workes, the new magnificence of this our age, can hardly match. Now though Brutus,[25]

---

[19] *husband . . . woman*] Livy i.46.3, 5–9 and 47.1–6; also 48.5–8. This
was Tullia, daughter to Servius and formerly married to Tarquin's brother.
After Servius had been slain by Tarquin's agents, Tullia 'came riding in her
coach into the common place of assemblie, & nothing dismaied or abashed at
the presence of so many men, there met together, called forth hir husband out
of the Senat house, & was the first that stiled him with the title of king. By
whom shee being willed to depart away out of that throng and uprore, as she
returned homeward . . . the coachman . . . suddainely staied for feare, and
reined in his horses, and shewed unto his ladie and mistresse, *Servius* lying there
murdered. And hereof followed (as the report goeth) a beastly part, and beyond
all sence of humanitie . . . the raging and frantike woman *Tullia*, harried with
the furies and haunted with the ghosts of her sister and husband, caused (men
say) her chariot to be driven over her fathers dead corps; and being her selfe
bespreint and beraied with the bloudie chariot, caried home with her some part
of it in token and witnesse, that her hand was in this parricide and murder of
her owne father' (Holland, D5ᵛ).

[20] *a man . . . peace*] Livy i.53.   [21] *of whom . . . lessons*] Ibid., i.49.
[22] *let him . . . Turnus*] Ibid., i.50–1.

[23] *his stratageme . . . Gabians*] Ibid., i.53.4–11; 54.

[24] *because . . . citie*] Ibid., i.55.1–9 and 56.2.

[25] *Brutus*] Lucius Junius Brutus, son of the king's sister Tarquinia, contrived
to escape the tyranny of the king (Livy i.56.7–8): 'And therfor composing and
framing himselfe of purpose to counterfeit a noddie and a verie innocent, as

after in a popular and sedicious oration, to incite the multitude to rebellion, debased this worthie worke of his, saying he wasted the treasure of the realme, and tyred and toyled out the people, *in exhauriendis cloacis,* in emptying of Jaxes[26] (for that was his word) yet it appeares by the historie, that if his sonne[27] had not defloured the chast *Lucrece* (the mirror of her sex[28]) Brutus with his fayned folly, true value, and great eloquence, could never have displaced him.[29] For even with all his faults you see, that Brutus his owne sons[30] would have had him againe; who laying their heads together, with many young gallants, that thought themselves much wiser then their fathers; concluded among them selves, that a king was better then a Consul, a Court better then a Senate; that to live onely by lawes, was too strict and rigorous a life, & better for pesantly then princely dispositions: that Kings could favour, aswell as frowne, reward, aswell as revenge, pardon, aswell as punish, whereas the law was mercilesse, mute, and immutable; finally, they concluded it was ill living for them, where nothing but innocencie could protect a man.[31] Lo Brutus, how eloquently thy sons can pleade against their father; but thou hadst[32] a Jurie of sure free-holders, that gave a verdit against them, and thy selfe wast both judge and shiriffe, and hastenedst execution.[33]

---

suffering himselfe and all that he had to fall into the kings hands as an escheat, he refused not to be misnamed *Brutus,* a name appropriate to unreasonable creatures; that under the shadow and colour of that surname, that courage of his lying close hid, which should one day set free the cittie of Rome, might abide the full time and appeare in due season' (Holland, E2).

[26] *popular . . . Jaxes*] Livy i.59.8–9. 'Moreover he laid abroad the pride of the king himselfe, the miseries, the infinite toyle and pains of the commons, buried as it were under the ground, with cleansing and casting of ditches, voiding and ferming of the sinkes' (Holland, E3ᵛ).

[27] *his sonne*] Sextus Tarquinius.

[28] *had not defloured . . . sex*] Livy i. 57.6–11 and 58.

[29] *Brutus . . . him*] Ibid., i.59.4–6; 12. 'Thus rehearsing these and other matters, much more grievous and horrible . . . he so mightily inflamed the multitude, that he caused them to depose the king, to deprive him of his royall state and dignitie, yea and to decree and enact, that *L. Tarquinius* with his wife and children should be banished for ever' (Holland, E3ᵛ).

[30] *Brutus his owne sons*] Titus and Tiberius.

[31] *who laying . . . man*] Livy ii.3–5.   [32] hadst] hast *B*

[33] *Lo Brutus . . . execution*] The conspiracy on the part of Brutus's sons and the other young gallants to return Tarquinius having been revealed by a slave, the traitors were condemned to be put to death (Livy ii.5.5–9): 'Which suffering

O brave minded Brutus![34] I wil not call thee *primus Romanorum*, because one was shent[35] for calling one of thy posteritie, *ultimus Romanorum*,[36] but this I must truly say, they were two Brutish parts both of him, & you; one to kill his sons for treason, the other to kill his father[c] in treason; and yet you would both make us beleeve you had reason, and why so? forsooth because *Victrix causa placet superis, sed victa Catoni*.[d][38] That is to say in English, You had great fortune, &

---

[c] Caesar called Brutus son, and sayd to him when he stabd at him, καὶ σὺ τέκνον.[37]

[d] Lucan. li.1.[39]

---

of theirs was the more notable, for that the father by his place and vertue of his office [as consul], was bound and charged to see execution done upon his owne children: and he who otherwise ought not to have bene a spectator and looker on, even he (such was his fortune) was forced of necessitie to be the principall actor in this tragicall execution' (Holland, E5ᵛ–E6).

[34] *O . . . Brutus*] i.e., Lucius Junius Brutus.   [35] *shent*] Blamed.

[36] *for calling . . . Romanorum*] This must refer to the trial in A.D. 25 of Cremutius Cordus for having published a history which eulogized Marcus Junius Brutus and termed Cassius 'the last of the Romans' (Tacitus *Annals* iv.34). Plutarch, however, ascribes to Brutus himself the phrase calling Cassius ἔσχατον ἄνδρα Ῥωμαίων ('Brutus' 44.1).

Cassius and Brutus were kinsmen but only by marriage—Junia, the wife of Cassius, was Brutus's half-sister (Tacitus iii.76).

Harington, in order to play on the *primus . . . ultimus Romanorum* theme, here uses the phrase which the historians had applied to Cassius as if it applied to Brutus, thus reinforcing the parallelism between Lucius Junius Brutus (*primus*) who killed 'his sons for treason' and Marcus Junius Brutus (*ultimus*) who killed 'his father in treason.'

That Harington is perfectly aware of conflating the two is indicated by the passage in the *Apologie* where he calls two of his own detractors who 'had bene likened to Brutus and Cassius' *'ultimi Ruffianorum* [panders]' (p. 258).

It would appear that, not only in this passage but throughout the section dealing with the Roman rulers, Harington's historical citations have overtones of contemporary reference. That is, in carefully calculated remarks he directed gibes at his contemporaries; but he has so skilfully worked them in with the classical sources he is quoting it is impossible to be certain of the contemporary referents. Indeed, it must have been difficult for sixteenth-century readers, unless they were thoroughly aware of the vagaries of the courtly world; hence his protection from charges of libel.

[37] συ τεχνον *A. Caesar called . . .*] Suetonius 'Julius' 82.3. Holland has annotated this passage: 'This may have reference to that which is reported before, how in his youth, he [Caesar] loved Servilia, the mother of Brutus: for his age falleth out to agree fitly with that time: in so much as he was commonly thought to be a sonne of his. And yet this attribute *Fili*, may sort well with the familiaritie that was betweene them' (Holland, tr. 1606, ed. C. Whibley, London, 1899, I, 248).

[38] Catoni *A*   [39] *om. A, B. Pharsalia* i.128.

your cosin had great friends; yet neither died in bed, but both in battell, onely his death was his enemies advancement, and thy death was thy enemies destruction.[40] But to omit these trifles, and to returne to my tesh; whereas thou raylest against so great a Prince, for making of so sumptuous a Jakes, this I cannot endure at thy hands; and if thou hadst played me such a sawcie part here in my country, first of mine owne authoritie,[e] I would have granted the good behaviour against you: secondly, Tarquinius him selfe might have *Scandalum magnatum*[42] against you: and thirdly, a bill should have bene framed against you in the Starre chamber,[43] upon the statute of unlawful assemblies[44]: and then you would have wisht you had kept

---

[e] It seems the writer hereof would faine be thought a Justice of peace.[41]

---

[40] *onely his death . . . destruction*] *i.e.*, the death of Marcus Brutus resulted in the tyranny of Augustus while the death of Lucius Brutus had resulted in the Roman Republic. This same concept later appears in the *Discourses upon Cornelius Tacitus* by Virgilio Malvezzi (1622), translated by Sir Richard Baker (1642), where the third discourse is entitled 'A Parallell between the conspiracy of *Marcus Brutus* against *Caesar*, and that of *Lucius Brutus* against *Tarquin*: whereby we may see why the one [Lucius Brutus] brought in libertie; the other [Marcus Brutus], tryanny' (C5–D1).

[41] In 1584 Harington was named among those qualified to serve as justice of the peace (*L&E*, p. 12, citing Lansdowne MS 737). From the records of the Privy Council it is clear that Harington was serving in this capacity in 1588, again in 1593, and, apparently, from his marginal comment here and again in the *Apologie* (p. 209), in 1596. The directives issued by the Privy Council, missing for the period from 26 Aug. 1593 to 1 Oct. 1595, do not specify the names of the justices of the peace for Somerset during 1596 (*APC*, XVI, 232; XXIV, 219).

[42] *Scandalum magnatum*] 'The especiall name of a wrong done to any high personage of the land, as Prelates, Dukes, Earles, Barons, and other Nobles: and also of the Chanceler, treasurer, clerk of the privy seale, steward of the kings house, Justice, of the one bench or of the other, & other great officers of the realm, by false news: or horrible & false messages, whereby debates and discords betwixt them and the commons, or any scandall to their persons might arise' (John Cowell, *The Interpreter*, 1607, 3N2ᵛ). Harington's appropriation of the term to a literary context is earlier than the instance cited in the *OED*.

[43] *a bill . . . chamber*] 'Routes, Riots' and other 'Misdemeanures' not sufficiently provided for by common law were tried in the Court of the Star Chamber (Cowell, 3Q1ᵛ). Harington originally wrote, 'and thirdly, Mʳ Atturney showld have framed a bill agaynst yow in the star chamber,' which reinforces the notion that this section carries topical overtones.

[44] *statute . . . assemblies*] In his handbook for justices of the peace, William Lambard summarizes the legislation and punishment as follows: 'If any persons (above the number of two, and under twelve) beeing assembled, have intended unlawfully with force to murder or stay anie of the Queenes subjects:

your eloquence to your selfe, and not when a man hath done but two good workes in all his life, you to stand rayling at one of them. For suppose that Tarquin had given me but a fee, thus would I pleade for him. Maister Brutus you have made us beleeve all this while, you were but a foole; but I see now, if one had begged you,[45] he should have found you a Bygamus.[46] And whereas you seeme to disgrace my honorable clyent, for making of A Jax, I dare undertake to prove it, that your owne lawes, your religions, your customes, yea your conscience, is against you, and shewes, it is but a meere calumniation. For to omit Dame *Cloacina*, so lately deified, did not the noble Hercules, whom you Brutus honor as a God, farre ancienter then *Quirinus*,[47] and *Romulus*, among those many labors that eternized his memory, make cleane Augeus dunghils.

> *Quis non Eurysthea[48] durum*
> *Aut illaudati nescit Busiridis aras.*[49]

If the work have a basenesse, Tarquinius but with his purse, Hercules with his person effected it, leaving a patterne to posteritie both of labour and wit, for by turning a streame of water on the micksons,[50] he scowred away that in a weeke, that an hundred could scant have done in a yeare. Then would I end with some exclamation, and say, *O tempora, ô mores!*[51] Oh times, oh manners! If a man be not popular, you wil straight say, he is proud; if he keepe good hospitalitie, you wil

---

Or to cutte or cast downe anie inclosure, or bankes of anie Fishponde, or conduite head, or pipe . . . and have not departed upon proclamation, but have attempted to doe any of those things,' they shall incur 'one yeeres prisonment, and treble damages to the partie grieved, and costes' (*Eirenarcha*, 1592, 2D4–2D4ᵛ).

[45] *if one had begged you*] To petition the Court of Wards for the custody of a minor, an heiress, or an idiot. See p. 123 and n. 72.

[46] *Bygamus*] In ecclesiastical law applied to one who married a second time and was so applied by Harington to bishops (*A Short View*, p. 15 and *A Supply or Addicion*, p. 46).

[47] *Quirinus*] The name given to the deified Romulus (Plutarch 'Romulus' 28.2 and 29.1).

[48] Euristea *A*   [49] *Quis . . . aras*] Virgil *Georgics* iii.4–5.

[50] *micksons*] Place where refuse or dung is put.

[51] *O tempora, ô mores*] A favourite exclamation of Cicero, *e.g.*, *I Oratio in Catilinam* i.i.

say, he doth but fill many Jaxes; if he[52] build goodly vauts for sewers, you will say, he spends his treasure *in exhauriendis cloacis.* Or rather I would say, O Hercules come and bend thy bow against Brutus, that shootes arrowes thorow thy sides to slay Tarquinius. But now let me leave playing the lawyer,[f] and lawyerlike be friends immediatly with him whom even now I talked against so earnestly, I meane with Brutus; because indeede saving in this one case, I never meane to be of counsell with Tarquin: for such proud clients will speak us passing faire while we serve their turnes, and after picke a quarrell against us when we sue for a reward. Now therefore go forward with the storie.

When this valiant Brutus had thus discharged[54] the Kings and Queens out of the packe, and shewed himselfe indeed a sworn and vowed enemie to all the coate cardes,[55] there crept in many new formes of governement, & every one worse then other, namely, *Consuls, Dictators, Decemviri, Tribunes, Triumviri,*[56] till at last after oft enterchanges, it came to the government of Emperours. In all which times, there were not onely lawes, and speciall caveats given to the great officers in time of warre and danger, *Ne quid respub. detrimenti caperet,*[57] to looke to the safetie of the maine chance (the common wealth) but also there were officers of good account, as *Aediles, Praetores urbis,* that made inquiries *de stillicidiis, de aquae ductibus,* of reparation of houses, of watercourses, or common sewers, of which I could recite out of the 43. booke of the *Digest. tit.* 23. *de cloacis.* where you shall find, it was lawfull for any man

---

[f] Martial. 505. *Carpere causidicus fertur mea carmina. qui sit Nescio. si sciero vae tibi causidice.*[53]

---

[52] he] *om. MS*

[53] 505] *MS uncertain;* carmina qui *A;* Nescio si *A;* ve *A, B, MS cropped.* In modern editions this is v.33.

[54] discharged] *B;* discarded *A,* discharded *MS*

[55] *coate cardes*] A playing card bearing a 'coated' figure, *i.e.,* king, queen, or knave.

[56] Triumviri] *B;* Triumviris *A, MS*

[57] *Ne quid . . . caperet*] A well-known formula by which unlimited power was granted to the consuls, provided that (*ne quid. . .*). Cf. Cicero *pro Milone* 26.70.

purgare & reficere cloacam.[58] What officers were to licence him
that would *privatam cloacam facere, quae habeat exitum in
publicum.*[59] What speciall care was to be had of *Tubus* and
Fistula. Lastly, that *novam cloacam facere is concedit, cui
publicarum viarum cura sit.*[60] That is, that no man might make
a new Jakes, but he that had licence of the wardens of high
ways. With much more which I wold cite, if it were not to avoyd
prolixitie. And from them no doubt was derived our commission of sewers,[61] of which, the best of us all I hope, will
take no scorne: which commission, though in our country it is
chiefly intended to keep open the chanels of rivers in the deepe
countrey, that the water may have free passage. Yet the very
name imports, that therein is comprised the subject of my
present Discourse, which in populous townes had as much
neede to be looked to, as the other, infection being fit to be
avoided aswell as inundation. But now I hasten to Imperiall
examples: for though I have shewed already some authorities
for my text out of the practise of the lawes, the provident care
of Magistrates, the magnificent cost of kings, the religion
(though false) of the[62] pagans, yet[63] until I have added to all
these, the majestie of Emperours, and the veritie of Scriptures,
I suppose some carping mouthes will not be stopped.

The first example I meet with among the Emperours, was a
matter rather of curtesie then cost: and if any man will say,
that I draw this into my Treatise, as it were *obtorto collo,*[g] I
answer, that in my understanding, the tale falleth so fit and
proper unto this discourse, as indeede to have brought it into
any discourse saving of[65] A Jax, I would say it were unproper
and uncivill. The argument holds *à minore ad maius.* Now

---

[g] Some of our rude countrimen English this *obtorto collo,* hanging an arse.[64]

---

[58] *purgare . . . cloacam*] Justinianus, *Digestorum Seu Pandectarum,* Florence,
1553, II, 3V6ᵛ.

[59] *privatam . . . publicum*] Ibid., 3X1.   [60] *novam . . . sit*] Ibid.

[61] *commission of sewers*] 13 Elizabeth, c. 9 (*Statutes of the Realm,* IV, Pt. I,
543–4).

[62] the] *MS; om. A, B*   [63] pagans. Yet *A*

[64] Apparently a pun via *cul* on *obtorto collo* (with a wry neck) and the
proverbial 'hanging an arse.' See Tilley A384 where he explains the proverb as
signifying 'a reluctance' or 'hanging back.'

[65] of] on *MS*

hearken to my tale. Claudius Emperour of Rome, and husband
to that filthie *Masselyna*[h], (*Vilissima quae fuerunt vel sunt.*)
she that was worthy, for the commonnesse of her bodie (be it
spoken with saving the reverence of all women that are or
were, save her selfe) to have bin metamorphized into A Jax,
rather then poore *Hecuba*, for barking at him that kild her
sonne, into a bitch.[67] This Claudius I say, though not for cost
(as Tarquin) yet for his curtesie was greatly to be commended:
for a Gentleman one day being talking with him, and falling
suddenly into a grievous fit of the cholicke, the poore Gentleman would not for good maners sake breake wind, which might
presently have eased him, and after the disease increased so
sore on him that he died. The Emperour enformed of his
death, was much grieved thereat, specially hearing of the cause,
and immediatly thereupon made it be solemnly proclaimed,
that if any man herafter should be troubled with the cholicke,
it should not be taken for ill maners to break wind, though it
were in the Emperours owne company.[68] Now it may be, some
man in disgrace of this proclamation, will say, that this Claudius
was but a cuckold and a foole.[69] I answer, that for the cuckold,
that was none of his fault, and if it were a fault, God forbid all
our faults should be seene on[70] our forheads. And for the foole,
the old proverbe may serve us, *Stultorum plena sunt omnia*, the
world is ful of fools.[71] But take heede how you begge him for a

---

[h] Agrippa saith of her, that she lay with 22. severall men in 24. houres, at
the common stews: *& tandem lassata viris non satiata rediit.*[66]

---

[66] *Note not in MS*; 24 houres *A*; stews. *& A*. Either Harington suffered a
lapsus memoriae or the printer made an error, as Agrippa says 'quinto & vigesimo
concubitu' (*de Incertitudine & Vanitate Scientiarum & Artium*, Antwerp,
1534, L4); *& tandem . . . rediit*] From Juvenal 6.130 and incorporated by
Agrippa in his text.

[67] *Hecuba . . . bitch*] Ovid *Metam.* xiii. 404–7.

[68] *and immediatly . . . company*] Suetonius 'Claudius' 32. Harington
includes a reference to this same edict in his translation of *The School of
Salernum*, p. 79.

[69] *Claudius . . . foole*] Suetonius 'Claudius' 26.2, 3; 27.1, 2.

[70] on] of *MS*

[71] *Stultorum . . . fools*] Cicero *Epistulae ad Familiares* ix.22.4 and Tilley
W896.

foole,[72] for I have heard of one that was begged in the court of wards for a foole, and when it came to triall, he proved a wiser man by much, then he that begged him.[73] And though I have small skill in the law, specially in these prerogative cases,[74] (for I must confesse I studied Littleton[75] but to the title of discontinuance)[76] yet me thinke I should find out[77] a quirke, to make them that should begge him have a cold sute in the court of wards. For I take it to be a ruled case, that though a man hold wholly[78] *in Capite*,[79] put the case by a whole Knights service,[80]

---

[72] *how you begge . . . foole*] Ask to be his guardian. From the time of Edward I, the crown claimed the wardship of any natural fool, identified by the inability to give his age, to name his father or mother, to count to 20*d.*, or to beget children; his property could then be leased out and the individual sold to a guardian. The wardship of fools as well as of heirs (if under age) of tenants holding property in chief by knight's service came under the provenance of the Court of Wards and Liveries, of which Burghley was master from 1561–98 (H. E. Bell, *An Introduction to the History and Records of the Court of Wards & Liveries*, Cambridge, 1953, Ch. 6). Cf. Harington's epigram 'To a great Magistrate, in Re and in Spe,' apparently addressed to Burghley (*L&E*, p. 276). Cf. Tilley F496.

[73] *for I . . . him*] Perhaps an allusion to a current case. In comparison with other wardships, keeping a fool was considered unprofitable. Cf. Thomas Powell: 'Be assured that your selfe is somewhat the wiser man, before you goe about to beg him [the fool], or else never medle with him at all, lest you chance to play at *handy dandy*, which is the Gardian, or which is the foole? and the case alter *e Converso ad Conversum*' (*The Attourney's Academy*, 1623, quoted in Bell, p. 131).

[74] *prerogative cases*] Cases that came within the jurisdiction of the prerogative court held by an archbishop for the settling of inheritances.

[75] *Littleton*] John Littleton '*aliàs Westcote* the famous Lawier, Justice in the Kings Bench in the time of King Edward the Fourth, to whose Treatise of Tenures the students of our Common Law are no lesse beholden, than the Civilians to *Justinians Institutes*' (Camden, *Britain*, 3B3ᵛ). The *Tenures* was probably written c. 1475–80.

[76] *title of discontinuance*] 'Signifieth in the common law, nothing els but an interruption or breaking of: as discontinuance of possesion, or discontinuance of proces. And the large discourse that *Litleton* hath about this (*Discontinuance*) is rather to shew cases wherein it is, or wherein it is not, then to define the thing' (Cowell, Z2). Harington had entered Lincoln's Inn 27 Nov. 1581 (*The Records of the Honorable Society of Lincoln's Inn*, London, 1896, I, 94); he discontinued his studies after the death of his father in 1582.

[77] out] *om. B*   [78] wholly] alltogether *MS*

[79] *in Capite*] Holding a tenure directly from the crown.

[80] *Knights service*] 'That service, which the tenent by reason of his fee, oweth unto his Lord' (Cowell, 303).

or half a nights service, yet if he be covert Baron,[81] as Claudius was (for I am sure his wife ware the breches) & being at his foole age of 31.[82] the *Custodia* must of course be graunted to the wife, although the man be *plus digne de sang*. And thus much wee say, saving to our selves all advantage of exception to the unsufficiencie of the bill,[83] &c. And without that[i] the sayd Claudius did fondly to cause a mans hand to be cut off upon the motion of a stranger,[84] and without that[85] he had almost marred all the pastime he & his friends should have had at a Naumachia or sea-game, with resaluting the slaves that should have fought, in good Latine.[86] And lastly, without that the sayd Claudius at his being in England[j] (though he was counted

---

[i] Two partes why Claudius was esteemed a foole. Looke Sueto.

[j] Claudius was in England.[87]

[81] *covert Baron*] The legal status of a married woman who is under the protection of her husband (*potestate viri*—Cowell T3ᵛ); here used humorously to describe Claudius's marital position. The earliest instance of this application cited in the *OED* is in Florio's *Montaigne*, 1603.

[82] *at his foole age of 31*] A play on the legal term *full age* ('21. yeres'—Cowell, C2) and the proverbial saying that after thirty a man is either a fool or a physician (John Ray, *A Collection of English Proverbs*, 1670, p. 35 and Tilley M125).

[83] *unsufficiencie of the bill*] Variant of insufficiency; Harington's usage here is earlier than the instance cited in the *OED*.

[84] *And without ... stranger*] Suetonius 'Claudius' 15.2. Perhaps this passage is intended to recall the punishment meted out to the gallant John Stubbes after the publication in 1579 of his *Discoverie of a Gaping Gulfe* attacking the Queen's projected marriage to Alençon. After his right hand had been smitten off, Stubbes doffed his hat with his left and said in a loud voice, 'God save the Queen.' That Harington, although unsympathetic with Puritanism, had been particularly interested in the case of Stubbes is attested by his preservation of a number of papers relating to the case—Stubbes's petition to the Queen, to the Privy Council, his words on the scaffold, etc. (*NA*, I, 143–165).

[85] *that*] that that *MS*

[86] *and without ... Latine*] Suetonius 'Claudius' 21.6. 'When he was about to let out the water of the mere Ficinus, he exhibited in it a navall fight before: and as they who were to fight this battaile, cryed out unto him, "*Ave Imperator*, etc., *i*. All haile O Emperour; they salute thee and wish thy life who are ready to dye": and he againe made answere, "*Avete vos*." After which word given, as if he had pardoned them this skirmish, there was not one of them would fight' (Holland, II, 76). Harington, using a tag Latin phrase, has annotated the Sheffield copy: 'by saying es / tote salvi vos / and they tooke / yt for a dis / charge.'

[87] Suetonius 'Claudius' 17.1; according to Dio Cassius, Claudius spent sixteen days in England (*Roman History* lx.23). This, together with Harington's note, reinforces the suggestion of a covert contemporary allusion.

one of the best freeholders in Middlesex) could forfeit any land that he held by the right of his sword, either in fee-simple, or fee-taile, either by the socke, or the smocke, to anie other Ladie, but to[88] the Ladie his wife. But alas Claudius, thy friends may say, that I am a bad lawyer, for al this while I have done litle better then confesse the action, but I care not seeing thou art dead, *Mortui non mordent*,[89] and it were fitter now to preach for thee, then to pleade for thee: well then for thy gentle proclamations sake, loe what in sadnesse (if I were to make thy funeral sermon) I would say for thee, that howsoever some writers have wronged thee with the name of a foole,[k] in one of thy judgements I may liken thy wisdome to Salomon,[l] and in one of thy jests, I can compare thy wit with Diogenes.[94] Asse for example, a woman on a time disclaiming her sonne, and pretending that for conscience sake she must needes confesse a truth, viz. how her owne child died, and this was a *Supposititius*, a substitute in his place, for avoyding of her husbands displeasure, no evidence appearing to the contrarie, and the next heire following the matter verie hard, by complot with the mother, who remained obstinate in the tale, Claudius then sitting in judgement, seems to beleeve it, and seeing the man a comely young man, & she no old woman, & oft protesting she maliced him not: he commanded her immediatly in his presence to marrie him. The malicious mother driven to that unlookt for

---

[k] He was[90] called foole to his face. But hereby hangs a tale.[91]

[l] Claudius his[92] judgement like that of Salomon.[93]

---

[88] to] *MS*; *om. A, B*

[89] *Mortui non mordent*] Plutarch attributes this saying to the sophist Theodotus of Chios when he urged that Pompey the Great be put to death ('Brutus' 33.3).

[90] was] *MS*; is *A, B*

[91] *He . . . face*] Suetonius 'Claudius' 4. Cf. 15.4 where Suetonius tells the story of the Greek lawyer who, pleading a case before Claudius, let slip the remark: 'Thou art both old and a fool besides.'
But . . . tale] Tilley T48.

[92] his] *not in MS*

[93] I Kings 3:17-27. For the parallel story in Suetonius, see 'Claudius' 15.2.

[94] *and in . . . Diogenes*] Harington probably has in mind Diogenes's remark—that the great thieves were taking off the little thief—when he saw the officials of a temple take away a man who had stolen a bowl (Diogenes Laertius 'Diogenes' vi.45). The remark became proverbial, see Tilley T119.

pinch, openly confessed her unnatural malice, to avoyd so unnaturall a mariage: and thus much for his justice; now let us here what his jest is. A certaine Gentleman[95] that had his fingers made of lime twigges,[96] stole a peece of plate from Claudius one day at a banket; the conveyaunce was not so cleanly, but one had spied it, and told the Emperour, and offered to accuse him of it, whereby his goods might have bene all confiscate: but this good Prince wold neither head him nor hang him, no nor so much as once suffer him to be troubled; onely the next time he came, he[97] caused him to be served in an earthen dish. The Gentleman being abashed at it, for the dish gave him his dinner,[98] Claudius was so farre from laying his crime in his dish,[99] that he sayd, be of good cheare man, and fall to thy meate, and when thou hast dined put up that dish too: for I will spare thee that with a better will then the last, for perhaps thou hast a minde to poke up thy dish[100] when thou likest thy meate well. And so farewell good Claudius, & when any of my friends are troubled with the collicke, I hope I shall make them remember thee.

The next Emperour that is fit to bring into this discourse, is Vespasian, though his predecessour Vitellius, who is noted to have bene a passing great eater, would (I thinke) have taken it in good part, to have bene offred a cleanly & easie place for egestion after his good digestion.[101] But to the purpose. Vespasian before he was Emperour had borne some other offices, among the which, one was *Aedilis*, and it is written of him, that he incurred great displeasure with Otho then Emperour,[102] because he had not seene better to the keeping

---

[95] *A certaine Gentleman . . .*] Suetonius 'Claudius' 32 and elaborated by Harington.

[96] *his fingers . . . twigges*] Tilley F236.   [97] he] *not in MS*

[98] dinner. *A*   [99] *laying . . . dish*] Tilley T155.

[100] *to poke up thy dish*] To put into a poke or bag; this is the earliest instance cited in the *OED*.

[101] *his predecessour . . . digestion*] Suetonius 'Vitellius' 13.1–3. 'But being given most of all to excessive bellie cheere and crueltie, he devided his repast into three meales every day at the least, and sometime into foure, to wit, Breakefast, Dinner, Supper and rere-bankets, able to beare them all very well, hee used to vomit so ordinarily' (Holland, II, 196).

[102] *Otho then Emperour*] According to Suetonius, it was Gaius Caesar Caligula who chided Vespasian for his negligence in office. See 'Vespasian' 2.3 and 5.3 where Vespasian's disgrace is listed among the portents of his imperial rank.

sweete of the streets, and caused the filth of them (according to his office) to be caried to the places appointed for the same. But afterward himselfe coming to be Emperour (though the Citie of Rome was before his time sufficiently furnished of Jaxes) yet it seemed there wanted other places of neare affinitie to them (which he found belike when he was Aedile by experience) I meane certaine pissing conduites[103]: and therefore he caused diverse to be erected in the most populous and frequented places of the Citie, and saved all the urine in cesternes, and sold it for a good summe of money to the Dyers.[104] But though I tell you the tale thus plainly, you must imagine that[105] the matter was much more formally & finely handled, and namely, that there was an Edict set out in this sort.

By the Emperour C. Flavius Vespasianus,
pater patriae, semper Augustus, &c.

Forasmuch as his Majestie hath bene enformed by sundrie credible men, that great abuse is committed by the irreverent demeanure of diverse persons, ill brought up, who without all due respect of civilitie and reverence, in most unseemely maner, shed their urine, not only against the wals of his royal pallace, but also against the temples of the Gods and Goddesses. Whereby not onely ugly and lothsome sights, but filthie and pestiferous savours are dayly ingendred, his Majestie therfore as well of a fatherly care of his citizens, as of a filiall reverence to the gods, hath to his great charges, & of his princely bountie & magnificence, erected diverse & sundrie places of faire polished marble, for this speciall purpose, requiring, and no lesse straightly charging all persons, aswell citizens as strangers, to refraine from all other places, saving these especially appointed, as they tender his favour, &c.

Thus could I have penned the Edict, if I had bene secretarie.

---

[103] *there wanted . . . conduites*] A water fountain in London located near the Royal Exchange, characterized by its small stream of water, was called the pissing conduit; cf. *2 Henry VI*, IV.vi.1–5.

[104] *and therefore . . . Dyers*] Suetonius 'Vespasian' 23.3. In his annotation to this passage, Holland refers to the use that 'Fullers, Walkers, and Diers' made of this commodity (II, 284).

[105] that] *MS; om. A, B*

For it had not bene worth a figge,[106] if they had not artificially covered the true intent (which was the profite) and gloriously set forth the goodly and godly pretence (that was least thought on) viz. the health of the people, and cleane keeping of the temples. But I doubt, notwithstanding this goodly Edict, it will be objected, that it was condemned for a base part, by a judge whose sentence is above all appeale: I meane that noble *Titus, deliciae humani generis*, he that thought the day lost in which he had done no man good[107]: to answer which, I would but say as was said to him, when the pissing mony was put into the perfumed purse, *suavis odor lucri*, the smell of gaine is sweet.[108] And I dare undertake, this answer wil satisfie[109] my Lord Mayor of London, & many of the worshipful of the Citie, that make sweete gaines of stinking wares,[m] & will laugh and be fat,[111] and say:

> *So we get the chinks,*
> *We will beare with the stinks.*[112]

But I must finde out a better answer for courtly wits, and therefore I say to them, that according to the discipline and custome of the Romanes (in my opinion, under reformation of their better judgements) this was so honourable a part of Vespasian, that he was therefore worthy to have bene deified. For if Saturnus were allowed as a God, by the name of *Ster-*

---

m Oyles, oad,[110] tarre, &c.

---

[106] *not bene . . . figge*] Tilley F211.

[107] *Titus . . . good*] Suetonius 'Titus' i.1 and 8.

[108] *when . . . sweet*] 'Vespasian' 23.3. 'When his sonne Titus seemed to finde fault with him for devising a kinde of tribute, even out of urine; the monie that came unto his hand of the first paiment, hee put unto his sonnes nose: asking withall, whether he was offended with the smell, or no, and when he answered No: "And yet," quoth he, "it commeth of Urine" ' (Holland II, 223). Cf. Tilley G3.

[109] satisfe *A*

[110] Or woad. The plant *Isatis tinctoria*, the leaves of which, powdered and fermented, were used in preparing a blue dye. A proclamation in 1585 forbade the sowing of woad within eight miles of the Queen's residences and within four miles of cities and market towns (Camden, *Elizabeth*, 2A5; cf. *CSP, Dom.*, XII, Addenda 1580–1625, 207–8, for a subsequent modification).

[111] *laugh and be fat*] Tilley L91, where Harington's example is the earliest cited.

[112] Cf. Tilley C350, where Harington's example is the earliest cited.

cutius, as is before alledged, for finding a profitable use of all maner soyle, I see a good reason (*à paribus*) that Vespasian should aswell be deified, for finding a meanes to make money of urine, and accordingly to be named *Urinatius*, of *Urina*, as the other[113] is, of *Stercus*, *Stercutius*. Furder Vespasian was famous for two true miracles[114] done by him, greater then all their gods beside ever did. Now if any take exceptions to his face, because the foole told him, he looked as if it went hard with him:[115] trust me it shall go hard with me too, but I will find somewhat to say for him; and first I will get some of the painting that comes from the river of Orenoque, which will wonderfully mend his complexion.[116] Secondly, I will say this, how bad soever his face was, he had something so good, that a handsome woman gave him a thousand crownes, for putting his seale with his label to her pattent, and yet she exhibited the petition (as I take it) *in forma paper*,[117] for she was starke

---

[113] the other] tother *MS*

[114] *Vespasian . . . miracles*] Suetonius 'Vespasian' 7.2. 'It fortuned that a certaine meane commoner starke blind, another likewise with a feeble and lame leg, came both togither unto him as hee sat upon the tribunall, craving that helpe and remedie for their infirmities which had beene shewed unto them by Serapis in their dreames: That hee should restore the one to his sight, if he did but spit into his eyes: and strengthen the others legge, if hee vouchsafed onely to touch it with his heele. Now when as hee could hardly beleeve, that the thing anie way would finde successe and speede accordingly, and therefore durst not so much as put it to the venture: at the last through the perswasion of friends, openly before the whole assembly, hee assayed both meanes, neither missed hee of the effect' (Holland, II, 212).

[115] *Now if . . . him*] Suetonius 'Vespasian' 20.1. See also n. 130, p. 107.

[116] *and first . . . complexion*] Harington clearly is remembering a passage in Raleigh's *Discovery of the Large, Rich, and Beautiful Empire of Guiana*, also published in 1596: 'Where there is store of gold, it is in effect nedeles to remember other commodities for trade: but it hath towards the south part of the river, great quantities of Brasill woode, and of divers berries, that die a most perfect crimson and Carnation: And for painting, al *France*, *Italy*, or the east Indies yeild none such: For the more the skyn is washed, the fayrer the cullour appeareth, and with which, even those brown and tawnie women spot themselves, and cullour their cheekes' (Hakluyt Society III, London, 1848, p. 113).

[117] *in forma paper*] Harington is punning on *in forma pauper*, derived from the legal expression *in forma pauperis*. Cf. his similar pun in the epigram '*To my Lady* Rogers *of her servant* Paine' (*L&E*, pp. 180–1). As a result of the statute enacted 11 Henry VII, c. 12, a poor person was allowed to sue or defend in a court of law 'in the form or guise of a pauper' and as a consequence was not liable for costs (*Statutes of the Realm*, II, 578).

naked. Once this I am sure Suetonius writes,[118] that when his steward asked him, how he should set downe that 1000 crownes on his booke, he bad him write it among his other perquisites, in some such sort.

> *It. for respit of homage*[119] *from a*
> *loving tenant to her lovely Lord* } 1000. *crowns*
> *for a whole knights fee, recepi. . .*

Now for his wit,[120] though I could tell you two excellent tales, how he deceived a groome of his chamber, of his brother,[121] and how he would needes be halfe with his horse-keeper, for setting on a shoe on a horse that lacked none[122]:

---

[118] *Suetonius writes . . .*] 'Vespasian' 22. 'Having yeelded at length to a certaine woman enamoured of him, and readie as it were to dye for pure love, when she was brought to his bed, and had given him fortie thousand sesterces for lying with her, his Steward comes to put him in minde in what manner and forme hee would have this summe of money to bee set downe in his booke of accompts. "Marie thus," quoth he, "*Vespasiano adamato,*" *i.* Item, given to Vespasian beloved' (Holland, II, 222). According to another reading, it is Vespasian who, despite the lady's importuning him, gives the reward.

Cf. the following passage in the *Ulysses*: 'But you privelye gird likewise at patents (I meane not the father and the sonne both wittie and learned gentlemen) who (as I am inspired) are the very *Genii* and good angells in furthering your best studies' (E7ᵛ); the author of the *Ulysses* then continues with a reference to Harington's attack on monopolies (p. 167 ff.).

[119] *respit of homage*] 'The forbearing of homage, which ought first of all to be performed by the tenent, that holdeth by homage. Which respight may be occasioned upon divers good reasons: but it hath the most frequent use in such as hold by Knights service *in capite*' (Cowell, 3L3ᵛ). There is of course the same pun as on p. 123.

[120] *his wit*] Suetonius 'Vespasian' 22. 'For given exceedingly hee was to skoffs, and those so skurrile and filthy, that he could not so much as forebeare words of ribaudrie. And yet there bee many right pleasant conceited jests of his extant' (Holland, II, 221).

[121] *how he deceived . . . brother*] Suetonius 'Vespasian' 23.2. 'A Minister and servitour about him, whom hee loved deerely, made suite in the behalfe of one as his brother, for a Stewardship. When hee [Vespasian] had put him off to a farther day, hee called unto him the partie himselfe, that made meanes for the thing: and having exacted so much monie at his hands, as hee had agreed for with the Mediatour aforesayd, without more delay, he ordained him Steward. Soone after when the Servitour interposed him selfe, "Goe your wayes," quoth he, "seeke you another to be your brother: for, this fellow whom you think to be yours is become mine" ' (Holland, II, 222–3).

[122] *and how . . . none*] Suetonius 'Vespasian' 23.2. 'Suspecting that his mulitier who drave his carroch alighted one time, as it were to shoo his Mules, thereby to winne some advantage of time and delay, for one that had a matter in lawe and was comming unto him: hee asked the Mulitier what might the

yet I omit them both, because many wil be too apt to follow the president, and I will keepe me very strictly to my tesh, and specially because I hasten to a most royall example. I meane of Trajan. There is no man (I thinke) that hath either travelled farre countreys, or read forraine stories, but hath either heard of the famous exploits and victories that he had, or seene some of the stately & sumptuous monuments that he made. This Trajan was Emperor of Rome, and then Emperor when Rome stood at her highest pitch of greatnesse, a man whose conquests were most glorious, whose buildings were most gorgeous, whose justice was most gracious, he that stayed his whole armie, to right the cause of one widow,[123] he that created a magistrate, & delivering him the sword for justice, sayd to him, use this for me as long as I governe justly, but against me when I governe otherwise,[124] he in whose time no learned man was seene want,[125] no poore man was seene begge,[126] he that wold

---

shooing of his mules cost [the soliciting party], and so covenanted with him to have part of his gaines' (Holland, II, 223).

[123] *he . . . widow*] There appears to be no classical source for the story of Trajan and the widow, which exists in several different versions although the central element remains the same. Dio Cassius relates a comparable episode about Trajan's successor Hadrian (*Roman History* lxix.6).

During the Middle Ages the story was added to the cluster of legends associated with Trajan, appearing in its earliest form in the *Life of St. Gregory* by Paul the Deacon, c. 787 (Arturo Graf, *Roma nella memoria e nella immaginazione del medio evo*, Turin, 1882–3, II, 3).

Whatever Harington's original source, there is a version recorded in Antonio de Guevara's *Chronicle, conteyning the lives of tenne Emperours of Rome*, translated by Edward Hellowes, 1577 (a work which Harington had read as is revealed by his subsequent remarks on Trajan): '*Trajane* being on horsebacke, and upon the voyage of the seconde warres into *Datia*, there came a woman and saide unto him: Emperour *Trajane*, I am poore, olde, and a widowe: and having but one daughter, one of thy housholde servaunts hath ravished her. *Trajane* answered: poore woman, be not importune with mee: for I sweare unto thee, by the immortall Gods, that beeing returned from the warres, I will do thee justice: to this the olde woman did replye: and what suretie hast thou *Trajane*, to returne from the warres: hearing so byting an aunswere, presently he lighted on foote and deferred his departure, until he perfourmed justice with the poore olde woman' (C3ᵛ).

[124] *he that . . . otherwise*] Dio Cassius *Roman History* lxviii.16.

[125] *he in whose . . . want*] 'Although *Trajane* were not much learned, he was moste truely a greate friende unto learned men: whome he did promote unto honours and to estates, and did much joy to holde them for his friendes: in suche wise, that in his house and court, a learned man was never seene in necessitie' (Guevara, B6ᵛ).

[126] *no . . . begge*] 'He forbad any poore man to goe from doore to doore, but

boast of Nerva his predecessor, of Plotina his wife, of Plutarke his counseller:[127] finally, this Trajan was so well accomplished a Prince in all princely vertues, as no storie, no time, no memorie, in all points can match him. This most renowmed Emperor, hearing there was a town in Bithinia, farre off from Rome, and in a place where he was never lyke[128] to be troubled with the ill[129] savour, that was much annoyed for lacke of a good conveyance of the common privies, thought him selfe bound (as a father to all his subjects) to provide a remedie for such an inconvenience, and of his owne purse he tooke order for making a vault of great cost and charge in the citie. And for full satisfaction of the reader herein, I will set downe the two Epistles, as I find them in the tenth booke of the Epistles of *Plinius Secundus* to *Trajan*.[130] ep. 99."

   C. Plinius Secundus Traiano Imp. S. Amestrianorum civitas, domine, & eligans & ornata habet, inter praecipua opera pulcherrimam, eandemque longissimam plateam, cuius à latere per spatium[132] *omne porrigitur, nomine quidem flumen re vera cloaca foedissima.*[133] *Quae sicut turpis & immundissima aspectu ita pestilens est odore teterrimo. Quibus ex causis non minus salubritatis quam decoris interest eam contegi, quod fiet si permiseris*

   ⁿ *Argumentum quaerit an, contegenda sit aqua quae per civitatem Amestrianorum fluit.*[131]

---

that all which were impotent, should be succoured of the common treasure: and unto such as could traveile, they gave them whereon to worke from the Senate' (*ibid.*, B5ᵛ).

   [127] *he that wold . . . counseller*] 'Many *Romaines* on a time murmuring of the insolencies of the Emperour *Domitian, Trajane* sayde unto them: The intention wherwith *Domitian* hath intreated me, the Gods have to judge: for of his works which he hath done, I may not complaine, since he hath bene the occasion that I have recovered *Nerva* for my father, *Plutarche* for my maister, & *Plotina* for my wife, and above al the rest, he brought me acquainted with adverse Fortune: for that afore I presumed of nothing but to commaund: but now only to serve' (*ibid.*, B3ᵛ).

   [128] *never lyke*] *MS*; like never *A, B*   [129] *ill*] *MS*; evill *A, B*

   [130] *the Epistles . . . Trajan*] Pliny the Younger was appointed legate to the province of Bithynia, c. A.D. 111. The record of his official correspondence with Trajan constitutes Bk. x of his *Letters*, published after his death. This is Letter 98 in modern texts.

   [131] Argumentum . . . an] *transf. to text B;* contegenda . . . fluit] *Markham-Wrenn; not in MS, A, B;* Amestrianorum] I have retained Harington's spelling of this proper noun in both the Latin and the English.

   [132] spacium *A*   [133] fedissima *A*

*curantibus nobis ne desit pecunia operi tam magno quam neces-
sario.* Which is thus in English.[o]

Caius Plinius to Trajan the Emperor greeting. The Citie of
the Amestrians (my Lord) being both commodious and
beautifull, hath among her principall goodly buildings, a very
faire and long streete, on the side whereof runneth through the
whole length of it, a brooke, in name (for it is called so) but
indeed a most filthie Jakes; which as it is foule & most uncleanly
to behold, so is it infectious with the horrible[136] vile savour,
wherefore it were expedient, no lesse for wholsomnesse then
for handsomnesse, to have it vaulted, which shall be[137] done
if it please you to allow it, and I will take care that there shall
be no want of money for such a worke, no lesse chargeable then
necessarie. Thus writes *Plinius Secundus*, a Romane Senator,
and as it were a deputie Lieutenant in the province of Bithinia,
to the great Trajan, and I do half marvell he durst write so, for
had it bene in the time of Domitian, Commodus or Nero,
either Martiall should have jested at him with an Epigram, or
some secretarie that had envied his honest reputation, should
have bene willed to have answered the letter in some scornefull
sort, and would have written thus.

Maister Plinie, my Lord God the Emperour, not vouch-
safing to answer your letter him selfe,[p] hath commanded me to
write thus much to you, that he marvels you will presume to
trouble his divine Majestie with matters of so base regard, that
your father being held a wise man, and a learned, might have
taught you better manners, that his Majestie hath matters of
greater import, concerning the state of the Empire, both for
warre & peace, to employ his treasure in. Thus much I was
commanded to write. Now for mine owne part, let me say thus
much to you, that I heard my Lord God the Emperour say,
that if the ill savour annoy you, you may send to your Mistresse

---

[o] The contents is, whether he shal cover the water that runs by[134] the towne
of[135] Amestris.

[p] *Che scrisse*[138] *taccia et piu no l' faccia.*

---

[134] by] *Margin cropped in some copies of B*
[135] of] *Margin cropped in some copies of B*
[136] horrible] terrible *MS*   [137] de *A*
[138] scrisse] fece *MS*

for a perfumed handkerchif to stop your nose, and that some Physicians say, the smel of a Jakes is good against the plague. Some such answer as this, had bene like to have come from some of those beastly Emperours, & their filthie followers. But how did Trajan answer it? I will set you down his owne letter, out of the same booke, in the same language.

Argumentum.
Permittit confornicari cloacam.[139]

Tr. Plinio S.

Rationis est, mi Secunde carissime,[140] *contegi aquam istam quae per civitatem Amestrianorum fluit, si detecta salubritati obest. Pecunia*[141] *ne huic operi desit, curaturum te secundum diligentiam tuam certum habeo.* Thus in English. It is good reason, my dearest Secundus, that the water be covered that runs by the citie of the Amestrians, if the want of covering may breed infection. And for money for the worke, I make no question, but you according to your accustomed diligence, will make provision. Short & sweet,[142] yea most sweet indeed, because it was of an unsavorie matter. But I had almost forgot to English the argument, & then folks might laugh indeede at me, and thinke I were *Magister incipiens* with an *s*,[143] and say I could not English these three words, *permittit confornicari cloacam*; what the good yere,[144] what is this same *confornicari*? trust me there is a word I never read in Homer nor Artistotle, mary indeede they wrote but ill Latine, no nor in Tully, in Livie, in Tacitus, nor in all the Poets: what a straunge word is this? Ho sirra bring hither the Dictionarie. Which of them,

---

[139] *Argumentum . . . cloacam*] Harington adds the Argument in order to make his jest on p. 135. In modern editions this is Letter 99.

[140] secunde Charissime *A*   [141] obest, Pecunia *A*

[142] *Short & sweet*] Tilley S396.

[143] *Magister . . . an s*] A play on *incipiens*, from the phrase *incipiens in artibus* applied to a qualified candidate for the degree of M.A. (*Pedantius*, ed. G. C. Moore Smith, *Materialien zur Kunde des älteren Englischen Dramas*, Louvain, 1905, n. 626, p. 115) and *insipiens*, foolish.

[144] *what the good yere*] An imprecatory phrase analogous to 'what the devil.' Cf. pp. 213, 243.

134

Cooper?[145] No no, *Thomas Coperus omisit plurima verba.*
Which then, that with the French afore the Latin,[146] or *Thomas
Thomas?*[147] Yea,[148] bring me them two. What hast thou
brought the two dictionaries? I meant but the two *Thomases.*
Come old friend *Tom, Tom,*[q] *Qui fueras quondam clarae
praepositor*[150] *aulae,* you have made rods to jerke me withall
ere now, I thinke I shall give you a jerke, if you do not helpe
me to some English for this word. Looke it sirra there in the
dictionarie. *Con, con.* Tush what dost thou looke in the French?
thou wilt make a sweete peece of looking, to looke for *confornicar*
in the French: looke in the Latin for *fornicor. F, fa, fe, fi, fo,
for, for, foramen, forfex,*[151] *forica, forma, fornicator,* (now I
think I am neare it) *fornix, fornicor, aris, are.*[r] There, there,

---

[q] A great officer among the boyes at Eaton, Maister of the rods.[149]

[r] Eliots dictionarie and Coopers placed these 2. wordes, too neare together.[152]

---

[145] *Cooper*] Thomas Cooper, after having for the 'third time corrected'
Sir Thomas Elyot's *Bibliotheca Eliotae,* published his own *Thesaurus Linguae
Romanae et Britannicae* in 1565, a work which is said to have so pleased the
Queen that she resolved to give its author all due advancement.

In his account of Cooper in 'A Supplie or Addicion,' Harington states that
this work 'was in those days accompted a great prayse to him, and a chiefe
cause of his preferment.' Later, in speaking of advancement by means of
literary effort and perhaps recalling his own disappointed hopes of becoming
Archbishop of Dublin and Lord High Chancellor of Ireland, he states the
Queen 'gave Doctor Cooper the bishoprick of Lincolne, only for making
a dictionarie, or rather but for mending that which Sir Thomas Eliot had
made before' (*NA,* II, 88, 224).

[146] *that with . . . Latin*] The celebrated *Dictionnaire français-latin* of Robert
Estienne was published in 1529.

[147] *Thomas Thomas*] Like Harington, Thomas attended both Eton and
King's College, Cambridge, where he became the first printer to the University.
His popular *Dictionarium,* which had gone through fourteen editions by 1644,
was originally published in 1587 (*The Eton College Register 1441–1698,* ed.
W. Sterry, Eton, 1943, p. 331).

[148] Yea] I *MS*   [149] *Note not in MS*

[150] *praepositor*] A name given to seniors at Eton who were entrusted with
much of the discipline of the school. Thomas attended Eton from 1565 to 1571;
Harington, who was enrolled in 1571, would thus have come under his discipline.

[151] forfex *A*

[152] In imitating the process of word hunting, Harington illustrates a kind of
selective serendipity, picking out items that have a suggestive relevance to his
text. In defiance of alphabetical order—as well as that of Elyot and Cooper—
he inserts the passive form *fornicor, fornicaris* 'to commit fornication' before the
active *fornicare* 'to make an arche or a vault,' thus permitting his observation
that Elyot and Cooper place these two words 'too neare together.' A 'vaulting
house' was one of the cant terms for a brothel.

what says he of that ?[153] A vault or Arche,[154] to vault or arch any thing with a compasse. Well said, carrie away the bookes againe, now I have it: then thus it is, He alloweth[155] the vaulting or arching over of the Jakes. Marie Gods blessing on[156] his heart for his labour, and I love him the better for it. Wherefore (most noble Trajan) thou mayest well be called the patterne of all princely qualities, comely, bountifull, martiall, mercifull, a lover of learning, moderate in private expences, magnificent in publike, most goodly of stature, amiable, not onely in thy vertues, but even in thy vices. For to say the worst was ever said of thee, these were al thy faults, ambition, or desire of glorie in warres, love of women, and persecuting of religion. For so they joyne thee, *Nero, Domitianus, Traianus, Antoninus,*[157] *Pontifices Romanos laniarunt.* To which thus I aunswer without a fee, but with all my heart: that thy ambition was so honorable, and thy warlicke humour so well tempered, that thou didst truly witnesse of thy selfe, that thou didst never envie any mans honour, for the confidence thou haddest of thine owne woorth: and all the world can witnesse, that thou never didst make unjust warre, nor refuse any just or indifferent peace. For that same sweete sinne of lecherie,[158] I would say as the Frier sayd, a young man and a young woman in a greene arber in a may morning; if God do not forgive it, I would. For as *sir Thomas More* saith of *Edward* the fourth: he was subject to a sin, from which, health of bodie in great prosperitie of fortune, without a speciall grace, hardly refrayneth.[159] And to speake uprightly of him, his lusts were not furious, but friendly, able with his goodly person, his sweete behaviour, and his bountifull gifts, to have wonne *Lucretia.*[160] Besides, no

---

[153] There . . . that ?] *MS*; There, what is that ? *A, B*

[154] or Arche] *MS*; *om. A, B*

[155] alloweth] allowes *MS*   [156] on] of *MS*

[157] *For so . . . Antoninus*] Trajan is included by St. Augustine among those who persecuted the Christians. In his commentary Vives refers to the letter from Pliny to Trajan asking how he should deal with the Christians and Trajan's reply: '*Trajan* biddeth him not seeke them out, but if they bee accused unto him punish them, unlesse they will recant &c.' and he adds, 'O would wee christians could use this moderation unto others' (*Citie of God*, Bk. xviii, Ch. 52, 3R6ᵛ).

[158] *For that . . . lecherie*] Cf. p. 84.

[159] *as sir Thomas . . . refrayneth*] *The English Works*, I, 400.

[160] Lucrecia *A*

doubt his sin was the lesse, in that he ever loved his wife most
dearely, and used her most respectively: for I have ever maintained this paradox, it is better to love two too manie, then one
too few. Lastly, for the persecution of thy time, though I dare
not defend it, yet there is a maxime, *invincibilis ignorantia
excusat*,[161] and sure thou didst not know the truth, and thy
persecution was verie gentle, and halfe against thy will, as
appeareth[162] by the 98. epistle[163] of the tenth booke of Pl.
epistles, where thou doest utterly reject all secret promoeters,[164]
and dost pronounce against the strict inquisition, *Conquirendi
non sunt, &c.* Wherefore I doubt not to pronounce, that I hope
thy soule is in heaven, both because those thou didst persecute
prayed for thee, wishing to thee, as *Tertul.* saith; *Vitam
prolixam, imperium securum, domum tutam, exercitus fortes,
Senatum fidelem, populum probum, orbem quietum.*[165] A long life,
a happy raigne, a safe dwelling, strong armies, a faithful
Senate, honest people, and a quiet world. Further, it is written
by authors of some credite,[s] that thy soule was delivered out of

---

[s] S. Damascen[166] S. Brigid[167] write this of Trajan, beleeve them who list,
for though it seem Popish, yet it ministers an argument against some Popish
opinions.[168]

---

[161] excusat] *MS, Lumley-Folger;* recusat *A, B; invincibilis . . . excusat*] Cf.
Nashe: 'Ignorantia, si non excusat a toto, saltem excusat a tanto.' McKerrow
states that this is untraced and probably derives from some manual of theology
(*Works*, II, 35, and IV, 216). Cf. the standard legal maxim: 'Ignorantia juris non
excusat a toto sed a tanto' (John Hawarde, *Les Reportes del Cases in Camera
Stellata*, ed. W. P. Baildon, 1894, pp. 25, 35, 79).

[162] appeareth] appeers *MS*

[163] *98. epistle*] X.97.

[164] *promoeters*] Professional informers, a species against which Harington
constantly inveighed. Cf. p. 243 and ff. and his epigram, '*Against Promoters*':

> Base spies, disturbers of the publike rest,
> With forged wrongs, the true mans right that wrest:
> Packe hence exil'd to desart lands, and waste.
> And drinke the cup that you made others taste.
>   But yet the Prince to you doth bounty show,
>   That doth your very lives on you bestow.
>
>   (*L&E*, pp. 181–2.)

[165] *Tertul . . . quietum*] *Apologeticus* 30.4.

[166] The reference to the prayer of Pope Gregory the Great in behalf of
Trajan is found in the homily *De Iis Qui in Fide Dormierunt,* a work doubtfully
assigned to St. John of Damascus (*Patrologiae Graecae*, ed. Migne, XCV, 262–3
and Graf, II, 7).

[167] *Revelationes celestes*, IV, 13, K3[v] [Nuremberg, 1517]. St. Bridget or

hell, at the prayer of great S. Gregorie, which though I am not bound to beleeve, yet as in love, I had rather love too manie then too few, so in charitie, I had rather beleeve too much then too litle. As for that Scripture, *ex inferno nulla redemptio*,[169] I have heard it oft alleadged by great clerkes, but I thinke it is in the Epistle of S. Paule to the Laodiceans, or in Nicodemus Gospel: for I never yet could find it in the Bible. Wherefore this I will frankly say for Trajan, that where soever I find a Prince or a Peere with so great vertues, and so few vices, I will honour him, love him, extoll[170] him, admire him, and pronounce this of him; that the armie is happie that hath such a Generall, the Prince happie that hath such a counseller, the Mistresse happy that hath such a servant,[171] and thus I end my prophane authorities, and now I come to the devine, wherin I thinke I shall serve you in the banket I have promised you as my self have bene served many times at our commencement feasts, and such like in Cambridge, that when we have bene in the midst of some pleasant argument, suddenly the Bibler hath come,[172] and with a lowd and audible voyce begunne with *Incipit libri Deuteronomium, caput vicesimum ter-tium*.[173] And then suddenly we have bene all *st*[174] *tacete*, and hearkened to the Scripture, for even so must I now after all our pleasant stories, bring in as I promised, some divine authorities,' to the which I pray you let us with all due reverence be attentive.

' Authorities of Scripture.

Birgitta (d. 1373; canonized 1391), the patron saint of Sweden, was the founder of the Order of the Most Holy Saviour. The *Revelations*, of which St. Bridget experienced some six hundred, were translated into Latin by her confessors and first published at Lübeck in 1492; they were widely circulated thereafter both in Latin and vernacular versions (*Butler's Lives of the Saints*, ed. Thurston and Attwater, N.Y., 1956, IV, 54–9).

[168] opininions *A*

[169] *ex inferno . . . redemptio*] A theological commonplace. Cf. Nashe, III, 192, and Tilley R60, where Harington's example is the earliest cited.

[170] extoll] follow *MS*

[171] *Wherefore . . . servant*] Harington's tribute to Essex, see p. 141 ff.

[172] *the Bibler hath come*] It was the custom at Eton for the Bibler to read a portion of scripture in the hall at dinner, and this same practice apparently obtained at Cambridge. Cf. Nashe, 'The gentleman he brings in reading a Chapter (Colledge fashion at dinner time)' (*Works*, III, 128).

[173] ter–cium *A*   [174] st] *MS*; s't *A*

In the aforesaid[175] 23. Chapter of Deuteronomie in the 12. verse, I find this text

12 *Habebis locum extra castra ad quem egrediaris ad requisita naturae.*

13 *Gerens paxillum in balteo, cumque sederis fodies per circuitum, & egesta humo operies quo relevatus es.*

14 *Dominus enim Deus tuus ambulat in medio castrorum, ut eruat te & tradat tibi inimicos tuos, & sint castra tua sancta, & nihil in eis appareat foeditatis, ne derelinquat te.* That is.

12 Thou shalt have a place without thy tents, to which thou shalt go to do the necessities of nature.

13 Carying a spade staffe[u] in thy hand, and when thou wilt ease thee, thou shalt cut a round turfe, and thou shalt cover thy excrements therewith, in the place where thou didst ease thy selfe.

14 For the Lord thy God walketh in the midst of thy tents to deliver thee, and to give thy enemies into thy hands, that thy tents may be holy, and that there appeare no filthinesse in them, lest he forsake thee.

But me thinke some may say upon hearing of this text, What is it possible there should be such a Scripture, that handleth so homely matters? I can hardly beleeve it; I have always had a Bible in my parlour thus[176] many yeares, and oft time when the weather hath bene foule, and that I have had no other booke to reade on,[177] and have wanted company to play at cards or at tables with me, I have read in those bookes of the old Testament, at least halfe an houre by the clocke,[178] & yet I remember not anie such matter. Nay further, I have heard a Preacher, that hath kept an exercise a yeare together upon the bookes of Moses, and hath told us of Genesis, & genealogies, of the arke and the propitiatorie, of pollutions, of washings, of leprosies, but I never heard him talke of such a homely matter as this. I answer, It may be so very wel. And therfore now I pray you, sith the text is so strange to you, give me leave to put you in mind of two vertuous and honest

---

[u] Or a trowell.

---

[175] aforesaid] foresayd *MS*   [176] thus] *MS*; these *A, B*
[177] on] of *MS*   [178] by the clocke] by clocke *MS*

observations out of this (how homly so ever) yet holly[179] Scripture. One, to be thankful to our Saviour[180] for his mercies[181]; the other, to be faithfull to our Soveraigne[182] for her merites.[183] We may thanke God that all these servile ceremonies, which S. Paule calleth[184] the works of the Law,[185] as Circumcision, New moones, Sabbaths, washings, cleansings, with touch not, handle not, eate not, &c. are now taken away & quite abolished by the Gospell, which hath now made *Omnia munda mundis*.[186] And as S. Augustine saith, in steed of ceremonies, combersome, infinite, intollerable,[187] unpossible, hath given Sacraments, easie, few, sweete, and gracious,[188] & hath taught us in steed of hearing *Fac hoc & vives*,[189] to say now to him, *Da Domine quod jubes*.[190] Secondly, whereas it seemes you never heard this text preached on,[191] you may blesse in your soule, & pray for her Majesties so peaceable and prosperous raigne, this text being not fit for peace & a pulpit, but only for warre and a campe. And therefore though I hope we shal never have cause to heare such a Scripture preached of in England, yet those that serve in other countreys, both have and shall heare it thus applied (and that oft not without neede) viz. that though now to the cleane all things are cleane, yet stil we must have a speciall care of cleanlinesse, and wholsomnesse, even for the things here spoken of, and if for such things, how much more for rapes, thefts, murthers, blasphemies, things (as God knowes) too common in all our campes. *Ne Dominus Deus noster, qui ambulat in medio*

---

[179] holly] *MS, Lumley-Folger, Sheffield*; wholly *A, B*

[180] our Saviour] god *MS*

[181] *One . . . mercies*] Ps. 100:3–4.   [182] our Soveraigne] Her Matie *MS*

[183] *the other . . . merites*] Rom. 13:1–4; I Pet. 2:17.

[184] calleth] calls *MS*   [185] *which . . . Law*] Ga. 2:16.

[186] *Omnia . . . mundis*] Titus 1:15.   [187] intollerable] untollerable *MS*

[188] *And as . . . gracious*] Augustine expresses this idea in several places— Letters 54.1; Letter 55.35; and in his exposition of Psalm 73:2, 'Mutata sunt sacramenta; facta sunt faciliora, pauciora, salubriora, felicora' (*Corpus Christianorum* XXXIX, 1006).

[189] *Fac hoc & vives*] Luke 10:28.

[190] *Da Domine . . . jubes*] Harington is perhaps recalling Augustine's 'Da quod jubes, et jube quod vis' (*Confessions* X.29).

[191] on] of *MS*

castrorum derelinquat nos. Least the Lord our God, that walketh[192] in the midst of our tents, should forsake us. And even in the time of the sweetest peace, me thinks I could also say, here at home, that it is an unreverent thing, for Churches ordained for prayer, and church-yardes appointed for buriall, to be polluted and filed as if they were kennels & dunghils.

And I have thought sometime with my selfe, that if I were but halfe so great an officer under our most gracious Emperesse, who is indeed worthy, and onely worthie to be Trajans Mistresse, as Plinius secundus was under that Trajan; I would write for the mending of such a lothsome fault in my neighbour town of Bath (where many noble persons are oft annoyed with it) as Plinie did for Amestris. Yet[193] whie may I not by *Poetica licentia*, and by an honest & necessarie figure (in this age) called *Reprehensio*,[194] imagine my selfe for halfe an houre to be *Secundus*, and suppose some other, that perhaps at this houre is not farre from Trajans countrey, to be that worthiest Trajan?[195] For though in the English Grammer, the feminine gender is more worthie then the masculine,[196] the which rule I wish long may hold, yet[197] lest old Priscian should say I brake his head[v]

---

[v] There is a Comedy called *Priscianus vapulans*,[198] wher if one should say *ignem hanc*, *Priscian* wold cry, his head were broken.[199]

---

[192] walketh] walks *MS*   [193] *MS lacking from* Yet *to* Secundus

[194] *Reprehensio*] *i.e.*, refutation. Cf. Cicero *de Inven.* i.42.78.

[195] *and suppose . . . Trajan*] As has been recognized, this is quite clearly a commendatory reference to Essex who was one of the commanders of the expedition to Cadiz which set sail from Plymouth on June 1 and returned at the end of the first week in August (Stow, *Annales*, 1615, 3S6ᵛ–3T3ᵛ).

[196] *For though in . . .*] In order to insert a compliment to the Queen (and perhaps to offset his addressing of Essex as Trajan) Harington goes counter to the familiar tenet concerning agreement of nouns and adjectives in Latin set forth in William Lily's authorized grammar: 'Where note, that the Masculine gendre is more worthy then the Feminine, and the Feminine more worthy then the Neuter.' The example given is 'Rex & Regina beati (*A Shorte Introduction of Grammar*, 1567, Scholars' Facsimiles & Reprints, N.Y., 1945, C5).

[197] hold. Yet] *A*

[198] Published at Strasbourg in 1580, *Priscianus Vapulans* by Nicodemus Frischlin[us] (1547–90) is described on the title page as a 'Comoedia Lepida, Faceta & utilis, in qua demonstrantur soloecismi & barbarismi, qui superioribus seculis omnia artium & doctrinarium studia, quasi quodam diluvio inundarunt: scripta in laudem huius seculi.' The passage to which Harington refers occurs in IV.2.

[199] *Priscian wold . . .*] Puttenham explains this proverbial expression: 'Your

when I never came neare him, I will keepe me in this my pleasant imitation, within such an honest limitation, as shalbe free from all just reprehension, and write, in steed of *C. Pl. Secundus Traiano Imp. Salutem.*

> *Haec tibi Traiano, terraque maríque remoto,*
> *Scribit Misacmos, nulli pietate Secundus.*

" The Citie[200] of Bath (my Lord) being both poore enough "and proud enough, hath since her highnesse being there,[201] "wonderfully beautified it selfe in fine houses for victualling and "lodging, but decayes as fast in their ancient and honest trades "of merchandise and clothing: the faire Church her Highnes "gave order should be reedified, stands at a stay, and their "common sewer, which before stood in an ill place, stands now "in no place, for they have not any at all. Which for a towne so "plentifully served of water, in a countrey so well provided of "stone, in a place resorted unto so greatly (being at two times "of the yeare, as it were the pilgrimage of health to all Saints)[202]

next intollerable vice is *solecismus* or incongruitie, as when we speake false English, that is by misusing the *Grammaticall* rules to be observed in cases, genders, tenses and such like, every poore scholler knowes the fault, & cals it the breaking of *Priscians* head, for he was among the Latines a principall Grammarian' (p. 251). Cf. Tilley P595.

[200] *The Citie . . .*] This letter illustrates Harington's prolonged interest in the reparation of the Abbey Church at Bath. The site, originally devoted to a temple to Minerva and Hercules, was first used for an abbey in the eighth century; some four centuries later the Bishop of Wells translated his seat to Bath and rebuilt both the town and the abbey. During the Reformation the church, which had been rebuilt in the reign of Henry VII, was offered to the city for five hundred marks. Although the citizens declined to buy it, they showed no scruples in plundering it of the bells, glass, iron, and lead which were shipped to Spain; the despoiled property passed into private hands. However, in 1572 Edmund Colthurst, then the owner, granted the church described in letters patent as 'totam illam ecclesiam ruinosam sive templum ruinosum' to the City of Bath. And in 1583 the 'ruinated church,' partially rebuilt, became a parish church. As late as 1610 Harington was still soliciting funds for its renovation. (See *NA*, II, 132–42; *The Municipal Records of Bath*, ed. King and Watts, pp. 51–3; *L&E*, pp. 141–2.)

[201] *hath . . . there*] The Queen visited Bath in 1574 and in 1592 (*Municipal Records*, p. 38 and Nichols, *Progresses*, III, 250).

[202] *being at . . . Saints*] Camden refers to the biannual visits to Bath: 'This Citie hath flourished as well by clothing, as by reason of usuall concourse thither for health twice every yeere' (*Britain*, V3). In an epigram, '*To* Leda,' Harington again describes Bath as 'the pilgrimage of Saints' (*L&E*, p. 231).

"me thinke seemeth an unworthie and dishonorable thing,
"wherfore if your Lordship would authorise me, or some wiser
"then me, to take a strict account of the money, by her
"Majesties gracious graunt gathered and to be gathered, which
"in the opinion of manie, cannot be lesse then ten thousand
"pounds (though not to wrong them, I thinke they have
"bestowed upon the point of 10000. pounds abating but one
"cipher) I would not doubt, of a ruinate church to make a
"reverent church, and of an unsavorie town a most sweet
"town.

"   This I do the rather write, because your Lordship, and the
"rest of her Majesties most honorable counsel, thought me once
"worthie to be Steward of that towne, but that the wiser counsel
"of the town thought it not meet, out of a deeper reach, lest
"being already their pore neighbor, this increase might have
"made my estate too great among them.[203] For indeed the fee
"belonging to it, & some other commodities annexed, might
"have bin worth to me *de claro*[204] *viis & modis, per annum.*
"*CCCC lxxx.d.*

"   Moreover I am to certifie your Lordship, that the spring
"taken out of the hot bath into the private, doth not annoy or
"prejudice the vertue of the hote bath, as her Majestie hath
"bene lately enformed. And it is not unnecessarie, for some
"honorable persons that come thither, somtimes to have such

---

[203] *This I do ... them*] On 29 May 1593 the Privy Council directed the
mayor and aldermen of Bath 'to elect Mr. John Harrington of ———— in the
countie of Sommerset, esquior, Steward of that towne, the place being presentlie
void and in their guift' (*APC*, XXIV, 266).
    Although Harington was not elected, his interest in the reparation of the
church continued. Writing in 1608, he describes the progress of the renovation:
'Collections have bene made over all England, with which the chauncell is
covered with blew slate, and an alms-house built, *ex abundantia*; but the whole
body of the church stands bare, *ex humilitate*. The rest of the money never
comming to the townsmens hands, is laid up (as I suppose) with the money
collected for Paul's steeple, which I leave to a *melius inquirendum*. And thus the
church lies still, like the poore traveller mentioned in the 10. of Luke, spoiled
and wounded by theeves' (*NA*, II, 142–3). Camden likewise refers to the money
that had been collected throughout England for this project, which owing to the
'late avarice of some' had been 'craftily conveied ... another way' (*Britain*,
V2ᵛ).

[204] *claro*] 'In re pecuniaria vocant id, quod, solutis debitis, reliquum est'
(Du Cange, *Glossarium Mediae et Infimae Latinitatis*, 1954).

"a private bath.[205] But now I pray you let us hearken to the
Scripture, for the Bibler is not yet come to *Tu autem*.[206]

I find also in the second and third chapters of[207] Nehemias,
which some call the second booke of Esdras,[208] where he telles
how no bodie but he and his asse went to survey the citie.
*Et ingressus sum ad portam vallis nocte, & ante fontem draconis,
& ad portam stercoris, & considerabam murum Ierusalem
dissipatum, & portas eius consumptas igni.* And in the third
chapter shewing who repaired all the ruines, *Et portam vallis
aedificavit Hanum & habitatores Zanoe, ipsi aedificaverunt eam,
& statuerunt valvas eius, & seras, & vectes, & mille cubitos in
muro usque ad portam sterquilinii. Et portam sterquilinii aedificavit Melchias filius Rhecab princeps &c.* And the gate of the
valley built Hanum & the inhabitants of Zanoe, they built it,
and they made the leaves of the gate, and the lockes, and the
hinges, and a thousand cubites in the wall, even to the doung
gate, and Melchias sonne of Rhecab being prince of Betha-
charam built the doung gate. I would have said, save-reverence[w]

---

[w] There is a noble & learned Ladie, dowager to the Lord John Russell,[209]
that will not name love without save reverence.[210]

---

[205] *that the spring . . . bath*] The main baths were the King's Bath (private),
the Hot Bath (common), and the Cross Bath. Harrison describes the King's
Bath as 'verie faire and large, standing almost in the middle of the towne, at
the west end of the cathedrall church. It is compassed about with a verie high
stone wall, and the brims thereof are mured round about, where in be two and
thirtie arches for men and women to stand in separatlie, who being of the
gentrie for the most part, doo resort thither indifferentlie, but not in such
lascivious sort as unto other baths and hot houses of the maine, whereof some
write more a great deale than modestie should reveale, and honestie performe'
(Holinshed's *Chronicles*, 1587, I, T5ᵛ).

[206] *Tu autem*] *domine miserere nostri.* Found at the end of the office of prime
(*Breviarium Romanum*, Venice, 1570, B4). Brewer states that the words intro-
duced the final clause of a lengthy grace used at St. John's College, Cambridge
(*Dictionary of Phrase and Fable*, Philadelphia, 1894).

[207] chapter of the booke of] *MS*

[208] *which some . . . Esdras*] Nehemiah is the form adopted in the Genevan
version; the Bishops' Bible and the sixteenth-century vulgates, although
indicating both names at the beginning, use II Esdras as the running title. The
use of Nehemias was first applied by Jerome.

[209] Lady Elizabeth Russell, one of the three learned daughters of Sir Anthony
Cooke, to whom Harington had addressed a letter shortly after he penned 'this
fantasticall treatise' asking that she send a copy to Lord Burghley—her
brother-in-law (*L&E*, pp. 65–6). Lady Elizabeth's first husband had been
Sir Thomas Hoby and their eldest son, Edward, had attended Eton with
Harington; in 1574 she married John Lord Russell, heir of Francis Russell

the doung gate, but that Nehemias who was a Gentleman well brought up, and a courtier, and had bene a sewer and cupbearer to Artaxerxes, writes it as I have recited it.[211]

But now to the purpose, perhaps you will say, that this makes nothing to the present argument, that the gate is called doungate, for we have a gate in London called Dougate,[212] that with a little dash with a pen will seem to be the same gate,[213] and yet hath no great affinitie with the matter, and on[214] the other side, there is a place hath a glorious title of Queene Hive, and yet it was ordained for my Ladie *Cloacina*.[215] I grant it might be so, for so there is a parish by London called Hornsey, which is an ungracious crooked name, and yet I verily perswade me, that the most glorious or gracious streete in London hath more hornes in it somtime either visible or invisible then all the other parish.[216] But concerning the gate in Jeruselagim

---

the Second Earl of Bedford. In 1584 Lord Russell died, after which the title passed to his nephew Edward Russell who in 1594 married Lucy, the daughter of Harington's cousin Sir John Harington of Exton. See *Apologie*, p. 226.

[210] *Note not in MS.* Cf. Mercutio in *R&J*:

> weele draw thee from the mire
> Or, save your reverence, love, wherein thou stickest
> Up to the eares. . . .

$$(F_1 \text{ I.iv.41–3, with } F_4 \text{ punctuation.})$$

[211] *but that . . . it*] Neh. 1:11. The cupbearer served both as taster of the king's wine and guardian of the royal apartment; the dates of Artaxerxes I are 464–423 B.C. (*The Interpreter's Bible*, N.Y., 1954, III, 670–1).

[212] *Dougate*] One of the old watergates of the city located west of London Bridge (E. H. Sugden, *Topographical Dictionary*, Manchester, 1925, p. 157).

[213] *that with a . . . gate*] *i.e.*, in accordance with the regular practice of the Elizabethans of putting a straight mark (or tilde) over a vowel to indicate the omission of the following *n*.

[214] on] of *MS*

[215] *Queene Hive . . . Cloacina*] Or Queenhithe, the name of a ward and also a quay located on the north bank of the Thames, a little west of Southwark Bridge, in which was 'a common Way to a common Jakes' (Stow, *A Survey of the Cities of London and Westminster*, ed. J. Strype, London, 1754, I, 26; 700).

[216] *or gracious streete . . . parish*] The street, running between Cornhill and Eastcheap, took its name from the parish church 'called Grasse Church, of the Herbe market there kept'; the street was filled with 'many faire houses for Marchants, and artificers, and many fayre Innes for travellers' (Stow, ed. C. L. Kingsford, Oxford, 1908, I, 213; 175).
This is clearly a scandalous allusion. Cf. the *Ulysses*: 'Why into Gracious street? Because of al streets in London you have thought this the best market to make proclamation of cuckoldry. Now sir what *John* of himself, or *John* by constraint know you there that hath inheritance in Cornhil, whom you so pretilie intitle to Hornden? Mum budget not a worde' (E8).

called *Porta Stercoris*, I find it was so called, because it lay on the East side of the Citie, toward the brooke Cedron, whither all the raine water of the Citie, and all other conveyances ran, as they do out of the city of London into the Thames: and that being so, and the City so populous, the gate might well be called *Porta Stercoris*.[217] Now without the Citie I find mentioned another place ordained for the like purpose, to carrie out all such filth as the raine could not wash away, and had no common passage, and that was the valley of Hinnon, which seemes by the map to lye Southeast and by South to the Temple, and thither, I say, the Scavengers caried their loding, as they do at London[x] beyond Golding lane.[218] And therefore in the new Testament it is called *gehenna*, and taken for hell, and if you have a mind to know how I come by this divinitie, trust me if you will, I come by it as true men come by their goods. For so it is, that not long since there dwelt in Bath a schoole-maister, a man whom I favoured much, for his sake that sent him thither.[220] But he had not bene there long, but

---

[x] The Brickils.[219]

---

[217] *But concerning . . . Stercoris*] Harington's information here and for what follows seems to be derived from the *Theatrum Terrae Sanctae et Biblicarum Historiarum* of Christian Adrichomius (1533–85). The section giving the historical and topographical account of the city of Jerusalem was translated by Thomas Tymme as *A Briefe Description of Hierusalem and of the Suburbs therof, as it florished in the time of Christ*; this appeared in 1595, enriched with a 'lively and beawtifull mappe.'

Adrichomius locates the *Porta Stercoris* to the east: 'THE DOUNG GATE, on the east side of the cittie, toward the corner gate, on the north-east, caried all the doung and filth of the cittie which the raine gathered together, into the brooke *Cedron*. Where upon it was rightly called the doung gate' (Tymme, K4ᵛ).

Modern scholarship places the Dung Gate on the southwest side of the city (L. H. Grollenberg, *Atlas of the Bible*, tr. and ed. J. M. H. Reid and H. H. Rowley, London, 1956).

[218] beyond Golding lane] to yᵉ Leastalls of yᵉ citty *MS*; *Golding lane*] A street running north from the east end of Barbican, opposite Red Cross Street, to Old Street (Sugden, p. 226).

[219] *not in MS*

[220] *For so it is . . . thither*] The reference is to Alexander Hume, M.A. (from St. Andrews; incorporated in Oxford 1581, Wood, *Fasti Oxon.*, ed. Bliss, London, 1815, I, 217), about whom little is known other than that he wrote some schoolboy grammars and two works on religious topics, all of which were published in Scotland. His involvement in the dispute over Christ's 'descention' is established by Hume's ministerial opponent, Adam Hill, who tauntingly refers to him as 'Schoolemaister of Bath' (*The Defence of the Article: Christ descended into Hell*, 1592, I4).

a controversie arose betwixt[221] him & some preachers ther-
about,[222] among whom we have too manie that studie nothing
but the controversies, and it came after manie disputes on[223]
both sides, at last to writing and publishing of books. And the
schoole-master (though being no Preacher) wrote a booke with
this title, *that Christ descended not into hell*:[224] the verie sight of
which title, being flat contradictory to an article of the Creed,[225]

A key to the identity of the individual who had helped Hume secure his
teaching position at Bath is perhaps to be found in Hume's dedication of his
Rejoynder to Doctor Hil (1593) to the Earl of Essex.

[221] betwixt] between *MS*

[222] therabout] heerabowt *MS*   [223] on] of *MS*

[224] *But he had not . . . hell*] The general outline of the controversy, one of
several years' duration, is preserved in the published accounts of the two main
disputants: the established custom at Chippenham, Wilts., had been for certain
preachers to lecture on market days; accordingly, on 14 Feb. 1589/90, M. Wisedom, one of the local preachers, spoke against the article that Christ descended
into hell; this stirred the vicar of Chippenham to an immediate protest and the
promise of a countering attack the following week, which was duly delivered.
However, the week after (28 Feb.) when it was M. Wisedom's turn to answer
the vicar, his place was taken by M. Hill being nearby 'by accident, or of set
purpose' who concluded his sermon in defence of the article with a challenge to
any of the learned to confute him. Alexander Hume thereupon wrote an answer
in Latin which, with due moderation, he did not send to his opponent until the
following Nov. In the meantime, however, a copy of his first draft which Hume
had translated into English for a 'freend' fell into Hill's hands, whereupon he
'fumbled' up an answer. This answer—a point by point confutation of Hume—
was published in 1592 as an addendum to the original sermon: *The Defence
of the Article: Christ descended into Hell*.

Hume followed with his *Rejoynder to Doctor Hil*, containing his original
comments and Hill's confutation of them which Hume, in turn, confuted as
'fallacies and deceits in reason' to the number of six hundred, 'and yet not half
reckoned.' This publication stirred the authorities to action, and in Dec. 1594
'one barrell and ii firkins of bookes of ALEXANDER HUMES Doing of
CHRISTES Descention into hell' were, according to warrant, seized from a
ship 'that came forth of Scotland' and delivered into the hands of Dr. Bancroft
at Lambeth Palace (*S.R.*, II, 40).

[225] *the verie . . . Creed*] The controversial article 'descendit ad inferos,'
although not found in earlier Western creeds, was introduced into the Roman
symbol sometime after the fifth century. Vividly set forth in the apocryphal
Gospel of Nicodemus, the descent was a traditional part of church doctrine
until the Reformation. In England this article which had been approved by the
Convocation of 1553 appeared with a slight omission in the Thirty-Nine Articles
(Latin—1563; English—1571), and it was of course familiar to all through the
Edwardian and Elizabethan Prayer Books (Philip Schaff, *The Creeds of Christen-
dom*, 6th ed., N.Y., 1931, I, 615–6; II, 46; III, 487–514). Its lack of precise
scriptural authority led to a variety of interpretations and debates; these
centred not only on the meaning of the Greek *hades* and *gehenna* and the

I remember I said of the man as Heywood saith in his
proverbes, that hereafter

> *He might be of my Pater noster indeed,*
> *But sure he should never come in my Creed.*[226]

And therefore I might repute him as a good humanist, but I
should ever doubt him for a good devine. Now as I say,
hearing in these disputes & sermons, diverse names of hell
throughly sifted, as[227] *Ades, Tartaros, Infernum, Stagnum*
ardens, and last of all *Gehenna,* which last I was most used to,
as having an old verse when I was at Eaton, of a peacocke:[228]

> *Angelus in penna, pede latro, voce gehenna.*
>
> *A bird that hath an Angels plume,*
> *A theevish pace, a hellish tune.*

Consequently, I observed, that our honest and learned preacher
of Bath M. R. M.[229] first proved hell to be a locall place (if not
circumscriptivè,[230] yet at least *definitivè*).[231] Then he shewed

---

Hebrew *sheol* (interpreted variously as 'abode of the dead,' 'place of the damned,'
'the grave,' 'torments of the soul,' etc.) but also on the motivation for Christ's
descent. From 1560 on, the controversy was pursued in an endless series of
sermons, expositions, and defences with the various Protestant factions ranged
in opposition to the official Anglican doctrine. For a summary of the conflicting
views preserved among Burghley's papers, see Strype, *The Life and Acts of*
John Whitgift (London, 1882), II, 364–7.

That Harington maintained both an interest in the question and his present
view is shown by his remarks on the subject some twelve years later (*NA,*
II, 101–3; 201–2).

[226] *as Heywood . . . Creed*] Cited with slight modification from *A dialogue*
conteynyng . . . proverbs, Pt. II, Ch. 9, 195–6. Heywood expanded it into a
four-line epigram in *Three hundred Epigrammes,* No. 118.

[227] sifted. As *A*   [228] peacocke. *A*

[229] *our honest . . . M. R. M*] 'Mᵣ Meri- / dith'—Harington annotation in the
Lumley-Folger copy. In 1584 Master Richard Meredith (he was not granted
a B.D. degree until 1606) was presented the living of the parish church of
SS. Peter and Paul, Bath. However, in 1590 he demised to the mayor, aldermen,
and citizens the rectory of the church with all tithes, payments, and appur-
tenances thereto belonging (reserving to himself the parsonage house within the
city with its barn, garden, and orchard) at a rent of £52 (*Municipal Records,*
p. 54 and Appendix A, xxvi). The only sermons of Meredith's extant appear
to be two preached before King James in 1606/07. In 1607 he was appointed
King's Chaplain and Dean of Wells.

[230] circumscriptive *MS, B*   [231] definitivè, *A,* definitive. *MS, B*

the etymologie of the word *gehenna* to be derived in Greek of
γῆ καὶ ὶννόν[232] that is, the earth or valley of Hinnon: then he
told, that this place was as it were the common dunghil or
mickson of the whole towne, that the Jewes[233] had used in this
valley, to make their children passe through the fire, as a
sacrifice to the Devill, according to the Psalme of David, *they
offred their sonnes and daughters unto devils.*[234] Finally, that our
Saviour to make a more fearefull impression in their hearts, of
the paines of hell indeed, which they knew not, used the name
of this hellish place,[235] which they knew that had in it these
hatefull hellish properties, smoke, stinke, horrible cries, &
torment. But least you should thinke I speake as a parrot,
nothing but what I have heard an other say, let me adde
somewhat of mine owne poore reading, and that shall be this,
that this valley of Hinnon was once for the sweete ayre, fine
groves, faire walkes, and greene and pleasant fields, comparable
with anie place about Jerusalem,[236] but when the obhominable
Idoll of Moloch[237] was erected in it, whose purtraiture was like

---

[232] γη και ιννον A. The Greek *gehenna*, the fiery hell or place of future
punishment, literally means the 'valley of Hinnon.' A ravine stretching southwest of Jerusalem, it was the site where the Israelites worshipping Moloch
caused their children to pass through the fire. According to a medieval Jewish
commentator on the Psalms (Kimchi, c. A.D. 1200), it later became the dumping
ground for the refuse of the city. The fire which burned there constantly and
the worms which fed on the refuse became symbolic of the torments inflicted
on the wicked. Hence in later Jewish literature, gehenna became the popular
name for the place of future punishment. Although in the N.T., *gehenna* was
carefully distinguished from *hades* (O.T. *sheol*), this distinction was not
preserved in the English translation, thus partially accounting for the controversies concerning the descent of Christ into hell (Orchard *et al.*, *A Catholic
Commentary on Holy Scripture*, London, 1953, 920, and *The Interpreter's Bible*,
VIII, 222).

[233] Jewes] Idolatrows Jews *MS*   [234] *Psalme . . . devils*] 106:35.

[235] *Finally . . . place*] Matt. 5:22.

[236] *let me . . . Jerusalem*] Cf. Augustine's description, 'Comm. in Evangelium
Matthei,' I, x.

[237] *but when . . . Moloch*] Adrichomius describes Moloch: 'the greatest
abhomination and moste hated unto God. . . . It was an Idoll the matter whereof
was brasse; made in the likenesse and similitude of a king, it was hollow within,
and had a head like to the head of a Calfe, the other partes or members of the
body having the shape and fashion of a man, the armes whereof were stretched
out' (Tymme, L3ᵛ).
   The worship of Moloch, a wide-spread cult in the Semitic East characterized
by child sacrifice, was introduced to the Israelites by Solomon (I Kings 11:7)
and continued uninterruptedly until the reformation of Josiah (II Kings 23)
(*The Interpreter's Bible*, III, 323, and below).

a king having the head of a calfe, all of brasse, & hollow within:
unto which (most inhumanely) they sacrificed humane flesh,
yea their owne children, and to the end that the wicked parents
might not feele remorse of the wofull cries of the wretched
children, they daunced a strange medley about the fire, having
musicke sutable to such mirth, of drummes and Jewes harpes[238]
(for I thinke hornepipes and bag-pipes were not then found out)
I say these abhominations being there committed, the good
Josias,[239] driven to use an extreme medicine to so extreme a
maladie, first burned & brake all to peeces the horrible Idoll,
and then in detestation of the abuses there committed, cut
downe the fine groves, tare up the sweet pastures, defaced the
pleasant walks; and to the end that all passengers should flie
from it, that were wont to frequent it, he caused all filthie
carrion, dead dogs and horses, all the filth of the streetes, and
whatsoever hatefull and ugly things could be imagined, to be
caried thither. And this ô Josias was thy zelous reformation:
but alas how little do some that pretend thy name, participate
thy nature.[y] They pull downe Moloch, but set up Baal

---

[y] A reverend Bishop told me, that the Brownistes have written a book called
Josias reformation, to this zealous purpose.[240]

---

[238] *and to . . . harpes*] 'Amiddest these horrible tormentes where with they
were thus tormented, the miserable Clamor of the children could in no wise bee
heard, whereby the parentes mighte in any sorte bee moved to pittie or com-
passion, for that the priestes of this Idole *Moloch*, during the whole time of the
sacrifice, did usually make an exceeding greate noise both with the trumpettes
and drums' (Tymme, L4).

[239] *the good Josias . . .*] 'The which detestable madnesse, the godly kinge
Josias seeking at the length to redresse, brake in peeces the image of *Moloch*,
cut downe his Groves, and defiled the place thereof with the filthinesse of dead
Carcasses, of bones, and of other uncleane thinges, and appointed it to bee a
perpetuall dunghil for ever' (Tymme, L4).
See II Kings 23 and II Chronicles 34:3–7.

[240] *om. B. The Reformation of Religion by Josiah* (STC: 14815), an octavo
consisting of thirteen leaves, appeared without imprint in ?1590 (entered to
T. Man 22 June 1590). Its intent was to inspire the Queen and all who wished
to reform to follow the example of Josias, who at the age of twenty had thrown
down the 'monuments of Idolatrie,' whereas the church and people of England
despite thirty-two years' delivery out of 'Romish Egipt' were still living in a
woeful spiritual state (*passim*).
Whether the author of *Josiah's Reformation* was actually a Brownist is not
clear from the work itself, since he seems to dissent from a separatist doctrine.
However, the growing strength of the movement appeared sufficiently menacing
for the government to introduce a severe anti-Brownist bill in the Parliament of

Peor[241] & Beelsebub, their leane devotion thinkes the hill of the
Lord is too fat, their envious eye serves them like Aretinoes
spectacles,[242] to make all seeme bigger then it should be,
they learne the Babylonians song in the Psalmes.

> Downe, downe with it at any hand,
> Make all thing plaine, let nothing stand.[243]

They care neither for good letters nor good lives, but onely out
of the spoiles to get good livings, our good Lord Bishops must
be made poore Superintendents, that they might superintend
the goodly Lordships of the[244] rich Bishopricks, & then we
that be simple fellowes, must beleeve, that they offer us Josias
reformation, whereas indeed it savors not of that in any thing
but the ill savour: for as Josias defaced a faire field, and made it
spurcitiarum latrinam, so they would ruinate our cathedrall
churches, and make them *Speluncam*[245] *latronum,*[246] as my

---

1592/93, thus occasioning Raleigh's statement that there were nearly 20,000
Brownists in England (M. M. Knappen, *Tudor Puritanism,* Chicago, 1939,
303–15). The figure of 20,000 derives from D'Ewes *Compleat Journal* (1693),
p. 517, but cf. J. E. Neale's *Elizabeth I and Her Parliaments 1584–1601,* London,
1957, p. 289, where the figure attributed to Raleigh is 10–12,000. No source is
given.

[241] *Baal Peor*] An idolatrous god worshipped by the Israelites. See Num.
25:1–9.

[242] *Aretinoes spectacles*] I have not traced this.

[243] *Downe . . . stand*] These two lines with slight modification appear in the
Countess of Pembroke's translation of Ps. 137 preserved by Harington in his
collection of poems (*NA,* II, 407–8). Harington made his own translation of the
same psalm in briefer compass sometime before 19 Dec. 1600, when he sent a
copy of the Countess of Pembroke's translation together with his own effort to
Lucy, Countess of Bedford (*L&E,* p. 87; *NA,* II, 406).

[244] the] *MS;* om. *A, B*   [245] Speluncam] *MS;* Spelunca *A, B*

[246] *so they . . . latronum*] See Matt. 21:13. The same charge which Harington
here levels at anti-episcopal groups was even more frequently leveled at the
nobility, both lay and spiritual. On 2 Jan. 1595, Dr. Roger Goad, Vice Chancellor
of Cambridge, wrote to Burghley complaining that one William Covel, Fellow
of Christ's College, had preached a sermon on this text and 'in applying and
inveighing against those that did *facere speluncam latronum,* in our church, did,
offensively and extraordinarily, so charge the noblemen of this land especially;
and in some sort also the bishops' (Strype, *Annals of the Reformation,* IV, 323).
    That Harington consistently opposed the spoliation of church lands and
revenues is indicated by his generous detailing to Prince Henry of specific
instances (*NA,* II, *passim*).

good friend Harry-Osto, or mine Host Hary saith of the pagan Rodomont, after his host had ended his knavish tale.

> He makes the Church (*oh horrible abuse*)
> Serve him for his prophane ungodly use.[247]

Wherefore let them call them selves what they list, but if they learne no better lessons of Josias, but to turne sweete fields to stinking dunghils, they shall make no new Jaxes in England by my consent, and I hope my devise shall serve to mend manie that be now amisse, with an honester and easier reformation, and I doubt not but the Magistrate that hath charge to see *ne quid respub. detrimenti capiat*, will provide, lest our receipts prove deceipts, our auditors frauditors, and our reformation deformation, and so all run headlong to gehenna, where the sport will be torment, the musicke clamors, the prospect smoke, and the perfume stinke. Which two last, I mean smoke & stinke,[z] I have verily perswaded me, are two of those paines of hell, which they call *poena sensus*[249]: which paine S. Augustine[250] affirmes may also torment aerie or spirituall bodies, as partly appears in the story of Tobias,[251] where a wicked spirit was driven away with the smoke of a broyled liver; & therefore I have endevored in my poore buildings to avoid those two inconveniences as much as I may. As for the two other annoyances, that the old proverbe joyneth to one of these, saying, there are three things that make a man weary of his house, a smoking chimney, a dropping eves, and a brauling woman.[252] I would no lesse willingly avoid them, but when stormes come, I must as my neighbours do, beare that with patience, which[253]

---

[z] Esa. cap. 3. *Et erit pro suavi odore foetor.*[248]

---

[247] *He . . . use*] '28 Canto / of Ariosto / Stan. 89,' Harington annotation in the Lumley-Folger copy.   [248] Isa. 3:24.

[249] *poena sensus*] The established theological divisions of punishment were *poena sensus* and *poena damni*: 'grief for that we feel, or for that we forego' (Launcelot Andrewes, 'Of the Passion,' *Ninety-Six Sermons*, Oxford, 1841, II, 143). Harington has a number of admiring references to 'learned *Androes*,' *L&E*, pp. 285; 272; *NA*, II, 189–95.

[250] Augnstine *A*; *de Civitate Dei*, Bk. XXI, ch. 10.

[251] *as partly . . . Tobias*] See Tobias 5–8.

[252] *a smoking . . . woman*] Tilley H781 and S574.   [253] which] *not in MS*

I can not reforme with choler, & learne of the good Socrates, who when Xantippe had crowned him with a chamber-pot, he bare it off single with his head and shoulders, & said to such as laughed at him for it.

> *It never yet was deemd a wonder,*
> *To see that raine should follow thunder.*[254]

And to the intent you may see, that I am not only groundedly studied in the reformation of A Jax, which I have chosen for the project of this discourse, but that I am also superficially seene in these three other matters of shrewd importance to all good house-keepers, I wil not be dangerous[255] of my cunning, but I will venter my pen and my paines, if you will lend but your eyes or your eares,[256] though I perhaps shall have more fistes about my eares then mine owne for it. First therefore for the house, I will teach you a verse for it, that I thinke M. Tusser taught me, or else now I may teach it his sonne.[257]

> *To keepe your house dry, you must alwayes in sommer*
> *Give money to the mason, the tiler and plummer.*

For the shrewd wife, reade the booke of taming a shrew,[258] which hath made a number of us so perfect, that now every one can rule a shrew in our countrey, save he that hath her.[259]

---

[254] *It . . . thunder*] This anecdote derives from Diogenes Laertius 'Socrates' ii.36 and was frequently cited in the sixteenth century (*e.g.*, Erasmus, *Apophthegmes*, Ci[v] and 'Mery Tales, Wittie Questions and Quicke Answeres,' No. 49 in *Shakespeare Jest-Books*, I, 65).   [255] *dangerous*] Chary.

[256] *lend . . . eares*] Cf. Tilley E18. Harington's example antedates those listed.

[257] *that I thinke . . . sonne*] Cf. Tusser's advice for June:

> Thy houses and barns would be looked upon,
>   and all things amended, ere harvest come on:
> Things thus set in order, in quiet and rest,
>   shall further thy harvest, and pleasure thee best.

(*His Good Points of Husbandry*, ed. Dorothy Hartley, London, 1931, p. 76.)

[258] *reade . . . shrew*] *A Pleasant Conceited Historie, called The taming of a Shrew* was printed by Peter Short in 1594 and again in 1596, 'As it was sundry times acted by the *Right honorable the Earle of Pembrook his servants*' (W. W. Greg, *A Bibliography of the English Printed Drama to the Restoration*, Oxford, 1939, I, 120). This is one of the plays included in Harington's collection (*N&Q*, s. 7, IX, [1890], 382–3).   [259] *that now . . . her*] Tilley M106

But indeed there are but two good rules. One is, let them never have their willes; the other differs but a letter, let them ever have their willes,²⁶⁰ the first is the wiser, but the second is more²⁶¹ in request, and therfore I make choice of it.

Lastly for smoking chimneys, manie remedies have bene studied, but one excellent and infallible way is found out

among some of the great Architectes of this age, namely to make no fire in them, and by the same rule they may have very sweet Jaxes too.ᵃᵃ But the best way I have found, is out of Cardan²⁶² partly, but as I thinke mended by practise of some of my neighbours of Bath: who make things like a halfe cloke²⁶³ about the toppes of the chimneys, with a fane to

---

ᵃᵃ One taught an excellent rule to keepe a chimnie from smoking, & a privie from stinking, viz. to make your fire in your privie, and to set the close stoole in the chimney.

---

²⁶⁰ *One is . . . willes*] Harington expressed this idea in an epigram addressed to his mother-in-law, '*An infallible rule to rule a wife*' (*L&E*, p. 199).

²⁶¹ more] most *MS*

²⁶² *But the best . . . Cardan*] Girolamo Cardano (1501–76) offers the ingenious idea of constructing a chimney equipped with eight conduits or 'canales' to counter winds from any direction, and in order to ensure safety he encloses the top of the chimney in a sheath. There is a cut of the device in Cardano's text (*De Subtilitate Libri XXI*, Lyons, 1559, D2ᵛ).

²⁶³ a halfe] *MS*; halfe a *A, B*

turn round with the winde, which because they make of wood, is dangerous for fire, but being made of thinne[264] copper plates, or of old kettels will be as light and without all[265] daunger, but this is supererogation, and more than I promised you. But now to come home againe, though home be never so homely, the fourth annoyance though it be left out of the proverbe, may compare with two of the other three, which is a stinking privie, which makes a man wish sometime, save for an ornament of the face (as Heywood saith) to have no nose.

> *Most of our savours be more soure then sweet,*
> *A nose then or no nose, which is most meet ?*[266]

And for reformation of this, manie I doubt not, have ere this beaten their braines and strained verie hard, to have found out some remedie, but yet still I find all my good friendes houses greatly annoyed with it.

But yet ere I come to discover this exact & exquisite forme that I have promised, let me adde a word or two out of the good and wholsome rules of physick, both for authorising the homely wordes so oft used, as for proving that the matter in their facultie is specially regarded; for diverse, that are otherwise very daintie and curious, yet for their healths sake, will endure both to heare homely language, to see sluttish sights, to tast dirtie drugs, and to shew secret sores; according to the Italian proverbe,

> *All confessore medico & advocato,*
> *Non deve tener cosa celato.*[267]
> *From your confessor, lawyer, & phisition,*
> *Hide not your case on no condition.*[268]

No man therefore is either so ignorant, or so impudent, as either not to know or not to confesse, that the honourable

---

[264] of thinne] thinne of *B* [265] all] *MS*; *om. A, B*

[266] *Most . . . meet*] The last two lines of Heywood's epigram 'Of a nose' with slight modification, *The firste hundred of Epigrammes*, No. 31.

[267] *All . . . celato*] Florio in his *Giardino di Ricreatione* gives an abbreviated version: 'Al medico, & avvocato, non tener' il ver celato' (*Second Frutes, to which is annexed his Gardine of Recreation*, 1591, B1).

[268] *From . . . condition*] Tilley P261.

science of physicke, embaseth it selfe oft-times about the care of this businesse. For whereto serveth[269] I pray you, *fiant clysteria, fiant pillulae,*[270] *fiant potiones, fiant pessi.* But fye on't, it makes me almost sick to talke of them, sure I am the house I treat of, is as it were the center to which they must all fall first or last, and many times I thinke first were wholesomer of the two. But to enforce my proofes, though shortly yet soundly, I will not bring any peculiar prescripts out of Galen and Hipocrates, least you should oppose against them Asclepiades[271] or Paracelsus, nor stand long to dilate of the Empiricall physicke, or the dogmaticall and the methodicall.[272] Of all which if I should say all I could, I feare me not so much, that Physitions wold take me for a foole, as that fooles will take me for a Physition.[273] I will therefore set downe as it were certaine autenticall rules, out of a provinciall[274] Councell of Physitions, and that sent by common consent to a great King of England,[275] against which if any Doctor should except, he

---

[269] serveth] sarves *MS*   [270] *pillulae*] Late Latin form of 'pilula.'

[271] *Asclepiades*] Fl. second century A.D. Called, according to Pliny, the 'Cold-water Physician': 'hee withdrew mens minds from the opinion they had of former practise, and overthrew all . . . bearing men in hand, that there were but five principall remedies which served indifferently for all diseases' (*The Historie of the World*, tr. Philemon Holland, 1601, Tome II, Y2).

[272] *the Empiricall . . . methodicall*] Agrippa mentions among the various medical sects the 'Dogmaticall' (also called the 'Rationall' or 'Sophisticall'), approved by Hippocrates and later by Galen, 'who following Hippocrates more then others reduced the whole Arte of Phisicke to the knowledge of causes. . . .' Another sect 'altogeather gainefull and servill' was divided into the 'Empericall' and 'Methodicall,' the Empirical consisting, in practice, 'of experimentes' while the Methodical was a reduction of this method to certain set rules, such as those followed by Aesclepiades (tr. Sanford, 1569, 2N4–2N4ᵛ).

[273] *I feare . . . Physition*] Playing on the proverb 'Every man is either a fool or a physician.' See Tilley M125 and p. 124 above.

[274] provinciall] *Lumley-Folger*; generall *MS, A, B*

[275] *Councell . . . England*] This was the *Schola Salernitana* or *Regimen Sanitatis Salernitanum*, a very popular medical poem of the Middle Ages which Harington later translated, perhaps for Prince Henry. Setting forth simple precepts for the preservation of health, the work was described by Arnald of Villanova, its earliest commentator (d. 1313), as a composite effort of the physicians of Salerno. It was written according to tradition for Robert, Duke of Normandy, the eldest son of William the Conqueror. Although Robert never became king of England *de facto*, his hereditary claim to the crown and the fact that on his return from the siege of Jerusalem he spent a year in Salerno under-going treatment for a fistulous wound have been used to support the traditional view. However, the traditional dating, source, and intent of the poem have

must *ipso facto* be counted an hereticke. This therfore I find of my text in that booke that begins

Anglorum regi scribit schola tota Salerni.

For when he hath bene advised to make choyce of three Physitions,

Haec tria mens laeta, requies, moderata diaeta.[276]

Doctor Diet, Doctor Quiet, & Doctor Meryman.[277] Then they admonish him of many particulars, for his health, for his food, for his house, &c. Which if they might with good maners write to a king, then I may without incivilitie recite to a kinseman.

Si vis incolumem, si vis te vivere sanum,
Curas tolle graves irasci crede profanum,
Parce mero caenato parum nec sit tibi vanum,
Surgere post epulas somnum fuge meridianum.
Nec mictum retine, nec comprime fortiter anum.[278]

The Salern schole doth by these lines impart
Health to the British king, and doth advise,
From cares thy hed to free, from wrath thy hart,
Drinke not much wine, sup light, and soone arise,
After thy meate, twixt meales keepe wake thine eyes.
And when to natures needs provokt thou art,
Do not forbeare the same in any wise:
So shalt thou live long time with litle smart.[279]

---

come under attack, and the most recent scholarship assigns the work to the latter half of the thirteenth century (*Regimen Sanitatis Salernitanum*, ed. Sir Alexander Croke, Oxford, 1830, p. 24, and Introduction to Packard and Garrison's edition, pp. 57 ff; and P. O. Kristeller, 'The School of Salerno,' *Bulletin of the History of Medicine* XVII, 1945, 138–94).

The existence of many and varied MSS of the text, ranging in length from some three hundred to two thousand lines, as well as the numerous printed editions and translations attest to its popularity during the Middle Ages, the Renaissance, and the seventeenth century.

[276] diaeta] *Markham-Wrenn*; diet *A*

[277] *Doctor . . . Meryman*] Tilley D427.   [278] anum. *& A*

[279] *The Salern . . .*] Harington's translation here of the opening lines varies slightly from his 1607 version where he uses a stanza form riming abababccdd (Packard and Garrison reprint, p. 75).

Lo what a speciall lesson for health they teach, to take your oportunitie so[280] oft as it is offered of going to those businesses. Then soone after to let you know how wholsome it is to breake wind, they tell foure diseases that come by forbearing it.

> *Quatuor ex vento veniunt in ventre retento,*
> *Spasmus, hydrops, colica, vertigo, quatuor ista.*[281]

But most especially making for my purpose, both for word and matter.

> *Aer sit mundus, habitabilis ac luminosus,*
> *Infectus neque sit, nec olens foetore cloacae.*

Which as a principall lesson, to be learned by builders, I will set downe in verse.

> *A builder that will follow wise direction,*
> *Must first foresee before his house he makes,*
> *That th' aire be cleare, and free from all infection,*
> *And not annoyd with stinch of any Jakes.*[282]

For indeede let your house be never so well apparelled, never so well plaistered and painted, if she have a stinking breath I shall never like of my lodging. Lastly, there be two other verses, with which I will end these schoole authorities.

> *Multiplicant mictum, ventrem dant aescula strictum,*
> *Post pyra da potum, post pomum vade cacatum.*[283]

---

[280] so] as *MS*

[281] *Quatuor . . . ista*]

> Great harmes have growne, & maladies exceeding,
> By keeping in a little blast of wind:
> So *Cramps* & *Dropsies, Collickes* have their breeding,
> And *Mazed Braines* for want of vent behind.   (*Ibid.*, p. 79.)

[282] *A builder . . .*] See *School of Salernum*, p. 87 for considerable variation in the rendering.

[283] *Multiplicant . . . cacatum*] Characteristically, Harington juxtaposes two disparate lines of the original. His advice in 1607 on eating medlars—the small apple-like fruit of the *Mespila Germanica* eaten when excessively ripe—was as follows:

> Eate *Medlers*, if you have a loosenesse gotten,
> They bind, and yet your urine they augment,
> They have one name more fit to be forgotten,
> While hard and sound they be, they be not spent,
> Good *Medlers* are not ripe, till seeming rotten,
> For medling much with *Medlers* some are shent.   (P.102)

And thus I take it, I end this part of my discourse, with a well chosen verse to the purpose: yet ere you go, take this with you in prose, that many Physitions doe hold, that the plague, the measels, the hemorhoids,[284] the small poxe, & perhaps the great ones too,[285] with the *fistula in ano,* and many of those inward diseases, are no way sooner gotten, then by the savour of others excrements, upon unwholsome privies. Wherefore I will now draw to the conclusion of this same tedious discourse: for it is high time now to take away the boord, and I see you are almost full of our homely fare, and perhaps you have bene used to your dainties of *Potatoes,* of *Caveare, Oringos,*[286] *plums of Genowa,*[287] all which may well increase your appetite to severall evacuations, we will therefore now (according to the phisicke we learned even now) rise & stretch our legges a litle, and anon I will put on my boots, and go a peece of the way with you, and discourse of the rest: in the meane time my self wil go perhaps to the house we talk off, though maners would, I offred you the French curtesie, to go with me to the place, where a man might verie kindly finish this discourse.

THE THIRD SECTION,

shewing the forme, and how it *may be reformed.*

Nowe therefore to come where wee left last, for I know you would fain have your enstructions ere you go home, as soon as I have given my horse some breath up this hill, I will ride along

---

Shakespeare likewise alludes to the popular name that 'maids call medlars when they laugh alone.' (*R&J,* ii.1.36.)
Harington's advice on eating pears and apples:

> Drinke after Peares, take after Apples order
> To have a place to purge your selfe of ordure.

(P. 100)

[284] hemorhoids] emralds *MS*

[285] *the great ones too*] 'The Great Pox; *Il mal Francese;* La verole; le mal de Naples; *Las bubas*' (James Howell, *Lexicon Tetraglotton,* London, 1650, 7D2).

[286] Oringos] *MS;* Caveare Eringus *A, B. Potatoes . . . Oringos*] Regarded as aphrodisiacs. Cf. Harington's epigram '*Against an old Lecher*' where he gives the same list (*L&E,* p. 244).
Oringos] The candied root of the sea holly.

[287] *plums of Genowa*] I am unable to explain this; but cf. Nashe's use of 'plum tree' (*Works,* iii, 113, and McKerrow's note iv, 359).

with you, so you will ride a sober pace: for I love not to ride with these goose chasing youthes, that post still to their journeys end, and when they come thither, they cannot remember what businesse they have there, but that they had even as much in the place they came from.

These inconveniences being so great, and the greater because so generall, if there be a way with litle cost, with much cleanlinesse, with great facilitie, & some pleasure to avoyd them, were it not rather a sinne to conceale it, then a shame to utter it? Wherefore shame to them that shame thinke,[1] for I will confesse frankly to you, both how much I was troubled with the annoyance, & what I have found for the remedie. For when I found not onely in mine owne poore confused cottage, but even in the goodliest & stateliest pallaces of this realme, nowithstanding all our provisions of vaults, of sluces, of grates, of paines of poore folkes in sweeping and scouring, yet still this same whorson sawcie stinke, though he were commanded on paine of death not to come within the gates, yet would spite of our noses, even when we would gladliest have spared his company, prease to the faire Ladies chambers. I began to conceive such a malice against all the race of him, that I vowed to be at deadly fewd with them, till I had brought some of the chiefest of them to utter confusion. And conferring some principles of Philosophy[a] I had read, and some conveyances of architecture I had seen, with some devises of others I had heard, and some practises of mine owne I had payed for:[3] I found out at last this way that is after described, & a marvellous easie and cheape way it is, and I dare speake it upon my credit, not without good experience, that though it be neither farre fetched, nor deare bought, yet it is good for Ladies, & there be few houses that may not have the benefite of it. For there be few great & well contrived houses, but have vaults and secret passages made under ground, to convey away both the ordure & other noisome things, as also the raine water that falles into[4] the courts, which being cleanly in respect of the eye, yet because

---

[a] The principles ar these, *Aer non penetrat aquam. Natura non patitur vacuum.*[2]

---

[1] *shame . . . thinke*] Tilley S277.   [2] *Note not in MS*

[3] *for. A*   [4] *into*] in *MS*

they must of force have many vents, they are oft noisome in regard of the smell. Specially in houses of office, that stand high from the ground, the tuns[5] of them drawing up the aire as a chimney doth smoke. By which it comes to passe manie times (specially if the wind stand at the mouth of the vaults) that what with fishwater coming from the kitchins, bloud and garbage of fowle, washing of dishes, and the excrements of the other houses joyned together, and all these in moyst weather stirred a little with some small streame of raine water. For as the proverbe is,

> Tis noted as the nature of a sinke,
> Ever the more tis stird, the more to stink.[6]

I say these thus meeting together, make such a quintessence of a stinke, that if Paracelsus were alive, his art could not devise to extract a stronger.[7] Now because the most unavoidable of all these things that keepe such a stinking stirre, or such a stinke when they be stirred, is urine and ordure, that which we all carie about us (a good speculation to make us remember what we are, and whither we must) therefore as I sayd before, many have devised remedies for this in times past, some not many yeares since, and I this last yeare, of all which I will make choice onely of two beside mine owne to speake off, because men of good judgement have allowed them for good, but yet (as the ape doth his young ones)[8] I thinke mine the properest of them all.

The first and the ancientest, is to make a close vault in the ground, widest in the bottome, and narrower upward, and to floore the same with hot lime and tarris,[9] or some such drie

---

[5] tuns] i.e., pipes or conduits. The OED defines tun as 'a chimney pot' or 'a part of a chimney, particularly that extending above the roof' and cites this precise passage, although the reference in Harington which would properly illustrate that definition appears on p. 163.

[6] Tis . . . stink] Harington's more decorous adaptation of the common proverb: 'Res satis est nota: foetent plus stercora mota' (Binder, Novus Thesaurus Adagiorum Latinorum, 2959). Cf. Tilley T603.

[7] quintessence . . . stronger] 'The quinta essentia is that which is extracted from a substance—from all plants and from everything which has life—then freed of all impurities and all perishable parts, refined into highest purity and separated from all elements' (Paracelsus, Selected Writings, ed. J. Jacobi, tr. N. Guterman, N.Y., 1951, Bollingen Series XXVIII, 219–20).

[8] as the ape . . . ones] Tilley A270 where Harington's usage is the earliest example cited.

paving as may keepe out all water and aire also: for if it be so close as no aire can come in, it doth as it were smother the savour, like to the snuffes or extinguishers wherewith we put out a candle, and this standes with good reason, that seeing it is his nature to make the worse savour the more he is stirred, and nothing makes him keepe a more stinking stirre, then a little wind and water, surely there can be litle or no annoyance of him in this kinde of house, where he shall lye so quietly. But against this is to be objected, that if there be a little crannie in the wall as big as a straw, or if the ground stand upon winter springs or be subject as most places under ground commonly[10] are, to give with moyst weather, then at such times it must needes offend.

Besides in a Princes house where so many mouthes be fed, a close vault wil fil quickly; and that objection did my Lord of Leicester make to Sir John Young,[11] at his last being at Bristow, who commended to my Lord that fashion, and shewed him his owne of a worse fashion, & told him that at a friends[12]

---

[9] *tarris*] Variant of tarras—a kind of rock used for mortar or cement. Harington's usage is earlier than the example cited in the *OED*.

[10] commonly] *MS*; om. *A, B*

[11] *Besides . . . Young*] One such taxing situation experienced by Sir John Young 'where so many mouthes' had to be fed occurred when the Queen, attended by Leicester and others of her household, visited the city of Bristol in 1574 and lodged at Young's house from August 13 to August 21. It was during this progress that Sir John was knighted (Nichols, *Progresses* I, 393–408, and E. K. Chambers, *Elizabethan Stage*, Oxford, 1945, IV, 60–1).

[12] a friends] Mrs Penns *MS*; *that at a . . .*] Harington has annotated the Lumley-Folger copy: 'Mrs Penne.' Cf. his epigram:

> *Of casting out Spirits with fasting, without Prayer*
>
> A vertuous Dame that for her state and qualitie,
> Did ever love to keepe great Hospitalitie,
> Her name I must not name in plaine reciting,
> But thus the chiefest instrument in writing,
> Was, by Duke *Humfreys* ghests so boldly haunted,
> That her good minde thereby was shrewdly daunted.
> She sighing said one day to a carelesse Jester,
> These ill bred ghests my boord and house so pester,
> That I pray God oft times with all my heart,
> That they would leave this haunt, and hence depart:
> He that by his owne humor hap'ly ghest,
> What manner sprite these smel-feasts had possest,
>   Told her, the surest way such spirits out-casting,
>   Was, to leave prayer awhile, & fall to fasting.
>
> (*L&E*, p. 185.)

house of his[13] at Peter hill in London, there was a very sweet privie of that making.

Another way, is either upon close or open vaults, so to place the sieges or seats as behind them may rise tunnes of chimneys,[14] to draw all the ill aires upwards: of which kind I may be bold to say, that our house of Lincolnes Inne,[15] putteth[16] downe all that have bene made afore it, and is indeed both in reason and experience, a meanes to avoid much of the annoyance that is wont to come of them, and keepeth[17] the place all about much the sweeter. But yet to speake truly, this is not safe from all infection or annoyance while one is there, as my sense hath told me, for

Sensus non fallitur in proprio obiecto.[18]

Or perhaps by the strict words of the statute[19] it ought to be so, and that but two parts may be devised away, and a third

---

In the copy presented to Prince Henry, Harington has annotated this: 'Mr^s Pen. / mother to S^r / Michel Hix / and Sr Babtist / Hix' (p. 60). A reference in his 'Apologie of Poetrie' allows us to identify one of these 'ill-bred ghests' as 'Justice *Randoll* of London, a man passing impotent in body but much more in mind, that leaving behind him a thousand pounds of gold in a chest full of old boots and shoes . . . many a good meale he did take of his franke neighbour the widdow *Penne*' (*OF*, 1634, $5^v).

Cf. also the letters addressed to her by the poet Thomas Churchyard and by Sir Robert Cecil in which Cecil makes mention of her son 'Mr. Mich. Hycks' (reprinted in Thomas Wright, *Queen Elizabeth and Her Times,* London, 1838, II, 414–16; Wright mistakenly identifies Mrs. Penne as Michael Hicks's mother-in-law).

G. Moore Smith reprinted two of Churchyard's letters to her (including the one in Wright) and a letter from Mrs. Penne to the Earl of Oxford, but, following B. M. Ward, he too stated that she was the mother-in-law of Michael Hicks. However, he related Harington's epigram to the passage in the *OF* and the letter he had written to her as a ten-year-old student at Eton (*L&E*, p. 61; noting that the letter had formerly been in possession of Sir Michael Hicks, secretary to Lord Burghley, McClure simply conjectured that she had been a member of Burghley's household.) See Smith, 'Taking Lodgings in 1591,' *RES*, VIII, 1932, 447–50, cited in Nashe, Supplement, V, 23.

[13] of his] *not in MS*   [14] *tunnes of chimneys*] See p. 161, n. 5.

[15] *our house . . . Inne*] See p. 123, n. 76.   [16] putteth] puts *MS*

[17] keepeth] keeps *MS*

[18] *Sensus . . . obiecto*] The ultimate source of this idea is Aristotle *de Anima* ii.6.418a and *passim*.

[19] *the statute*] The Statute of Wills, 32 Henry VIII, c. I (further elaborated 34 and 35 Henry VIII, c. 5), allowed those holding lands of the king by knight's service to devise [dispose of by will] two-thirds of this property while reserving to the king 'the full and clere yerely value of the thirde parte thereof' (*Statutes of the Realm*, III, 745; 901–3).

must remaine to the heire,[20] for I dare undertake, go thither when you will, your next heire at the common house, whatsoever charge he is at in the sute, I am sure he may be made a savor, at least[21] for the *tertiam partem* above all reprises, if the fault be not his owne. And further, when the weather is not calme, the wind is so unruly, that it will force the ill aires downe the chimneys, and not draw them up, as we see it doth in chimneys where fire is made, force downe the smoke, notwithstanding that the verie nature of fire helpeth[22] to enforce it upward, whereas these moist vapours are apt (even of their owne nature) to spreade abrode, & hang like a deaw about every thing. Wherfore though I am but a punie[23] of Lincolnes Inne, and the builder hereof[24] was a grave[25] bencher,[26] yet I will under reformation, preferre my devise afore his, either because it is better, or else out of the common fault of young men in this age, that we thinke our devises wiser then our elders. Yet with this respective modestie, that because my devise is with water, where that cannot be had, or where houses stand on[27] an exceeding flat, there I will leave the worke to his oversight, but where anie convenient current is, and no want of water, there I would be surveyer,[28] and so to devide the regiment, that if for the dry land service he be generall, for the water service I will be Admirall. Yet by the way, I hope all the Innes of court will gratulate the present flourishing estate of our

---

[20] *and that . . . heire*] *i.e.*, two parts of the 'infection or annoyance' may be disposed of, but a third part will remain to the heir: air.

[21] at least] at the least *B*   [22] helpeth] helps *MS*

[23] *punie*] *i.e.*, puisne, a junior student.

[24] hereof] of this *MS*   [25] grave] *MS*; *om. A, B*

[26] *builder . . . bencher*] *i.e.*, a member of the governing body who had been called from the Bar of the Inn to the Bench. According to the author of the *Ulysses*, this is a reference to James Dalton: 'Forsooth and please you, the last part of his learned treatise, is the maner & meanes how to build cleane, handsome and necessary privies, not altogether of *M. Daltons* built [*sic*], whom he [Harington] handles (as *Horace* did *Maecenas*) scarce cleanly for his curtesies' (D5ᵛ).

Dalton entered Lincoln's Inn in 1555, was expelled on the suspicion of heresy during Mary's reign, readmitted, and called to the Bar in 1563 and to the Bench in 1569 (*The Records of the Honorable Society of Lincoln's Inn, The Black Books*, ed. W. P. Baildon, London, 1897, I, 323; 339; 408; 456).

Cf. the allusion in Marston to 'the glorious *Ajax* of *Lincolnes Inne*' (*What You Will* III.i, ed. H. Harvey Wood, II, 260).

[27] on] of *MS*   [28] surveyer] the survayor *MS*

Lincolnes Inne[b]: not so much for furnishing the realme with most honourable, upright and wel learned magistrates, great sergeants, grave counsellers, towardly barresters, yong gallants of worth and spirit *sans nombre*, but also (that I may now deale with mine[29] equals, & not with my auncients) with two such rare enginers, me for this one devise, & Maister Plat[c] for verie many. Or if envie will not suffer them to give us due honor, let us two M. Plat, at least grace one another: and I am the willinger to offer this kindnesse to you, because I was advised by some to have recommended this devise to your illustrations, which I was verie like to have done, save that we are of no great acquaintance, and beside I have a litle ambitious humour of mine owne to be counted a deviser, though to cleare me of pride, you see my first practice is upon so base a subject, as I hope no body will envy me, or seeke to take it from me: as the sweet Zerbino said to Marfysa, of the ugly Gabrina.

> *You have so sweet a peece to carrie by you,*
> *As you are sure that no man will envy you.[d]*

---

[b] A true praise of Lincolnes Inne.   [c] M. Plat set forth a booke of engines.[30]
[d] Ariost Cant. 20.[31]

---

[29] mine] my *MS*

[30] *M. Plat . . .*] Hugh Plat (or Platt), later Sir Hugh, the son of a prosperous London brewer, having received his degree from St. John's College, Cambridge, was admitted to Lincoln's Inn in 1571/72 and called to the Bar in 1581. In the last decade of the sixteenth century he devoted his energy and ingenuity (which were considerable) to 'sundry new and rare inventions' in the varied fields of agricultural and household economy, natural science, and mechanics. Plat then published accounts of these inventions in a series of pamphlets which were designed both to create a market for his earlier works as well as to herald forthcoming publications by tantalizing promises.

Although Plat has been commended for a number of his ideas, particularly in respect to the fertilization of soil, many of his 'rare and profitable inventions' must have proved irresistible to the scoffing wits of the day. Plat, in fact, admitted that his public included many sceptics, and he assumed an increasingly querulous tone and became increasingly chary of divulging the secret of his inventions. He, accordingly, adopted the somewhat truculent motto: *Nec omnes nec omnia mihi placuere, cur ego omnibus?* Harington is undoubtedly referring to *The Jewell House of Art and Nature,* published in 1594, a work consisting of five sections, three title pages, and individual pagination, obviously for ease of separate publication of the sections. His first and more modest effort, *A Briefe Apologie of certaine new inventions,* had been published in 1593 by Richard Field.

[31] '80 st.': Harington annotation in the Lumley-Folger copy. He has slightly modified his original translation (1591).

And after he had played a word or two with them, he concluded,

Ben siate accopiati Io iurerei,
Se come essa e bella tu gagliardo sei.

No doubt you are a fitly matched paire,
If you as lustie be, as she is faire.[32]

But when they had done breaking of jests one on another, and that it came to breaking of staves, the peerelesse Prince (for his othes sake) was fain to take that most hatefull hagge into his protection. And so I suppose, that some may play in like sort upon me and my writing, and say;

The writer and the matter well may meete,
Were he as eloquent as it is sweete.

But if they do, let them take heed, that in one place or other of this pamphlet, they do not pull themselves by the nose,[33] as the proverbe is. But that you may see M. Plat, I have studied your booke with some observation: if you would teach me your secret of making artificiall cole, and multiplying barley[34] (though I

---

[32] *No doubt . . . faire*] 'ibid. 83 / st.': Harington annotation in the Lumley-Folger copy.

[33] *they do . . . nose*] Tilley N237; Harington's usage is the earliest cited.

[34] *if you . . . barley*] Plat's secret was often heralded but reluctantly disclosed. The concluding section of the *Jewell House* offers certain 'new inventions, *which the Author will bee readie* to disclose upon reasonable considerations, *to such as shall be willing to entertaine* them, or to procure some Priviledge for them,' and the first item is his elusive invention of '*A new kinde of fire.*' There is a woodcut depicting the fire, its merits are described as well as a plan for distributing the projected profits, but the basis of its composition is carefully *not* revealed.

In 1595 Plat published a brief treatise entitled *A Discoverie of certaine English Wants* (reprinted in *The Harleian Miscellany*, ed. Thomas Park, London, 1812, IX, 105–10) setting forth a scheme for the correction of the social and financial ills of England by the use of his inventions, particularly of his artificial coal. He suggests 'that whatsoever might be saved in fewel and fire by some such art *as I would discover and make manifest, in most plaine and naked tearmes*' (p. 107, my italics) be brought together into a common treasury to which would be added 'the one third of al other fires, which may also be saved in al such shires where any seacoale is usually burnt, at the rate of 8 *s.* the chawdren, or upwarde.' Of the many advantages that would accrue, in addition to the employment of 'lazie and loytering rogues' in making 'colebals,' not the least would be the encouragement of the author and others of his consort who would 'most royally both enrich and beautifie this little iland, with their admirable and most profitable inventions.'

feare me both the meanes will smell a litle of kin to M. A Jax)*
I assure you I would take it verie kindly: and we two might
have a sute together for a monapole, you of your cole, as you
mention in your book, and I of M. reformed A Jax: and if you
wil trust me to draw the petitions, you shall see I will get some
of the presidents of the starch and the vineger,[36] and make it

---

* Some conjecture, that stale & cowdoung must effect both these multiplica-
tions.[35]

However, the support he craved was not forthcoming, and Plat did not reveal
his secret until 1603 with the publication of *A new, cheape and delicate Fire of
Cole-balles.*

The 'multiplication' of barley is recounted in *Diverse new sorts of Soyle*,
published in 1594 and then included in the *Jewell House*. Plat describes 'an
eare of Summer barlie' grown at his home in Bishops Hall, 'the stalke whereof
together with the eare was measured to bee an ell, and three inches in length,
from the ground to the summitie thereof' (G2ᵛ).

[35] For Plat's prompt reaction to 'M. Ajax' and his 'stale marginal notes,'
see p. 191 below.

That Harington was substantially right, however, in his conjecture is attested
by Plat's remark in *A new, cheape and delicate Fire of Cole-balles* some seven
years later: having set forth his basic composition (powdered seacoal mixed
with a 'thin pap' of loam and water and formed into balls), Plat then offers
various modifications. 'Many have thought my fire to consist of seacole and
Cowdunge, and one among the rest hath so adventured to publish the same, as
beeing assured of my composition: but now you may see that rash pens do soone
run riot. Yet I do not utterly dislike this mixture, because it may also have a
place amongst my cole-bals: but the matter thereof not being substantial enough
to match with a seacole, cannot bring forth so lasting a fire as my first is, and
the same having also some use already in the enriching of grounds, can hardly
be spared in some places to be consumed into firebals. Yet (to speake truly of it)
it maketh a sweete and pleasing fire: and if you bestow labor enough therin you
may make colebals, with it and seacole, without any other bande' (C1ᵛ–C2).

[36] *of the starch and the vineger*] Harington's gibe is directed at two of the
monopolies which had particularly stimulated a vigorous public reaction since
they represented established industries handed over to individuals as rewards
for personal service. Richard Young, the notorious J.P. for Middlesex whose
busy ferreting out of religious suspects had made him odious to Catholic and
Puritan alike, received by letters patent dated 15 April 1588 'full power, lycence
and aucthorytie for the making, bringing in and selling of starch' (*APC*, XXIII,
45–6). This lucrative monopoly, the profits of which were estimated from £400
to £7,240, aroused the ire of the Company of Grocers, and there were many
infringements, prosecutions, and extortions as a result. In 1594 the monopoly
was transferred to Sir John Packington with a residual interest remaining to
Young which ultimately was taken over by the Queen as partial payment for a
debt of £9000 which Young owed her. Young died in 1594/95 and Packington
remained the patentee. (See *APC* for the period, *passim*; *Salisbury MSS*, IV,
250–1; 261; 276; 499; 614; V, 532–3; XIII, 559; W. H. Price, *English Patents of*

carrie as good a shew of reason, and good to the common wealth as theirs doth. As first for yours I would frame these reasons: I would shew the excellent commodity of iron-milles[37] (for if you speake against them your sute will be dasht straight). I would prove how they reduce wild and savage woods, to civill and frutefull pastures. I would alledge, they are good for maintenance of navigation, in respect that everie ship, what with his cast peeces, ankers, bolts and nailes, hath halfe as many tunne of iron as timber to it. I would say, it is a commoditie to the subject, considering they sel it for twelve or fourteene pound the tunne, and when it came out of Spaine or Holland, it was sold but for eight pound. The like also I would say for glasse[38]: and so concluding, that the woods must needes be spent upon these two (as doubtlesse they will in a short time) then your devise for artificiall cole, of how homely stuffe soever you make it, will be both regarded and rewarded. And thus perhaps making some great man your halfe, you may have an imposition of a tenth or a fift of everie chaldron of your fewell. And though it should poison all the towne with the ill savour (as the brew house by White hall doth her Highnes owne house, and all Channon row) yet what for necessitie, and what for favor, it shuld be suffred. And never feare that the price of

---

Monopoly, N.Y., 1906, p. 15, n. 1.) See the *Apologie*, pp. 243–44 for Harington's subsequent remarks on Young.

The vinegar monopoly was granted to Richard Drake, an equerry of 'her Majesty's Stable,' for 'his long service, and in consideration of recompense of a portion due to him in Sir Francis Drake's voyage' (*Salisbury MSS*, IV, 457–8). E. W. Hulme termed this grant to Drake as 'typical of the Elizabethan monopoly system at its worst' ('The History of the Patent System under the Prerogative and at Common Law,' *Law Quarterly Review*, XVI, 1900, 50). Cf. the *Apologie*, p. 253 for Harington's later remarks on Drake.

[37] *iron-milles* . . .] Harington's ironic comments here give expression to a recurrent sixteenth-century economic concern. See, for example, the report of Edward VI's commissioners on the iron mills in Sussex where the same points are made about the consumption of timber, the spoiling of forests, increased cost of iron, etc. (*Salisbury MSS*, XIII, 19–24). Harrison also makes the same charges about both iron and glass in his *Description of England* (*Chronicles* I, P3ᵛ and X4ᵛ).

[38] *The like . . . glasse*] The destruction of woods by the glassworks was also a recurrent complaint (*HMC*, Rept. 3, 5; Rept. 13, Pt. 4, 75–6). See the request for a patent for glassmaking by George Longe in which he promises to repress all but two of the fifteen glasshouses in England in order to *preserve* the woods and to erect others in Ireland in order to *waste* the superfluous forests (*Original Letters*, ed. Henry Ellis, 2nd s., London, 1827, III, 157–9).

your cole will[39] fall by cherishing of woods, for now Sir Walter Mildmay[40] is dead, you shal have few men wil busie them selves about anie of these publique inconveniences, or if his honest*f* successor[41] would attempt it, he should I feare me, have small hope to prevaile, in that which so honest a predecessor could not.

Now for my Monapole, I would aske but this trifling sute, and I would make these goodly pretences. First, because I have proved by good authours, that M. A Jax is lineally descended of the ancient house of *Stercutius*, and to have lived long under protection of *Dea Cloacina*, & to have bene prayed for by so manie holy Saints, I would procure (if the traffique were as open with Rome as it hath[42] bene) that as his progenitor *Stercutius* was allowed for a God, by one of the first Romane *Pontifices Maximi*, so M. A Jax might be allowed for a Saunt by Pope Sisesinke,[43] *Sextus quintus* (I would have said) or one of his successors (which if it be so easie a matter, as Boccacio,*g* & other Italian authors write, will not be verie chargeable) & then

---

f The Author could have said honorable of both, but he takes honestie in this place for the higher title.

g Boccacio writes that *S. Ciapielleto* was canonized.[44]

---

[39] colewill *A*

[40] *Sir Walter Mildmay*] Appointed Chancellor of the Exchequer in 1566, Sir Walter was, according to Camden, 'a man of remarkable piety and singular wisedome,' who 'discharged all the offices of a good Citizen and a good man' (*Elizabeth*, 2K2). He died in 1589. See the Notes to Bk. xxii, *OF*, where Harington quotes a stanza, together with his own translation, of a Latin poem by Sir Walter.

[41] *his . . . successor*] 'S^r Jo Foskue' [Fortescue]: Harington annotation in the Lumley-Folger copy. Camden describes him as 'an upright man, excellently well learned in *Greeke* and *Latin*, who was overseer of the Queenes liberall studies, and Master of the Queenes Wardrobe a long time, and gave me light in some things as I was writing hereof' (*Elizabeth*, 2K2).

[42] hath] has *MS*

[43] *Pope Sisesinke*] A pun on sice cinque—'a throw at dice turning up a six and five'—and sink, 'privy.'
Taking the name Sixtus V, Felix Peretti became pope in 1585. He was especially odious to the English because of what Burghley called a 'roaring hellish bull' issued in 1588 which reaffirmed the edicts of Pius V and Gregory XIII, 'excommunicated the Queene, deposed her from her throne, absolved her subjects from all allegeance, and published his Croisado in print, as against *Turkes* and Infidels' (*CSP, Dom.*, ii, 1581–90, 493; Camden, *Elizabeth*, 2G6).

[44] *Decameron* I.1.

with some of the mony that you gain with the perfumed cole, (if you wil lend it me, & I wil morgage my Bull to you when I have it, for paiment)[45] I will erect in London & elsewhere, diverse shrines to this new Saint, and all the fat offerings shall bee distributed to such poore hungrie fellowes as sue for Monapoles, which being joyned to the ashes of your cole, wil be perhaps not uncommodious for land, and you and I will begge nothing for our reward, but you as I said afore, a fift part of everie chaldron, and I but the sixt part of an assis[46] a moneth, of all that will not be recusants, to do their daily service, at these holy shrines.[h] Now if anie do object it is too great a sute (for I thinke it would be the richest office in England) and say that it would amount to more than Peter pence, & Poll pence[48] too, I would first to stop their mouthes quickly, promise them a good share in it, then I would amplifie the service, that in this devise I do in some respects to the state of Christianitie, in a matter that S. Peter nor Paul neither never thought of. For it is a common obloquie, that the Turks (who still keepe the order of Deuteronomie for their ordure) do object to Christians, that they are poisoned with their owne doung, which objection cannot be answered (be it spoken with due reverence to the two most excellent Apostles) with anie sentence in both their Epistles, so fully to satisfie the miscreant wretches, as the plaine demonstration & practise of my device must needs answer them. What thinke you M. Plat, is not here a good plat layd, that you and I may be made by for ever? onely I feare one let, & that is this: I heare by report there is a worthie Gentleman,[49] somtime of our house, that hath now the

---

[h] If I had such a graunt, he that were my *heres ex asse*,[47] would be the richest squire in England.

---

[45] paiment] repayment *MS*

[46] assis] *MS, Markham-Wrenn, Lumley-Folger, Sheffield*; assise *A, B*

[47] *I.e.*, sole heir; the *as* was the basis used in designating portions in any division of inheritance (*Bouvier's Law Dictionary*, ed. W. E. Baldwin, Cleveland, 1948).

[48] *Poll pence*] Punning on Paul and poll—to rob or plunder.

[49] *a worthie Gentleman*] 'Egerton now / Lo. Keeper of / Lincolns In': Harington annotation in Lumley-Folger copy. In a letter dated 9 May 1596, Anthony Bacon remarks on the favourable response to the Queen's appointment of Egerton after the death of Sir John Puckering: 'into whose place with an extraordinary speed her majesty hath, *ex proprio motu & speciali gratiâ*, advanced

keeping of the great seale, & these sutes cannot passe but by his privity, & they say (see our ill hap) he hath ever[50] bene a great enemie to all these paltry[51] concealements & monapolies,[i] and further they say of him, that to beguile him with goodly shews is very difficult, but to corrupt him with gifts is impossible; wel, if it be so, all our fat is in the fire,[53] and let the leane go after. You may make a great fire of your gains, & be never the warmer: and I may throw al mine into A Jax, and be never the poorer. Let us then make a vertue of necessitie, & sith we cannot get these monapolies, let us say we care not for them, and a vengeance on[54] them that begge them, and so we may have millions say Amen to us, & we shall be thought the honester men, and seeing I have had so ill luck in this, I wold no body might ever have any more of them, till I make such an other sute. And if M. Plat will follow my advise, he shall impart his rare devises gratis, as I do this, and so we may one day be put into the Chronicles, as good members of our countrey, more worthily then the great Beare that caried eight dogges on him[j] when Monsieur was here.[55] But to leave

---

[i] I protest Misacmos & all his friendes love him the better for it. If you call this flatterie, I would you would all deserve to be so flattered.[52]

[j] A worthie matter to be put[56] into a Chronicle, & fit for such worthy historiographers.[57]

Sir THOMAS EGERTON, with a general applause both of court, city, and country, for the reputation he hath of integrity, law, knowledge, and courage' (Thomas Birch, *Memoirs of the Reign of Queen Elizabeth*, London, 1754, I, 481). The favorable response to Egerton's appointment stemmed in part from the fact that the former Lord Keeper had been disgraced by the 'briberies and corruptions of his servants, in selling of Church livings' (Camden, *Elizabeth*, 2Q6).

[50] ever] allways *MS*   [51] thesepaltry *A*   [52] flatteree *A*

[53] *all our fat is in the fire*] Tilley F79.   [54] on] of *MS*

[55] *when Monsieur was here*] i.e., the vist of Alençon to England in 1581-2. Stow remarks on the more familiar designation: 'By this time [1581] his Picture, State, & Titles, were advaunced in every Stationers shopp, and many other publique places, by the name of *Frauncis* of *Valois*, Duke of *Alanson*, heire apparant of Fraunce, and brother to the French Kinge: but he was better knowne by the name of *Monsier*, unto all sorts of people, then by all his other Titles' (*Annales*, 3M2).

[56] to put] *MS*

[57] I have not found any other mention of this feat. Elizabethan writers frequently alluded to the bears by name: 'Harry of Tame' and 'great Ned' (Nashe, I, 281) perhaps identical with 'Harry Hunkes' (Sir John Davies,

M. Plats cole, which kindled this fantasie in me, and to turne
to my tesh, though I called my selfe by metaphor an Admirall
for the waterworkes, yet I assure you, this devise of mine,
requires not a sea of water, but a cesterne; nor a whole Tems
full, but half a tunne full, to keepe all sweete and savorie: for
I wil undertake, from the pesants cottage, to the Princes pallace,
twise so much quantitie of water as is spent in drink in the
house, will serve the turne: which if it were at Shaftsburie,
where water is dearest of anie towne I know, that is no great
proportion. And the devise is so litle combersome, as it is
rather a pleasure then a paine, a matter so sleight, that it wil
seem at the first incredible, so sure, that you shall find it at all
times infallible. For it doth avoide at once all the annoyances
that can be imagined, the sight, the savor, the cold: which last,
to weake bodies, is oft more hurtfull then both the other,
where the houses stand over brookes, or vaults daily cleansed
with water. And not to hold you in too long suspence, the
devise is this; You shall make a false bottome to that privie
that you are annoyed with, either of lead or stone, the which
bottome shall have a sluce of brasse to let out all the filth,
which if it be close plaistered[58] all about it, and renced with
water as oft as occasion serves, but specially[59] at noone and at
night, will keepe your privie as sweet as your parlour, and
perhaps sweeter too, if Quaile and Quando[60] be not kept out.
But my servant Thomas[61] (whose pensil can performe more in
this matter then my pen) will set downe the forme of this by
it selfe in the end hereof, that you may impart it to such
friends of yours, as you shall thinke worthie of it, though you
put them not to so great penance as to reade this whole
discourse.

And that I may now also end your penance that have taken
all this paynes to read this, that for your pleasure you would

---

Epigram 43) and 'Ned Whiting' (Jonson, *Epicoene* III.I., cited by McKerrow
IV, 170–1). 'Sacarson' is mentioned by Davies as well as Shakespeare, *MWW*
I.I.307.

[58] *close plaistered*] *i.e.*, tightly. The earliest example of this usage cited in the
OED is a similar passage in the *Anatomie*, p. 193.

[59] speeially *A*

[60] *Quaile and Quando*] Clearly the names of dogs, see p. 110 above.

[61] *Thomas*] *i.e.*, Thomas Combe whose contribution appears in the *Anatomie*.

needs perswade me to write; I will not end abruptly here, but
as friends that are uppon parting in a jorney, chuse a clenly
place in the high way to take their leaves one of another, and
not in the dirt and myre: so I, ere we part, will first for the
ennobling of this rare invention, tell you somewhat of the
place, of the company, of the means, and of the circumstances,
that first put so necessary a conceyt in my hed. For I remember
I have read that Archymedes the excellent enginer, (a man[62] in
his time fully[63] as famous in Syracusa, as our M. Plat is here in
England,) was sayd to have disgraced him selfe by an untemperat
or rather untempestive[64] joy that he tooke of a very worthy
and memorable invention of his. The story is thus.[65] Archimedes
having long beaten his braines to fynde some way by art how
to discover, what quantitie of counterfaite mixture was put into
a crown of massy gold, not dissolving the mettals, and fynding
no meanes in long study, at last washing him selfe naked in a
bathing tubbe, he observed still that the deeper he sunke the
higher the water rose, and forthwith he conceived (which after
he performed in deed) that by such a meanes the true quantity
of each mettall might be found, and the frawd discovered: with
joy whereof he was so ravished, that starke naked as he was, he
ran out into the streets crying, εὕρηκα εὕρηκα[66] I have found it,
I have found it. At which for the tyme all the people were
amazed, and thought him mad, till his invention after proved
him, not onely sober, but also suttle. What if some plesant
conceited fellow shold give out by way of supposition, that
possibly the deviser of this rare conveyance, was at the time of
devising thereof, sitting on some such place, as the godly father
sate on at his devout prayers, or the godles king sate on at his
devillish practise? as put the case on the stately stinking privy
in the Inner Temple, (where many grave aprentices of the
law put their long debated cases to homely uses) and that with
joy of so excellent invencion he ran out with his hose about
his heels, and cried, εὕρηκα εὕρηκα[67] so might I be likened to
Archimedes, and there be some perhaps would be so very

---

[62] a man] and a man *MS*   [63] fully] *not in MS*

[64] *untempestive*] Variant of intempestive; it does not appear in the *OED*.

[65] *The story is thus . . .*] Vitruvius *de Arch.* ix. Preface 9–10.

[66] ευρεκα, ευρεκα] *A*   [67] ευρεκα, ευρεκα *A*

fooles to beleeve it. But lest any idle headed felow should devise, or any shalow braind people beleeve such a tale, I do before hand give the word of disgrace to any that shall so say, and will make it good on their persons with all weapons from the pin to the pike, that whether it were by my good guiding, or my good fortune, in the invention hereof, nor in the execution I never receaved such a disgrace as that of Archimedes. For I assure you the devise was first both thought of and discoursed of, with as brode termes as any belongs to it, in presence of six persons, who were (all save one) enterlocutors in the dialogue, of which I was so much the meanest, that the other five, for beuty, for birth, for vallew, for witt, and for wealth, are not in manie places of the realme to be matched.[68] Neither was the place inferior to the parsons, being a castle, that I call, the wonder of the West,[69] so seated without, as England in few places affoords more pleasures: so furnished

---

[68] *the other five . . . matched*] 'Erl of Southāp. / Sʳ Mat. Arundel / Count Arundel / La Mary Arundel. / Sʳ Hary Davers': Harington annotation in the Lumley-Folger copy.

Mary Wriothesley, sister of the Earl of Southampton (well known as Shakespeare's patron), had married Sir Matthew Arundell's son and heir, Thomas, in 1585. A valiant soldier of fortune, Thomas, with the Queen's recommendation and the approbation of his father, had left behind 'his studious solitary life of Southampton House' and gone to fight against the Turks in Hungary. For this military service the Emperor Rudolph II rewarded him with the title of Count of the Holy Roman Empire. Returning to England in the spring of 1596, Thomas found his new title of Count begrudged by the nobility and openly disapproved of by the Queen who stated: 'I would not have my sheepe branded with another mans marke; I would not they should follow the whistle of a strange Shepheard.' As a result, he was briefly imprisoned in the Fleet, forbidden attendance at court upon his release, and threatened with disinheritance by his father who by the end of July, however, had sufficiently overcome his fear of the Queen's displeasure to receive him and his family. Under James, Thomas was granted a baronetcy. (See *Salisbury MSS*, v, 480; vi, 78–9; 129–30; 240; 301–2; Camden, *Elizabeth*, 2Q5–2Q6.)

Harington's earliest acquaintance with Sir Matthew Arundell and his family would have come about through his parents, since Lady Margaret, like Harington's mother, had been an attendant to the Princess Elizabeth at Hatfield. See *Apologie*, p. 233. Thomas Arundell and Harington had also been fellow students at Eton (*OF*, Notes to Bk. xlv).

For Sir Henry Danvers's connection with Southampton and Arundell, see p. 59, n. 29. This enables us to place the time of this jocular conversation—and hence the genesis of the *Metamorphosis*—sometime before Oct. 1594 when the murder of Henry Longe and the consequent flight of the Danverses occurred.

[69] *the wonder of the West*] 'Warder [Wardour] castle': Harington's annotation in the Lumley-Folger copy. Sir Matthew Arundell's seat in Wiltshire.

within, as China nor the West Indies scant allowes more
plenty. Briefly, at the very coming in, you wold think you were
come to the *Eldorado* in *Guiana*.[70] And by this I hope both the
invencion and execution herof may be sufficiently freed from
basenesse.

Yet there remains one easie objection against the merit of
my good servis herein, I mean easy to make, but it will not
seeme so easie to answer, and that is that some may say, this
may fortune to do wel in many places, but yet there is no
depth in the invention: for it is nothing but to keepe down the
ayre with a stopple, & let out the filth with a scrue, which some
will mislike, and will not endure to have such a businesse every
time they come to that house. To which I answer, that for depth
in the invention, I affect it not (for I wold not have it in all
above two foot deep.) And though the proverbe is, the deeper
the sweeter,[71] that is to be intended in some sweeter matters,
for the deeper you wade in this, you shal find it the sowrer.
And if it seem too busie, he that hath so great hast of his
busines, may take it as he findes it, which cannot be very ill at
any time. But the old saying was, *Looke ere you leap*,[72] & the old
custome was, that if a man had no light to looke, yet hee would
feele, to seeke that he would not finde[k], for feare least they
should finde that they did not seek.[74] Further the paines being
so litle as it is, I should thinke him a sloven that would not by
him selfe or his man leave it as clenly as he found it: specially
considering that in Deuteronomie you are told, God mislikes
sluttishnesse, and every cat gives[75] us an example (as housewifes
tell us) to cover all our filthines, & if you wil not disdain to
use that which cometh from the Muske Catte,[76] to make your

---

[k] Martin.[73]

---

[70] *Eldorado in Guiana*] According to Raleigh, the name applied by Johannes
Martines to the fabulous city of Manoa (*Discovery of Guiana*, pp. 20–1). For
Harington's familiarity with Raleigh's account, see p. 129, n. 116.

[71] *the deeper . . . sweeter*] Tilley D188 where Harington's example is the
earliest cited.

[72] *Looke ere you leap*] Tilley L429.   [73] Martin] *MS*; *om. A, B*

[74] *least . . . seek*] Tilley H385 where Harington's example is the earliest
cited.

[75] gives] geve *MS*

[76] cometh from the Muske Catte] come from the Catte of Mowntayn *MS*

selfe, your gloves, and your clothes the more sweet, refuse not
to follow the example of the Cat of the house, to make your
entries, your staires, your chambers, & your whole house, the
lesse soure. Indeed for the devise I grant it is as plaine as
dunstable high way,[77] and perhaps it will be as common to,
but neither of them shal be any disgrace to it. For I heard an
Italian tell that in Venis, after they had had the great losse by
fire[78] in Maximillians time, when their Arsenall was burnt with
gunpowder they had long consultation, how to keep their store
powder from danger of fire, for feare of like mischaunces, at
last a plaine fellow (like my selfe) came and told, that he had
devised a way, and prayd to have[79] audience. Then he told
them a long tale, but all to this short purpose, that gunpowder
was made of iii. simples, viz. saltpeeter, brimston, & cole, that
ech of these severally,[80] would be easily kept from fire, and be
quencht if they were kindled, but being compound, it blew up
all in a moment, if the least sparke did but meet with it; then
he shewed that the causes could not be so sudden of using
powder, but that the simples being ready, it might soone be
made; lastly that saltpeeter did grow rather than wast with
lying, whereas being made into powder, it doth consume &c.[81]
All which though every man there knew before, yet because
they had not offerd to put it in practise, they gave him a
reward for his devise, and followed therein his advise, placing
these simples in several houses, which are so daungerous when
they are compound, and since that time they have bene more
annoyd with water then with fire. Wherfore I assure me the
Magnificoes of Venice wold allow of the devise, & if I had
some idle mony, I might hap be so idly disposed, to put out
more then I will speake of, upon this returne, when one of the
sonnes and daughters of S. Marke had put my devise in

---

[77] *as plaine . . . way*] Part of the ancient Roman road called Watling Street,
its long even stretches made it proverbial, see Tilley D646.

[78] *in Venis . . . fire*] On 13 Sept. 1569, fire broke out in the arsenal, and the
consequent explosion of the powder magazine caused the entire city to vibrate
while the flames were visible as far as Verona (W. C. Hazlitt, *The Venetian
Republic*, London, 1915, II, 117). Harington had earlier remarked on this
mishap in the Notes to Bk. IX of *OF*.

[79] hane *A*   [80] severally] *MS*; severall *A, B*

[81] consume. &c. *A*

execution, specially if that *Molto Magnificentissimo*[1] were yet alive, that when his wife was sick, and the phisition was to see her water, he knew not how to bid her make water, in words seemly for his high state and her fine ears, that had never heard so fowle a word as that in her life, till his man tooke on him the matter, and found a phrase, by circumlocution to signifie pissing, and never once to name it, in this[83] sort; *Chara*[84] *signora vi prego fate quello che fate dinanzi al cacare.* But see see, I would faine have bid you farewel, & now we are againe in our dirty common place; well Ile goe with you yet a coits cast[85] farder, and then upon the next[86] green we will bid farewel, and turn taile,[87] as they say: wherefore now I will make you only a briefe repetition of that I have sayd. You see first how I have justyfied the homely words & phrases with authorities[88] above all exception. I have proved the care ever had of the matter with examples above all comparison. Lastly, I have expressed to you a cleanly[89] forme of it above al expectation. Neither do I praise it as Marchants do their wares, to rid their hands of them,[90] for I promise you, how high so ever I praise it, I meane not to part with it: for were I to praise it upon mine oth, as we do houshold stuffe in an inventary, I wold prayse it in my house, to bee worth 100 pounds, in yours 300 poundes, in[91]

---

[1] The Mag. of Venice are called *Figliuoli de S. Marco.*[82]

---

[82] *not in MS*   [83] in this] of that *MS*

[84] *MS lacking from* Chara *to end of section*

[85] *coits cast*] The distance to which a quoit—a flat disc of stone or metal—was commonly thrown in an exercise of skill.

[86] nexr *A*

[87] *and turn taile*] Tilley T16 where Harington's example is the earliest cited.

[88] authorities] *B*; autoritie *A*   [89] cleanly] cleane *B*

[90] *as Marchants . . . them*] Cf. the epigram '*Why* Paulus *takes so much Tobacco*':

. . . .
Thus while proud *Paulus* hath Tobacco praised,
The price of ev'ry pound, a pound is raised.
And why's all this? because he loves it well?
No: but because himselfe hath store to sell.

(ll. 21–4, *L&E*, pp. 199–200.)

[91] poundes in *A*

Wollerton[92] 500 pounds: in Tibals,[93] Burley,[94] and Holmbie[95] 1000 pounds, in Greenwitch, Richmond & Hampton court[96] 10000. And by my good sooth, so I would thinke my selfe well payd for it. Not that I am so base minded to thinke, that wit and art can be rated at any price, but that I wold accept it as a gratuitie fit for such houses and their owners.

For I tell you, though I will not take it upon me, that I am in *dialecticorum dumetis doctus,* or *in rhetorum pompa potens,* or *coeteris scientiis saginatus,* as doth our *Pedantius* of Cambridge,[97] yet I take it, that in this invention I shal shew a great

---

[92] *Wollerton*] *i.e.,* Wollaton. The imposing residence of Sir Francis Willoughby in Notts., which was said to have been erected at a cost of 'four-score thousand Pounds' (Lady Middleton and C. F. G. Cumming, 'In the Old Muniment Room of Wollaton Hall,' *The New Review,* I, 1889, 641). Cf. the *Apologie,* p. 234.

[93] *Tibals*] *i.e.,* Theobalds, Lord Burghley's 'faire and elegant' house in Herts. (Camden, *Britain,* 2L4ᵛ).

[94] *Burley*] The Rutlandshire estate of Harington's cousin, Sir John Harington, with its 'stately and sumptuous house' (*ibid.,* 2X3ᵛ).

[95] *Holmbie*] *i.e.,* Holdenby, Sir Christopher Hatton's mansion in Northants. Reputed the finest house in England, it was modeled after the Lord Treasurer's country seat at Theobalds and dedicated to the Queen. Hatton at one point declined even to view his 'shrine' until 'that holy saint' had visited it. In 1579 Burghley paid an admiring visit; he immediately expressed his approval in a letter to Hatton which concluded with the wry comment, 'God send us both long to enjoy Her, for whom we both meant to exceed our purses in these' (*Memoirs of the Life and Times of Sir Christopher Hatton,* ed. Sir Harris Nicolas, London, 1847, pp. 155; 126). Cf. Harington's remark about the 'poore neighbour' who 'once dwelt at Holmeby,' *Apologie,* p. 228.

[96] *Greenwitch . . . court*] Of these three royal palaces, Hampton Court was the most extensive, containing 'five severall inner Courts passing large, environed with very faire buildings wrought right curiously, and goodly to behold' (Camden, *Britain,* 2M4ᵛ).

[97] *that I . . . Cambridge*] *Pedantius,* that 'exquisite Comedie,' as Nashe calls it, satirizing Gabriel Harvey, 'where, under the cheife part, from which it tooke his name, as namely the concise and firking finicaldo fine School-master, hee was full drawen & delineated from the soale of the foote to the crowne of his head' (*Works,* III, 80).

G. Moore Smith who edited the text of the first printed edition (1631) has argued, relying in part on an earlier reference of Harington in the Notes to Bk. xIV of the *OF,* but overlooking this passage, that a likely date for its first performance at Trinity College was 6 Feb. 1580/81. He was subsequently able to verify its author as Edward Forsett whose name appears on a manuscript of the play in the library at Caius College, Cambridge (*TLS,* 10 Oct. 1918).

Although electing to reprint the 1631 text rather than Caius MS 62, Moore Smith felt that 'neither is in all points nearer to the original form of the play than the other' (Introduction, p. III). However, the Latin phrases Harington

practise uppon the grammer, and upon this point I will chalenge all the gramarians, viz. I say, & I will make it good that by my rare devise I shall make *Stercutius* a nowne adjective.[98] Now I know you will set your sonne William[99] to answer me, and he shall say no no, and come uppon me with his grammer rule *ut sunt divorum Mars Bacchus Apollo, virorum &c.*[100] and hereby conclude, that he is both a substantive & that a substantiall one too, and a Masculine.

But all this will not serve, for I have learned the grammer too, and therefore *Come grammer rules, come now, your power show*, as saith the noble Astrophill.[101] First therfore I say, his no no is an affirmative.

For in one speech two negatives affirme.[102]

Secondly tel me prety Wil, what is a nown substantive? That that may be seene, felt, heard, or understood. Very wel, now I wil joyne issue with you on this point, where shall we trie it?

---

quotes are to be found in the Caius MS in Pedantius's description of himself (recorded in the textual notes of Moore Smith's edition, ll. 1694–6), whereas the 1631 version includes only 'in Rhetorum pompa potens,' l. 1695.

Despite his remarks here, Harington's sympathy in the Nashe–Harvey controversy seems to have been with Harvey. See the epigram '*To Doctor Harvey of Cambridge*' (*L&E*, p. 199).

[98] *I shall . . . adjective*] Harington is again playing upon the familiar rules of Lily's grammar: 'A Noune Substantive is that standeth by him selfe, & requireth not an other word to be joyned with him' whereas a noun adjective 'can not stand by himselfe' (*A Shorte Introduction*, A5).

[99] *your sonne William*] 'Will: Shel- / don': Harington annotation in the Lumley-Folger copy. The eldest son and heir of Harington's cousin Edward Sheldon, the Philostilpnos of the prefatory letter, 'prety Wil' was born in 1588/9 and was thus seven years old when the *Metamorphosis* was published; four years later he was to enter Gloucester Hall, Oxford. Eventually, he married Elizabeth, daughter of William, second Lord Petre, and became the father of the noted antiquary and literary patron Ralph Sheldon (*Visitation of the County of Worcester*, XXVII, 127–9, and Joseph Foster, *Alumni Oxoniensis 1500–1714*, Oxford, 1892, IV, 1343).

[100] *with his grammer . . . &c*] A familiar tag illustrating the rule for masculine proper names (Lily, *Brevissima Institutio*, A6ᵛ).

[101] *Come grammer . . . Astrophill*] The opening line of Sonnet LXIII of Sidney's *Astrophel and Stella*, first published surreptitiously in 1591. Harington is remembering somewhat imperfectly or, as his wont, modifying to make his point more directly (*Complete Works*, ed. A. Feuillerat, II, 267).

[102] *For . . . affirme*] Line 14 of the same sonnet: 'That in one speech, two negatives affirme.'

Not in Cambridge you will say, for I thinke they will bee parciall on my side. Well then in Oxford be it, & no better Judge then M. *Poeta*, who was cheefe Captayn of all the nowns in that excellent comedie of *Bellum gramaticale.*[m] For without all peraventure when he shal here that one of his band & so nere about him, is brought to that state, that he is neither to be seene, smellt, hard, nor understood,[104] he wil swere gogs nowns[105] he wil thrust him out of his selected band of the most substantiall substantives, and sort him with the rascal rablement of the most abject adjectives. But now sir that I have brought you to so faire a town as Oxford and so sweet a companion as your sonne William, I will leave you to him that made you.

Now (gentle Reader)[n] you have taken much paine, and perhaps some pleasure, in reading our Metamorpho-sis of A Jax: and you supposed by this time to have done with me: but now with your favour I have not done with you. For I found by your countenance, in the reading and hearing hereof, that your conceit oft-times had censured me hardly, and that somewhat diversly, and namely in these three kindes.[o]

---

[m] This Comedy was playd at her Majesties last being at Oxford.[103]

[n] The Epilogue or conclusion.   [o] Three reproofs of this pamphlet.

---

[103] When the Queen visited Oxford in 1592, she was entertained on 24 Sept. with a performance of this play at Christ Church (Nichols, *Progresses*, III, 155), but it was obviously not a new production as Harington had earlier referred to it as 'full of harmeless myrth' in his 'Apologie of Poetrie' (Chambers, *Elizabethan Stage*, IV, 374).

The original source was the Latin prose narrative of Andrea Guarna which had been translated into English in 1569 by William Haywarde, a clerk of the Court of Chancery. The dramatic version, according to an entry in the S.R. was by 'Master. SPENSE' (*S.R.*, IV, 317), but this is very probably an error. Anthony Wood had been told that its author was Leonard Hutton, who received his M.A. degree from Christ Church, Oxford, in 1582. In his recent census of neo-Latin plays, Leicester Bradner lists a 1635 edition by 'Leonardus Huttenius' (*Studies in the Renaissance*, IV, 63).

The subject is 'the horrible and bitter contentions in the most fertile region and countrey of grammar, by variance that grew betwixte two high and mightie princes, possessors of the same, the Noune and the Verbe' (Haywarde, reprinted in *A Collection of Scarce and Valuable Tracts*, ed. Scott, London, 1809, I, 533 ff.).

[104] *that he ... understood*] 'A Noune is the name of a thinge, that may be seene, felte, hearde, or underst[oo]de' (Lily, A5).

[105] *gogs nowns*] An example of Harington's technique of varying his expletives to give humour or point to the particular situation. Cf. *Apologie*, pp. 239,243.

First you thought me fantastical; secondly, you blamed my scurrilitie; and thirdly, you found me satyricall. To which three reproofes, being neither causlesse nor unjust, do me but the justice to heare my three answers.

I must needes acknowledge it fantastical for me, whom I suppose you deeme (by many circumstances) not to be of the basest, either birth or breeding, to have chosen, or of another mans choise, to have taken so straunge a subject. But though I confesse thus much,*p* yet I would not have you lay it to my charge, for if you so do, I shall straight retort all the blame, or the greatest part of it, upon your selfe: and namely, I would but aske you this question, & even truly between God and your conscience, do but answer it. If I had entituled the booke, *A Sermon shewing a soveraigne salve for the sores of the soule.* Or, *A wholsome haven of health to harbour the heart in.* Or, *A marvellous medicine for the maladies of the minde.*[106] would you ever have asked after such a booke ? would these grave and sober titles have wonne you to the view of three or foure tittles ?[107] much lesse three or foure score periodes.[108] But when you heard, there was one had written of A Jax, straight you had a great mind to see what strange discourse it would prove, you made enquirie who wrote it, where it might be had, when it wold come forth. You prayed your friend to buy it, beg it, borow it, that you might see what good stuffe was in it. And why had you such a mind to it ? I can tell you; you hoped for some meriments, some toyes, some scurrilitie, or to speake plaine English, some knaverie. And if you did so, I hope now your expectation is not altogether frustrate. Yet give me leave briefly to shew you what pretie pils you have swallowed in your

---

p Answer to the first objection, of fantasticalnesse.

---

[106] *A Sermon . . . minde*] Harington here mocks the craze for alliterative titles. Cf. *A Sovereigne Salve for a Sick Soule* by David Chytraeus, Englished by W. F. and published by Richard Field in 1590, and *The Haven of Health*, Thomas Cogan's popular medical work, which Field reprinted in 1596.

[107] *tittles*] Points used in writing.

[108] *periodes*] Although the usual meaning of *period* at this time is 'a complete sentence,' in view of the possible pun this may be an early example of its usage as a 'point marking the end of a sentence,' the earliest example of which cited in the *OED* is 1609.

pleasant quadlings,[109] & what wholsome wormewood was enclosed in these raisins of the sunne.

Against malcontents, Epicures, Atheists, heretickes,[110] & carelesse & dissolute Christians, and especially against pride and sensualitie, the Prologue & the first part are chiefly intended.[q] The second gives a due praise without flatterie, to one that is worthie of it,[111] and a just checke without gall to some that deserve it. The third part as it teacheth indeed a reformation of the matter in question, so it toucheth in sport, a reprehension of some practises too much in custome. All which the reader that is honorable, wise, vertuous, and a true lover of his countrey, must needes take in good part. Now gentle reader, if you will still say this is fantasticall, then I will say againe, you would not have read it except it had bene fantasticall, and if you will confesse the one, sure I will never denie the other.

The second fault you object, is scurrilitie, to which I answer, that I confesse the objection,[r] but I denie the fault, and if I might know whether he were Papist or Protestant that maketh this objection, I wold soone answer them: namely thus; I would cite a principall writer of either side, and I would prove, that either of them hath used more obscenous, fowle, and scurrill phrases,[s] (not in defence of their matter, but in defacing of their adversarie) in one leafe of their bookes, then is in all this. Yet they professe to write of the highest, the holiest, the waightiest matters that can be imagined, and I write of the basest, the barrennest, and most witlesse subject that may be described.

Quod decuit tantos cur mihi turpe putem?[112]

I forebeare to shew examples of it, least I should be thought to disgrace men of holy and worthie memorie.

---

[q] A briefe sum of the true intent of the booke.
[r] Answer to the second objection of scurrilitie.
[s] This cannot be denied.

---

[109] *quadlings*] Variant of codling—a hard variety of apple.
[110] Atheists heretickes, *A*
[111] *The second . . . it*] The Earl of Essex. See notes to p. 141.
[112] *Quod . . . putem*] Adapted from Ovid *Amores* ii. 8.14.

For such as shal find fault that it is too Satyricall,[t] surely I suppose their judgement shall sooner be condemned by the wiser sort, then my writings. For when all the learned writers, godly preachers, and honest livers over all England (yea over all Europe) renew that old complaint,

Regnare nequitiam & in deterius res humanas labi.[u]

When wee heare them say daily; that there was never under so gracious a head so gracelesse members, after so sincere teaching, so sinfull living: in so shining light, such workes of darkenesse. When they crie out upon us, yea crie indeed, for I have seene them speake it with teares, that lust and hatred were never so hote, love and charitie were never so colde: that there was never lesse devotion, never more division: that all impietie hath all impunitie: finally, that the places that were wont to be the samples of all vertue and honor, are now become the sinks of all sin & shame. These phrases (I say) being written and recorded, sounded & resounded in so manie bookes and Sermons, in Cambridge, in Oxford, in the Court, in the countrey, at Paules crosse in Paules church-yard: may not I as a sorrie writer among the rest, in a merie matter, and in a harmlesse maner, professing purposely, *Of vaults, & privies, sinks and draughts to write,* prove according to my poore strength, to draw the readers by some pretie draught, to sinke into a deepe and[114] necessarie consideration, how to amend some of their privie faults?[v] Beleeve it (worthie readers, for I write not to the unworthie) A Jax when he is at his worst, yeelds not a more offensive savour to the finest nosthrils, then some of the faults I have noted do, to God and the world. Be not offended with me for saying it, more then I am with some of you for seeing it. But this I say, if we wold amend our privie faults first, we should afterward much the better reforme the open offences, according to the old proverbe:[115] *Everie man mend one, and all*

---

[t] Answer to the third objection, that it is too Satyrical or sharpe against the faults of the time.

[u] Seneca.[113]   [v] Allusion to the former words.

---

[113] *de Beneficiis* i.10.1 with slight omission.

[114] aud *A*   [115] proverbe. *A*

would be mended.[116] Trust me, they do wrong me that count me satyricall. Alas I do but (as the phrase is) pul a haire from their beards[117] whose heads perhaps by the old lawes & canons should be shorne. If you will say there is salt in it, I wil acknowledge it, but if you will suspect there is gall in it, I renounce it. I name not manie, & in those I do name, I swarve not far from the rule,[w]

> *Play with me, and hurt me not:*
> *Jest with me, and shame me not.*[118]

For some that may seeme secretly touched, and be not openly named, if they will say nothing, I will say nothing. But as my good friend M. Davies said of his Epigrams, that they were made like dublets in Birchen lane,[119] for every one whom they will serve: so if any man find in these my lines any raiment that sutes him so fit, as if it were made for him, let him weare it and spare not, & for my part I wold he could weare it out.[120] But if he wil be angry at it, then (as the old saying is) I beshrew his angrie hart[121]: & I wold warne him thus much (as his poore friend) that the workman that could with a glaunce onely and a light view of his person, make a garment so fit for him, if the same workman come and take a precise measure of him, may make him another garment of the same stuffe (for there neede go but a paire of sheeres betweene them)[122] that in what sheere soever he dwelleth, he may be knowne by such a coate[123] as long as he liveth. Well, to conclude, let both the writer and the readers endevor to mend our selves, & so we

---

[w] A fit rule to be kept, and breedes all misrule when it is broken, specially by honorable persons.

---

[116] mended] amended *B.* Tilley M196.

[117] *pul a haire . . . beards*] Tilley H22.   [118] *Play . . . not*] Tilley P400.

[119] *Birchen lane*] The site of many second-hand clothing marts (Stow, ed. Kingsford, I, 198–9).

[120] *so if . . . out*] This, of course, becomes a standard declaration with the satirists. See the 'Post-script' to Hall's *Virgidemiarum* (*Poems*, ed. A. Davenport, Liverpool, 1949, p. 98) and Marston, *Scourge of Villainy* (*Works*, ed. A. H. Bullen, London, 1887, III, 382).

[121] *I beshrew . . . hart*] Not recorded in Tilley.

[122] *for there . . . them*] Tilley P36.

[123] *coate*] Garb indicating professional class, order, sort, or party.

shall the easier amend others, and then I shall thinke my labour well bestowed in writing, and you shall thinke yours not altogether lost in reading. And with this honest exhortation I would make an end, imitating herein the wisest lawyers, who when they have before the simplest Jurers, long disputed their cases to litle purpose, are ever most earnest and eager at the parting, to beat into the juries head some speciall point or other, for the behoofe of their client. For so wold I, howsoever you do with the rest of the matter: I would I say, faine beate still into your memorie this necessary admonition (which my new taken name[x] admonisheth me of) to cleanse, amend, & wipe away all filthinesse. To the which purpose, I could me thinke allegorise this homely subject that I have so dilated, & make almost as good a sermon, as the frier did before the Pope, saying nothing but *Matto San Pietro*[y] three times, & so came down from the pulpit again: & being afterward examined, what he meant to make a Sermon of three words, but three times repeated before the triple crownd prelat and so many Cardinals. He told them, they might find a good Sermon in *Matto San Pietro*; as namely, if heaven might be gotten notwithstanding all the pride, pleasures, and pomp of the world, with ease, sensualitie & epicurisme, then what a foole was S. Peter to live so strict, so poore, so painful a life. With which it is possible his auditory was more edified, or at least more terrified, then they would have bene at a longer sermon. But I wil neither end with sermon nor prayer, lest some wags liken me to my L. (   ) players, who when they have ended a baudie comedy, as though that were a preparative to devotion, kneele down solemnly, and pray all the companie to pray with them for their good Lord and maister.[124] Yet I

---

[x] *Misacmos.*

[y] That is to say, What a foole was S. Peter?

---

[124] *my L. . . . maister*] Harington seems to have intended a specific reference here. Chambers, who cites this passage, observes: 'A practice of offering up a prayer for the lord's well-being at the end of a performance was probably of ancient derivation, although whether it survived in the public theatres may perhaps be doubted' (*Elizabethan Stage*, I, 311).

That it was a regular custom (at least outside of London) is supported by the statement of Gervase Holles: 'It will not be amisse to remember (because even in those times unusuall amongst the greatest subjectes) that he [Sir William Holles of Houghton, Notts., 1509–90] alwais kept a company of stage players of

will ende with this good counsell, not unsuting to the text I have thus long talked of.

To keepe your houses sweete, cleanse privie vaults,
To keepe your soules as sweete, mend privie faults.

---

his owne wch presented him masques and playes at festivall times and upon dayes of solemnity. In the summer time they usually acted abroad in the country; and olde Alderman Fotherby has tolde me that he hath heard them act many times, alwais at the end of the play praying (as the custome then was) for the Queene's Matie, the Councill, and their right worshippfull good Maister Sir William Holles' (*Memorials of the Holles Family 1493–1656*, ed. A. C. Wood, Camden, 3rd s., LV, 42).

AN ANATOMIE OF THE
METAMORPHO-SED AJAX.

WHEREIN BY A TRIPERTITE METHOD is plainly, openly, and demonstratively, declared, explaned, and eliquidated,[1] by pen, plot, and precept, how unsaverie places may be made sweet, noysome places made wholesome, filthie places made cleanly. Published for the common benefite of builders, housekeepers, and house-owners.

By T. C.[2] Traveller, Aprentice in Poetrie, Practiser in Musicke, professor of Painting; the mother, daughter, and[3] handmayd of all Muses, artes[4] and sciences.

Invide quid mordes? pictoribus atque Poetis.
Quidlibet audendi semper fuit aequa potestas.[5]

---

[1] *eliquidated*] *i.e.*, made clear. This is the sole example cited in the *OED*.
[2] T. C.] Thomas Combe *MS*
[3] and] The *MS*   [4] Muses artes *A*
[5] *pictoribus . . . potestas*] Horace *Ars Poetica* 9-10.

To M. E. S. Esquier.[6]

Sir, my master having expresly commaunded me, to finish
a straunge discourse that he had written to you, called the
Metamorpho-sis of A JAX, by setting certaine pictures therto;
there came unto my minde a tale I had heard, perhaps more
merry then mannerly. How a plaine, or rather a pleasant
Servingman, wayting on his master at the Popes Court,
happened to be present one day, when the Gentleman, after
long attendance and great meanes, had obtained the favour to
kisse his holinesse foote. The man seeing what his master did,
first stale out of the chamber, & then ranne out of the house,
hyding himselfe for a pretie space. The Gentleman hearing of
it, pittied his mans simplicitie (who perhaps was craftie knave
inough for all that) and asked why he went away? Alas Sir said
he, when I saw that a man of your woorth and worship, in so
publique a place, might kisse but his toe, I doubted they would
have made me, have kist him in some homlyer place, and so I
might have bin shamed for ever.

If that servingman had cause to runne out of the house, my
thinke I may seeme to have more reason, to runne out of my
wits,[7] to have so strange a taske appointed me; for when the
verie face, & head, or title of the booke, seemed so fowle and
unsaverie, what might I thinke the feete or tayle thereof were
like to prove? Wherefore I would gladly have shunned so base[8]
an office: but having my masters example joyned to his com-
mandement, I tooke hart to me, and first I read over the
discourse, to see what was promist therein on[9] my behalfe
(viz. certaine pictures).[10] But I assure you in the reading of it,
whether it were the wel handling of the matter, or my partiall
opinion (a fault that I am seldome charged withall) my minde
was altered, and I compared the homely title of it, unto an

---

[6] Master Edward Sheldon of Boeley, Worc. See notes to p. 58.

[7] wits] witte *MS*   [8] base] homely *MS*

[9] on] of *MS*   [10] behalfe. (viz. certaine pictures.) *A*

ilfavored vizer,[a] such as I have seene in stageplayes, when they daunce Machachinas,[12] which covers as sweet a face sometimes as any is in the companie. And even presently therewithall, as if I had bene inspired with the spirite of A JAX, me thought I durst have adventured with my pen and pensill upon any thing. For, as the saying is,

> Painters and Poets, clayme by old enrolment,
> A charter, to dare all, without controlment.[13]

Wherefore by the Priviledge of this Charter (as also by a Pattent I have of serving two prentiships) I will go somewhat beyond the bare wordes of my commission, and yet not swarve much from the charge that is layd upon me. For Sir, I would you knew it, though I never troubled the schooles at Oxford, with any disputes or degrees, yet I carried there[14] a good schollers bookes after him,[15] and I trust I gat some quaynt phrases among them, as namely in steed of praying the Cobler to set two patches on my shoes, I could have said, *set me two semicircles upon my suppeditals*,[16] with much other eloquence beyond the common intelligence, and that I may bee bolde to say that I have herd as good schollers thear as any (I must not compare with Cambridg[17]) but as any bee in Europe.[18] And yet notwithstanding all these great vaunts, I will not take upon me, that I am able to say so much of the Metamorpho-sis,

---

[a] Or to a toad or a snake made in suger,[11] that lookes unsightly, but tasts sweetly.

---

[11] suger. *A*

[12] *Machachinas*] A dance performed by matachins (sword dancers) dressed in fantastic costume. This is the earliest example cited in the *OED*. Cf. *OF* VI.61 where Harington speaks of the dancers as 'masking Mathachinas all disguised.'

[13] '*A Poets Priviledge*' (*L&E*, p. 168, printed from BM Add. MS 12049). It is also included in the MS copy of the Epigrams presented to Prince Henry.

[14] there] *not in MS*

[15] *yet . . . him*] Perhaps an allusion to Harington's brother Francis who received his A.B. from Corpus Christi 7 Nov. 1581.

[16] *set me . . . suppeditals*] A recurrent joke, found first in that source book of Beatrice's wit, *A C. Mery Talys*, with the form *subpedytales*, and later in Lodge's *Wits Miserie* with the form *suppeditaries* (*Shakespeare Jest-Books*, I, 20; *Complete Works of Thomas Lodge*, IV, 29).

[17] cambridg *MS*

[18] and that . . . Europe.] *MS*; intelligence. *The rest om. A, B*

the Etimologie, and the reformation of Don A JAX-house, as my master hath said, or defend[19] the wordes, illustrate the matter, and dilate of the forme as he hath done, for who can stand against such an army of Emperours, Kings, Magistrats, Prophets, Poets Allhallowes, and all prophanes, even from the Bible to the Bable, as are by him brought for enobling of his argument?[20] yet for Anatomysing as it were of the shape and bodie therof, bycause he hath handled that point (in M. Plats opinion)[b] somewhat too briefly for common understandings I

---

[b] M. Plat in his booke against famine, *fol. ultimo penultimo.*[21]

[19] defend] to defend *B*

[20] argument] *MS*; arguments *A, B*

[21] *Sundrie new and Artificiall remedies against Famine;* although not entered in the S.R. until 23 Aug., the work clearly was in print prior to 3 August when Harington dated the dedication of his complete text, including the *Anatomie*, to Thomas Markham. See Introduction, pp. 25–6.
Stung by Harington's gibes, Plat decided to retaliate at once by sprinkling references to 'M. Ajax' in the last three leaves of this brief pamphlet setting forth various means of counteracting the dearth—a work which he perhaps had ready at hand. In 'A petition to the curteous Reader,' Plat asks his public to bear with him for the present for not disclosing the secret of his 'coleballs' and other inventions and to disregard the 'censures of those ignorant, or malicious spirits of our age, who presuming to know the simples of my fire, may happily range into base and offensive matter, and thereby labor to discredite that secret, whose composition they could never yet reach unto, nor, if they had the particulars, were they able to combine & knit them with their lefthanded workmanship' (D4ᵛ).
Heralding his next 'new and profitable' invention (for the benefit of the maltsters), he again mentions Harington: 'And that I could fal into *M. Ajax* veine, and had some of his glib paper, & gliding pens, I might soon scribble ten sheets, and sell everie sheet for two pence, towarde necessarie charges: and in the end conclude the expectation of manie leaves, in a few sweeter lines then he hath done before me: but because I will bind my selfe to no such privy presidents, I will deliver my conceipt in as plain and naked tearmes as I may' (E1).
Finally, offering to disclose 'a new and extraordinary meanes for the inriching of arable grounds,' Plat adds one last sally: 'I will here (without praying in aide of M. *AJAX*, or his stale marginal notes, whose reformation hath already more offended the eares of Honorable persons, then his first falts could ever offende their noses) make a publike offer to all those Gentlemen and Farmers of England . . . how they shall bee sufficientlie furnished, with a newe and plentifull *Compost* . . . whose nature is so transmuted and disguised, as that one neighbor, yea M. Ajax himselfe, though he were present at the disposing or scattering thereof, shall not be able to discerne what his next neighbour hath doone to his ground' (E1ᵛ–E2).
For a defence of Plat, see the *Ulysses*, E5–E6.

must heare a litle better open it: for as the old saying is, (*bonum quo communius eo melius*)[22] and the old verse is,

Scire tuum nihil est, nisi te scire hoc sciat alter.[23]

Goodnesse is best, when it is common showne,
Knowledge were vayne, if knowledge were not knowne.

Wherefore now, seriously & in good sadnesse to instruct you, and all Gentlemen of worship, how to reforme all unsaverie places of your houses,[c] whether they be caused by privies, or sinkes, or such like (for the annoyance comming all of like causes, the remedies neede not be much unlike) this you shall do.

" In the Privie that annoyes you, first cause a Cesterne[d]
"containing a barrell or upward, to be placed either behind the
"seat, or in any place, either in the roome, or above it, from
"whence the water may by a small pype[e] of leade of an inch be
"convayed under the seate in the hinder part therof (but quite
"out of[27] sight) to which pype you must have a Cocke or a
"washer to yeeld water with some pretie strength, when you
"would let it in.

" Next make a vessell[f] of an ovall forme, as broad at the

---

[c] If that which followes offend the reader, he may turne over a leafe or two, or but smell to his sweet gloves, and then the savor will never offend him.

[d] This Cistern in the first plot is figured at the letter A. and so likewise in the second plot.[24]

[e] The small pype in the first plot at[25] D. in the 2. E, but it ought to lye out of sight.[26]

[f] This vessell is exprest in the first plot H. M. N. in the 2. H. K.

---

[22] *bonum . . . melius*] Not in Tilley, and I have not traced the source. Lodge, who cites it in *Wits Miserie*, terms it an axiom of Aristotle (*Works*, IV, 17). Ray includes it in his *Collection of English Proverbs*: 'For as it is said of *Bonum, quò communius eò melius*; So by the rule of contraries, What is ill, the further it spreads the worse' (1670, p. 51).

[23] *Scire . . . alter*] Persius *Sat.* I.27.

[24] plot] *not in MS*   [25] at] *not in MS*

[26] it ought to . . . sight] but bying close under ye seat yt should not bee seen *MS*

[27] of] *MS; om. A, B*

"bottome as[28] at the top, ii. foote deep, one foote broad,
"xvi. inches long, place this verie close to your seate, like the
"pot of a close stoole, let the ovall incline to the right hand.
"   This vessell may be brick, stone, or leade, but whatsoever it
"is, it should have a Current[g] of 3. inches, to the backe part of
"it, (where a sluce of brasse must stand) the bottome, and sides
"all smooth: and drest with pitch, rosin, and waxe,[h] which will
"keepe it from taynting with the urine.
"   In the lowest part of this vessell (which[30] will be on the right
"hand), you[31] must fasten the sluce or washer of brasse with
"soder or Ciment, the Concavitie[i] or hollow thereof, must be
"ii. inches and ½.
"   To the washers stopple, must be a stemme of yron as bigge
"as a curten rod,[j] strong and even, and perpendicular; with a
"strong skrew at the top of it, to which you must have a hollow
"key with a woorme[32] fit to that skrew.
"   This skrew[k] must, when the sluce is downe, appeare through
"the planke not above a strawsbredth &[33] on the right hand,
"and being duly placed, it will stand three or foure inches
"wyde of the midst of the backe of your seate.
"   Item, that Children & busie folke, disorder it not, or open
"the sluce, with putting in their hands, without a key,[l] you
"should have a little button, or scallop shell,[m] to bind it downe
"with a vice pinne,[36] so as without the key it will not be
"opened.
"   These things thus placed: all about your vessell and els-
"where, must be passing close plastered with good lyme and

---

g The Current[29] is exprest in the second plot K.

h A speciall note.   i In the 2. plot I. L.

j In the first plot G. F. in the 2. F. & I.

k In the first plot betweene G. I.

l This showes in the[34] first plot K. L.

m In the[35] 2 G. Such are in the backside of watches.

---

28 bottomeas A   29 *Current*] Slope or fall.
30 vessell (which] MS; vessell; which A
31 hand you MS; hand, you A   32 *woorme*] Thread.
33 strawsbredth &] MS; strawbreadth A, B   34 the] *not in MS*
35 the] *not in MS*   36 *vice pinne*] Screw.

"hayre, that no ayre come up from the vault," but onely at your "sluce, which stands close stopt, and ever it must be left, after "it is voyded, halfe a foote deepe in cleane water.

" If water be plentie, the oftener it is used and opened, the "sweeter; but if it be scant, once a day is inough, for a need, "though twentie persons should use it.

" If the water will not run to your Cesterne, you may with a "force[37] of twentie shillings,[o] and a pype of eighteen pence the "yard, force it from the lowest part of your house to the "highest.

" But now on the other[39] side behold the Anatomie.

Here are the parts set downe with a rate of the pryses, that a builder may guesse what he hath to pay.

A. the cesterne stone or bricke, prise		0.6.8.[40]
B. D. E. the pype that comes from the cesterne with a stopple to the washer.		0.3.6.
C. a wast pype.[41]		0.1.0.
F. G. the stem of the great stopple with a key to it.		0.1.6.[42]
H. the forme of the upper brim of the vessell or stoole pot.		
M. the stoole pot of stone or lead, pryce of stone.[43]		0.8.0.[44]
N. the great brasse sluce, to which is[45] three inches current, to send it down a gallop into the Jax.		0.10.0.[46]

---

[n] Else all is vayne.

[o] These forces as also the great washer you shall buy at the Queenes Brasiers in Lothbery[38] at the Bores head.

---

[37] *force*] The plunger of a force-pump. This is the earliest example cited in the *OED*.

[38] *Lothbery*] A street in Colman Street Ward, 'possessed for the most by Founders that cast Candlestickes, Chafingdishes, Spice mortars, and such like Copper or Laton workes' (Stow, ed. Kingsford, I, 277).

[39] the other] tother *MS*   [40] bricke prise o 6.8. *A*

[41] pype, *A*   [42] o.1 6 *A*

[43] of stone or lead . . . stone] *MS*; of stone prise *A*

[44] o.8.o *A*   [45] to which is] with *MS*

[46] o.10,o *A*

[47] *forest bill*] A thick knife or chopper with a hooked end used for pruning.

[48] And . . . cakes] *not in MS*

[49] *peke devaunt*] A short beard trimmed, in Nashe's inimitable phrase, to a 'prety polywigge sparrows tayle peake' (*Works*, I, 312).

[50] the whole charge] *not in MS*   [51] yet . . . like] *not in MS*

[52] Memorandum the *A*

This is Don A JAX house, of the new fashion, all in sunder, that a workeman may see what he hath to do.

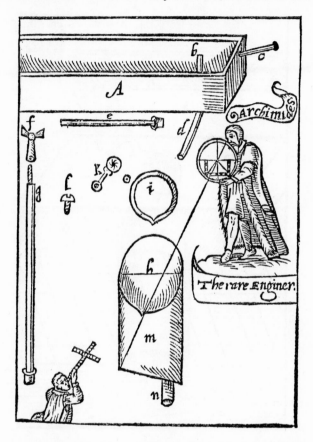

And least you should mislike with this phrase, I had it in a verse of a grave author that was wont to walke up and downe the Court, with a forest bill,[47] I have forgot how it begun (like a beast as he was) but it ended in ryme.

> *O that I were at Oxenford, to eate some Banberie cakes.*[48]

I. the seate with a peke devaunt[49] for elbow roome, the whole charge[50] 30. shillings eight pence, yet a mason of my masters was offred thirtie pounds for the like.[51] Memorandum, the[52] scale is about halfe an inch to a foote.

(*For Footnotes see page* 194.)

Here is the same all put together, that the workeman may see if it be well.

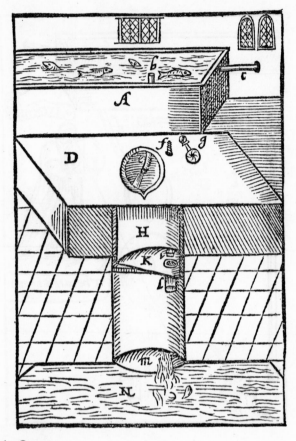

A. the Cesterne.

B. the little washer.

C. the wast pipe.

D. the seate boord.

E. the pipe that comes from the Cesterne.

F. the Screw.

G. the Scallop shell to cover it when it is shut downe.[53]

H. the stoole pot.

I. the stopple.

K. the current.

L. the sluce.[54]

M. N. the vault into which it falles: always remember that (   )[55] at noone and at night, emptie it and leave it halfe a foote deepe in fayre water. And this being well done, and orderly kept, your worst privie may be as sweet as your best chamber.

(For Footnotes see page 197.)

But to conclude all this in a few wordes:[56] it is but a standing close stoole easilie emptyed.

And by the like reason (other formes and proportions observed) all other places of your house, may be kept sweet.

Your worships to commaund

T. C. traveller.[57]

But pah: what have I talked off all this while? of A JAX? Pa-pe, what an unsavorie argument is this?[p] Nay fie, I marvell you would reade it. I have lost all my credite with our[60] wenches, if they heare that my penne hath thus polluted my paper. But alas, tis[61] but my fortune and not my falt; I am forced hereto,[62] when the Maister is in the Imperative moode, the man must obey in the Present tense, though he should be thought for his labour, *As in praesenti, perfectum format in avi,*[q] *ut no nas knavi*[63] &c. Well, yet you see I have not forgot all my Grammer. Iwis it were better for us servingmen[r], if you Maisters, would do more in the Dative case, and speake lesse in the Imperative moodes. If you will be lecherous, we must be bawdes; if you will be quarellous, we must be ruffians[s]: and

---

[p] All this is sweetened with this one sentence. *Humani nihil à me alienum puto.*[58] Or, *dulcia non meruit qui dedignatur amara.*[59]

[q] *Fidelis servus perpetuus Asinus.*

[r] *Quae mala sint Domini,*[64] *quae servi commoda nescis, Condile, qui servum, te gemis*[65] *esse diu.*[66]

[s] By your leaves Masters.[67]

---

[53] shut downe] drawn *MS*

[54] the sluce- *A*

[55] ( )] the chamberlain *MS*

[56] wordes it *A*

[57] Your . . . traveller] *not in MS*

[58] Terence *Heauton Timorumenos* I.77.

[59] *Or . . . amara*] *not in MS.* More commonly with *non gustavit* for *dedignatur,* as in *OF,* 1634, margin Y2[v].

[60] our] the *MS*

[61] tis] it is *B*

[62] hereto] thereto *B*

[63] *As . . . knavi*] A recurrent jest derived from Lily's rule for forming the perfect tense in Latin:

> As in pręsenti, perfectum format in avi,
> Ut no nas navi, vocito, vocitas, vocitavi.

(*Brevissima Institutio,* C6). Cf. Nashe, I, 282, and Marston, *What You Will* II.I. (ed. Wood, II, 255).

[64] Dominini *A*

[65] gemis] *MS;* genus *A, B*

[66] Martial ix.92.1–2.

[67] By . . . Masters] *not in MS*

now my Maister playes the Physition, I must be Potycarie. If
he cast the water, I must minister the clyster, what is the
remedie ?

> *Delirant domini, famuli plectuntur: iniquum est.*[68]

> *The men still beare their Maisters sin,*
> *But little justice is therein.*

But a great many of my Masters betters, may say for themselves,

> *Meae* (*contendere noli*) *stultitiam patiuntur opes.*[t]

> *To strive with us it is but vaine,*
> *Our wealth our follies will sustaine.*

Wherefore now to say somewhat for my selfe, and as it were
to play one bout in mine owne defence (for, if *Zoilus* have
already bitten at my Masters banket, it may be, some *Momes*
will mocke me for my short pittance.) First therfore to answer
some Ciceronians, that maintaine that such a word as *Stercutius*
should not be named in civilitie. (To omit, that where he[70]
condemnes it, there he useth it,[u] and in one place beside[v]) but
I would aske some Rhetoricke Reader (for somtimes, *Eloquence
hath thought it good, to give the sword and buckler place*) whether
it be not as civill a phrase to say, *Stercutius* is made a Nowne
Adjective,[75] as these fewe that I will here recite, which if I
should English, they wold make some perhap cast up their
gorges. Against *Piso*,[w] a great noble man, his better in birth,
his equall in office.

---

[t] Horace.[69]

[u] *Nolo stercus curiae dici Glauciam.*[71] De orat. 157.[72]

[v] *Supra stercus iniectum.*[73] De divina. 92.[74]

[w] *Oratio in Pisonem.*[76]

---

[68] Apparently adapted from Horace *Epistle* i.2.14: 'quidquid delirant reges,
plectuntur Achivi.'

[69] *Epistle* i.18.28–9.   [70] *he*] Cicero.

[71] Nolo . . . Glauciam] *not in MS*; glauciam *A*. 'Tul:' Harington annotation,
Lumley-Folger copy.

[72] De ortat. *A*;   de Orat. iii.41.164.

[73] Supra . . . iniectum] *not in MS*   [74] de Div. i.27.57.

[75] *Stercutius . . . Adjective*] See p. 179, n. 98.

[76] In the passage quoted, T. C. telescopes and selects to suit his purpose.
See 1–6 *passim* and 16.37.

Cum hac me peste & labe confero ? Meministi caenum; nescio quo e gurgustio[77] *te prodire obvoluto capite soleatum ?*[x] *foetidam nobis popinam exhalasti. Unde tu nos partim turpissimè respondendo, partim foedissimè eructando eiecisti.*[y]

And against the worthy *Anthonie* (whom so noble pennes have celebrated)[78] marke what he saith, & where ? even in the Senat: But first, you must imagine that[79] *Anthonie* had had a litle mischaunce, while he sate in Judgement on the Bench (perhaps some foolish Orator, that could not tell a slovenly tale cleanly had bin arguing, of *purgare* and *reficere cloacam.*) Whereby the noble man being queysie, layd open his stomacke,[80] and *Tullie,* owing him a grudge, a yeare after, layes it in his dish in these sweet wordes.

Orem non modo visu foedam; sed etiam auditu[z] &c. *In coetu po. R. negotium publicum gerens, cui ructare turpe esset, is frustis esculentis, vinum, redolentibus, gremium suum, & totum tribunal implevit.*[82]

Thus you see your *M. T. C.* when it[83] pleased him, to

---

[x] *Pauci tua lutulenta vitia noveramus.*

[y] *Epicure ex hara producte.*

[z] O matter slovenly to be seene, to be heard hatefull,[81] &c.

---

[77] egurgustio *A*

[78] *whom . . . celebrated*] Apart from classical writers, foremost to an Elizabethan would have been the Countess of Pembroke whom Harington was later to call 'that Excellent Countesse, and in Poesie the mirrois of our Age' (*L&E,* p. 87). Her *Antonius,* a translation of Robert Garnier's neo-classical tragedy, was first published in 1592.

The use of the plural 'noble pennes' perhaps raises the question whether Fulke Greville's tragedy dealing with Antony and Cleopatra had been written at this date and, if so, whether Harington had been among 'those few' who had seen it before its author prudently consigned it to the fire. In speaking of his literary efforts, Greville's statements are vague, but he seems to indicate that they stemmed from a period of his youth and that this particular tragedy had been destroyed at the time of the Essex uprising (1601) because those who had seen it felt that it might be 'construed, or strained to a personating of vices in the present Governers, and government' (*Life of Sir Philip Sidney,* ed. Nowell Smith, Oxford, 1907, pp. 150–61). (For Harington's subsequent remarks on Greville and his father, see *Apologie,* pp. 241–2).

By extension, the remark could be taken to include the tragedy of *Cleopatra* published in 1594 by Harington's 'good friend Master Samuel Daniel.'

[79] that] *not in MS*

[80] queysie . . . stomacke] queasy-stomaked layd open his mynde *MS*

[81] hateull *A*

[82] *Orem . . . implevit*] II *Philippic* 25.63.   [83] it] *not in MS*

displease others, would use wordes as bad as the best of us.[84]
But I smyle at some whose manners proove that thear mynds
admit all wickednes, and yet forsooth theyr ears cannot brooke
a litle scurrilytye. Ys[85] it not pittye that men of so fyne ears
should *male audire*. Yf[86] one name a merd they thinke they are
mard but a fylthyer thing then that mard them. What[87] doe
they with Rabbles and Aretyne in theyr studyes?[88]

But to argue succintly (as they call it) I say, that that some
call scurrilitie, in this booke, is indeed but a checke to
scurrillitie. I wil[89] prove it. Teachers of all sortes,[aa] when they
will teach one to mend his fault, will shewe the fault in themselves first. Also the incomparable Poet of our age, to give a most
artificially reproofe of following the letter too much, commits
the same fault of purpose.

> *You that do Dixionary method bring,*
> *Into your rymes, running in ratling rowes.[bb]*

Further this booke, where it seemes most loose, marke if it
do not stoppe[cc] rather then open all gaps[92] of lasciviousnesse.

But least some bad disputers confessing the premisses to be
true, should denie the conclusion, let me deale *Sillogisticè*[93] in
moode and figure.[dd] And that the Sillogisme may be sutable to

---

[aa] Grammarians. Musitians. Daunsers. Fensers.[90]

[bb] *Syr P. Sid.*[91]

[cc] A good triall of what spirit a booke is written.

[dd] This is to you that be Schollers.

---

[84] but alasse wee have had some would belche backward upon the benche.
Marginal n. MS; om. A, B   [85] ys *MS*

[86] yf *MS*   [87] what *MS*

[88] But I . . . studyes.] *MS; om. A, B because of space*

[89] I wil] Ile *MS*

[90] Daunsers. Fensers.] Dauncing fensing. *MS.* Fenfers *A*

[91] Sonnet xv, ll. 5–6, *Astrophel and Stella* (*Works*, II, 248).

[92] gaps] *MS, B*; gapes *A*

[93] *Sillogisticè*] This form does not appear in the *OED*, but Plat had earlier
used it in his attack on Harington (*Sundrie new and Artificiall remedies*, D4ᵛ).

the proposition, let it be in the third figure the 5. moode called[94] *Bocardo.*[ee]

Some homely wordes in necessary matters are not to be condemned.[ff]

But all ages, all writers, all states, have used these wordes in these matters.[gg]

Ergo, the title of the booke should not be condemned.[hh] Now if any be in so fierse a figure, and in so angrie a moode, that he will reduce all to *Barbara,* I thinke we should chop logicke best with such a one[96] in *ferio.*

But if an argument be brought against us in the 2. figure, in a sober moode, and in the[97] sacred name of *Cesare*; in this wise.[ii]

No wordes obscenous, scurrill, and sordidous,[98] should come to modest, chast, and vertuous eares;   1

But all words concerning the subject of the booke, are obscenous, scurrill, and sordidous: 2

Ergo, no part of the booke is approvable. Faith, then we are all *non plus.* I would our *festino*[99] had bene *caelarent*; for there is no denying nor replying to that moode,[100] but only say, God save the Queene, & pray for the Psalme of mercy.   3

Well, yet I trust how ever my master speeds, I shall do wel inough. *Aquila non capit muscas.*[jj] Wherefore to conclude, and to grace my selfe a litle with you and your friends, let me tell

---

[ee] A Sillogisme in Bocardo.[95]   [ff] *Maior.*

[gg] *Minor.*   [hh] Conclusion.

[ii] A Sillogisme in the first moode of the second figure.

[jj] Egles stoope not at flyes.[101]

---

[94] called] *not in MS*

[95] *Bocardo*] See p. 91, n. 48. As stated, T.C.'s example does not have the pattern of a syllogism in the third figure where, in Thomas Wilson's words, 'the double repeate' [middle term] should be the 'former parte in both Propositions' (*The Rule of Reason,* 1580, I1ᵛ–I2).

In the following passage, T.C. is apparently punning on the mnemonic terms and the classical Latin forms.

[96] with . . . one] *not in MS*   [97] the] a *MS*

[98] *sordidous*] This antedates the earliest example cited in the *OED.*

[99] festino: *A*

[100] *caelarent . . . moode*] Since its conclusion is a universal negative.

[101] *Note not in MS. Aquila . . . muscas*] Emblem XXXII in Combe's *Theater of Fine Devices* illustrates this common proverb. The posy reads:

> Great persons should not with their might,
> Oppresse the poorer, though they might.

you some of my adventures. A servants boast you know[102] is to be like his master, loe then how many wayes I can liken me
1 to him.[kk] First[104] we are neare of an age, past our foole age,[105] neither young nor old.[106]

2 Both of a Complexion, enclining to the orientall colour of a Croydon sanguine.[107]

3 Like in Disposition, not idle, nor well occupied.

4 One of my kin did teach him at Eaton, & one of his kin taught me at Oxford.

5 We have bene beyond sea, but never out of the Queenes dominions.[108] In England beyond Wales.[ll] In Irland, on[109] this side England,[mm] where we saw young children mothers at xi. young women old at 23. We[111] saw some fayre with litle dressing, fat with scant feeding, and warme with thin clothing.

Excellent Religion; Masse in the morning; common prayer

[kk] This I learne of my cosin M. Tomas Cicero to prayse my selfe.[103]

[ll] Milford.

[mm] Waterford because it is on[110] this side the English pale.

The device showing an eagle amidst a swarm of flies is followed by an ottava:

> Who notes the noble bird, that doth command,
> All feathered fowles subjected to the skies,
> And hath the Eagles princely nature scand,
> Which doth disdaine to litigate with flies;
> Hereby may weigh and wisely understand,
> In base contention little honour lies.
> For he that striveth with th' inferiour sort,
> Shall with dishonour reape an ill report.

For the identification of Thomas Combe of the *Anatomie* with the translator of the *Theater of Fine Devices*, see Introduction.

[102] you know] *not in MS*

[103] Ciceto *A*. For some examples of Cicero's inveterate self-adulation, see *Brutus* 317–24; *Orator* 102 ff.; *Orat. in Pisonem, passim.*

[104] him, First *A*   [105] *foole age*] See p. 124, n. 82.

[106] old.] old and yet older then god a myghty. *MS*

[107] *Croydon sanguine*] Sallow.

[108] *We have . . . dominions*] Combe apparently accompanied his master to Ireland in 1568 when Harington, his brother-in-law Edward Rogers, and six others were authorized as 'undertakers for the repeopling and inhabiting of the province of Munster' to take £1,000 of lawful English money for the necessary use of 'themselves, their company, servants, and followers' (*CSP, Ireland*, III, (1586–8), 113).   [109] on] of *MS*

[110] on] of *MS*   [111] 23. we *A*

at noone; common daunsing at night[nn]; we went as undertakers thither; we came backe overtaken, as for those that mockt us so, God and our Lady, and one more go with them.

Since this travell we have bene both Poeticall, and I [6][112] Musicall & Pictoricall,[113] & though we may lye and steale by authoritie,[114] yet we are taken for true men, and have holpe to hang theeves.[115]

At this houre some of our friends, thinke us worthy of better 7 fortunes then we have, but none is our friend so much to helpe us to them.

We have playd, and bene playd with, for our writings. *Si* 8 *quis quod fecit, patiatur ius erit aequum.*[116] If you do take but such as you give, it is[117] one for another, but if they that play so, would give us but a peece of gold for everie good verse we thinke we have made; we should leave some of them, but poore felowes.[oo] But soft, if I shold tell all, he wold say, I am of kin

---

[nn] The 1. they call Gods service. The 2. they call the Queenes service. The 3. some thinke the devils service.

[oo] Now if the man such prayse will have. Then what must he that keepes the knave? Dametas in *Arcadya*.[118]

---

[112] *Numbers 6, 7, 8 not in MS.*

[113] *Pictoricall*] This is the earliest example cited in the *OED*.

[114] *we may . . . authoritie*] In reference to the fact that both Harington and Combe's published works were translations. Cf. Harington's epigram '*Of honest Theft. To my good friend Master* Samuel Daniel':

> Proud *Paulus* late my secrecies revealing,
> Hath told I got some good conceits by stealing.
> But where got he those double Pistolets,
> With which good clothes, good fare, good land he gets?
> Tush, those, he saith, came by a man of warre,
> That brought a Prize of price, from countries farre.
> Then, fellow Thiefe, let's shake together hands,
> Sith both our wares are filcht from forren lands.
> > You'le spoil the Spaniards, by your writ of Mart:
> > And I the Romanes rob, by wit, and Art.
>
> > > (*L&E*, p. 196.)

[115] *and have . . . theeves*] A reference to Harington's official duties as a J.P. and sheriff.

[116] aequum] *MS;* equum *A, B*   [117] it is] tis *MS*

[118] *Note not in MS.* The alarming appearance of a bear having disrupted the Arcadian scene, the loutish Dametas thrust himself into a bush from fear, 'for, like a man of a very kind nature, soone to take pittie of himselfe, he was full

to *Sauntus Ablabius*. It is[119] no matter, since he makes me to write of *Sauntus Acacchius*.

But now, that you may know I have bene a dealer in Emblemes, I will conclude with a devise[120] not sharpe in conceyt, but of venerable antiquitie, and yet by my masters owne computation, it is not so auncient as Dame *Cloacyna*, by 1800. yeares[121] and more. Now riddle me what name is this.[pp]

The (*grace of God*)[123] *guides well both age and youth,*
Fly sin with feare, as harmlesse (hare) doth hound,
Like precious (ring) embrace, more precious truth,
As (tunne) full of good juyce, not emptie sound,
In these right scand, Mysacmos name is found.[124]

[pp] It is good to set a name to the booke: For a booke without name may be called a libell.[122]

---

resolved not to see his owne death.' After his apprentice, the disguised Musidorus, has slain the bear and rescued him, Dametas joyfully sings:

> Now thanked be the great God *Pan*,
>   which thus preserves my loved life:
> Thanked be I that keepe a man,
>   who ended hath this fearefull strife:
> For if my man must praises have,
>   what then must I that keepe the knave?

(*Complete Works of Sir Philip Sidney*, I, 119–23.)

[119] It is] tis *MS*   [120] a devise] an emblem *MS*   [121] yeares] yeer *MS*
[122] It is ... libell] A booke withowt name may be counted a libell. *MS*. The absence of a name seems to have been accepted as a salient factor in determining a libel. When John Hales was being examined in respect to the Marprelate controversy, he denied that Penry's *Supplication to the Parliament* was a libel 'for he subscribed his name' (*State Trials*, ed. T. B. Howell, London, 1816, I, 1267). Martin makes the same point in *The Epistle* (*The Marprelate Tracts 1588, 1589*, ed. W. Pierce, London, 1911, p. 81). Cf. *CSP, Dom.*, III, 1591–4, 410 and the *Apologie*, p. 214.
[123] *grace of God*] 'Joannes sig- / nifies gracia / Dei,' Harington annotation in the Lumley-Folger copy.   [124] *no parentheses in MS*

AN APOLOGIE[1].

1. *Or rather a retractation.*
2. *Or rather a recantation.*
3. *Or rather a recapitulation.*
4. *Or rather a replication.*
5. *Or rather an examination.*
6. *Or rather an accusation.*
7. *Or rather an explication.*
8. *Or rather an exhortation.*
9. *Or rather a consideration.*
10. *Or rather a confirmation.*
11. *Or rather all of them.*
12. *Or rather none of them.*

WHEN I HAD FINISHED the precedent pamphlet, & in mine owne fantasie very sufficiently evacuated my head of such homely stuffe, of which it might seeme it was verie full charged, and shewed how litle conceit or opinion I had of mine owne ability to handle stately matters, by chusing so meane a subject to discharge my selfe upon: I thought now to rest me a while, and to gather some strength, by feeding on some finer meates, & making some cullesses[2] and restoratives for my selfe out of some other mens kitchins, & not open this vaine any more. But I laboured all in vaine to stop such a vaine: for certaine people of the nature of those that first dwelt in the Canaries,[a] have forced me to a further labour. For whether it were over-watching my selfe at primero,[4] or eating too much venison,

---

[a] Canaries were so called, of the dogges that were found in them.[3]

---

[1] *MS missing from p. 205 to p. 251,* you have read

[2] *cullesses*] Strong broths.   [3] Pliny *Natural History* vi.38.205.

[4] *primero*] A fashionable card game. See Harington's epigram '*The Story of* Marcus *life at Primero*' (*L&E*, pp. 227–8).

which they say is a verie melancholie meate[5]: I know not how, but betimes one morning when we use commonly to take our sweetest sleepe, namely betweene eight and halfe houre past ten, I was either in so straunge a dreame, or in so strong[6] a melancholie, that me thought there came to me a nimble dapper fellow (I can not hit on his name) one that hath pretie petifogging skill in the law, and hath bin an under-shiriffe (but not thrise[b]) and is now in the nature of an Atturney, this honest friend told me this solemne tale; I was (saith he) yesternight at ( ) Ordinarie, and there met M. Zoilus, M. Momus, and three or foure good natured Gentlemen more of the same crew, and toward the end of supper they fell to talking (as their maner is) of certaine bookes lately come foorth. And one of them told how Lipsyas the great Politicke (that learned to speake so good English but a while since[8]) had written a booke *de Cruce*,[9] protesting that though he understood not the language, yet it offended his conscience, to see so manie crosses

---

[b] The saying is Thrise an undershiriffe & ever a knave.[7]

---

[5] *venison . . . meate*] See Sir Thomas Elyot, *The Castel of Helth*, 1541, F3^v–F4.

[6] strong] straunge *B*

[7] un dershiriffe *A*. Not in Tilley. A paradox based upon it appears in Part Two of the *Gesta Grayorum* printed by Nichols: 'An Under Sherife thrice may be noe knave; for he doth naught without warrant' (*Progresses*, III, 338). According to W. W. Greg, this 'so-called second part' is a 'composition of some twenty years later having no immediate connexion with the original entertainment' (*Gesta Grayorum*, Malone Society Reprint, London, 1914, p. viii).

[8] *how Lipsyas . . . since*] Apparently a puff for the recent translation by W. Jones of the *Sixe Bookes of Politickes or Civil Doctrine* of Justus Lipsius which Richard Field had printed in 1594. From the translator's address to the reader, it is clear that this version was intended to supplant an earlier and unsatisfactory one: 'And although I had at the beginning, great reasons to disswade me from the enterprise (as a matter over-difficult, the same having bene attempted by two or three, and perished, with one, in the bud, with another in the blossome, and with the third, being no sooner ripe, but foorthwith it was rotten.)' (A3).

Multiple entries in the *S.R.* support Jones's statement: an English version of the work was entered to John Wolfe on 15 Nov. 1589; on 13 Jan. 1590 another entry to Wolfe was recorded for both the Latin and the English; and again on 10 July 1590 an English translation was entered, this time to Edward Aggas (II, 534; 537; 554).

[9] *de Cruce*] Lipsius's study of the historical origins of the cross as a Christian symbol, published at Antwerp in 1593, included illustrations of the various kinds of crosses.

AN APOLOGIE

in one booke, and he have so few in his purse[10]; then they
spoke of M. Raynolds booke against Bellarmine,[11] but they
could find no fault with it, for they said it was of a matter they
used not to trouble themselves withall: thirdly they descanted
of the new Faerie Queene & the old[12] both, and the greatest
fault they could find in it, was that the last verse disordered
their mouthes, and was like a tricke of xvii. in a sinkapace.[13]
Finally they ran over manie mens writings, saying some wanted
rime, some wanted reason, and some both.[14] One they sayd,
was so young, that he had not yet learned to write, another so
old, he had forgotten to write, & was fit now to be *donatus rude*,
as Horace[15] saith. But to make short, at last one of them pulled

---

[10] *to see . . . purse*] A perennial jest on coins marked with a figure of the
cross. Cf. Nashe, II, 223; III, 75.

[11] *M. Raynolds . . . Bellarmine*] *De Romanae Ecclesiae Idololatria*. See notes
to p. 104 above.

[12] *the new . . . old*] Bks. I–VI were printed in 1596 by Richard Field; the first
three had originally appeared in 1590.

[13] *like a tricke . . . sinkapace*] A *cinquepace* was a lively dance related to the
galliard; it was elaborated by various 'tricks' and 'turns.' Cf. Sir John Davies:

> So Musick to her owne sweet tunes doth trip
>   With tricks of, 3, 5, 8, 15, and more:
> So doth the Art of Numbring seeme to skip
>   From ev'n to odd in her proportion'd score.

(*Orchestra*, st. 95, *The Poems*, ed. Clare Howard, N.Y., 1941; for other
references, see Supplement to Nashe, v, 34–5.)

[14] *manie mens . . . both*] This passage dealing with the discussion of current
literature by young gallants over the supper table seems to have been utilized
by John Davies of Hereford in an epigram in *Wits Bedlem* (1617); from the
epigram addressed to Harington in the same work, we know Davies was familiar
with the *Metamorphosis*.

> *Tis merry, when knaves meet.*
>
> Conceipted youths, when they at wine are met
> Mong other matters lightly they inquire
> What well pend Pamphlet lately out is set?
> What merry *Epigrams* or soure *Satire*?
> . . . .
> All that can say this as their *Pater noster*
> Have seene the Lions, sweet well seasoned youths
> About the *Muses* Minions still they muster
> To get some swelling lines to fill their mouthes:
> But for their owne *Muse* it doth ever sing,
> *Rime* without *Reas'n* a common English thing.

(Quoted by L. Ennis in *HLB*, XI, April, 1937, 18–19.)

[15] *donatus . . . Horace*] *Epistle* i.1.2. The *rudis* was a staff or foil given to a
gladiator as a symbol of honourable discharge.

out of his bosome, a booke that was not to be sold in Paules churchyard, but onely that he had borowed it of his friend, and it was intituled *The metamorpho-sis of A JAX*, at which they began to make marvellous sport: and because it was a rainie night, they agreed to read over the whole discourse to passe the time with. First they read the authors name, & though they understood it not, yet that it might not passe without a jest, they swore that it signified *Myse in a sack of mosse.*[c] They read the letters, and stumbling once or twice on a figure called *Prolepsis* or prevention,[16] they were angrie their scoffes were so prevented. But when they found *Rabbles* named, then they were at home, they looked for pure stuffe where he was cited for an author. The letters being ended, they perused the pictures, they swore they were fit for a gongfarmer[17] and a chimney-sweeper.[d] Then they fell to the Metamorpho-sis, it pleased them well, they sayd it was scurrill, base, shallow, sordidous; the dittie, the dirge, the etymologie, the pictures, gave matter of jest, of scorne, of derision, of contempt. At last, they came to the true intent (as they thought) of the whole discourse of reforming Maister AJax ill breath, why, they were so pleased with it, they were readie to untrusse, and thought to have gone to it presently; but when they came to the exposition of the name *Misacmos*, and found it was a hater of filth, it was such a jerke, that they were halfe out of countenance with it; swounds saith one of them, this fellow is an enemie to us, for we are counted but filthie fellowes among the grave gray-beardes. But at last, when they were come to the double distichon,[18] directly entituled to them by name, they had no sooner read it, but there was such spitting & spalling,[19]

---

[c] Misacmos.

[d] And they both be honester occupations, then Zoylus and Momus.

---

[16] *Prolepsis or prevention*] The refuting of objections in anticipation (Quintilian *Inst.* iv.i.49). The Elizabethans more frequently used the term *procatalepsis* for this technique (Puttenham, pp. 231–2 and Henry Peacham, *The Garden of Eloquence*, 1593, 2B4). Harington's usage is earlier than the example cited in the *OED*.

[17] gongfarmer] dongfarmer *B*   [18] *double distichon*] See p. 80.

[19] *spalling*] Or spawling—spitting out with force. This antedates the example cited in the *OED*.

as though they had bene halfe choked,[e] they thought they should never get the tast out of their mouthes, yet they tooke immediatly fiftie pipes of Tabacco between five of them, and an ownce or two of kissing comfits.[21] And soone after, swearing over a Pater noster or two, and cursing two or three Credoes, (I meane the poxe & three or foure smal curses) they vowed a solemne revenge, and taking pen and inke, they fell[22] to quoting of it, meeting with some matter almost in everie page, either to deride or to carpe at, and when they had done (for it wold make a booke to tell all that passed among them) at last one of them, that had some more[23] judgement, but not lesse malice then the rest, said in great choller, Doth this idle headed writer, because he can tel a tale of old *Stercutius* out of S. Augustine, think that his wit wil serve him to find meanes to amend the ill savours in Ritchmond and Greenwich? No, if Hercules that served *Augeus*, if *Atlas* that sustained the world, if S. Christopher that is painted at Richmond with his cariage, *qui tollit peccata mundi*, if all these should joyne with him, I doubt if it could be done. Yet said another of them (in scoffe) we may thanke him for his good meaning. Nay rather, said a third man in earnest, let us plague him for his mallapertnesse. In conclusion[24] they all layed their heads together as neare as they could for their brow antlers, and devised to indite you at a privie Sessions.[25] Some said, you could not be indited, except you were put out of the peace first[f]; but straight one alledged a president in Wiltshire, of a Justice indyted for a barreter.[27] Now therefore (sayd my litle Atturney) advise you

---

[e] Martial saith *Quincunces puto post decem peractos.*[20]

[f] That they found in the [118.][26] page.

---

[20] Quincuncies *A.* i.27.2.

[21] *kissing comfits*] Sweetmeats to sweeten the breath. Falstaff (*MWW* V.v.22) couples them with snow eringoes, considered an aphrodisiac.

| [22] fell] fall *B* | [23] more] *om. B* |
| [24] couclusion *A* | [25] *privie Sessions*] A double pun. |

[26] 44. page *A*, 41. page *B*

[27] *of a Justice . . . barreter*] i.e., a justice of the peace charged with disrupting the peace. A barrator 'is a common wrangler, that setteth men at ods, and is himselfe never quiet, but at brawle with one or other' (Cowell, 13[v]).

This is perhaps an allusion to the wrangling of two notable Wiltshire families—the Danverses and the Longes—which prefaced the murder of Henry Longe to which Harington had earlier alluded. See p. 59 and n. 29.

how to answer it, for the Session will be a purchased Session[28] sooner then you looke for.[29] He had but newe ended his speech, and I had scarce leasure to thanke him, when me thought there rushed into my chamber, a thicke well trussed fellow, with a badge just over his heart, and commaunds me in the name that I love above all names, to go immediatly with him. I must say truly, that though I blessed the name he used, and the badge he ware; yet I beshrewed his heart for bringing me no better newes next my hart, but with him I went (for needes he[30] must go whom the Devill drives)[31] and yet why should I bely the Devill? I thinke for fortie shillings more then his fee, he would have bene seeking me a moneth in every place save where I was.[32] But to proceed, me thought this gentle pursevant brought me before an austere and grave Magistrate, whom I greatly loved and honored, to answer to diverse objections and articles that I never expected to be charged with, I comforted my selfe as well as I could with an old adage or two, *qui vadit plane vadit sane*, the plaine way hath the surest footing,[33] and *magna est veritas, & praevalet*, great is the truth, and prevaileth,[34] and then answered my accusers as I could.

The maner of the accusation, was not much unlike the assault of a towne: for first they skirmished as it were with smal

---

Both Sir John Danvers (father of the murderer) and Sir Walter Longe (elder brother of the victim) had served as justices for Wiltshire—Sir John almost continually from 1576 to 1592 and Sir Walter from 1588 to 1592 ('Minutes of Proceedings in Sessions in 1563 and 1574 to 1592,' *Wiltshire Arch. and Natural History Society*, IV, 1949, *passim*). From a declaration 'of the ground of the conceaved mislike of Sir Walter Longe, knighte, & Henry Longe . . . againste Sir John Danvers, knighte, his Sonnes & Followers,' we learn that the quarrel originated in Sir John Danvers's having prosecuted two servants of the Longes for robberies. As a result 'Sir Walter Longe was by the Justice of Assizes sharpelie reprehended for undue proceeding in matter concerning the said Robberie,' and, ultimately, 'committed to the Fleete, for his undue Course againste the said Sir John Danvers, for his due proceeding in Hir Majesties service' (Hawarde, *in extenso*, pp. 391–3; *CSP, Dom.*, IV, 1595–7, 34; cf. *Salisbury MSS*, VI, 267–8).

[28] *purchased Session*] i.e., one for which proceedings have been instituted; in legal terminology, *to purchase* means 'to commence an action.'

[29] for.] for it. *B*   [30] he] *om. B*

[31] *for needes . . . drives*] Tilley D278.

[32] *I thinke . . . was*] Cf. Stubbes, Pt. I, 117–18.

[33] *qui vadit . . . footing*] Cf. 'Chi va piano, va sano, va lontano' and Tilley W9.

[34] *magna est . . . prevaileth*] III Esdras 4:41 and Tilley T579.

shot, which I bare off with the armour and shield of plaine dealing and honest simplicitie, but finding their forces increase, I was glad to retire me into the castle of innocencie, where they made a sore batterie, with Rabbinets, Minions, Sakers, & Demicannons.[35] For as God wold have it, they had no Cannons,[g] but thus they objected, and thus I answered.

Some layd to my charge, I was an idle fellow, and shewed 1[36] by my writings I had litle to do. Alas said I, it is too true, and therefore if you know any man that hath an office to spare, you may doe well to preferre me to it: for it were a bad office that I would not chaunge for this I have taken upon me; and if I had another, I would be content this were devided among you.

Some said I was such[37] a foole to thinke seriously the devise 2 worthie to be published and put in practise; as a common benifite, trust me that is true to.

Some supposed, that because my writings now lay dead, and 3 had not bene thought of this good while; I thought (as Alcibiades cut of his dogs tayle, to make the people talke of his curtall[38]) so I wold send my Muse abroad, masking naked in a net[39] that I might say.

Nunc iterum volito viva per ora virum.[40]

Of my honor that is not true. Will you deny it on your oth? No by our Lady, not for a thousand pounds.

---

[g] Cannons signifie rules of law. Nowe they are not right cannons but bastard cannons, that batter innocencie.

---

[35] *Rabbinets . . . Demicannons*] Various kinds of ordinance. See Harrison's classification, Holinshed's *Chronicles*, I, S2[v].

[36] *om. A, B*

[37] such] *all presentation copies, B; but A*

[38] *as Alcibiades . . . curtall*] 'Alcibiades had a marvelous fayer great dogge, that cost him three score and tenne minas, and he cut of his taile that was his chief beawtie. When his friendes reproved him, and tolde him how every man blamed him for it: he fell a laughing, and tolde them he had that he sought. For, sayeth he, I would have the ATHENIANS rather prate upon that, then they should saye worse of me' (Plutarch 'Alcibiades,' tr. North, Shakespeare Head Press, Stratford, II, 116–17).

[39] *masking . . . net*] Cf. 'You dance in a net and think nobody sees you,' Tilley N130.

[40] *nunc . . . virum*] Adapted from an epigram of Ennius quoted by Cicero *Tusculanae disputationes* i.15.34.

4   Some said plainly, because my last work was an other mans invention, and that some fine phrase-making fellowes, had found a distinction betweene a versifier and a Poet,[41] I wrate this to shew I could be both when I listed, though I meane to be neither, as Thales Milesius, by making himselfe ritch in one yeare shewde his contempt of ritches.[42] The devill of the lye that is.

5   Some surmised against me, that because the time is so toying, that wholesome meates cannot be digested without wanton sauce, and that even at wise mens tables, fooles have most of the talke, therefore I came in with a bable to have my tale heard, I must needs confesse it.

6   Some said that in emulation of outlandish witts, and to be one of the first English, that had given the venter to make the title of his worke the worst part of it; I was perswaded to write of such an argument, I will never denie that while I live.

7   Some affirmed that I had taken this laughing libertie to grace som that have favord me, and grate against some that had galled me, *guiltie my Lord*.

Alasse poor Gentleman (say the standers by) he will be condemned certainly for this that he hath confest already, if he be not saved by his booke:[43] let us heare what he will answere to the rest of the inditement.

---

[41] *and that . . . Poet*] Predominant in Harington's mind would have been George Puttenham whom he designates in his 'Briefe Apologie of Poetrie' by the terms 'unknown Godfather' and 'Ignoto' but whom he had earlier identified by name in a written direction to Richard Field, their mutual printer (*N&Q*, 11 s., I, 1910, 404).

Although taking cognizance of Puttenham's distinction set forth on the opening page of his *Arte of English Poesie*, Harington declines to bestow any long time in discussing 'whether Master *Faire* translating *Virgil*, Master *Golding* translating *Ovids* Metamorphosis, and my selfe in this worke that you see, be any more then versifiers,' but to the young translator, having completed his stint of 32,000-odd lines, the distinction must have appeared a trifle supererogatory. In any case, he retaliated by pointedly observing that Puttenham's own poetry decisively proved the assertion of 'M. *Sidney* and all the learneder sort' that poetry is a gift and not an art (*OF*, 1634, §3). See also his sonnet '*To the Earle of Essex, of one envious of* Ariosto *translated*' (*L&E*, pp. 176–7).

[42] *as Thales . . . ritches*] Aristotle *Politics* i. 4.5–6. Also Cicero *de Divin.* i.49.111–12. Thales, reproached for poverty which resulted from his interest in philosophy, countered the charge by cornering the market in olive presses and making a fortune.

[43] *if he . . . booke*] Punning on *by the book*, a phrase used in claiming 'benefit of clergy.'

You did meane some disgrace in the letter afore the booke 8
and in many passages of the booke it selfe, to Ladies and
Gentlewemen. Who I? God damne me if I love them not, I
feare more to be damned for loving them too well.

You did thinke to scoffe at some Gentlemen that have 9
served in some honorable services, though with no great good
successe. As I am a Gentleman not guilty: neither do I meane
any, but such as will needs be called M. Captains, having
neither caried out with them, nor[44] brought home with them,
worth, wealth, or wit.

You did seeke to discredit the honest meaning & laudable 10
endevours of some zealous & honest men, that seeke for
reformation, & labour faithfully & fruitfully in the word. To
this in all & everie not guiltie, provided they rayle not against
bishops nor against the Communion book.

You did intend some scorne to great Magistrats & men in 11
authority, either alive or deceassed, under covert names to cover
som knavery. Knavery? no as God Judge me my Lord, not
guiltie, the good yeare of all the knaverie and knaves[45] to for
me. By whom will you be tryed? By the Queene and the Ladies,
by the Counsell and the Lordes. What sawcie younker will not
meaner tryall serve you? No good faith my Lord, I loved
alwayes to be the worst of the companie.[46]

Well sirra this is the Judgement of the Court, that because
there is hope you may proove a wiser man hereafter, and that
you have some better friendes then you are worthie of, you
shall have this favour; if the inditement[47] happen to be
found,[48] you shall travers it, and you shall chuse xii. free
holders *bonos & legales homines*,[49] that shal enquire of the

---

44 nor] *B*; not *A*   45 and knaves] *om. B*

46 *I loved . . . companie*] Cf. the epigram 'Misacmos *of himselfe that loves to
be worst in the company*' (*L&E*, p. 305).   47 indiment *A*

48 *if the inditement . . . found*] A written accusation of a criminal or penal
offence was exhibited to the jurors and if 'by their verdict found and presented
to be true,' it was declared a *billa vera*, signifying 'that the presentor hath
furnished his presentment or denunciation with probable evidence, and [it is]
worthy of farder consideration. And thereuppon, the party presented by the
same bill, is said to stand indicted of the crime, and so tyed to make answer
unto it, either by confessing, or traversing the indictment' (Cowell, 2B2ᵛ and K3).

49 *bonos & legales homines*] Used to describe jurors who should 'bee of good
fame and *Legales homines*, that may dispende yeerely twentie shillings of
Freehold, or twentie six shillings eight pence of Copyhold' (Lambard, 2H1ᵛ).

qualitie of your discourse, and bring in their verdict *quindena Paschae*[50] & if they find you guilty, you shall have a hole bored in your eare.[51] What to do? to weare my M^rs. favour at? Now, God save your M^rs. life my Lord. Clarcke of the peace draw his endytement upon the foure last articles that he denied, & upon the Statute of *Scandala,*[h] for I tel you we must teach you to learne the lawes of the Realme, as well as your rules of Poetrie. Lawes? I trow I have the law at my fingers endes.

Aures perdentes super & sint Pillory stantes,
Scandala[53] *rumantes in Regis consiliantes,*
Aut in magnates nova sediciosa loquentes,
Non producentes autores verba ferentes.[54]

Their eares must on the Pillory be nayld',
That have against her highnesse counsell rayld',
Or such as of the Peeres fowle brutes do scatter,
And cannot bring their autor for the matter.

Wherefore you shall find I will keepe me safe enough from scandaling. And if you do, it is the better for you.

What is your name? *Misacmos.* What it is a Welche name I thincke? of whence do you write your selfe? *Misacmos* of Carnarvan Gentleman. Who made you of Carnarvan? She that made you of England.[55] Well you shall fare never the worse for

---

[h] *Anno 1. 2. Ph. M. Cap. 3. Anno. 23. Elis. Cap. 2.*[52]

---

[50] *quindena Paschae*] One of the five 'returnes' in Easter term when the sheriff or bailiff returned a writ to the court certifying what he had done touching the serving of the writ (Cowell, 3L4^v).

[51] *you shall . . . eare*] The standard punishment for a rogue or vagabond (Cowell, 3M3^v and Harrison R1^v). Among the various punishments for libel and slander were fines, imprisonment, whipping, the pillory, loss of the ears, nailing the ears (see below), and wearing papers (A. K. R. Kiralfy, *A Source Book of English Law*, London, 1957, pp. 320–32).

[52] *Statute of Scandala*] See p. 118, n. 42.

[53] Scandala] *Lumley-Folger, Nares-Folger;* Scanda *A, B*

[54] ferentes] *B;* serentes *A*

[55] *Misacmos . . . England*] On 11 May 1579 the Queen had granted Harington the constableship of Carnarvon Castle in North Wales in reversion after his father with a fee of sixty pounds a year, a reward, according to Harington, for his 'father and mothers .22. years servyce' (*CSP, Dom.*, XII, Addenda 1580–1625, 424; *L&E*, p. 138).

that, but looke to the answering of your endytement I advise
you. What must I have no counsell? Straight a bigge fellow
with a beggin[56] on his head, and his gowne of of one shoulder,[57]
cryes no, the Queene is a partie.[i] But I had rather your gown
were of the other[59] shoulder & your head after, then you should
make her a partie against me, & yet as ill as I love you, I wold
my second sonne had chaunged possibillities with your eldest
for a thing that I know, and thus after a few wrangling wordes,
me thought the Court rose for that time, and suddenly my man
came bussling into my chamber and told me, that all the
Gentlemen that had bene riding on the heath were come backe
againe, and that it was neare xi. of the clocke, and straight I
called for my sute of Abrizetta,[60] and made all the hast I
could to make me readie, not so much as tarying to say my
prayers, least I might not come time enough to the peace of
God at the closet, and so I might be in daunger to loose my
dynner.

But having somewhat better ponderd with my selfe this
foresaid fancie, I was somewhat troubled with it, not so much
for those hanging Metaphors, for as a good Knight of our
country[61] sayd, gogs soule sirs, the best Gentleman of us all
need not forsweare hanging,[62] but that I thought that my Genius

---

[i] I meane no Lawyer of our time, but one that Martiall speakes of.[58]

---

[56] *beggin*] Or biggin, the coif of a sergeant-at-law.

[57] *and his gowne . . . shoulder*] Perhaps identifiable to Harington's contemporaries on this account.

[58] 'Quod semper clamas quodque omnibus obstrepis Heli / Non facis hoc
gratis accipis ut taceas': Harington annotation in the Lumley-Folger copy.
Martial i.95 with slight variation.   [59] *other, A*

[60] *Abrizetta*] I am unable to explain this.

[61] *a good Knight of our country*] 'Sr George / Sidnam,' Harington annotation
in the Lumley-Folger copy. Possessed of much property in Somerset, Sir
George mainly resided at Combe Sydenham. He had been sheriff of Somerset
in 1576 and one of the commanders in the county of the 3,000–4,000 men
readied for defence in 1588. His only daughter had married Sir Francis Drake.
Lady Jane Rogers, Harington's mother-in-law, was related to the Sydenham
family, and it is to be noted that the Haringtons named one son George and
another Sidenham (G. F. Sydenham, *History of the Sydenham Family*, Surrey,
1928, pp. 124–5; 160; 411–12; *Misc. Gen. et Her.*, n.s., IV, 192).

[62] *the best . . . hanging*] Stressing that Englishmen often boasted that members
of their family had been sent to the stake or the gibbet, a Venetian recorded the
story of a foreigner who asked an English captain whether any one of his family

hereby presaged to me some perill to my reputation, of the sundrie sensures I should incurre by letting such a Pamphlet fly abroad at such a time, when everie thing is taken at the volley,[63] and therefore I held it not unnecessarie, as much as in me lay, to keep it from the view and censure of all such as were like to deride it, despise it, or disgrace it, and to recommend it onely to all such as I thought wold allow it & approve it. For to confesse the truth frankly to you my good cosins ὁ καὶ ἡ φιλοστιλπνος I desire not altogether to have it concealed, least som hungrie promoting[64] fellowes should beg it as a concealement,[65] and begge the autor also, for writing a thing that he were ashamed to shew, but if I might governe the matter as I would, I would generallie recommend it only to such as have houses and families of their own. For I remember I have read of a certaine king[66] of the Lacedemonians, that being one day privat in his garden, was teaching one of his sonnes of five yeares old to ride on a sticke, and unawares a great Ambassadour came to speake with him, & found him in the manner[67]: at which, both the king, and the Ambassadour in the kings behalfe began to blush at first; but soone after, the king put away the blush, & the hobbie horse together, and with a pretty smile asked the Ambassadour, if he had any litle children of his owne? He answered no. Then said he, I pray you tell not what you found me doing, till you have some litle ones of your owne, and then tell it, and spare not.

---

had been hanged and quartered. When the captain responded that he did not know of any, another Englishman whispered, 'Don't be surprized, for he is not a gentleman' (*CSP, Venetian*, VI, Pt. 3, 1672; cited in H. W. Chapman, *The Last Tudor King*, London, 1958, p. 39).

[63] *at the volley*] i.e., without due consideration. Harington has written 'folly' in the Markham-Wrenn copy to indicate the pun.

[64] *promoting*] i.e., informing. See p. 137 above and 243 ff. below.

[65] *should . . . concealement*] Harington is again playing upon legal terminology, here with respect to the inheritance of property held of the crown in chief. Before an heir could sue out his livery, the Court of the Wards adjudicated the claims of the heir *vs.* the claims of the crown. Should he attempt to conceal the extent and value of his property, there were professional informers ready to reveal the fact and seek the concealed lands as a reward.

[66] *a certaine king . . .*] Plutarch 'Agesilaus' 25.5. This popular anecdote appears, for example, in Puttenham, pp. 279–80, and in Thomas Cogan's *Haven of Health* (reprinted by Richard Field the same year as the *Metamorphosis*); Cogan, however, relates it of Socrates (B1ᵛ–B2).

[67] *in the manner*] Proverbial for 'caught in the act,' Tilley M633.

For even so, I would request men to forbeare reading of this discourse, or at least reproving of it; till they had of their owne that, that would make them know the commoditie and cleanlynesse of it, & for those that will not, I would but wish them (as Martiall wishes to Charinus. *Quid imprecabor ô Severe liventi.*[68] *Opto Mulos habeat & suburbanum*)[69] so I would, they could ride on their footcloth,[70] and had a house, and A Jax of their owne. Yet surely it may be, it were the wisest way to show it to none at all, and so I halfe wish sometimes, but because everie generall rule must have his exception,[71] you shall see whom I would be content both the discourse, and the devise may be shewed unto.[j]

First to a good and judicious scholer, for he will reade it, 1 eare he will judge of it, and say *omnia probate*; & then perhaps after he hath read it, he will smile, and say it is some young schollers worke, that would have shewed more wit if he had had it; but it is well, *ridentem dicere verum quis vetat,*[72] &c: and then he wil say, it were good, some of his friends would advise him to spend his talent, and his time on some better subject. But some supercilious fellow, or some stale scribe, that thinke men will not judge them to be learned, except they finde faults; they will sweare, a man would have written as well, that had read but *Marcus Aurelius.*

Secondly, I would have it shewed to a housekeeper, that 2 hath[73] much resort to him, for it were not onely a deede of charitie to helpe such a one, but a sinne to hide it from him; for else he may picke a quarrell (and say) that this same companie hath so stencht up his house, that he must be forced to lye at London, till his house be made sweeter.[k]

---

[j] Directions for shewing the booke.

[k] A common excuse of such as breake up house.

---

[68] severe Liventi *A*

[69] *Quid . . . suburbanum*] *not run-on in B.* Martial viii.61.8–9.

[70] *footcloth*] A richly ornamented cloth laid over the back of a horse, hanging to the ground on each side; it was considered a mark of dignity.

[71] *everie . . . exception*] Tilley R205.

[72] *ridentem . . . vetat*] Adapted from Horace *Satire* i.1.24.

[73] hath] had *B*

3   Thirdly, if one be a builder and no house-keeper, let him see
it to, for he loves to have all fine for his heire; and perhaps I
would be content for the love I have had to that humour, that
my master his sonne, were maried to his mistres my daughter;
as Heywood saith of a lustie old widower that woed a young
woman, and boasting how well he would provide for his sonne.

> *In a short tale, when his long tale was don:*
> *She pray'd him go home, & send her his son.*[74]

But if one be a builder, & a housekeeper both; then I will
come home to his house to him, I will reade him a lecture of it,
I will instruct his workemen, I will give him plots and models,
and do him all the service I can:[75] for that is a man of my own
humor, & a good common wealthsman; but yet I will give him
a caveat in his eare, that I learned of Sir Thomas More, if his
purse be not well furnisht.

> *Aedificare domos multas, & pascere multos,*
> *est ad pauperiem, semita laxa nimis.*[76]

> *The way from wealth, and store, to want, and neede,*
> *Is much to build, and many mouthes to feed.*

---

[74] *as Heywood . . . son*] Last two lines of No. 66 of *The firste hundred of Epigrammes* with slight variation.

[75] *then I will . . . can*] That his invention was utilized in the palace at
Richmond is indicated by Harington's epigram '*To the ladies of the Queenes
Privy-Chamber, at the making of their perfumed privy at* Richmond' (*L&E*,
p. 165).
In 1602 when Cecil House was in process of being constructed, Harington
also sent his device to Sir Robert Cecil: 'I have sent yowr honor by the bearer
hereof a homely present, and thowgh the mettle thearin bee neyther gold nor
sylver, yet yf Master Controller of the works or I can judg owght yt will bee
worth gold and sylver to yowr howse. In my ydle discowrse on this subject,
(yf yowr honor can remember), I valewd this devyse for my own poor howse to
bee worth one hunderd pownds, and in Theballs (as myght be in proportion)
worth a thousand. . . . The errors of some dull workmen have made that in
some places yt hath not done so well as yt myght, but Master Basyll and my
selfe will geve that dyrection for yowrs as neyther fayr nor fowl wether shall
annoy' (*L&E*, p. 93). Cf. also his letter to the Earl of Shrewsbury on the same
subject (*L&E*, pp. 94–5).

[76] *Aedificare . . . nimis*] No. 4 of the *Progymnasmata*; identified by Bradner
and Lynch as No. X. 119 of the *Anthologia Palatina*. Harington's text varies
slightly from all sixteenth-century editions in reading 'laxa' for 'recta.'

Fourthly, if you would know whether you should show it to 4
Ladies ? Yea in any wise to all maner of Ladies, of the Court,
of the country, of the City, great Ladies, lesser Ladies, learned
ignorant, wise simple, fowle welfavoured, (painted unpainted)
so they be Ladies, you may boldly prefer[77] it to them. For
your milkmayds, & country housewives, may walke to the
woods to gather strawberies, &c. But greater states cannot
do so; & therfore for them it is a commoditie more then I will
"speake of, yet for a touch upon this point,[78] make me but a good
"ryme to this line after[79] dinner.

"*Within yon tower, there is a flower, that holds my hart.*

Howbeit, you must now show it after one fashion to all,
but to the wise and sober, after a plaine fashion; to the wanton
and waggish, after another fashion; as namely, if they cry (fie for
shame) when they heare the title read, or such like; do but you
say (for company) that it is a mad fantasticall booke indeed,
and when you have done hide it away, but where they may
finde it, and by the next day, they wilbe as cunning in it as you:
for this is not the first time that I have said of such a kinde of
booke.[80]

In Brutus presence, Lucrece will refuse it,
Let him but turne his backe, and sh'ill peruse it.[81]

Fiftly, you may shew it to all amorous young youthes, that 5[82]
wil scratch their head but with one finger at once (as Cato
noted of Caesar)[83] and had rather be noted of three disorders
in their lives, then of one in their lockes; and specially[84] if
they be so cleanly, that they will not eat pottage (no not alone)
but that they will wipe their spone between everie spone-full,
for feare least their[85] upper lip should infect the neither: for I

---

[77] pre fer (*on two lines, no hyphen*) A

[78] yet . . . point] yet upon a touche of this point B   [79] after] afore B

[80] *for this . . . booke*] OF, 1634 edition, $6.

[81] *In . . . it*] Martial xi.16.9–10.   [82] *om.* A, B

[83] *that wil . . . Caesar*] Plutarch 'Caesar' 4.4, where the observation,
however, is attributed to Cicero not Cato.

[84] specially] especially B   [85] their] the B

would thinke certainly, that such a one, if he be so cleanly as he would seeme to be, would make great account of A Jax so well reformed. But yet the world is so full of dissimulation, and hypocrisie, that we of the plainer sort may be easily deceived; for I heard of one the last day, in a towne a hundred myle from London, that had engrossed[86] all the fine fashions into his handes; of the curling, perfuming, wyping the spone, &c: and yet after all this cleanlynesse, went to as common, and as deformed A Jax of the feminine gender, as any was in the towne, and then alas, what will such a one care for my device. Lastly, I would have it shewed to all good fat corpulent men,[l] that carry with them a writ of *Corpus cum causa*,[87] for they are commonly the best natured men that be; without fraud, without trecherie, as *Caesar* said of *Anthonie*, and *Dolobella*, that he never mistrusted them for any practise, because he saw they were fat, but rather *Casca* and *Cassius*, that were leane hollow fellowes, and cared not for a good dinner[88]: And therefore I would be censured by those good fellowes that have lesse gall, and the rather, because I looke every day for presse money from the Captaine,[89] to be imployed in the conquest of that country,[m] and this engyn of mine is like to be

---

[l] Prayse of fat men.

[m] Lubberland.[90]

---

[86] *engrossed*] The earliest figurative use cited in the *OED* is *I Henry IV*, III.ii.148.

[87] *Corpus cum causa* 'A writ issuying out of the Chauncerie, to remove both the bodie and the record touching the cause of any man lying in execution, upon a judgement for debt into the Kings bench, &c. there to lye untill he have satisfied the judgement' (Cowell, T2–T2ᵛ).

[88] *as Caesar . . . dinner*] Harington errs in citing Casca for Brutus. Plutarch repeats Caesar's remark three times: 'Caesar' 62.5; 'Antony' 11.3; and 'Brutus' 8.1. Nicholas Udall vividly translates Caesar's comment: 'Tushe, no no (quoth Caesar) I feare not these ruddie coloured and fat bealied feloes, but yonder same spare slender skragges, & pale salowe coloured whoresoonnes, shewying with his finger Brutus & Cassius' (*Apophthegmes* of Erasmus, 2B1–2B1ᵛ).

[89] *from the Captaine*] 'Doctor Gif- / ford. / to,' Harington annotation in the Lumley-Folger copy. Dr. Roger Giffard, a man of wide culture, well read in French, Italian, and Flemish literature, served as physician to the Queen and president of the College of Physicians. In 1590 as one of Her Majesty's physicians, he was granted the goods of Germane Poole, forfeited by reason of his continuation beyond the seas (*DNB* and *CSP, Dom.*, II, 1581–90, 705).

[90] Cockaigne, the imaginary land of plenty.

in great request for those services. But me thinkes, you may say that here is a marvellous restraint made of showing this discourse of mine; not much unlike to our stage keepers in Cambridge, that for feare least they should want companie to see their Comedies, go up and downe with vizers, and lights, puffing and thrusting & keeping out all men so precisely; till all the towne is drawne by this revell to the place; and at last, tag and rag, fresh men and subsizers,[91] & all be packt in together, so thicke, as now is scant left roome for the Prologue, to come upon the stage: for so you may suppose, that I would barre all from this Pamphlet of mine, save those, that can write, or read, or understand. But if you take it thus, you do much mistake it; for there be divers[n] from whom I would keepe it, as I would from fire and water, as for example.

First, from a passing proud fellow, such a one as Naaman 1 the Syrian,[92] that would disdaine to wash in Jordan, though it would cure him of the Leprosie, or the pox; & to such for my "part, I would wish they might lay all in their gold breeches, "rather then to abase their high conceits, so much, as to thinke "upon poore Master A Jax.

Secondly, from all manner of fooles and jesters, whether they 2 be artificiall, or naturall; for these be so dull, they cannot tast the salt, in a peece of well powdred writing; and those be so tart, they will rather loose a friend then a jest[93]: yet if their railing were allaide a litle, with the two excellent vertues, of flattring, and begging; one might hope for some kindnesse at their hands.

Thirdly, if you spie a fellow with a bay leafe in his mouth, 3 avoyd him, for he carieth a thing about him worse then Maister A Jax, that all the devises we have cannot reforme.[94]

---

[n] Foure sortes of men, that will mislike of the book.

[91] *subsizers*] At Cambridge a needy undergraduate ranking below a sizar.

[92] *Naaman the Syrian* . . .] II Kings 5:10–12.

[93] *they will . . . jest*] Tilley F708.

[94] *Thirdly . . . reforme*] Although the virtues of the bay leaf were many and varied (*e.g.*, placed under the pillow, it induced sleep; eaten in the morning, it warded off drunkenness), the only allusion I have found to its being carried in the mouth is that set forth in Theophrastus's description '*Of Superstition*': 'But he is superstitious, which with washt hands, and being besprinkled with holy water out of the Temple, bearing a bay leaf in his mouth, walketh so a whole day together' (*Characters*, tr. John Healey in Earle's *Microcosmographie*, London, 1899, p. 135).

4   Fourthly, if you see a stale leane hungrie poore beggerly thridbare Kavalliero, like to Lazorelloes maister, that when he dined at his owne house, came foorth with more crummes of bread on his beard, then in his belly, and that being descended of diverse Nobilities, wil do a meane gentleman the honour to borow ten shillings of him:[95] shew it not him, for though he can say nothing against it, yet he will leere under his hat, as though he could speake more then he thinkes. For such a one that mak's not a good meale at home once in a moneth, hath not a good stoole above once in a weeke, and then he will never say us Gramercie for it: and this I may say to you, is a consideration of no small importance, for though I must acknowledge, that this[96] is not one of the meritorious workes I looke to be saved by, yet to have a prayer or two from some, that perhaps never say prayer any where else, would do me no hurt, nor them neither. And me thinke I might much better deserve a kn-ave Mery to be said for me, where my stately A Jax is admitted, & standes men in steed; then he, for whose soule the young Gentleman, the first time he consumated his mariage with his wife, said a *Pater noster*; and being asked for whom he prayed, he told his wife, it was for his soule that had taken the paines to make his way[97] so easie for him. Oh Sir said she, it is a signe you have travelled such wayes more then an honest man should have done that you are so cunning, and so they became good friendes. But ware ryot hoe,[98] whither am I running? I said I would keepe me from scandaling, but if I stop not betime, some will thinke to have their action in the case against me; yet it is good to cast the worst. Suppose that

---

[95] *Fourthly . . . him*] Of his (third) master, Lazarillo observed: 'I did like him well, but only that me thought he was to presumptuous, where I often wished that seeing hee so plainely perceived his owne povertie, hee wold something have hid his fantasticall pride. But as I thinke, it is a common rule amongst such as hee, which though they have not a crosse in the worlde, nor a Denier, the cappe must needes stande in his olde place' (*The Pleasaunt Historie of Lazarillo de Tormes*, tr. David Rouland, 1586, Percy Reprint No. 7, Oxford, 1924, p. 48).

[96] this] *Lumley-Folger*; *om. A, B*   [97] way, *A*

[98] *ware ryot hoe*] An interjection used in hunting, as 'ware hawk'; it was taken over into common speech. Cf. Skelton in 'Speke, Parrot': 'Ware ryat, Parrot, ware ryat, ware that' (ed. A. Dyce, London, 1843, II, 6; I owe this reference to Dr. William Nelson); *LLL* V.ii.43, 'Ware pencils, ho!' and *T&C* V.vii.12, 'Ware horns, ho!'

for my bad indyting, I should be indyted, as it is twentie to one but if the graund Jurie were packt[99] by a bad Shiriffe, out of those foure last mentioned sutes (and three of them, you shall have a full apparaunce in most Courts of Christendome) they[o] will sure say *billa vera,* though they should say of right nothing but *ignoramus.*[101] But see see, even with thinking of it I fall againe into my former melancholie, me thinke the indytement is found, I am arraigned, I plead not guiltie, I would still be tryed by the Nobilitie, by such as build stately pallaces and keepe great Courts, but it will not be graunted me, I must have none but freeholders; I chaffe at it, and would appeale; they cry it is not the course of the common law, I praise the Civill law; for there a man may hold play with appealing, if he have a litle idle money to spend, three or foure yeare. At last comes the litle dapper fellow my honest Atturney, that knew better the course of these matters then I did, and he roundes[102] me in the eare, and tells me that for fortie shillings to Maister high Shiriffes man that weares the[103] russet sattin doublet, and the yellow silke stockings, he will undertake, I shall have a Jurie of good freeholders: but for the Nobilitie it is out of their commission; & Sir (saith he) what need you to stand so much on the Nobilitie, considering you desire to have none, but great housekeepers, and builders? For suppose you could get 3. or foure to appeare: one[104] at Petworth,[105] an other hard by, there at Coudrey[106] (where in

---

[o] Proud Fooles, Beggers. [100]

---

[99] packt] prickt *B* [100] Fooles Beggers] *A*

[101] *ignoramus*] 'A word properly used by the grand Enquest empaneled in the inquisition of causes criminall and publique: and writen upon the bill, whereby any crime is offered to their consideration, when as they mislike their evidence, as defective or to weake to make good the presentment. The effect of which word so written is, that all farder inquiry upon that party for that fault, is thereby stopped, and he delivered without farder aunswer' (Cowell, 2N3).

[102] *roundes*] Whispers. [103] rhe *A*

[104] appeare. One *A*

[105] *Petworth*] In Sussex, the seat of Henry Percy, ninth Earl of Northumberland. Financial records which cover the period from Aug. 1590 to 19 May 1591 show that the Earl spent some time at Bath where he rented a house from Dr. Sherwood (cf. Harington's epigram '*To Doctor* Sherwood, *how Sack makes one leane,*' *L&E*, pp. 217–18). These records also show a payment of 40*s.* to Mr. Richard Percy 'at the christening of Mr. Harrington's child' (*HMC* 6th Rept., Pt. I, p. 227). This apparently was Harington's daughter Ellena

the old Vicounts time *Iupiter hospitalis*[107] is said to have dwelt)[108] and the young Lord I heare doth *patrisare*,[109] or rather I should say *Avisare*, (and that is a good word, if he will marke it.)[110] Say also another dwelt at Ragland[111] in Monmouth shire, where I heard a good Knight of Glostershire affirme, the most honorable house of that Realme was kept: & a fourth at Nonesuch, where the housekeeper for true English Noblesse and honour, deserves the name, better then the house.[112] But when you shal thinke to make up the *Tales*,[113] where wil you have them? some will be *non est inventus in*

(or Helena) who was baptized at Kelston 3 May 1591 (*Misc. Gen. et Her.*, n.s., IV, 192). Harington has annotated the Markham-Wrenn copy: 'Earl of Nor / thumberlād.'

[106] *an other . . . Coudrey*] Also in Sussex, the seat of Anthony Browne, second Viscount Montague.

[107] hospitales *A*

[108] *where . . . dwelt*] The first Viscount Montague (d. 1592) had been host to the Queen from 14 Aug. to 20 Aug. when her progress took her through Surrey, Sussex, and Hants. An account of the festivities at Cowdray was twice published in 1591 (Nichols, *Progresses*, III, 90–6, and Chambers, *Elizabethan Stage*, IV, 65; 106).

[109] patrysare *A*

[110] *and the young . . . it*] The fact that the first Viscount Montague was succeeded in 1592 by his grandson accounts for Harington's coinage of *avisare*—on the analogy of *patrisare*. The latter term appears to have expressed a favorite concept of Harington's as he used it in a letter to Sir Robert Cecil some six years later describing a message from his 'eldest sonne (of 12 yeer old) with news that my wyfe was delyverd of a sonne, and becawse my sonne must *patrisare* hee wrytte yt in this verse. *Gaude pater, quartum genetrix peperit tibi natum*' (*L&E*, pp. 92–3). Harington has annotated the Markham-Wrenn copy 'Vicount / Montegue.'

[111] *another . . . Ragland*] Edward Somerset, fourth Earl of Worcester, who had succeeded to the title in 1589. Harington's annotation in the Markham-Wrenn copy: 'Erl of Worster.'

[112] *at Nonesuch . . . house*] This country retreat in Surrey, begun by Henry VIII, was ultimately completed by Lord Lumley, son-in-law of the Earl of Arundell to whom the property had been alienated in 1556. Although the Queen purchased it in 1590/1, whence, according to Rowland White, it became her favourite house, Lord Lumley continued to live there as caretaker (Chambers *Elizabethan Stage*, I, II. n. 4., and Sears Jayne and F. R. Johnson, *The Lumley Library*, London, 1956, p. 9). 'Lord Lumley': Harington annotation in the Markham-Wrenn copy.

[113] *Tales*] 'Used in our common lawe, for a supply of men empaneled upon a jury or enquest, and not appearing, or at their apparence, chalenged by the partie . . . the Judge upon petition graunteth a supply to be made by the Shyreeve of some men there present, equall in reputation to those that were impaneled' (Cowell, 3S1ᵛ).

baliva,[114] some that you love best, will not be perhaps *intra quatuor maria*[115]; wherefore the Judge was your friend more then you were aware, that gives you choise of freeholders.

Beleeve me (said I) I thinke it is so in deede, hold thee my litle dappert knave, there is fortie shillings for Maister Shiriffes man, to buy him another paire of silke stockings,[p] and there is fortie pence for thy good counsell, and see you finde me a Jurie of substantiall free-holders, that are good house-keepers to trie my honestie by. He goeth and ere an Ape can cracke a nut (as they say)[116] he brings the names, and Maister Cryer he comes twentie shillings in his shoes, and cals them though he be sure they cannot heare him. As followeth.

John Harington of Exton, in the Countie of Rutland Knight, 1
aliâs John Har: of Burleigh, in the Countie aforesaid, *aliâs* of Combe, in the Countie of Warwick, *aliâs* of Ooston,[117] in the

---

[p] Wooden stockes were fitter for them then silke stockings.

[114] *non est . . . baliva*] A formula used in the return of a writ by a bailiff or sheriff, indicating that he has been unable to locate the specified person within his bailiwick. (See Cowell, H2[v] and Tilley N204.)

[115] *some that you love best*] 'Earle of / Essex,' Harington annotation in the Lumley-Folger copy. Essex had sailed from Plymouth 1 June with the expedition to Cadiz.
Harington explicates the Latin phrase in his *Tract on the Succession*: 'And all our old Records in England that talke of service to be done within these two countries [England and Scotland] have usually these Latyn wordes: *Infra* [sic] *Quatuor Maria:* or in French *Deins les quatre mere,* that is within the 4 seas.' He derives his explication from the old libel directed against Leicester which had originally appeared in 1584 under the title of *A Copye of a Letter written by a Master of Arts at Cambridge,* but it was more commonly known as *Father Parson's Greencoat* or *Leycesters Commonwealth* (1641 ed., S3).
Although the Queen and the Privy Council had endeavored to prevent its circulation, Harington makes clear that the libel circulated even within the premises of the court, for he describes how he had read 'the book called Greencoate, or the Life of Leycester' in the Tiltyard at Greenwich to four notable people of the court, including the Earl of Ormonde, 'and next day my Lo. of Ormond meerly, even in the Earle of Leicester's presence, bad me *Good morrow, Mr. Reader*; and when my Lo. of Leyster asked me what I had redd, I blushed (and, God forgive me for lieng), I aunswered they were certaine Cantoes of Ariost. But as Ovid saith *Heu, quam difficile est crimen non prodere vultu*' (*Tract on the Succession,* pp. 61; 44).

[116] *ere an Ape . . . say*] Not in Tilley.

[117] *John Harington . . . Ooston*] The eldest son and heir of Sir James Harington and Lucy, daughter of Sir William Sidney of Penshurst, Sir John was a prosperous landholder and builder of note. Although he and Harington addressed each other as 'cosin,' their precise relationship is uncertain. When queried about this relationship by King James after he had elevated Sir John

Countie of Leicester; come into the Court, or else, &c. Hath he free hold? Yea he is a pretie free-holder in all these shires: Sayth an other he is a great houskeeper.[118] Moreover saith a third man, though he be a free-holder; yet he hath maried his daughter to one,[119] that for a grandfather,[120] for a father,[121] for two uncles, & three or foure auntes,[122] may compare with most men in England. Lastly a fourth said, & foure hundred confirme it, that he relieves many poore, & sets them to worke; he builds not onelie his own houses, but Colledges, and Hospitals.[123] Mary Sir, then shall he be foreman of my Jurie with all my verie hart, a builder and a house-keeper both, you

---

of Exton to the peerage, Harington modestly responded that they were 'bothe branches of the same tree' (*L&E*, p. 110).

Exton—the family seat of the Haringtons in Rutland.

Burleigh i.e., Burley-on-the-hill, a manor adjoining Exton, settled on Sir John at the time of his marriage to Anne, daughter of Robert Kelway, Surveyor of the Court of Wards and Liveries (Ian Grimble, *The Harington Family*, London, 1957, p. 74).

Combe i.e., Combe Abbey in Warwickshire, the inheritance of his wife, Lady Anne (*ibid.*).

Ooston i.e., Oulston. Various lands belonging to the rectory, the late priory, and the manor of Oulston, Lincolnshire, had been granted in reversion in 1539 to Harington's grandfather, at that time an Esquire of the Royal Body (*L&P, Henry VIII*, XIV, Pt. I, 420).

[118] Sayth . . . houskeeper] *Markham-Wrenn, Nares-Folger, Sheffield; om. A, B*

[119] *to one*] 'the young / Erl of Bed- / ford,' Harington annotation in the Markham-Wrenn copy. The marriage of Lucy Harington to Edward Russell, the third Earl of Bedford, had taken place on 12 Dec. 1594.

[120] *for a grandfather*] Francis Russell, second Earl of Bedford, 'a true follower of religion and vertue,' according to Camden, died in 1585, 'the next day after that his soone *Francis* was slaine . . . upon the borders of *Scotland*' (*Elizabeth*, 2A5).

[121] *father*] Sir Francis Russell who was attending a meeting of the wardens was hit by a volley of shot when the Scots suddenly broke off the truce and, three thousand strong, attacked the English (*ibid.*, 2A1).

[122] *for two . . . auntes*] Each of the second Earl's three daughters in turn married earls—Anne, who had married Ambrose Dudley, Earl of Warwick, in 1565, was at this date a widow; Elizabeth was married to William Bourchier, Earl of Bath, and Margaret was married to George Clifford, Earl of Cumberland. The fourth aunt was that 'noble and learned Ladie, dowager to the Lord John Russell' to whom Harington had earlier referred (p. 144). (See Wiffen, *Historical Memoirs of the House of Russell*, London, 1833, I, *passim*.)

[123] *Colledges and Hospitals*] In 1594 a licence was granted to Sir John Harington and the Earl of Kent, the executors of Frances, Countess of Sussex, to erect a college in Cambridge to be called Sydney Sussex College (*CSP, Dom.*, III, 1591–4, 527). I have found no reference to his building of hospitals.

cannot devise to please me better. I would there were a *decem tales* in everie shire in England, & on that condition, I would be glad to be one of them. Well, what have you to say to Sir John Harington? Mary this. Here is one *Misacmos*, that is accused by some diligent officers and good[124] servants of the state,*ᵃ* to be a writer of fantasticall Pamphlets, to corrupt manners; the same suspected of divers untruthes, and treasons, not sparing the Majesties of Kings, and great Emperours (saying one was a cuckold and a foole, an other had an ill face, as in the Pamphlet it selfe more plainly appeareth) now because it seemes he is a Gentleman, and of reasonable good breeding; he craves to be tried by a substantiall Jurie, of which, for many respectes, he will have you to be the forman. He pleads to all the principall matters not guiltie, and justifies, that those things they call untruth, and treason, are truth, and reason. He is to be tried, by God and the[126] country,[127] which country you are, wherefore your charge is (if it please you) to read the whole Treatise at your leasure, and then to say how you like it. He saith further, he cares not to have you sworne, because your word will be taken for a greater matter then this, by ten thousand pounds without oth. Jurie Harington.

Who is next? Sir John Peeter of Stonden[128] in the Countie of Essex Knight, a good house-keeper, and a builder both. Hath he free hold? Yea so so, I thinke he may weare velvet

---

ᵃ But enquire what the good Lord of Bedford called them.[125]

---

[124] by . . . good] *om. B*

[125] *om. B*

[126] the] *Lumley-Folger; om. A, B*

[127] *by God and the country*] The standard response of an indicted person, indicating that he consents to be tried by a jury. The 'country' was to be represented by persons likely to know the facts; as a result of the statute 27 Elizabeth, c. 6, only two were required to be *de vicineto* (A. T. Carter, *A History of the English Courts*, London, 1944, pp. 131; 139).

[128] *Sir John Peeter of Stonden*] Son and heir of Sir William Petre who had been appointed in 1535 one of the visitors of the monasteries whence he derived a considerable estate. Sir John who served in Parliament and as a deputy lieutenant for Essex and the town of Colchester was considered sympathetic to the Catholics, his wife having been listed as a recusant in 1587 (*CSP, Dom.*, II, 1581–90, 573; Strype, *Annals*, III, Pt. 2, 597; *Records of the English Province of the Society of Jesus*, ed. H. Foley, London, 1877, Ser. II–IV, 586–8, n. 12).

Stonden—this should read Thorndon (West Horndon), where Sir John moved, probably c. 1575 (A. C. Edwards, 'Sir John Petre and his Household, 1576–7,' *Essex Review*, LXIII, No. 252, Oct. 1954, 190).

and sattin, by the Statute of (*4. & 5. Phil. Ma.*)[129] for he may dispend twentie markes a yeare *ultra reprisas*.[130] Well, because he is a builder and a house-keeper, I hope he will not deny me to be of my Jurie. The same charge, &c: that Sir John Harington tooke, you[131] &c: and so long may you keepe a good house. Jurie Peeter.

3   Sir John Spenser Knight, a good substantiall free-holder in Northampton shire, and a good house-keeper, and so was the father afore him[132]: Oh I remember him, he had a poore neighbour once dwelt at Holmeby,[133] that made foure verses if I have not forgot them, were fortie shillings out of his way.

> *Erupuit sors dura mihi, sors altera reddit,*
> *Haec loca quae veteri, rudere structa vides:*
> *Aeternos vivat, Magna Elisabetha per annos,*
> *Quae me tam grato, laeta favore beat.*[134]

---

[129] *by the . . . Ma.*] Harington again reverts to his habit of citing the calendar year [155]4–5 for the more usual regnal year, 1 and 2 Philip and Mary, c. 2 (*Statutes of the Realm*, IV, Pt. 1, 239).

[130] *for he . . . reprisas*] This is of course jesting understatement since the statute prohibited those who could not dispend 'xx. pounds by yeere' from the wearing of 'any maner of Silke' (Lambard, 2F3). In 1595 Sir John estimated his income from rent at £4000 (Edwards, 'Sir John Petre and his Household,' p. 191).

[131] tooke you, *A*

[132] *Sir John Spenser . . . him*] Representative of a conspicuously wealthy Northamptonshire family, Sir John Spencer had succeeded to the manor of Althorpe in 1586. Although the fortunes of the family, which derived from sheep raising, had been established early in the sixteenth century, Sir John's father had himself been a prudent husbandman and had made a prosperous alliance as well with Katherine, daughter of Sir Thomas Kitson, an eminent merchant prince. His son then followed his example by marrying Mary, daughter and heiress of Sir Robert Catlin (Mary E. Finch, *The Wealth of Five Northamptonshire Families, 1540–1640*, Oxford, 1956, pp. 38–65).

[133] *he had . . . Holmeby*] Since Holdenby bordered Sir John's estate, this is apparently a semi-ironic reference to Sir Christopher Hatton whose vast expenditures during his lifetime were offset by the vastness of his debts. Sir Robert Cecil in a letter to the former Lord Chancellor's friend and follower, Sir Henry Unton, commented that Hatton's debts amounted to '56,000 £, to the Queene, and to the subjecte 14,000 £; a huge somme' (*Correspondence of Sir Henry Unton, Knt.*, Roxburgh Club, LXIV, London, 1847, p. 174).

[134] *Erupuit . . . beat*] It was of course owing to the Queen's favor that Hatton had been enabled to 'rebuild his ancestors' homely manor-house' on such a palatial scale (Eric St. John Brooks, *Sir Christopher Hatton*, London, 1946, p. 155).

By S. Mary he had good cause to say, well fare a good Mistresse, or else Holmby had bin joyned to your freehold. How say you worthy Knight (& the best man of your name that is, but not that hath bene[r]) will you be of our Jurie ? You will say you know not this same *Misacmos*. It may be so verie well; for I thinke the fellow doth scarce know him selfe at this instant, and yet he learned γνῶθι σεαυτόν[136] twentie yeares ago. Well, I presume you will not refuse it: for though you never heard of him, it seemes he hath heard of you. I will tell you two or three good tokens, you have three or foure sisters,[137] good well favored, well featured, wel statured, well natured women, for plaine country wenches; and they were maried to men, a step, or two, or three, or foure, above the best yeoman of Kent[138] (wel fare all good tokens) and one of them is a widow, I beshrow their harts, & I would their wives were widowes that made her so.[139] I trow it was Sir James Harington, and your father, that went a begging to make a purse to marie

---

[r] There were Earles of the Spensers.[135]

---

[135] Like other Tudor gentry, the Spencers duly turned to pedigree hunting, and in 1595 the College of Arms obliged by tracing their descent from the ancient house of Despencer, earls of Gloucester and Winchester (Finch, p. 38).

[136] γνοστι *A*, γνοθι *B*. The well-known inscription on the temple at Delphi.

[137] *three or foure sisters* . . .] These included Elizabeth, married to Sir George Carey, newly succeeded as second Lord Hunsdon (July 1596); Katherine, married to Sir Thomas Leigh of Stonleigh, Warwickshire; Anne, who had married, first, William Stanley, Baron Monteagle, secondly, Henry, Lord Compton, and, lastly (1592) Robert Sackville, heir to Lord Buckhurst; Alice was the widow of Ferdinando Stanley, fifth Earl of Derby.

[138] *yeoman of Kent*] 'It passeth,' according to Fuller, 'for a plain man of plentiful estate, yeomen in this county bearing away the bell for wealth from all of their rank in England' (*Worthies*, London, 1952, p. 258). Cf. Tilley K163.

[139] *and one . . . so*] The Earl of Derby's death on 16 April 1594 aroused a furor because it was popularly believed to have resulted from witchcraft. Stow gives a detailed account of the physiological manifestations accompanying the Earl's last illness plus a listing *in extenso* of the 'reasons and conjectures, as caused many learned men to suppose him to be bewitched' (*Annales*, 3S4[v]–3S5[v]). A similarly detailed statement is preserved in the Talbot Papers (printed in Lodge, *Illustrations of British History*, London, 1838, II, 459–62). Camden more moderately observes that the death of the Earl in the flower of his youth was 'not without suspition of poison' (*Elizabeth*, 2O1[v]). Harington has annotated the Lumley-Folger copy 'La Derby.'

their daughters[140]; but you will make a hundred of us go a begging, if we should follow you: will you have any more tokens yet? you had a brother of Lincolnes Inne[141]; and an other they say keepes a good house, for I weene the best house-keeper in England was at his house[142]; yet one token more, you have a learned writer of your name, make much of him, for it is not the least honour of your honorable familie.[143] Jurie Spencer.

4   Thomas Stanop Knight,[144] of Shelford in the Countie of Notingham a house-keeper, a builder, a substantiall free-holder, come into the Court. Alasse Sir he is lame he cannot come. Is he so indeed? I am sorry for it: I have heard that he hath borne some sway in his country,[145] yet bid him not forget the old proverbe, a good friend in the Court, is worth a penie in the purse at all times.[146] Well, if he cannot come let us have

---

[140] *I trow . . . daughters*] Of Sir James Harington's eighteen children, no less than eight daughters entered into marriage, a fact duly noted on the monument erected in the church at Exton (Grimble, p. 73), while Sir John Spencer neatly approximated the feat by providing husbands for six, including the four note-worthy alliances above.

[141] *you had . . . Inne*] Two of the Spencer brothers attended Lincoln's Inn: Thomas, admitted 1564, obtained a fine legal training and became a bencher sometime before 1603; Edward was admitted 1576/7, but his death occurred before 1584 (*Records of Lincoln's Inn*, I, 72; 84, and Finch, pp. 57; 174).

[142] *and an other . . . house*] William Spencer of Yarnton, Oxford, had entertained the Queen on 23 Sept. 1592 (the year in which Harington had also entertained her). See Chambers, *Elizabethan Stage*, IV, 107.

[143] *you have . . . familie*] Harington nicely anticipates Spenser's own assertion, soon to be published, that he derived his name from 'an house of auncient fame' (*Prothalamion*, st. 8), an assertion that the poet did much to foster.

[144] *Thomas Stanop Knight*] Son and heir of Sir Michael Stanhope who had obtained the manor, rectory, and priory of Shelford as well as the priory of Lenton at the dissolution of the monasteries. During the next reign Sir Michael, a brother-in-law of Protector Somerset, was implicated in the conspiracy against the Duke of Northumberland and executed in 1552. However, his wife Lady Anne was allowed to retain Shelford.

[145] *I have heard . . . country*] Knighted at Kenilworth in 1575, Sir Thomas served in several parliaments as knight of the shire and also as sheriff for both Notts. and Derby (*Notices of the Stanhopes as Esquires and Knights* [London, 1855], p. 11).

[146] *the old proverbe . . . times*] Tilley F687.
Harington has in mind the almost incessant litigation which troubled Sir Thomas from 1591 until his death in 1596, stemming from the fierce enmity that existed between the Stanhopes and the Earl of Shrewsbury, together with the Earl's close relatives, the Cavendishes, and their numerous retainers.

an other. Oh Sir (saith one) stay but a *Pater noster* while,[147]
and you may have his sonne in his place. What (Maister
John Stanop my old Schoole-fellow, an honest & valiant

In 1591 Sir Thomas had stolen a march on the Earl by marrying his only
daughter Anne to John Holles (afterwards Earl of Clare), thus disrupting an
alliance between Holles and a kinswoman of the Earl which cost 'a great deale
of trouble and some mens lives' (Holles, p. 90).

The next year various incidents occurred in regard to a weir belonging to
Sir Thomas on the river Trent, and a petition for its removal signed by five
hundred inhabitants of thirty-nine towns was found to have been obtained by
'subornacion and bad practize' on the part of the Earl's followers. The Privy
Council thereupon directed the case to be referred to the Commission of
Sewers (*APC*, XXIII, 16–17; 148–50; 155–7).

The Earl next served two writs on Sir Thomas, one a charge of *scandalum
magnatum*; this latter, according to Nicholas Williamson - - a servant of the /
Earl's, he was found to be involved with Scottish Catholics - - had been certified
as a verbatim statement but had actually been revised according to the Earl's
dictates (*Rutland MSS*, I, 306; *Salisbury MSS*, V, 254–6).

Foul disorders committed against both Stanhope and Shrewsbury forced the
Council to intervene again in Feb. 1593, and the sheriffs and justices of Notts.
were directed to administer 'speciall and exemplar punishment' against those
'lewd persons that did deface the coach of Sir Thomas Stanhop, and likewize
those . . . that did set up certain vile pictures of the Talbot' (*APC*, XXIV, 77–8).
The defacing of the coach had been the act of young John Markham of
Sedgebrook, who was Sir Thomas's godson but in the service of the Earl.
Sir Thomas's immediate reaction was to scatter abroad unsigned doggerel
verses:

> Thou crook backte scabed scurvie Squyer
> Thou playest the knave for flatterie and hyer
> Thou shalt have to portion by this birthright
> The gallows, most fit for so scurvie a wight,
> And for the coach cuttinge and libels set up
> Thou art a calfe and a sheep's face, no wiser
>   than a tup [ram]
> A scurvie knave thou art, and so thou wilt dye.
> Farewell scabed crook back, not worth a flye.

(C. Markham, *Markham Memorials*, London, 1913, I, 130; for Markham's
railing retort, see pp. 131–2; see also *CSP, Dom.*, III, 1591–4, 410.)

On 'Easter Even' 1593, matters were climaxed when a 'greate and unlawfull
assembly' of persons gathered 'in tumultuous and ryotous manner' to pluck
down the weir. Sir Thomas as well as the Privy Council found it difficult to
obtain action against the offenders because of the great prestige and influence of
the Earl in the county, and the matter was referred to the Star Chamber.
Finally on 10 May 1595 fines ranging from 1,000 marks to £40 were imposed
on thirteen rioters (these were eventually mitigated, see *CSP, Dom.*, IV, 1595–7,
48 (2)), but the Earl 'known to be an apparent encourager of the riotous pulling
down of the Wear' was not suffered to be touched in the Star Chamber 'such
was her Majesty's favour towards him' (*Salisbury MSS*, V, 526–8).

---

[147] *Pater noster while*] Tilley P99.

Gentleman[148]) I will tarrie for him with all my hart. To the next.

5   Mathew Arundell Knight,[149] of Warder in the Countie of Wiltshire a good freeholder, and a builder. Tush he is no housekeeper, so said one that dwels three score myle to Trent Northward. Is it so? I will know within this moneth, if it be so or no. In the meane season, I will venter to take him if I can meet with him. For first I doubt, if he him selfe that said so, have spent so much in honorable services as this freeholders sonne hath done. Secondly, I have seene both Lords, and Ladies, as well intertained in his poore house, and served in as fine plate, and Porslin, as any is in the North. And admit he were no housekeeper, yet I would have him, because I heare he is a good horsekeeper,[s] a red deare keeper, a fallow deare keeper, and other such base things, as may enable him for my Jurie. Come on old father Peleus,[150] he lookes like Prester John in his furred night cap; but he hath more wit under that cap, then two or three of his neighbours. Will it please you Sir, to be of our Jurie? It shall cost the life of one of the bald faced buckes else. What are you angry, I call you *Peleus*? If I were but an other *Prometheus*,[151] I would sweare your fortune should

---

[s] Horse-keeper.

---

[148] *Maister . . . Gentleman*] He too had attended Eton, 1567–74 (*The Eton College Register*, p. 317). In March 1593 this 'honest and valiant Gentleman' was briefly committed to the Marshalsea for fighting in Fleet Street with Sir Charles Cavendish's men (*APC*, XXIV, 125; 135).

[149] *Mathew Arundell Knight*] Son and heir of Sir Thomas Arundell and Margaret, sister of Queen Catherine Howard, Sir Matthew was a distant kinsman of the Queen. His father, the first of the Arundells to own Wardour Castle, had been executed in 1552 along with Sir Michael Stanhope for involvement in the plot against Northumberland, but by letters patent dated 2 July, 1 Mary, Sir Matthew recovered all his father's property to which he made many additions. The family was Catholic. (J. P. Yeatman, *The Early Genealogical History of the House of Arundel*, London, 1882, pp. 265; 267–74.)

[150] *old father Peleus*] This would seem to establish the identity of the Peleus mentioned in four of Harington's epigrams: in three of these the epithet 'old Peleus' is used (*L&E*, pp. 149, 159, 216), and in the fourth the mention of Peleus's proffered gifts is in terms appropriate to Sir Matthew's interests:

> Then one shall have a Colt of his best race,
> Another gets a warrant for a Buck:
> (*L&E*, p. 275.)

[151] *Peleus . . . Prometheus*] 'Peleus son / a better man / then his fa- / ther,' Harington annotation in the Lumley-Folger copy, referring to Thomas the Valiant, Count of the Holy Roman Empire. See p. 174, n. 68. Cf. *Prometheus Bound* 768.

be, to be like *Peleus*: for the time was, that one wrate of your
Thetis, when she waited on Diana at Hatfield.

> *Who marketh well her grace, thereby may plainly see,*
> *A Laura in her face, and not a Willoughbee.*[152]

Whist ? peace (saith my litle Atturney in mine eare) you that
are so full of your Poetry, we shall have a new endytement
framed against you upon the Statute of *Rogues*.[153] For telling
of fortunes. Have you a verse for that too ? Yes Mary have I Sir.

> *Fati narrator, Ægiptus, Praestigiator,*
> *Aure perurantur, simul atque flagella sequantur.*

> *All fortune tellers, Jugglers, and Egiptions,*[154]
> *Are burnd in th'eare, or whipt by lawes prescriptions.*

Notwithstanding I trust a man may by *poetica licentia*, and by
example of *Virgill*,[155] tell fortunes that be past; yet litle said
is soone amended;[156] howbeit, I will not forget to be thankefull
to this good Knight, for one speciall favour he did me. And
that was; he made me go when I was with him at Warder, to

---

[152] willoughbee *A*;   *that* . . . *Willoughbee*] 'the Lady / Arundel a / wiloughby,'
Harington annotation in the Lumley-Folger copy. From the verses entitled
'The prayse of six Gentle-women attending on the Lady Elisabeth her Grace
at Hatfield' written by Harington's father. Since the versions published in the
editions of the *Nugae Antiquae* and in BM Add. MS 28635 vary considerably
from this, Harington has apparently in accordance with his habit adapted the
quotation to suit his context. Elsewhere he speaks of Lady Arundell as 'that
Venus plus quam venusta' (*L&E*, p. 91).

[153] *Statute of Rogues*] Much legislation in the sixteenth century was directed
against 'roags,' 'idle sturdie beggars,' and 'vagabonds calling themselves
Egyptions' (see, for example, *Statutes of the Realm*, IV, Pt. I, 242–3; 448–9;
590–8).
    The punishment for the first offence, as Harington indicates, was 'whipping,
and boring through the grissell of the right eare with a hot yron an inch in
compas'; for the second offence it was 'death as a felon' (Cowell, 3M2ᵛ).

[154] *Egiptions*] Egyptians were according to the 'statutes and lawes of *England*,
a counterfeit kinde of roagues, that being English or Welch people, accompany
themselves together, disguising themselves in straunge roabes, blacking their
faces and bodies, and framing to themselves an unknowne language, wander
up and downe, and under pretence of telling of Fortunes, curing diseases, and
such like, abuse the ignorant common people, by stealing all that is not too
hote or too heavie for their cariage' (Cowell, 2B1).

[155] *by example of Virgill*] Of the many *a posteriori* predictions in the *Aeneid*,
the most celebrated is that found in vi.851–3.

[156] *litle . . . amended*] Tilley L358.

as stately *AJAX house* (for a sommer house) and as sweete, as any can be; in a standing made in an Oke, that hanges over a ponde, and marvell not I call it stately: for this Maister A Jax, if you bring but an Angle rod, and a crosbow with you; will affoord choise of three royall sports, to kill deare, foule, and fish; now this I take it, was more than common kindnesse, and somuch for Jurie Arundell.

6 Frauncis Willoughby Knight,[157] of Wollerton in the Countie of Nottingham, a good freeholder, a housekeeper, and a great builder. Oh my neighbour, that dwels a hundred myle from me, & yet but a hedge partes our land;[158] good morrow neighbour, with the faire house,[159] the faire wife,[160] and the faire living. *Tout beau, tout beau.*[161] I pray you let us have a faire verdict from you in our matter; or else I will promise you, I will rather lye in the worst Inne in Notingham, then in the fairest bedchamber in your house; and if you will be of our side, I will pray that all your fayres, may be the fayrer,[162] one for an other. Jurie Willoughby.

---

[157] *Frauncis Willoughby Knight*] The second son of Sir Henry Willoughby and Margaret, daughter of Sir Robert Markham, Sir Francis acquired a vast territorial estate. In addition to being a landed baron, he was also an industrialist and speculator, fostering the industries of coal mining (whence his great wealth), iron smelting, and glass making (Finch, p. 54).

[158] *Oh . . . land*] The reversion of the site of Lenton Priory and various lands attached to the manor in Lenton and Radford had been granted by the Queen to Harington's parents in 1563 (*Cal. Pat. Rolls, Elizabeth*, II, 1560–3, 510–11). This property extended to within forty yards of Sir Francis's land, where, Harington observed in a letter to the Earl of Shrewsbury in 1604, Sir Francis had made a £1,000 a year out of coal (*L&E*, pp. 399–400).

[159] *the faire house*] At Wollaton, which he had erected, according to Camden, mainly from the profits of his 'Cole-pits' (*Britain*, 2Z2). See notes to p. 178.

[160] *the faire wife*] Sir Francis had married (c. 1565) Elizabeth, daughter of Sir John Littleton by whom he had six daughters. Her death occurred in 1594, following a period of estrangement. Then, having quarreled with his son-in-law Percival Willoughby, Sir Francis resolved to marry again and provide his own heir; accordingly, in Aug. 1595 he married Dorothy, the widow of John Tamworth. Ironically, in Nov. 1596, only a few months after this passage had appeared in print, Sir Francis died, and it was suspected he had been poisoned by his wife. He left Lady Dorothy with child and his heirs squabbling over the estate (Middleton and Cumming, 'In the Old Muniment Room,' *New Review*, I, 641–2; *Salisbury MSS*, VI, 526–7; *CSP, Dom.*, IV, 1595–7, 557).   [161] Tout beau, tout beau.] Tout beau. *B*

[162] *all your . . . fayrer*] Lenton, says Camden, was much frequented and famous in old time for its abbey, 'but now all the fame is onely for a Faire there kept' (*Britain*, 2Z2).

John Berin Knight,[163] of the same Countie, a great good 7
housekeeper. Marie Gods blessing on his hart for it. Indeede
I remember they would say, that Sir John Berin for Notingham-
shire, was as great a housekeeper, as Sir Edward Baynton[164] in
Wiltshire: and then I will be sworne, he was a good one. Well,
let us make much of him, for there is but a few of them left;
I trust he will not refuse me, for my Jurie. Jurie Berin.

George Sampoole Knight,[165] a Lincolnshire man, and a 8[166]
Lincolnes Inne man; a good freeholder, & keepes a good house
in his country (as I heare) but I know my neighbours of Bath
will affirme, that he kept good hospitalitie there: and that he &
his faire Ladie[167] both, are a worthie, vertuous, & godly
couple. Well, let them be as godly as they may, and as perfect
in the Scripture as *Priscilla* and *Aquila*[168]; I hope they will not
denie, but I have good authorities, for my teshe, and give a
friendly verdict. Jurie Sampoole.

Raph Horsey Knight, the best housekeeper in Dorsetshire, a 9

---

[163] *John Berin Knight*] Sir John Byron of Newstead served as justice of the
peace and sheriff for both Notts. and Lancashire (*APC*, XIII, 148; XXI, 353;
CSP, Dom., I, 1547–80, 375, 379). His son and heir Anthony attended Cambridge
at the same time as Harington, where his secret marriage in 1576/7 caused a
flurry of excitement and his subsequent disinheritance. Harington's youthful
observations on this matter are recorded in a letter to Sir Edward Dyer wherein
he asserts *he* will not do anything contrary to the will of his tutor (*L&E*,
pp. 61–2).

[164] *Sir Edward Baynton*] Sir Edward inherited a great mansion at Bromham
which his father had built during the reign of Henry VIII; it was reputed to
have been almost as large as the palace at Whitehall, and the ironwork alone
was said to have cost £5,000 (*Victoria History of Wiltshire*, London, 1953,
VII, 179–81; 226). According to the *Wiltshire Visitation Pedigrees, 1623* (Pub. of
the Harleian Society, CV and CVI, London, 1954, 7), Sir Edward died in
1592/3, but the *Victoria History* states 1597. From this passage the latter
would seem to be correct.

[165] *George Sampoole*] A member of a well-established family in Melwood,
Lincolnshire, Sir George had been admitted to Lincoln's Inn in 1580 (Camden,
Britain, 2Y6ᵛ; *Records of Lincoln's Inn*, I, 91). He was one of a 'good troupe of
gentlemen' directed to accompany the Earl of Lincoln to Scotland to honour
King James's marriage (*APC*, XVIII, 89–90).

[166] *Numbers 8, 9, 10, 11, 12*] *Markham-Wrenn; om. A, B*

[167] *his faire Ladie*] He married Frances, the daughter of Sir Christopher
Wray, Lord Chief Justice (*Lincolnshire Pedigrees III*, Pub. of the Harleian
Society LII, London, 1904, 846).

[168] *Priscilla and Aquila*] Acts 18:26.

good freeholder, a Deputie Lieutenant.[169] Oh Sir, you keepe haukes, and houndes, and hunting horses; it may be some mad fellow[*] will say, you must stand in the Bath up to the chinne,[172] for spending five hundred pounds, to catch hares, & partridges, that might be taken for five pounds. But if you do come to Bath (so you will be one of my Jurie) I will stand as deepe in the bath as you, and it is odds, but at the spring and fall, we shall meet good company there. I pray you give a friendly verdict, for old acquaintance between Kings Colledge, and Trinitie Colledge.[173] Jurie Horsey.

10   Sir Hugh Portman of Orchard,[174] in the Countie of Somerset Knight, a good housekeeper, a builder, and a substantiall

---

[*] According to the tale, in the[170] hundred merie tales.[171]

[169] *Raph Horsey . . . Lieutenant*] Son and heir of George Horsey of Digwell, Herts., Sir Ralph served as M.P. for Dorset in 1586–7 and as a deputy lieutenant in 1596 (Venn, *Alumni Cantab.*, Pt. 1, 11, 410; *Salisbury MSS*, VI, 137; *APC*, XXVI, 445). In this same year (1596) Sir Ralph's wife, the 'vertuous and chaste' Lady Edith, received the dubious distinction of being addressed as the patron of Peter Colse's *Penelope's Complaint*. This puzzling work was written to counter *Willobie His Avisa*, a work even more puzzling because of its allusion to the 'old player' W.S. (Reprinted Alexander Grosart, *Occasional Issues*, XII, pr. pr. 1880.)

[170] the] *om. B*

[171] This is taken from *Mery Tales, Wittie Questions and Quicke Answeres*, LII (reprinted in *Shakespeare Jest-Books*, I, 68–9; Hazlitt also errs in referring to this story as appearing in *A C Mery Talys*, pp. viii–ix).

[172] *it may be . . . chinne*] In reference to the Italian who was accustomed to curing madmen by plunging them into a gutter or ditch in his house 'some to the midell legge, some to the knee, and some dypper,' according to their degree of madness. One who had been cured by this method chanced to see a gentleman riding by with his hawks and hounds and queried what they cost him a year; on being told forty ducats, he then asked what they profited him. The answer was four ducats, whereupon the mad man retorted, 'Gette the lyghtlye hense . . . for, if my mayster come and fynde the here, he wyll put the in to the gutter up to the throte.'

[173] *Kings . . . Colledge*] He matriculated as a fellow commoner from Trinity in 1577 but did not graduate (*Admissions to Trinity College*, Cambridge, ed. W. W. R. Ball and J. A. Venn, London, 1913, II, 113). Harington was in residence at King's from 1576 to 1581.

[174] *Sir Hugh . . . Orchard*] The son of Sir Henry Portman and Joan, daughter of Thomas Michele, Sir Hugh had served as sheriff in 1590, immediately preceding Harington's tenure of office (Collinson, I, xxxvii). The family estate was located near Taunton, an area which stirred Camden to high praise: 'The Countrey here, most delectable on every side with greene medowes; flourishing with pleasant Gardens and Orchards, and replenished with faire Mannour houses; wonderfully contenteth the eyes of the beholders' (*Britain*, T3).

freeholder. Marie Sir I might ill have spared him. Come my good Knight, I have kept you in store for a dead lift[175]; I hope you will sticke close to us, for the Law; for you have as much if you list to shew it, as some that weare coyfes. Besides, you have that same soveraigne medicine against the consumption, called *aurum potabile*:[176] & I know your neighbours of Taunton say, you are liberall of it; and for your good hospitalitie, your neighbours of the Court wil say, you are no niggard of your meate.[177] Yet I remember one day, when I told a good friend of yours; that I was sure you never tooke usurie: well (saith he) though I graunt he doth many men kinde pleasures, yet he doth them not all *gratis*. I promised him I would tell you so, and to pick a further thanke,[178] I will tell you what I answered him. (For I guessed at his meaning, by meanes I had once some smattering of the Latin toung) if your *gratis* (quoth I) be an adjective, the fault is theirs, & the prayse is his."

Well Sir Hugo, I will come shortly and see your new builded Orchard[179] (I thinke there is not two better Orchards in England, and put Kent to it) and when we have conferred, for reforming one fault there (you can smell my meaning I am sure) then would I aske your opinion, which makes a man happier, *to be wise, or ritch*. I asked a Philosopher once, and (he said) he could not tell, because he still saw[180] the wise men wayte, at the ritch mens doores. Well happie are you if you can decide this question, and happier if you cannot decide it. A

" *Gratis* signifieth to thankfull persons. But *gratis* the adverbe signifies freely.

---

[175] *a dead lift*] *i.e.*, a dire situation; cf. Tilley L271.

[176] *you have . . . potabile*] In recounting the news to Sir Robert Sidney 22 Dec. 1595, Rowland White speaks of Sir Hugh as 'the rich gentleman' who was 'knighted by the Queen at Kew' (A. Collins, *Letters and Memorials of State*, London, 1746, I, 384).

[177] *and for your . . . meate*] Of four epigrams Harington addressed to Sir Hugh, two make mention of his hospitality: in one Harington refers to his entertaining forty guests, in the other, to his table furnished with 'venison, snytes [snipes], quailes, larks' (*L&E*, pp. 161; 254).

[178] *to pick . . . thanke*] *i.e.*, to curry favour by tale-bearing.

[179] *your new builded Orchard*] Cf. Harington's epigram '*Of the growth of Trees. To Sir* Hugh Portman' (*L&E*, pp. 226–7).

[180] still saw] saw stil *B*

ritch man, a wise man,[181] a builder, and specially a bacheler. *Franco, sciolto, slegato, ô che felice stato.* Wherfore keepe you so still, and beleeve me it is the happiest state, yet tell not my wife that I say so, for (of my honestie) she will make me unsay it again, with all my hart. Jurie Portman. Cryer count them.

Sir John Harington, one. Sir John Peeter, two. Sir John Spencer, three. Sir Thomas Stanop, foure. Sir Mathew Arundell, five. Sir Frauncis Willoughby, six. Sir John Berin, seven. Sir George Sampoole, eight. Sir Raph Horsey, nine. Sir Hugh Portman, ten: whop, why how now Maister K. Shiriffes man? Here is but ten; give[182] me a noble, of my 40. shillings backe againe. Oh speake soft Sir, you shal have a *tales* for two more, the best we can get, but we can finde you no more Knights. There is two names more for you. Who have we here? Raph Sheldon of Beeley, in the Countie of Worcester Esquire.[183] Thomas Markham Gentleman.[184] First let us see what this same[185] Sheldon is. Hath he freehold?[186] Yea Sir. He is a good freeholder, a great house-keeper, a builder, an excellent common wealthes man as any is in all his country; I will warrant you, he will be for you. Not too much of your warrants.[187] What said Harry[188] Tuttle to his grandfather?[v]

---

[v] What is a knaves warrant worth? A by word of[189] Somerset shire.[190]

---

[181] *a wise man*] 'Skil in y[e] / law was / ever counted / wisdom, and / called by y[e] / Romans / Jurispruden / tia,' Harington annotation in the Markham-Wrenn copy.   [182] ten, Give *A*

[183] *Raph Sheldon . . . Esquire*] The son of William Sheldon who is credited with having introduced the art of tapestry weaving into England, Ralph inherited wealth and much property in Worcestershire and Warwickshire. He married Anne, daughter of Sir Robert Throckmorton, by whom he had ten children, nine daughters and one son, Edward, the Philostilpnos of the *Metamorphosis.*

[184] *Thomas Markham*] Harington's uncle, see below.

[185] same] *om. B*   [186] freehold] freeholdes *B*

[187] *I will warrant . . . warrants*] A reference to the many difficulties Sheldon encountered with the government because of his Catholic beliefs: having been summoned before the Privy Council in Aug. 1580, he was subsequently imprisoned in the Marshalsea for 'obstinancie in Relligion'; in Nov. because of ill health he was placed in the custody of the Dean of Westminster who was instructed to confer with him for the reforming of his error; in Dec. a discourse proving it lawful for a Catholic to attend a Protestant service was delivered to him, and by Jan. he had agreed to 'yielde himself duetifull and obedient' and to attend church (*APC*, XII, 166; 254–5; 301–2; *CSP, Dom.*, I, 1547–80, 691). However, in 1587 he was again in trouble: his name appeared in a list of

Give me leave I pray you a litle, I have heard he is an unthrift, I have forgotten at what game it was, but I am sure it was said; if he had not had[191] faire play played him, he was in daunger within these two yeares, to have lost his land, by one plea[192] or other.[193] By the masse[194] it is true, there was such a matter. Wel, let him thanke a guiltlesse conscience, & a gracious Princesse, that he sped no worse.[w] Oh these same *oves, & boves, & pecora campi*, a flocke of white sheepe in a greene field, and a new house on a high hill; I tell you, they be perillous tempting markes to shoot at.[196]

---

[w] And let him pray for Trajans soule with S. Gregorie.[195]

---

gentlemen who were to be excluded from the commission of justice of the peace with the notation, 'His wife a recusant, himself very wise, and a man of good sufficiency,' and he was again summoned before the Privy Council (Strype, *Annals*, III, Pt. 2, 458; *APC*, xv, 137).

[188] Harry] Henry *B*

[189] of] in *B*

[190] Not in Tilley.

[191] had not had] had not *B*

[192] plea] play *B*

[193] *I have heard . . . other*] In 1594 Sheldon's most serious difficulty occurred when he was implicated by a nephew, Richard Williams—a priest—in a purported plot to kill the Queen and offer the crown to the Earl of Derby. It was revealed that Dr. William Gifford [later archbishop of Rheims] was to come to England to 'resolve' Sheldon, that the conspirators intended to rely on his wealth, and that a servant of Sheldon's under colour of buying hawks in Ireland had carried letters to Cardinal Allen. As a result, Sir Thomas Lucy and Sir John Harington of Exton were instructed to search his house and Sheldon himself was to be interrogated on various points, namely, his intercourse with English fugitives, the books and libels which he had, and the fact that although he attended church he heard mass and received priests at his house (*CSP, Dom.*, III, 1591–4, 531–2, 540–1, 544–7, 554).

[194] *by the masse*] An example of Harington's sense of decorum. Cf. his epigram '*Against Swearing*' (*L&E*, p. 256). It was said to have been one of the Queen's oaths (*The Seconde Parte of a Register*, ed. A. Peel, Cambridge, 1915, II, 53–4).

[195] Since Trajan would not tolerate informers. See p. 137 and notes.

[196] *Oh these . . . at*] Harington here repeats a taunt that had been directed against Sheldon himself and applies it to those who had informed against him. This is made clear by a passage in Father Person's *Memoirs* where he mentions a book written by a Catholic layman which asserted it was lawful for Catholics to go to 'heretical churches' in order to avoid persecution. This had appeared in 1580 at a time when Sheldon and other important Catholics had been imprisoned: 'At the sight of this book several of the said gentlemen in prison began to waver, as for example Lord Paget [Thomas, third Baron Paget] who was a prisoner in Windsor Castle, and in London Ralph Sheldon, a very powerful and rich man, whose fall [*i.e.*, his promise to conform] caused so

It is straunge to see the world, not halfe a yeare before I heard one that was a great Courtier say, that he thought him one of the sufficientest wise men of England, and fittest to have bene made of the Counsell, but for one matter; and indeed by *Cornelius Agrippa* his rule,[197] that is a right Courtiers commendacion: For after they have roved three or foure idle words to praise a man, straight they mar all at the buts: I would to God for their own sakes, & mine too, they could leave it. Well Maister Sheldon, I pray you be of our Jurie, for you have made a fine house at Weston[198] (but I know one fault in it.)[199] Now though I praise your house like a Courtier with a but, you must bring in your verdict, like a plaine countryman, without the but.

12   Thomas Markham[200] Gentleman come to the Court;

---

much talk and scandal to the rest, that it was made the subject of pasquinades, one of which was:

> Sheldon is fallen; and do you ken why?
> Through *oves et boves et pecora campi.* '

(*Miscellanea*, Publications of the Catholic Record Society, IV, 4–5). The last line of the pasquinade is from Ps. 8:8.

[197] *Cornelius . . . rule*] Describing the professional courtier, Agrippa says, 'They sell all their favoure, they despise all vertue, and disteine other mennes praises with sundrie opinions, and artificiallye doo sclaunder every man behinde his backe, they prayse noman without exception, like as that oratoure saide, I confesse that *Julius Fortunatus* is a woorthy man, and it is manifestly knowen that he hathe atcheived many valiaunte enterprises, notwithstandinge if I had not knowen the force of his eloquence, I should muche marveile by what meane he escaped judgemente of briberie and extorcion' (tr. Sanford, 2G2ᵛ).

[198] *for you . . . Weston*] In 1532 Sheldon's father had purchased the manor of Weston-juxta-Cherington in Warwickshire and had been licensed to empark three hundred acres of land, meadow, pasture, and wood, which was to be called by the name of Weston Park forever. Here Ralph Sheldon built a fine manor house (E. A. B. Barnard, *The Sheldons*, Cambridge, 1936, pp. 16, 21).

[199] (but . . . it. *A*, (but) . . . it. *Lumley-Folger*

[200] *Thomas Markham*] The son of Sir John Markham by his third wife, Anne, daughter of Sir John Strelley and widow of Sir Richard Stanhope, Thomas Markham, like his sister Isabella (Harington's mother), had long been in the service of the Queen. Having inherited the manor of Ollerton in Notts., he became the founder of the Ollerton branch through his marriage to Mary, the daughter of Rice Griffin of Dingley, who was, in the words of a younger Markham 'a great inheritrix, wise, virtuous, & very religious (in her religion which is Popish) gentlewoman' Francis Markham, the second son of Robert Markham of Cotham, cited in *Familiae Minorum Gentium III*, 966).

which[201] Markham is this? black Markham[202] keeper of
Bescowd; why[203] he is a Squire, I trow I have a verse for it,
made by a most honorable Poet.[204]

To[205] *Thomas Markham the gentle Squire,*
Whom Sir Fulke Greevill[206] *cal'd a grim sire.*

---

[201] Court, which *A*

[202] *black Markham*] Apparently a common epithet applied to Markham, see
Rutland MSS, I, 344. Lodge refers to a manuscript in the College of Arms
which calls him '*Niger Markham*' (*Illustrations*, II, 393, n.), and his sons were
described as 'exceeding swarthy' (*Salisbury MSS*, XV, 193).

[203] Bescowd, why *A*. In 1567 the keepership of Beskwood, a royal residence,
with a fair lodge and a park well stocked with deer, was granted to Markham
(*CSP, Dom.*, VII, Addenda 1566–79, 31; *Thoroton's History of Nottinghamshire*,
ed. J. Throsby, London, 1797, II, 279). This was one of several grants that had
been made to him of parks, walks, and woods carved out of Sherwood Forest
which stirred the Earl of Rutland to envy. Beginning in 1578 and continuing
for more than twenty years, he endeavoured through controversy and persuasion
to obtain possession of certain of these; the Queen, however, steadfastly refused
to make any change during the lifetime of her 'old servant' (*Salisbury MSS* II,
227–8; XIII, 169–70; VII, 302; IX, 359; X, 104–5; *CSP, Dom.*, I, 1547–80, 689;
XII, Addenda 1580–1625, 22–4; *APC*, XIV, 4–5).

[204] *most honorable Poet*] 'The Erl of / Shrowsbery,' Harington annotation in
the Lumley-Folger copy. The friendship between the Earl and Markham was
such that the Earl felt compelled to write to Burghley in 1591 to counteract
the charge made by Sir Thomas Stanhope, 'one of the most ambitious, proud,
covetous and subtle persons that ever I was acquainted with,' that he was
unduly influenced by Markham. The Earl explains that the 'evil disposition'
of Stanhope toward him and his 'most malicious mind' toward Markham
'betwixt whom and me he well knoweth to have been dearness of good will and
friendship since I was of man's estate and before' has prompted the report that
he was wholly ruled by three people—his mother-in-law, his wife, and Thomas
Markham. As a result of new causes of enmity, Stanhope has again attempted
to impair his credit; the Earl goes on to assert that Markham 'though he be (as
of very long he hath been) my dear good friend, and as often and many ways
hath expressed the same unto me as ever any friend of mine to his power hath
done,' yet he himself is not so devoid of spirit as to be 'ruled by him or by any
one man living' (*Salisbury MSS*, IV, 112–15).

There is further evidence of this intimacy in a note of 'notorious Papists and
dangerous recusants in the household of, or in great account with, Lord
Shrewsbury. Thomas Markham, of Kirby Bellars [his seat in Northants.],
his chief friend and secret councillor, whose wife is chief companion to the
young Countess when she is in Nottinghamshire, and whom she calls sister'
(*CSP, Dom.*, III, 1591–4, 174).   [205] *To*] *om. B*

[206] *Sir Fulke Greevill*] of Beauchamp Court, Warwickshire. 'He was a
Gentleman, full of affabilitie and courtesie, and much given to hospitalitie,
which got the love of the whole countree. For in his time no man did bear a
greater sway in the countie of Warwick than himselfe. He was evermore
attended with a brave companie of gentlemen' ('The Genealogie, Life and
Death of Robert, Lord Brooke,' 1664, a Manuscript cited in F. L. Covile,
The Worthies of Warwickshire, London, 1870, 333).

Yea it is true; but the case is altered[207] since: for that same good Knight[208] is lame, or else I dare answere he would "have appeared on this Jurie him selfe (and his sonne is an "honorable Gentleman and a great states man may do a man "displeasure[209] about the Queene,[210] it is not good troubling "of him.) If it be that Markham I will none of him, for I heard a noble Philosopher[211] of the same coate[212] that the Poet was, say that he is a Stoicke, and I will no Stoickes of my Jurie; of the two extremes I would rather have Epicures. Besides that, I would have no such black fellowes, for we shall have some of these Poetrie men say, as one said of Sir Harry Goodyeare when he wrote *Candida sint comitum Goodyeeri nil nisi nigrum*,[213] he wrate underneath it. *Hic niger est, hunc tu*

---

[207] *the case is altered*] Tilley C111.

[208] *for that same good Knight*] *i.e.*, Greville.

[209] displeasure] pleasure *Markham-Wrenn*

[210] *and his sonne . . . Queene*] Friend of Sidney and Dyer, Fulke Greville was long a favoured courtier. Bacon says he 'had much and private access to Queen Elizabeth, which he used honourably, and did many men good; yet he would say merrily of himself; *That he was like Robin Goodfellow: For when the maids spilt the milkpans, or kept any racket, they would lay it upon Robin: So what tales the ladies about the Queen told her, or rather bad offices that they did, they would put it upon him*' (*Works*, 1872, XIII, 377).

[211] *a noble Philosopher*] 'The Earl / of Lincoln,' Harington annotation in the Lumley-Folger copy. Knighted in 1553 at the coronation of Queen Mary, he had succeeded to the earldom in 1585.

[212] *same coate*] *i.e.*, Catholic in sympathy. (See above and *Salisbury MSS*, v, 526–8).

[213] *Sir Harry Goodyeare . . . nigrum*] Known mainly today because of his patronage of Drayton, Sir Henry, the eldest son of Francis Goodere of Poles-worth, Warwickshire, was a courtier who had interested himself in the affairs of Mary Queen of Scots for some fifteen years. This interest brought him into periodic difficulties with the authorities. In 1569 he was examined about a plan to transport the queen to an abbey in his possession; in 1571 he was imprisoned and questioned about his share in conveying letters to her from the Duke of Norfolk; it also appeared that he had devised a cipher for her use. In 1583 it was asserted that the buttons of gold which he wore on his cap and doublet had been given to him by the Queen of Scots. However, his allegiance to Queen Elizabeth was sufficiently re-established so that in 1586 he was knighted by Leicester, and in 1588 he was listed with others as a colonel to lead an army for the defence of Her Majesty's person.

While imprisoned in the Tower for his support of the Scottish queen, Goodere had endeavoured to ease his plight by addressing Queen Elizabeth with a series of verses in English justifying his actions. These were followed by the words which Harington, who preserved a copy of the poem (Harington MS at Arundel Castle from BM Add. MS 28635, Nott's transcript of this), quotes:

Regina caveto,[214] a goodyeare on him for his good *caveat*, for he hath had since some young scholers[215] that have learned to put in the like *caveats*. *Cave credas* take heed you trust him not, but *Tullie* saith in his Oration *pro Ligario; nonne omnem humanitatem exuerunt*?[216] Have they not cast away all sence of humanitie? And a litle after saith the same *Tully* of *Cave*

Candida . . . nigrum. I am uncertain about the interpretation, but the *nil nisi nigrum* is perhaps intended to recall *de mortuis nil nisi bona.*

B. H. Newdigate who prints a portion of Goodere's poem in his book on Drayton gives the Latin gloss, which he does not explicate, as *candida sunt comitum, Goodereij nil nisi nigrum.* (*Salisbury Papers,* I, 458, 534, 535, 536; CSP, *Dom.,* I, 1547–80, 425–6; II, 1581–90, 124, 519; BM Add. MS 28635, fol. 55ᵛ; *Michael Drayton and His Circle,* Oxford, 1941, 25–39.)

[214] *he wrate . . . caveto*] One of the 'Poetrie men' employed by the government during the period covering Norfolk's trial was Thomas Norton, co-author of *Gorboduc,* translator of Psalms, and an ardent reformer. Whether he conceived of his effort as part of his official duties or not, Norton, utilizing a technique common in the period, wrote a travesty of Goodere's poem in which the defence is twisted into an accusation. This was followed with *Hic niger est . . . caveto,* an adaptation of Horace's *Satire* i. 4.85. Harington also preserved a copy of this (BM Add. MS 28635, fol. 56). Newdigate reprints the Latin gloss of Norton, whom he calls 'the epigrammatist,' from the Harington MS.

Apparently the poems must have had considerable circulation. Newdigate cites part of Goodere's poem from a Bodleian MS (which differs in various small details from BM Add. MS 28635, fol. 56), and refers to the Harington MS and to a third copy in Dublin. However, he completely misunderstands this passage in the *Apologie*: suggesting that 'the Rabelaisian author of *The Metamorphosis of Ajax* might well have inspired the austere Drayton with stern disgust,' he adds that 'in his *Apologie* he had written ungraciously of Drayton's patron, the elder Goodere, echoing Norton's sneer: *Hic niger est hunc tu Regina caveto*' (p. 67). This is obviously a distortion of Harington's meaning *and* point of view.

[215] *young scholers*] 'Justice / Young a pra / mooter,' Harington annotation in the Lumley-Folger copy. An example of the odium which Young aroused by his methods is to be found in a letter from the priest Anthony Tyrrel to the Queen, asserting that the false accusations he has made had been induced by Justice Young: 'Of whom I cannot but say, altho' I abide all the torments that he can procure me, if ever I come again under his hands, that he is a most cruel bloodsucker, a destroyer of your people, and a great abuser of your majesty; for his cruelty in shedding of bloud, it is too well known.' And he explains that if a suspect is to escape Young's recommendations for the gallows, he must furnish proof of allegiance by playing the spy and 'under the colour of godliness to practice all the knavery that he can.' As a result, 'How many false reports and lyes doth justice Young bring your majesty in a year, partly by his own devising, and partly by such as I have been!' (Strype, *Annals,* III, Pt. 2, 425–39, *passim.*) A rack in use at this time was called 'Younges Fiddle' (*Records of the English Province of the S. J.,* S. 5–8, III, 765).

[216] *Cave . . . exuerunt*] *Pro Q. Ligario Oratio* 5.14. Here, as below (5.16), Harington has altered the original (where Cicero is attacking Tubero, the prosecutor of his client) to the plural.

ignoscas; Haec nec hominis, nec ad hominem vox: qua qui apud te C. Caesar utetur, suam ipsi citius abiicient humanitatem, quam extorquebunt tuam, thus in England. Take heed you pardon not. O lewd speech, not fit to be spoken of a man nor to a man, which speech, whosoever shal use to thee (ô more then *Caesar*) shall sooner discover their own cruell inclination, then extort from thee thy naturall clemencie. O devine *Tullie,* is not this Christianly spoken of a heathen? were not that heathenishly spoken of a Christian? Well he that should put in such a *caveat* for me, I would follow presently a *quare impedit,*[217] why I might not present him for a *cnave* at litle Brainford[218] & lesse honesty.

Thomas Markham Gentleman, come to the Court. Yet[219] againe? I tell thee I will none of him, one said he lookt blacke on him: yea, but he that found such fault with his complexion, I heard one tell him was dead, and he answered verie charitablie; young he was, & poore he was, & knave he was, and so God have mercy on his knaves soule. Faith that is like enough to be his answer.[220] Then it may be he is cleare otherwise, though he look black. Cleare, yea on my word.[x] *Candido piu nel cuor che di fuor Cigno.* What is that? *Rara avis in terris nigroque simillima*

---

[x] *In memoria aeterna erit iustus.*[221] Not Justis Young that[222] accused him[223] and said, Lopus[224] had bid him say, he was a daungerous man, with *Cave credas. Tamquan stercus, memoria impiorum.*

---

[217] *quare impedit*] 'A writ, that lyeth for him, who hath pourchased a maner with an Advousen thereunto belonging, against him that disturbeth him in the right of his Advowsen, by presenting a Clerk therunto, when the Church is voide' (Cowell, 3G3).

[218] *litle Brainford*] Great Brainford [Brentford] was located at the junction of the Brent and the Thames, eight miles west of London (Sugden), and presumably 'litle Brainford' was near by.   [219] Court; Yet *A*

[220] *but he . . . answer*] Francis Markham also remarks on Thomas's inveterate habit of forthrightness: 'He had . . . reverence of the greatest Lords which he got by a kind of bluntness of speech, telling men their faults without dissimulation' (*Familiae Minorum Gentium III,* 966).   [221] Ps. 111:7.

[222] Not Justis Young that] *all presentation copies; om. A, B*

[223] him] *Markham-Wrenn, Nares-Folger, Sheffield; om. A, B*

[224] Dr. Roderigo Lopez, the Queen's physician, whose involvement in a plot against the Queen, largely brought to light by a determined Essex, had led to his execution in 1594.

Justice Young's accusation perhaps appeared among 'the Confessions, Examinations, Depositions, Declarations, Messages, Letters, Tickets, Tokens, Conferences, Plotts and Practyses taken, discovered and intercepted' which the

Cygno[225] just as Jermins lips,[226] now you have compared him well, as white as a blacke swan. Wel I have no minde to have him of my Jurie, he is but a poore freeholder, he hath no credit. No credit? why his bond hath bene taken for twentie thousand pounds. Hath it? more foole he, I will never trust him for halfe so much, I pray thee looke me some better freeholder. Why Sir? I advise you do you not scorne him, though he be no Knight, he had a Knight to his father,[227] & hath a Knight to his sonne,[228] you may well admit him of your Jurie. I tell thee my little knave, thou doest presse me beyond good maners, I wil not have him. Harke in your eare, they say he is *Mal-content.* Who saith so? Nay who saith not so? *Unton is undone,*[229] *Markham is mal-content.*[y] Who hath not heard that? Wherefore

---

[y] A lewd libell made at the death of the Lord Chancellour Hatton.[230]

---

government in order to avoid a 'long and unpleasant discourse' did not trouble to set down in its account (*A Collection of State Papers . . . from the Year 1571 to 1596*, ed. William Murdin, London, 1759, 673).

[225] Cigno *A*. Juvenal *Sat.* 6.165.

[226] *just as Jermins lips*] Used pejoratively. Thus, Wilson in giving an example of a syllogism incorrectly made up of more than three terms says, 'Therefore it hangeth together as Germaines lippes, as we use to saie' (*The Rule of Reason,* 1580, H1[v]). For other examples, see Tilley G87.

[227] *he had . . . father*] Knighted by Henry VIII at Tournay, Sir John Markham was a long-time servant of the king: he was among those summoned to be servitors for the coronation of Anne Boleyn and the reception of Anne of Cleves; he was a member of the Earl of Rutland's council in the Scottish wars; and he served as sheriff for Notts. and Derby. Under Protector Somerset he was appointed Lieutenant of the Tower (*Markham Memorials*, I, 32–4; *L&P, Henry VIII*, VI, 246; VII, 558; XIII, Pt. 2, 406).

[228] *a Knight to his sonne*] His eldest son, Sir Griffin, had been knighted by Essex at Rouen (Sir Thomas Coningsby, *Journal of the Siege of Rouen, 1591,* Camden Miscellany I, London, 1847, 27, 71).

[229] *Unton is undone*] Sir Henry Unton. See below.

[230] His death occurred 20 Nov. 1591. Lewd rimes and libels were of course a common phenomenon in the sixteenth century, and Harington himself preserved some few examples in the family collection of contemporary writings. I have not been able to trace this particular libel, but passages in the elegies on Hatton indicate he was so attacked. For example, in the dedicatory epistle of *A Maidens Dreame*, Robert Greene says, 'as *Virtutis comes est invidia,* so base report who hath her tong blistered by slanderous envie, began as farre as she durst, now after his death, to murmure, who in his life time durst not once mutter' and in the complaint, Religion is made to say:

> Then base report, ware what thy tongue doth spred,
> Tis sin and shame for to bely the dead.

(*Plays & Poems*, ed. J. C. Collins, London, 1905, II, 223, 232.) For details of the libel, see below.

make no more a do, but send me for his nephew Robert that came of the elder house, and of the bloud of Lancaster,[231] he that Maister Secretarie Walsingham gave the Arabian horse,[232] I would have him, he is a fairer complectioned man by halfe, and in sadnesse I wish him well. Hey hoe: what doest thou sigh? Alasse sir he wold come with all his hart, but he is busie sitting on a commission, (I have forgotten in what Benche it is)[z] and when he hath done there, he must go they say to an other Benche at Oxford.[aa] What Robert Markham of Cottam, so honest a Gentleman, so good a housekeeper, so well descended, so well affected in Religion, & become such a Bencher, that when he is called is forth comming, but not comming forth, I am sorie I can do him no pleasure, I would his best cosen did know it. The time hath bene that if he could[235] have walked with a litle sticke like a ragged

---

[z] Kings Bench.[233]   [aa] Penilesse Bench.[234]

---

[231] *his nephew . . . Lancaster*] Robert Markham of Cotham was the grandson and heir of Sir John Markham (the father of Thomas and Isabella). Owing to Sir John's three marriages, his grandson Robert, who inherited the property at Cotham, was almost the same age as Sir John's son Thomas, who inherited the property at Ollerton. Robert was thus the nephew of Thomas and Harington's cousin.

Sir John Markham's first marriage had been arranged by Margaret Beaufort, mother of Henry VII, to 'a kinswoman of hers, a lady of the blood-royal.' This was Anne, daughter of Sir George Neville, descended of Edmund Beaufort, Duke of Somerset. Hence Robert came of the elder house of Markham and of the blood of Lancaster (*Familiae Minorum Gentium III*, 968).

[232] *he that . . . horse*] Robert Markham had served as M.P. for Notts. in 1571 and as sheriff in 1571 and 1589. In a letter to Walsingham, Markham thanks him for his favours to the youth (apparently his eldest son Robert) who wished to serve in the Low Countries, adding that if his own services as captain of the horsemen in Notts. were not required he might be permitted to retire to private life to recover himself from his debts (*Markham Memorials*, I, 52; *CSP, Dom.*, II, 1581-90, 646).

[233] King's Bench Prison was used for debtors.

[234] *Both notes scored in Markham-Wrenn*. The name of a covered bench, one of which formerly stood near Carfax Church, Oxford, used by destitute wayfarers.

[235] *if he could . . .*] In reference to the heraldic badge which an individual selected for use as decoration and as a mark of ownership on his personal property and which was also worn by his servants and followers as livery buttons or embroidered on the front or back of a coat or on a sleeve. The crest which was properly an ornament upon the helmet worn only by the owner also came to be used as a badge, and during the sixteenth century the terms *badge, device, cognizance,* and *crest* were often used interchangeably. Moreover,

staffe[236] on his sleeve, or if he had had but a walking hynde,[237] or a ramping stag,[238] or the white birde, that is such a beautie to the Thamis,[239] he should not have layne so long after his resting. Well then I perceive the world goeth hard on all the Markhams sides; I thinke they be all *Mal-contents*, they shall none of them be of my Jurie, I pray God they do not say that I am of kinne to them, for indeede my name *Misacmos*[240] begins with an *M*. what if one should write *Misacmos* is *mal-content* ? I would leape upon the letter, & replie. By your leave you lye, like a lowt lewd Maister Libeller. But Markham is *mal-content*, how prove you it ? *Scriptum est enim*, for it is written, but it is in *libro fictitio*. I would you could name me your authour[241]; yet let us examine this *ignoto*, if he say true. Let us do him the favour that men do to Astronomers, if they tell but one true tale,[bb] beleeve him in a hundred lyes,[242] sure you lyed in all the rest good M. Libeller, for first[cc] he that you said was undone,

---

[bb] Agrippa.

[cc] The Libell is thus.[243] *Umpton is undone.*[244] *Markham is mal-content.*[245]

---

the fact that a badge was never a subject of official record leads to uncertainty of identification (A. C. Fox-Davies, *Heraldic Badges*, London, 1907, pp. 12–41).

[236] *a litle . . . staffe*] This had been used by Ambroise Earl of Warwick and by Leicester (Fox-Davies, pp. 121, 156). In 1604 when Robert Dudley was endeavouring to prove his claim to the earldoms of Warwick and Leicester he was charged with having 'gyven the Ragged staffe to his men that walke upon the Thames with the same' (Hawarde, *Les Reportes*, p. 169).

[237] *walking hynde*] Used by Sir Christopher Hatton (W. C. Metcalfe, *A Book of Knights . . .* London, 1885, 131).

[238] *a ramping stag*] I have not identified this.

[239] *the white . . . Thamis*] Used by, among others, Baron Hunsdon and members of the Stafford family (Fox-Davies, 115, 144).

[240] Miscamos *A*

[241] *for it . . . authour*] Harington again emphasizes the conjunction of anonymity with libeling. See p. 204, n. 122.

[242] *Let us . . . lyes*] Agrippa observes of astrologers that 'whereas in other men for makinge one lie, the faithe of him that speaketh is so muche mistrusted, that all the residewe beinge true are not regarded: contrarywise in these Masters of forgeries, one veritee spoken by happe, giveth credite to their common lies' (tr. Sanford, 1569, N3).

[243] Although I have been unable to trace this libel, two facts about it may be concluded from what Harington records: (1) all the individuals mentioned had been connected with Hatton and (2) most of them, if not all, had at various times been labeled as Catholic sympathizers, even as Hatton himself had been so labeled (Camden, *Elizabeth*, 2L4ᵛ; *Leycesters Common-wealth*, 1641, V3; *An*

lived to do more service for his country, then ever you will do, and many things are left undone by his death, that might perhaps have bin much better done; & he that you said fadeth,[dd] doth now florish with a guilt axe in his hand, in a much more honorable service,[247] & he that you said wayled,[ee] is well and

---

[dd] *Flower fadeth.*[246]

[ee] *Swale waileth.*[248]

Advertisement Written to a Secretarie of my L. Treasurers of Ingland, 1592, A7). This suggests the libeller represented an extreme Protestant faction.

[244] As early as 1584 and the appearance of *Leycesters Common-wealth* (with its charge that Unton had received letters from Rome stating Hatton to be of such credit and special favour in Rome, as if he were the greatest papist in England), Unton was accounted Hatton's servant (Wood, *Athenae Oxon.,* I, 647), and in 1591 Burghley in a letter to Unton terms him 'your singular good patrone.' Knighted by Leicester in 1586, Sir Henry became ambassador to France in 1591, from which post he wrote to the Lord Chancellor 'perplexed' at hearing of his 'wante of healthe, which bringeth wantes to many, and to me moste, whose whole and only comforte dependeth on your Lordships favor and goodnes, and who, I proteste, doth not desier to live after your Lordship' (*Correspondence,* 194, 152). Sir Henry himself died suddenly in 1596, while serving his second appointment as ambassador.

[245] Since Markham had served as the Standard Bearer for the Gentlemen Pensioners, he would have known Hatton from the latter's first appointment at court which was as a pensioner in 1564.

[246] Francis Flower was also a follower of Hatton's, interested in literature and printing. Besides penning some of the choruses, he helped direct the proceedings in 1588 of *The Misfortunes of Arthur* presented before the Queen by the Gentlemen of Gray's Inn (Chambers, *Elizabethan Stage,* III, 348–9); he also wrote commemorative verses to his patron which were placed on a tablet near his tomb (printed in Nicolas, *Memoirs of the Life and Times of Hatton,* London, 1847, Appendix, lxiv–lxv). Flower's connection with the publishing world is shown by his lucrative grant to print books in Latin, Greek, and Hebrew (*S.R.,* II, 15) and by his friend Thomas Newman's dedication to him in 1591 of the surreptitious first edition of Sidney's *Astrophel and Stella* (reprinted in Feuillerat, III, 369). In 1595–6 he was J.P. for Middlesex (*APC,* XXV, 156, 230).

[247] *guilt axe . . . service*] *i.e.,* as a member of the Gentlemen Pensioners. During Elizabeth's reign, the insignia of the band was a gilt battle-axe (Samuel Pegge, *Curialia,* London, 1784, Pt. II, 48).

[248] Richard Swale, also a servant of Hatton's, had had a stormy career at Cambridge because of his Catholic bias. After Swale became President of Gonville and Caius College in 1582, Burghley wrote to Hatton that 'both Doctor Legge the Master, and this Swale, hath, for my courtesy showed to them (they both deserving correction), abused me many ways, and specially have maintained covertly in the College a faction against the true religion received, corrupting the youth there with corrupt opinions of Popery' (Nicolas, p. 261). In 1587 he received his LL.D. and had a long tenure as Master in Chancery; after Hatton became Lord Chancellor he was said to have consulted Swale on all important cases (Nicolas, p. 63).

merie (he thankes you not) and he you said was bankrout,[ff] payes the Queene more subsidie, then you and I both, I dare lay a wager; and the other two, the one neede not go bare head, for want either of hat or haire,[gg] and the other will neither dodge nor doubt to shew his face as you do.[hh] Wherefore M. Libeller (though in this matter you are cited, & beleeved better then *S. Austen*) yet I beleeve you not in saying Markhams be *malcontents*; and yet at a venture, I would you had the causes of discontent that they have, so they had none of them; but thus[251] I will distinguish upon the authority alledged; that taking *Mal-content* as an honest man might take it; namely a man sorowfull for the grievous losse of his greatest friend;[252] the

---

[ff] *Bancroft is bankrout.*[249]

[gg] *Hatton is, Hat of.*   [hh] *Dodge doubteth.*[250]

[249] Richard Bancroft, the future Bishop of London and Archbishop of Canterbury, had served as Hatton's chaplain; as late as 1599 he still referred to 'mine old good lord and master, the late Lord Chancellor' (Nicolas, p. 371; *Salisbury MSS*, IX, 178). Bancroft early distinguished himself as an opponent of the Puritans, who thereupon, says Harington, 'maligned him in lybells and rymes, for they were voyd of reasons, laying the imputacion of papistry unto him' (*NA*, II, 28).

[250] *om. B.* 'Mr. Dodge, Sir C. Hatton's man' is recorded among those resorting to Mrs. Fuller's house, a place appointed in London for papists to hear mass (*Records of the English Province of S. J.*, I, 205, n. 2). An Edward Dodge is mentioned with Francis Flower in the *CSP, Dom.*, for 1581, II, 23.

[251] thus] this *B*

[252] *a man . . . friend*] Clearly a reference to the alienation between Markham and the Earl of Shrewsbury, an alienation known to have occurred but the genesis of which is somewhat difficult to trace. Although Markham was related to Sir Thomas Stanhope, the Earl's ancient enemy, a certain degree of hostility had existed between Markham and Stanhope (see notes to p. 230). However, in the course of the many quarrels between the Earl and Stanhope, it appears that Markham was asked to intercede (*Salisbury MSS*, V, 227) and, apparently, was ultimately won over to the Stanhopes' side. Thus in 1595 the (now-disaffected) agent of the Earl, Nicholas Williamson, testified that the Countess of Shrewsbury when speaking to him of the Earl of Derby's mysterious death (see p. 229) had said that 'if the like should happen to my lord—as if it doth, it must be by one of these three factions, either Sir Tho. Stanhope with Tho. Markham, or his [the Earl's] brethren, or the other (whom I understood to be those whom she thought to have poisoned my lord of Derby)' (*Salisbury MSS*, V, 251-4).

Francis Markham in his memoirs, written sometime after 1617, compressing many facts about his relative into a paragraph, simply says, 'for as in the beginning he [Shrewsbury] was his truest friend, & after, as I know, very unnecessarily lost . . . and being lost, Markham according to his usual bluntness railing on him, discovering what, imparted in former friendship, he knew that might disgrace him, & not daring a direct opposition (to his power), combining

ungratefull requitals of most kinde & 'friendly offices; the
unadvised revolt of his deare sonne,[253] the unaccustomed
frowne of his dread soveraigne,[254] if a man felt no discontent
in these, I would say he were a stock & not a Stoicke,[255] but
understanding it as I know you would be understood, that
they be *Mal-content* as ill affected to their Prince, I dare say
you lye in plaine English, but there is one will come home
shortly I trow, that will tell you, if you be so full of the French,
as I take you to be *Tu ments par la gorge.* But good M. Libeller
and your fellowes, I know your meanings, you would faine

[*sic*] with his adversaries, yea with those who for his own sake first became his
adversaries' (*Familiae Minorum Gentium, III*, 966-7).

[253] *the unadvised . . . sonne*] In Aug. 1592, Robert, his second son, educated
at Cambridge and Gray's Inn, and in the service of Burghley, fled to the
Continent to become a Catholic, intending thereby, as he wrote to his father,
to escape the 'odious name of a traitor . . . (besides the infinite trouble and
charge which I know it would bring unto you both), as I rather choose to leave
my country than to hazard the staining of our house and name with treason,
which as yet was never attainted.' Upon receipt of the letter, his father immediately sent it to Burghley together with his own expression of disappointment:
'My grief is the greater, for that expectation and opinion was so firmly settled
of his good and dutiful behaviour, both to her majesty and the state; beside the
former hope that I had to see him enable himself by his diligent study to serve
the same' (Strype, *Annals*, IV, 156-9). Francis Markham likewise attests to
Robert's singular qualities 'who for wisdom, valour, temperance, & justice,
was in mine openion the rarest gentleman that ever I knew' (*Familiae Minorum
Gentium III*, 966).

[254] *unaccustomed . . . soveraigne*] What occasioned the 'unaccustomed frowne'
I do not know, but the year 1592 was not without difficulties for Markham. In
Jan. when the commissioners for recusants in Notts. were intending to call
before them 'Mystres Markham, wyfe of Thomas Markham, esquire,' the
Privy Council ordered them to defer the examination since Markham was 'one
of her Majesty's auncyent servantes, and well knowne to theire Lordships to
be of good credytt and reputacion' (*APC*, XXII, 205-6).
   In Feb. they again sent similar instructions, this time in reference to his
wife's aunt, again commenting on Markham's well-known 'reputacion and
integritie' (*ibid.*, 257-8).
   However, in April Markham was prompted to send to Burghley an 'answer
to her Majesty's objection for leaving his office in time of her greatest danger,'
in which he recounts his services at various critical points in the course of her
reign (*Salisbury MSS*, IV, 189).
   Finally in Aug. his son's disaffection occurred, at which time writing to
Burghley, Markham concludes his letter with the humble request 'that her
majesty by your honourable means may not misconceive of me, but of her
princely and gracious wisdom rightly deem of me' (Strype, *Annals*, IV, 156-7).

[255] *a stock . . . Stoicke*] Cf. 'Let's be no Stoics nor no stocks, I pray,'
T. Shrew. I.i.31.

make *mal-contents*, and it grieves you you cannot, the water is to cleare for your fishing,[256] you catch nothing but goodgins,[257] the great fishes be too warie, & now you are faine to lesson your meashes contrarie to Statute,[ii] being willing to play any game rather then sit out. Or I thinke you have read the pollicie of Richard the third, who to give his wife a preparative to her death, gave out first she was dead, hoping that this corsive (cordial I would have said) might breake her hart,[259] as it did indeed. So you worthy members of your country (God amend you, for I was saying, the plague take you all) when you would make Mal-contents then your pollicie gives out first that they be so. Oh take heed[260] of such a one, he is a dangerous man. A Puritan, why so ? He will not sweare nor ride on[261] a Sunday, then he wishes to well to the Scottish Church, note him in your tables. An other is a Papist. How know you ? He said he hoped his grandfathers soule was saved. Tush but he goes to Church. Mary they be the most perillous men of all. And why so I pray you ? if they will venter their soules to please[262] their Prince, what do you suspect them of. Oh if they be Catholicke, they are Spanish in their harts, for he is their Catholicke king. By my fay that is somwhat you say, but I pray you, you that are not Spanish but all for the French, what Religion is the French

---

[ii] *Statute of fishing, anno. I. Elis. that the meashe must be two inches and a halfe.*[258]

---

[256] *the water . . . fishing*] The obverse of the proverb 'It is good fishing in troubled waters,' Tilley F334 where Harington's usage in the *OF* is the earliest example cited.

[257] *goodgins*] Gudgeon, a small fresh-water fish used for bait; hence a credulous person.

[258] *om. B*; 'An ACTE for the preservacion of Spawne and Frye of Fyshe,' I Elizabeth, c. 17 (*Statutes of the Realm*, IV, Pt. I, 378–9).

[259] *the pollicie . . . hart*] Cf. *Rich. III*, IV.ii.50–9; iii.39. This derives from Hall: 'But howsoever that it fortuned, either by inward thought and pensyvenes of hearte, or by intoxicacion of poyson (which is affirmed to be most likely) within a few daies after [the report that she was dead], the quene departed oute of this transitorie lyfe, and was with dewe solempnite buried' (*Chronicle*, London, 1809, 407; cited in *Richard III*, ed. J. D. Wilson, Cambridge, 1954, p. 222).

[260] *Oh take heed . . .*] This satirizing of intolerance is typical of Harington's salutary attitude toward the religious question. See p. 263 ff. and Ch. VIII of the *Tract on the Succession*.

[261] on] of *MS*　　　　　　　　　　　　　　　[262] please] pleasure *B*

king of?[263] Oh no more of that, you will answere that when Callis is French againe.[264] Fare you well Sir.

Thomas Markham Gentleman, come into the Court, and plucke up thy old spirits. Is not this he should have bene controuler, and now he is affrayd rather to be controlled. What evill hath he done? His second sonne grew so great he could not finde roome enough in England. Alas poore boy, God punisheth oft the sinne of the father on the children, but never but once that I have reade of, the sonnes offence on the father. Is there no body hath a sonne so farre of? I trow there is. And yet he a true and worthy Gentleman. Thomas Markham Gentleman her Majesties servant extraordinary,[265] come to the Court. Why was he once ordinarie? Yea that he was. Ask old Hatfield men, & aske them quickly to, for they be almost all gone. Why man he was standerd bearer to the worthie band of Gentlemen Pentioners. What did he leave such a place *gratis*? yea *gratis* the adverbe. Why wold he leave it? Because it asked such perpetuall attendance.[266] Oh now you have answeared me, he shall be none of my Jurie for that. Had he so litle wit? Well sir saith[267] my Atturney, I pray you dally no more but take him, for you may have a worse else. I say unto you he is a right English man, a faithfull, plaine, true, stout Gentleman,

---

[263] *what Religion . . . of*] In reference to Henry IV's politic religious vacillations; in 1593 he had officially adopted Catholicism.

[264] *when Callis . . . againe*] In April, 1596, the Archduke Albert led a Spanish force from the Netherlands against Calais. Immediately, says Camden, that 'the Queene heard by the fearefull messengers of the *French* King, that *Calis* was besieged, she commanded a power of men to be gathered that very day being Sunday, while men were at Divine service. . . . This army hastily raised, she committed to *Essex*: But before they were shipped, she had certaine advertisement that both the Towne and Castle were yeelded up into the *Spaniards* hands' (*Elizabeth*, 2Q1). Essex then turned his energies to preparing for the voyage to Cadiz (see above, p. 141).

[265] *servant extraordinary*] i.e., employed in addition to the regular staff.

[266] attendance? *A*. 'The Gentlemen Pentioners' made up a royal guard, consisting of fifty men under a captain, whose function was to attend the sovereign on all occasions. Although each man was allowed three months' liberty a year, only a third might be absent at one time, and for all important holidays the entire band was in attendance. Its members were usually prosperous men of good birth who sought experience and prestige at court. Sir John Holles is said to have observed that when 'he was pensioner to the Queene he did not know a worse man of the whole band than himselfe and that all the worlde knew he had an inheritance worth five thousand poundes a yeare' (Holles, p. 94).

[267] saith] sayes *MS*

& a man of honestie & vertue. Out asse. What doest thou tell
me of these stale fashions of the sword and buckler time?[268]
I tell thee they are out of request now, (honest, & vertuous) I
durst as leave you had told me a tale of an old Jakes. Of A Jax?
Marie that I can do to. I assure you he loves an easie cleanly
Jaxe marvelous wel, & he is a very good fellow at the Jax, for
if one be his deare friend, he will let him tarrie with him, while
he is at his businesse. I thinke he saith his prayers there, for I
wil[269] be sworne, I heard him say oft times, I thanke God I
have had a good stoole, &c.[270] May I beleeve this of your word?
Yea be bold of it, I can prove both this & all the rest by very
good witnesse. Why didst thou not say thus much at the first?
I would have had him, though I had gone to Barwick on foote
for him. What a good freeholder, a builder, and a house keeper,
and loves a sweet Jax too; though he cannot be *Alpha* of my
Jurie, yet he shall be *Omega*. Come on M. Markham, I must
crave lesse acquaintance of you as grim as you looke, did not a
Lady say once, that I should fare the better for that good face
of yours, and God thanke her for it, so I did indeede: yet now
some will make me beleeve, I fare the worse for it. Be of good
cheare man. What makes you so sad? I have commendations
for you from your old friend, Thomas of Ormond[ii] hath sent
you a hawke will make you live one yeare the longer. I cannot
make him look merily on me for all this, he seys[272] he can not
live long, he must thinke of his grave. Tush man though you
cannot live long, you may linger (an please God) as others have
done, some 3. or 4. and twenty yeares yet. What say you? no life?
M. Richard Drake[273] hath you commended, and wold have you
get the Queene an other gelding, for Gray Markham will have
his old maisters fault & fortune both, he wil be old, & then they
will not care for him. Not a word yet? I will make him speake

---

[ii] A most honorable Earle, and true friend.[271]

---

[268] *of the sword and buckler*] See note 61, p. 79.   [269] I wil] Ile *MS*

[270] *I heard him . . . &c*] Cf. p. 92.

[271] Thomas Butler, tenth Earl of Ormonde, called the 'Black Earl.' Popular
with the Queen, he spent several years at court beginning in 1565. Thereafter
he was mainly caught up in the turbulent Irish scene (*DNB* and *Carew MSS*,
II, 413–15).

[272] seys] *Markham-Wrenn*, Nares-Folger; sees *MS, A, B*

[273] *M. Richard Drake*] Equerry of the Queen's Stable, see p. 167, n. 36.

anone. You shal have your sonne joyned patent with you for
Bescood, if he will come home and be a true Knight to the
crowne. What say you to that ? Mary Gospell in your mouth[274];
and if he can be proved other, I renounce him for my sonne.
Oh have you found your toung now ? Wel Sir, I have a sute to
you, I pray you appeare on[275] my Jury, & give a good verdict
of our booke called M. A Jax. You know the booke well
enough, I read you a sleep in it once or twise as we went from
Greenewitch to Westminster. Out upon it, have you put it in
Print ? did not I tell you then, Charles Chester[276] & 2. or three
such scoffing fellowes would laughe at you for it ? Yes: & did
not I tell you again, that I would laugh too, and so we might all
be merie ? Well grim sire, let me have a friendly verdict, if it
be but for teaching you to mend a fault at Bescood, that I felt
there 24. winters ago; & if you do not say well of it, I will cause
one or other that hath bin at M. A Jax with you, report it in
Court to your disgrace,[277] & your Joane[278] shalbe disgraced
too for tying your Points, and sitting by you so homelie (yet I
would I had given 100. pounds she never had had worse nor
untruer tale told of her) & so fare you well good M. Markham,
and God send you manie a good stoole. And thus with much
a do the Jurie was Impanneld. Now began I to have a good
hope, nay rather a firme assurance of my acquitall; having got
a Jurie of so good sufficiencie, so great integritie, so sound
ability: but it is commonly seene that in matters depending in

---

[274] *Gospell in your mouth*] Tilley G379.　　　　　[275] on] of *MS*

[276] *Charles Chester*] Called by Nashe 'an odde foule mouthde knave,' Chester's
reputation for railing is several times referred to by the Elizabethans (Nashe
I, 190–1 and *N&Q*, 10th s., I, 381–3). In 1592 Justice Young, having apprehended him as a religious suspect, searched his chambers where in addition to
'some score of vain and papistical books, especially in the Spanish language,'
he found 'pictures, beads, mass-book, pax, shirt of hair, whips and other
trumpery, but not above 16s. in money.'
Chester thereupon wrote to the L. Admiral and Cecil recounting his past
history, largely a series of disgraces owing to 'false tales' and 'false tongues.'
He makes mention of Sir Walter Raleigh's friendship and, having been forsaken
of the great peers, 'his chief and last friend, Mr. John Stanhope' (*Salisbury
MSS*, IV, 210–11, 221–2).

[277] *I will . . . disgrace*] 'Yet Cato / entertaynd / King Ptolomy / of that
fa / shion / as homely,' Harington annotation in the Markham-Wrenn copy.
See Plutarch 'Cato the Younger' 35.2–3.

[278] *your Joane*] His daughter Jane married to John (later Sir John) Skinner,
the son of a Lord Mayor of London (*Familiae Minorum Gentium III*, 967).

controversie, the greatest danger is bred by too much securitie:
For the accusation was so hard followed, that some of the[279]
Jury began to be doubtfull of their verdict, the witnesses were
so manie, their allegations so shrowd, & the evidence so
pregnant. And not onelie the faults of this present Pamphlet
but my former offences which were before the pardon (contrarie
to the due course of all Courts) were inforced against me. As
first to prove I had wronged not only Ladies of the Court, but
all womens sex; they had quoted a Stanse in *Hary Osto*
beginning thus,

> *Yee Courtly Dames, that are both kind & trew*
> *Unto your Lords, if kind and true be any;*
> *As sure I am in all your lovely crew,*
> *Of so chast minde, there are not over many.*[280]

And after in the person of Rodomont.

> *Ungratfull, false, craftie you are, and crewell,*
> *Borne of our burning hell to be the fewell.*[281]

And lastly in this Pamphlet to compare, or rather to confound
bawdie houses & Jakes houses, Courtisans & Carters, with

---

[279] the] their *B*

[280] *OF* XXII.1.1–4. Harington has changed the 1591 reading in line 2 from
loves to *Lords*.
There follows in A, B: And after in the hosts tale if worse may be.

> *Now he began to hold his wife excused,*
> *His anger now a litle is relented,*
> *And though that she her body had abused,*
> *And to a servant had so soone consented,*

This passage is scored in MS and all presentation copies.

[281] *OF* XXVII.98.7–8, 1591 edition.
There follows in A, B:

> *Not her for this, but he the sex accused,*
> *That never can with one man be contented:*
> *If all (quoth he) with one like staine are spotted*
> *Yet on a monster mine was not besotted.*

Scored in MS and all presentation copies. These eight lines (st. 36, Canto 28)
appeared in the MS at the bottom of fol. 56[v] and top of 57. After scoring the
entire stanza, Harington added a substitute passage at the bottom of fol. 56[v].
The printer ignored the deletion, thus introducing two lines from Canto 27
into the middle of the ottava from Canto 28.

Angels & Hermits, there were 3. or 4. of the Jury*kk* (that said)
the time had bin, they would have thought it no good manners.
But *Alpha* & *Omega*[283] that have ever thought chastitie a
vertue, acquited me for this last,[284] saying, to scorne vice,
shewed a love of vertue. And for the rest I pleaded not onely a
generall but a special pardon. Yet least the standers by should
thinke I had bin guilty, or that I had bin burnt in the hand for
the like fact before,[285] I answered, that in the verse I did but
follow my author. The whole work being enjoyned me as a
penance by that saint, nay rather goddesse, whose service I am
only devoted unto.[286] And as for the verses before alledged,
they were so flat against my conscience, that I inserted somewhat, more then once, to qualifie the rigour of those hard
speeches. For example against railing Rodomont, I said thus,

> *I tremble to set downe in my poore verse,*
> *The blasphemies that he to speake presumes;*
> *And writing this, I do know this that I*
> *Oft in my hart, do give my pen the lye.*[287]

And in another place, to free me from all suspition of
pretended malice, & to shew a manifest evidence of intended
love, where my autor very sparingly had praised some wives,
I added of mine owne (   )*ll* so much as more I thinke

---

kk I will not tell you which foure, for a 100 pounds.[282]

ll Mine owne *subauditur*[288] verse or wife which you will.

---

[282] *Om. B*

[283] *Alpha & Omega*] *i.e.*, Sir John Harington and Thomas Markham, the
two relatives who begin and end the roll call of Harington's jury.

[284] for this last] *MS, Markham-Wrenn, Sheffield*; at last *A, B*

[285] before. *A*. 'Theeves that are saved by their bookes and cleargie, for the
first offense . . . are burned in the left hand, upon the brawne of the thombe
with an hot iron, so that if they be apprehended againe, that marke bewraieth
them to have been arraigned of fellonie before, whereby they are sure at that
time to have no mercie' (Holinshed's *Chronicles*, I, R2–R2ᵛ).

[286] *The whole . . . unto*] Harington's statement clearly confirms the tradition
(sometimes questioned) that, having translated and circulated the ribald 28th
canto, he had been ordered by the Queen to translate the whole as a penance.
(Cf. Letter 27, *L&E*, pp. 96–8, and Townsend Rich, *Harington and Ariosto*,
Yale Studies in English, XCII, New Haven, 1940, 23–4.)

[287] *OF* XXVII.99.5–8, 1591 edition, with *blasphemie* of line 2 made plural.

[288] sub auditur *A*. Used in grammar to indicate that a word or words must
be 'understood' to complete the sense. The earliest example cited in the *OED*
is 1803.

was never said for them, which I will here set downe *ad perpetuam rei memoriam*,[289] and that all posteritie may know how good a husband I would be thought.

> *Loe here a verse in laud of loving wives,*
> *Extolling still, our happie maried state,*
> *I say they are, the comforts of our lives,*
> *Drawing a happie yoke, without debate:*
> *A play-fellow, that far off all griefe drives,*
> *A Steward, early that provides and late;*
> *Faithfull, and kind, sober, and sweet, & trusty,*
> *Nurse to weake age, & pleasure to the lusty.*[290]

Further for the faults escaped in this fore alledged Pamphlet, I protested I was ready to make a retractation for their better satisfaction; as namely, First, for that homely comparison that I made betweene my Lady Cloacinas house, and my Lady Floras Nimphes, I take it not to hold in general, but with[291] this exception. Except it be a verie fowle & deformed harlot; or a very cleane and reformed AJAX.

Secondly for the rules of taming a shrew, that I commended for the wiser; I here protest against that rule: for if it have not bene followed within the first yere, or a day; it is too late to prove a new rule afterwardes. And therefore I hold it as a rule or maxime, proved by natural Philosophy, confirmed by ancient historie,*mm* and therefore may here be concluded in our poore Poetrie in this sort.

---

mm Aristotle ruled by his wife.[292] Semiramis asked leave to rule but a weeke, but you know what followed.[293]

---

[289] *ad . . . memoriam*] A legal formula used in bills to examine witnesses 'that their Testimonies may remain of Record' (William West, *The Second Part of Symboleography*, 1611, 2N5–2N5ᵛ).

[290] *Loe . . . lusty*] OF XXVII.108. Harington has modified the first three lines to make them more applicable to his context; line 7 varies from the 1591 edition (and subsequent ones). [291] with] within *B*

[292] Diogenes Laertius 'Aristotle' 5.4.

[293] Plutarch records this legend, one of many which clustered about the name of Semiramis: 'She was at first no better than a poore wench, servant and concubine to one of the great king *Ninus* slaves: but after that the king himselfe had set his eie and fancie upon her, he was so devoted unto her, & she againe so imperiously ruled over him, and with such contempt, that she was so bold to require at his hands, that he would permit her to sit one day upon her roiall throne, under the cloth of estate, with the diademe about her head, and so to

Concerning wives take this a certaine rule,
That if at first you let them have the rule,
Your selfe at last with them shall have no rule,
Except you let them evermore to rule.[294]

At this, the whole Jurie were mery & agreed all to quite me. And as for those that articuled[295] against me, some of them are so tickled with this answere as I am sure they wil never accuse me for an enemy to Ladies anie more.

The next Article was for abusing the name of a great souldier, both in that being a Graecian, I make him speake in *Latrina lingua*: & that having bin so renowned for his vallue in wars, I wold say his picture was set in so homely a place, that it[296] might also thereby seeme to have bin called after his name in English. Now this matter was followed verie hotlie by halfe a dosen gallant souldiers, that never saw naked sword out of Fleetstreet, and these came in swearing that I had touched them in honor, & they would therfore fight with me about it. The Jury seemed to make but light of the matter, but yet to satisfie the Gentlemen specially 2. of them, that had bene likened to Brutus and Cassius, and called *ultimi Ruffianorum*.[297] They wisht me to answer them, which I did in this sort. I said I was loth to fight for the jestification[298] of my wit: & further

give audience and dispatch the affaires of the kingdome in stead of him; which when *Ninus* had graunted . . . she caried herselfe with great moderation in her first commandements, to make triall of the pensioners and guard about her; and when she saw that they gainsaid her in nothing, but were very diligent and serviceable; she commanded them to arrest and apprehend the body of *Ninus* the king, then to binde him fast, and finally to doe him to death. Al which when they had fully executed, she reigned indeed, & for a long time in great state and magnificence ruled all *Asia*' (*The Morals*, 5C4ᵛ–5C5).

[294] rule, *A*. Included in his epigrams with slight modification (*L&E*, p. 199).

[295] *articuled*] Made specific charges.   [296] it] *not in MS*

[297] Ruffianorum] *B;* Ruffinorum *A, MS; that . . . Ruffianorum*] See notes to p. 117. This passage supports the view that in his account of Roman history Harington has inserted topical overtones. Although it is impossible to identify the two who had been likened to Brutus and Cassius, Harington is perhaps again alluding to the writer (or writers) of the anonymous libel directed against Hatton, Markham, etc. (p. 247 ff.), since in both cases he emphasizes a connection with French. In the earlier passage he had remarked that 'good M. Libeller,' with his fellows, was 'full of the French' and that one who would come home shortly [qu. Essex] would prove to him: '*Tu ments par la gorge.*' On p. 259 he again asserts that French seems their 'better language.'

[298] *jestification*] A coinage for the sake of the pun.

I could name them 2. honest Gentlemen that had offred
M. A Jax as great abuse as this, & he had put it up at their
hands; they[299] asked who they were ? I told them they were 2. of
his countrymen, one they called him M. Plato, the other
M. Plutark, of whom the one[nn] in his 10. booke *de Repub.* saith,
that the soule of A Jax went into a Lyon, & the other saith, it
had bin as good for it to have gone into an asse, & both agree
that it went into hell. And if reading of this will satisfie you, I
will turne you to the place, and lend you the booke in Latin or
in French, for that I thinke is your better language; & I protest
to you, it is an excellent chapter wherin the same Plutarke very
divinely sheweth how predestination, and freewill, and chance
may all stand together.[302] The pox on[303] Plutark & you to
(saith one of these fighting fellowes,) reade him who list, for
I will never reade him, but why should he or you either abuse
a souldiers name ? Oh sir said I, good words I pray you, though
I dare say you wish me no worse then you have your selfe: for
I know you are a Gentleman of 3. decents,[304] but if that be

---

[nn] *Plato 10. de Repub.*[300] *Plutark. 9. booke Symposeons. c.5.*[301]

---

[299] hands, they *A*

[300] According to the myth of Er, the souls of the dead, after the order of
choice had been established by lot, selected their pattern of life for the next
cycle of generation. Recalling the adjudication of the arms of Achilles, Ajax,
unwilling to become a man, chose the life of a lion (*Republic* x.620).

[301] sumposeons *A. Note om. B*

[302] *the same Plutarke . . . together*] 'for *Plato* alwaies toucheth three causes,
as being the philosopher who either first knew, or principally understood how
fatall destiny is mingled with fortune: and againe, how our freewill is woont
to bee joined with either of them, or is complicate with both . . . hee sheweth
excellently well, what power each of these causes hath in our humane affaires,
attributing the choice and election of our life unto free will, (for vertue and vice
be free, and at the commaund of no lord) and tying to the necessitie of fatall
destinie, a religious life to Godward in them, who have made a good choise,
and contrariwise in those who have made a choise of the worst: but the
cadences or chaunces of lots, which being cast at a venture, and lighting heere
and there, without order, befall to every one of us, bring in fortune, and
preoccupate or prevent much of that which is ours, by the sundry educations or
governments of commonweale, wherein it hapneth each of us to live' (*The
Morals*, 3V6). [303] on] *B*; of *A, MS*

[304] *a Gentleman of 3. decents*] 'homo trium / literarum': Harington annotation
in the Sheffield copy. According to the revised statutes of the Order of the
Garter, a person of three descents, provided there had been names and arms
on both sides, was declared a gentleman of blood (Major Henry Brackenbury,
The Nearest Guard, London, 1892, p. 24. n.).

beyond your reading, let me come within compasse of your study, I know you have read old Scogins Jests.[305] Did not he[306] when the French king said that he had set our kings picture in the place where his close stoole stands. Sir saith he, you do the better, for every time you looke on him, you are so frayd[307] that you have need of a close stoole. Now I hope I offer A Jax no greater scorne then that was, yet thankes be to God their successours remaine good friends. This did somewhat better answer them, but not fully. Nay Maisters (quoth I) if you stand on the puntillios with me: whomsoever this answere will not serve, let him send me the bredth of his buckler (I should say the length of his rapier) and draw himselfe as lineally from Captaine Medons grandfather[308] as I have derived A Jax from *Stercutius*, and I will presently make a recantation[oo] of all I have said. At last to take up the quarrell Sir M. A. and M. R. S.[309] set downe their order, that he should not be called any more Captaine *A JAX*, nor *Monsieur A JAX*, but *Don*

[oo] *Recantare*, is to sing the same song againe.

---

[305] *old Scogins Jests*] Entered in the S. R. 1565/6.

[306] *Did not he . . .*] Harington's paraphrase is more seemly than the original (*Shakespeare Jest-Books*, II, 144). Cf. Rabelais, Bk. IV, Ch. 67.

[307] frayd] afrayd *B*

[308] *Captaine Medons grandfather*] Although Medon appears in the *Odyssey* as a herald, this is apparently an allusion to a contemporary. Cf. Sir John Davies's epigram '*In Medonem*':

> Great Captaine *Moedon* weares a chaine of gold,
> Which at five hundred crownes is vallued,
> For that it was his graund-sires chaine of olde
> When great King *Henry Bulloigne* conquered.
>   And weare it *Moedon* for it may insue
>   That thou by vertue of this Massie chaine
> A stronger towne then *Bulloigne* maist subdue
> If wise mens sawes be not reputed vaine.
> For what said *Philip* King of *Macedon*?
> There is no Castel so well fortified,
> But if an Asse laden with gold comes on,
> The guard will stoope, and gates fly open wide.

(*The Works of Christopher Marlowe*, p. 630.)

[309] *Sir M. A. and M. R. S.*] Sir Matthew Arundell and Master Ralph Sheldon.

A JAX,[310] and then to this second article they all agreed not guiltie.

These swearing fellows being thus discharged, there comes a couple of formall fellowes in blacke cloaks faced with velvet, and hats sutable to the same; and under their hats litle night caps, that covered their Epimetheus, but not their Prometheus;[311] having special care to keep their braine warme[312] (yet one of them was said to be a hote brained fellow,) the other[313] had no great fault that I know, save that he would say too long a grace afore dinner, in so much that one of his owne coat[314] told him one day, that if he had thought to have hard a collation, he wold have sung a Psalme before it. These whisperd two or three of the Jury in the eare, and after having made a ducking curtesie or two, bad the Lord to guide their worships; and so went backe to their chambers (at the signe of the Bible:)[315] leaving a mad fellow their Atturney to urge the accusation they had brought, which was in shew verie sharpe and haynous, to this effect. That they supposed me to be in

---

[310] *Don A JAX*] 'Don Aiax / because of / Don Diego &c.,' Harington annotation in the Markham-Wrenn copy. His befouling of St. Paul's made Don Diego a figure of popular opprobrium, and as a result his name became generic for an obnoxious Spaniard. (See McKerrow's note to Nashe, v, 195, and the cross references to Webster, Heywood, and Fletcher.)

In a letter to one William Cotton written between Aug. and Oct. 1596, Nashe mentions Don Diego's actions in an abusive passage relating to the publication of the *Metamorphosis*. Nashe's antagonism perhaps stems from the unflattering epigram Harington had written during the Nashe-Harvey controversy (*L&E*, p. 199), but the extent of his remarks to Cotton suggests he felt he would be well received. A passage in Harington's 'Breefe Notes and Remembraunces' may perhaps explain the tone of Nashe's letter: 'I am to send goode store of newes from the countrie, for hir Highnesse entertainmente. I shall not leave behinde my neighbour Cotton's horn, for a plentifull horn it is.—Her Highnesse lovethe merrie tales' (*NA*, I, 166). (For conjectures as to Cotton's identity, see McKerrow's introduction to the letter, v, 192–3, and E. D. Mackerness, 'Thomas Nashe and William Cotton,' *RES*, xxv, 1949, 342–6.)

[311] *Epimetheus . . . Prometheus*] According to popular etymology, Epimetheus means *afterthought*, Prometheus *forethought*.

[312] warme] *MS, Markham–Wrenn, Lumley-Folger, Nares-Folger, B*; warne *A*

[313] the other] the tother *MS*

[314] *of his owne coat*] i.e., a puritan, see below.

[315] Bible: leaving *A*

hart a Papist.[316] Straight I searcht everie corner of my hart, and finding no such thought in it, I asked why any man should say so ?[pp] I know (said[318] I) some of you would see my hart out by your wils: but for that you shall pardon me. But this you know *ex abundantia cordis, os loquitur,* out of the abundance of the hart[319] the mouth speaketh.[320] And here I protest to you all, I never defended any opinion of Religion, either by way of argument or writing, that in any point gainsaith the Communion booke. Let my accusers say so if they can. Yes Sir, saith their zealous Atturney, I heard one testifie *viva voce* in a Pulpit, that you had defended a Popish opinion, of a second comming of Elias.[321] He lyes like an asse (said I) and so tell him.[322] And if I mistake him not much; I trow his good living grows not so fast with his new benefice, as his good name withers with his ill behaviour.[323] But if he use no better behaviour, then to tell me my faults at Bath, when I am at London; I may fortune play the bad horseman, and spurre him

---

[pp] All that defend the Queenes proceedings are counted no better then Papists with these hot fellows, and they call my Lord of Cant. our Pope.[317]

---

[316] *That they . . . Papist*] Some five years later Harington felt called upon to deny this same charge (*L&E*, 89), and in 1605 when he was suggesting he be appointed L. Chancellor of Ireland and Archbishop of Dublin, he spoke of it again in terms recalling this passage: 'This [appointment] I know wowld make great sport to som man in the world that in Queen Elisabeth's tyme traduced mee for a Papist, looking on all my doings with so envyous eys as now I fear both his inward and outward syght fayleth him, for yt will seem to him a straung *metamorphosis* that his Papist thinks no skorn to bee a *Superintendent*' (*A Short View of the State of Ireland*, p. 14).

[317] Papists] papist *MS*. 'For, may I not say that John of Canterbury is a petty pope, seeing he is so? You must then bear with my ingramness [ignorance]. I am plain; I must needs call a spade a spade; a pope a pope. I speak not against him, as he is a Councillor; but as he is an Archbishop, and so Pope of Lambeth' (*The Epitome, The Marprelate Tracts*, p. 118; cf. p. 331).

[318] said] say *B*   [319] the hart] *MS, B*; hart *A*

[320] *ex . . . speaketh*] Luke 6:45 and Tilley A13.

[321] *that you . . . Elias*] Included among Harington's miscellaneous papers is 'A Discowrse Shewing That Elyas must personally come before the Day of Judgment' (*NA*, II, 281–304).   [322] He lyes . . . him] *om. B*

[323] *I trow . . . behaviour*] 'this was / one Withers,' Harington annotation in the Markham-Wrenn copy. Perhaps the Puritan George Withers who was suspended from preaching at Bury St. Edmunds until he agreed to wear the 'cornered cappe.' In 1583 he became rector of Danbury in Essex, and in 1588 he published *A View of the Marginal Notes of the New Testament* with a dedication to Whitgift (*HMC*, 2nd Rept., 154–5, and Strype, *Annals*, III, Pt. I, 263–4).

at London for stumbling so ill favoredly at Bath. Or if I would ride like a hotspurre, he might hap like a dull Jade (asse he is) be wroung on the withers, as one of his coat was for such a matter in the same place. It may be he thinkes he hath advantage of me, because he can prate in a Pulpit *cum licentia*, but he shall see by this litle, that I have libertie if I list, to replie in Print *cum privilegio*. And my replication may fortune be as forcible as his answer.

More I would have said (for I was in choller) but some of the Jurie wished me (for satisfying of the companie,)[324] to tell what Religion I was of. It was a straunge question to be asked me afore such a Jurie[qq] (considering I came not thither to be Catachized) and therefore I determined to make them as straunge an answere, such as should please them all, or displease them all ere I had done. First I said, neither *Papist*, *Protestant*, nor *Puritan*. Then all said they would condemne me as a newter or *nulli fidian*, except I gave a better answer.

Then I said, I am a *protesting Catholicke Puritan*.[326] Tush say they, how can that be? Forsooth even thus, to beleeve well, do well, and say well, to have good faith, good workes, & good words, is not that a good Religion? Yes indeede, so done, were very well said. But said they, directly we expect your answere, what you count to be true Religion. Why then directly thus I answere; out of *S. Iustus Epistle* the two last verses,[327] you shall see who be of a wrong Religion, and who be of the right. *Iustus?* Oh, saith one by and by, I thinke he meanes James, and straight he puls a litle booke out of his sleeve, that looked like *Ianus* picture; with two faces[328] standing East and West (but it was a testament bound to the backside of Davids

---

[qq] For some of them I hope are but Protestantes of *anno primo Eliz.*[325]

[324] (for . . . companie,)] *B; no parenthesis A, MS*

[325] *I.e.,* they had necessarily been Catholic in the preceding reign. In referring to Elizabeth's accession, Harington says that she had been proclaimed Queen 'by general consent of Papists, for all were Papists' (*A Tract on the Succession,* p. 102).

[326] *Then I . . . Puritan*] Harington recalls this passage when speaking of himself in his *Tract on the Succession* as 'the protesting Catholique Puritan' (p. 108).

[327] *S. Iustus . . . verses*] James 1:26–7.

[328] *that looked . . . faces*] Tilley J37.

Psalmes) and turning to the place, he read as followeth. If a man thinke him selfe Religious, not refrayning his toung,*rr* but seducing his hart, this mans Religion is vaine. Pure Religion and undefiled before God, even the father, is this, to visite orphanes and widowes in their afflictions, and to keepe your self undefiled from the world. Why then, saith one, if you professe so pure a Religion, it seemes you are a Puritan. Even so. More time would have bin spent in this matter, but that sir H. P.[330] told them these things belonged to the high Commissioners, and therefore wisht them to proceede to the next. Now for the last article, because it was concerning onely the Pamphlet it selfe, the whole Jurie referred the censuring thereof to Syr H. P. to say if any thing therein were against the law, because he was well seene in the law.

He told them that indeede he had read it more then once: and that for ought he could observe in it, it did not in any point offend either common or Statute law. But (said he) there is a law (as I take it,) more common then Civill,*ss* that saith

---

rr To have a bad toung is bad[329] Religion.

ss Judge Markham would have bene of that opinion in the time of Ed. the iiii.[331] and Judge Portman your grandfather in Ed. the vi.[332]

---

[329] is bad] is a bad *MS*   [330] *sir H. P.*] Sir Hugh Portman.

[331] Appointed Lord Chief Justice in 1461 by Edward IV, Sir John Markham's integrity in resisting the will of the king is stressed by More: 'Whereof, I think, no man looketh that we should remember you of examples by name, as though Burdet were forgotten, that was for a word spoken in haste cruelly beheaded, by the misconstruing of the laws of this realm for the Prince's pleasure: with no less honour to Markham, then Chief Justice, that left his office rather than he would assent to that judgment, than to the dishonesty of those that either for fear or flattery gave that judgment' (*The English Works*, I, 440).

More's account had originally appeared in Grafton's continuation of Harding's *Chronicle* (1543) and in the two editions of Hall (1548; 1550); Hall, however, added a parenthetical statement detailing the story of Burdet's execution (p. 369 of 1809 reprint). Curiously, Edward Foss in his *Judges of England* (London, 1851, IV, 442–3), followed by the *DNB*, cites Fuller in saying Markham was removed from office because of a case involving Sir Thomas Cooke.

That his probity was freshly remembered is shown by the number of references to Markham: *e.g.*, *State Trials*, I, 894; *CSP, Dom.*, II, 1581–90, 293; Harington again alluded to him in the *Tract on the Succession* (p. 35), and Francis Markham recorded the tale of Burdet as he had heard it from William Fleetwood, the merry Recorder of London (*Familiae Minorum Gentium III*, 965).

[332] Knighted by Edward VI, Sir William Portman became a judge in 1547 and Lord Chief Justice in 1554 (*DNB*).

things must be as they be taken.[333] Yet for my part in my verdict I would not say any mans eares are hornes. What the rest said I could not tell, for I[334] was sent away, yet I over-heard one of them say, he would talke with a Counseller to informe him better of the law. But I finding that to grow so doubtfull, that I thought would have[335] bin so cleare, began now to thinke it my safest course to sue for a pardon." And with that I awaked, vowing I would never write any more such idle toys, if this were well taken: praying the readers to regard it but as the first lyne of Isops Fables.

Gallus gallinaceus dum vertit stercorarium invenit gemmam.[337]

FINIS.

[tt] *Sapientis est nihil praestare praeter culpam.*[336]

---

[333] *things . . . taken*] Tilley T31. [334] for I] for that I *B*
[335] would have] to have *B* [336] Cicero *Epistulae ad Familiares* ix. 16.5.
[337] Aesop's fable (I) of the dunghill cock.

INDEX

TITLES, in modern spelling, are indexed by author. A complete bibliographical reference will be found on the first page cited. Words are included only when Harington's usage is the first or antedates the first example cited in the *OED*; proverbs are starred when Harington's usage is the earliest or antedates the earliest example cited in Tilley. *MA* stands for *Metamorphosis of Ajax*.